THE PRIDE LIST

EDITED BY BISHAN SAMADDAR

The Pride List presents works of queer literature to the world. An eclectic collection of books of queer stories, poems, plays, biographies, histories, thoughts, ideas, experiences and explorations, the Pride List does not focus on any specific region, nor on any specific genre, but celebrates the great diversity of LGBTQ+ lives across countries, languages, centuries and identities, with the conviction that queer pride comes from its unabashed expression.

ALSO AVAILABLE IN

THE PRIDE LIST

MIREILLE BEST
Camille in October
Translated from the French by
Stephanie Schechner

MIREILLE BEST
Hymn to Moray Eels
Translated from the French by
Stephanie Schechner

KO-HUA CHEN
Decapitated Poetry
Translated from the Chinese by
Wen-chi Li and Colin Bramwell

JACOB ISRAËL DE HAAN
Pathologies
The Downfall of Johan van Vere de With
Translated from the Dutch
by Brian Doyle-Du Breuil

PAWAN DHALL
Out of Line and Offline
Queer Mobilizations in '90s Eastern India

PAWAN DHALL
Unfinished Equality
Discrimination, Resistance
and Hope in Queer India

VALENTIJN HOOGENKAMP
Antiboy
Translated from the Dutch by
Michele Hutchison

KIM HYUN
Glory Hole
Translated from the Korean by
Suhyun J. Ahn and Archana Madhavan

MU CAO
In the Face of Death We Are Equal
Translated from the Chinese by
Scott E. Myers

SUDIPTO PAL
Unlove Story
Translated from the Bengali by
Arunava Sinha

DANISH SHEIKH
Love and Reparation
A Theatrical Response to the Section 377
Litigation in India

OMAR YOUSSEF SOULEIMANE
The Last Syrian
Translated from the French by
Ghada Mourad

MICHAŁ WITKOWSKI
Eleven-Inch
Translated from the Polish
by W. Martin

CYRIL WONG
Beachlight

CYRIL WONG
Infinity Diary

Chapal Rani, the Last Queen of Bengal

THE LIFE AND TIMES OF A FEMALE IMPERSONATOR

SANDIP ROY

LONDON NEW YORK CALCUTTA

Seagull Books, 2026

First published by Seagull Books, 2026

ISBN 978 1 8030 9 551 6

British Library Cataloguing-in-Publication Data
A catalogue record for this book is available from the British Library

Typeset at Seagull Books, Calcutta, India
Printed and bound in the USA by Integrated Books International

CONTENTS

Introduction

The first time I saw Chapal Rani, he did not look like a queen at all.

It was at an LGBTQ+ art show in Kolkata. Section 377, which criminalized homosexuality, was still part of the Indian Penal Code but queer life seemed to be thriving in India. There were Pride parades, art shows, film festivals. I remember marvelling at the confidence of the young men in their flowing androgynous outfits and dangling earrings, their eyes lined with kohl. I had grown up in an India where queerness was furtive and secret, a dance in the shadows, where we took great pains to try and draw no attention to our gayness. I never wore bright colours, and preferred a palette of greys and blues, small checks and pin stripes. This, now, felt like a different country. Queer young people, comfortable in their brown skins, laughing, chatting, drinking tea, birds of paradise embracing each other.

Chapal Bhaduri was the guest of honour.

The former queen of jatra was now a queer icon. But he seemed to be the most strait-laced person in the room—a stocky man with thinning hair, dressed in a kurta and pyjama, sitting silently to one side. His face was broad, squarish, not particularly feminine. I could imagine him as a neighbourhood uncle sipping tea at the corner shop, or at the fish market with his shopping bag, inspecting fish. He smiled and nodded but appeared removed from the conversations swirling around him. He seemed out of place, a patch of beige in the rainbow in the room.

This was a very different Chapal Rani from the one whose performances I had seen in film clips and videos. That one wore gorgeous silk saris, parrot green or post-box red, saris with gold borders. Festooned with heavy necklaces, gleaming chokers and shiny bangles. The red of his luscious lips matching the bindi on his forehead. That Chapal's eyes, painted thickly black, could flash fire, narrow menacingly or turn limpidly tender at a moment's notice. One minute his finger raised in accusation, his eyes opened theatrically wide, he thundered, 'You cannot hurt even a little finger of Kaikeyi, but I can turn you into a pile of ash with just a flick of my sindoor.' Then, without missing a beat, he became a plaintive mother: 'Mother? Who called me mother? Madhu, Madhu, Madhu'—and broke into a tremulous lullaby as he collapsed with heart-wrenching sobs. At the end of a performance at the India Habitat Centre, New Delhi, he faced the audience and said, 'All I will say is I am alone, very alone. Being with all of you this evening fills my heart. If it made me too emotional, forgive me.'

Was that from his heart? Or part of his routine? It did not matter. Whether a queen from the epics or a mother in nineteenth-century Bengal, Chapal Rani belonged to the limelight. His diamonds were cut glass but they glittered nonetheless. The Chapal at the art show seemed the ersatz version in comparison.

Some people are born queer. Some have queerness thrust upon them. I felt Chapal was very much the latter. The LGBTQ+

movement was young in India. Hungry for a queer history, it seemed to have seized on Chapal Bhaduri to be its fairy godmother.

When we started on this book project, I met him weekly at the Seagull Books store in South Kolkata. His knees troubled him, and he moved slowly and haltingly. But he came without fail, always early and eager to talk after a cup of tea. At some point, though, he would invariably look around the room, point at all the art and books and say, 'I didn't finish school. And look at me now, sitting amid all these English books! I am so out of place.'

A few years ago, I went to a book launch in Kolkata. By then, I was well into his life story. Chapal was one of the panellists on stage. Everyone treated him with great deference, but the discussion was in English, and his grasp of the language was rudimentary. He sat silently at one end, staring into space with an air of polite attentiveness until a question was addressed to him in Bengali. After he answered it, he would lapse back into studied silence, and gaze at the ceiling while the panellists went back to discussing queer theory, heteronormativity and representation in literature. I felt bad for him—again, out of place. But then he turned towards me, caught my eye, nodded almost imperceptibly and mouthed, '*Thik aachhe*?'—was that OK?

I understood I was worrying in vain. Chapal was far cannier than I was about fitting into places where I assumed he did not belong. He was a performer through and through. At one time, he had acted as Sultana Riziya and Queen Kaikeyi. Then he had played Goddess Sitala on the streets. Now he was performing as gay icon and queer elder. I was of a generation that measured queerness via rainbow flags and the alphabet soup of identity. Chapal Bhaduri was queer in an older sense of the world, the proverbial square peg in a round hole. Yet he made it work. 'Acting is being what I am not,' he would often tell me.

He was a queer survivor.

'*Shob thik aachhe*,' I mouthed back with a nod. It's all OK.

Darling, You Don't Know Me Yet

Jatra, like queerness, always existed on the fringes of respectability in Bengal. A jatra performance lasted anywhere from six to twelve hours and drew audiences in the thousands, especially in the countryside. It was so popular that jatra scripts were not published while the show was on the boards because company owners feared rivals would steal their lines and songs. But the culturati found jatra embarrassing, tacky and over-the-top.

'The actors wore costumes that cost 1,800 rupees each, with hoses of German velvet, silk stockings, heavy wigs and glittering chapkans [long coats],' says Phanibhushan Motilal, one of the highest-paid jatra actors of his time, describing the early days of the jatra he had seen as a boy to theatre critic Samik Bandyopadhyay. 'There would be at least 60 songs, some of them lasting an hour. Prose or verse dialogues would alternate with the songs. As the singers sang, the actors would take off their wigs, loosen their clothes, smoke their hookahs and relax—in full view of the audience.'[1]

Jatra's origins were certainly respectable. *The Oxford Companion to Indian Theatre* says that the earliest recorded forms of jatra date back to the sixteenth century when devotees in Bengal's Nadia District recounted the stories of Lord Krishna,

---

1 Samik Bandyopadhyay, 'Theatre Traditional', *Hindustan Standard*, 28 October 1973, n.p.

blue-skinned and playing a flute, through 'song and dance woven together by dialogue, often extempore.'[2] 'The collective singing amidst the clash of gongs and fumes of incense produced a mass hypnosis and sent those singers into an acting trance,' writes Balwant Gargi. 'This singing with dramatic elements gradually came to be known as "jatra", which means "to go in procession".'[3]

Soon, stories about other gods were added to the repertoire—Ramjatra, Shivajatra and so on. Brothers Boko and Sadhu, who were Muslim, staged jatras based on the Hindu epic Ramayana.

Tales about gods, goddesses and legends from the epics were common because jatra was rural. It needed stories its audiences were familiar with. 'The theatrical representations were also called *jatra pala* (literally, "Jatra chapter" of well-known tales) and Palagan (*gan* meaning "song") for their operatic character,' says *The Oxford Companion*.[4] 'Thanks to their touring abilities, they were able to spread all over and became hugely popular,' says theatre scholar Ananda Lal, and editor of *The Oxford Companion to Indian Theatre*. 'They were never stuck in some time warp in a confined space.'[5]

As jatras became more popular, the themes became more secular. Stories about kings and queens, legendary robbers and

---

2 Kalyani Ghosh, 'Jatra', in Ananda Lal (ed), *The Oxford Companion to Indian Theatre* (New Delhi: Oxford University Press, 2004), p. 171.

3 Balwant Gargi, 'Jatra—Folk Theatre of India', Yakshagana; available at: https://yakshagana.com/jatra-folk-theater-of-india-by-balwant-gargi-continued/ (accessed 20 November 2025).

4 Ghosh, 'Jatra', p. 171.

5 Ananda Lal, interview with the author, 21 February 2025. Unless otherwise mentioned, all subsequent quotations from Lal are drawn from this interview.

brave social reformers were added to the mix. Jatra was no longer just about spreading the word of God. It was full-on entertainment. Clarinets—or *clarionets*, as jatra folk called them—alongside violins and table harmoniums joined the original minstrel orchestra of drums and cymbals. Then came the Vidya–Sundar stories, about the illicit romance between Princess Vidya and Prince Sundar, laced with a heavy dose of bawdy humour and double entendre.

For example, Malini, the flower-girl who promises to bring Vidya into the arms of Sundar, sings about her own talents as a go-between.

Jadu! Chintey to paro nai
Ami shukno dangay pansi chalai.
E noi re tor temon mashi
Sarbonashi, nimeshey Kashi–Macca dekhai
Ami jodi mone kori, phand pete chaand dhottey pari
Kuhak diye kuler nari bahir kori
Bahir kore bhelki dekhai

[Darling, you don't know me yet;
I can steer my pinnace across empty land.
I am no ordinary aunt. I'm dangerous;
I can show you Benaras and Mecca at the snap of my fingers.
If I want, I can trap the moon.
By my charm, I can bring out the chaste woman from her sheltered home.
Bring her out and amaze the world.][6]

---

6 Durgadas Lahiri, *Bangalir Gan* (Asitkumar Bandyopadhyay ed.) (Kolkata: Paschim Banga Bangla Academy, 2001 [1905]), p. 366, quoted in Sumanta Banerjee, *The Parlour and the Streets: Elite and Popular*

These were lapped up by both the villagers and the nouveaux riche of Kolkata, 'where foppish gentlemen babus—and their wives—depended on such women for the "arrangement" of their extramarital affairs,' writes Sumanta Banerjee in *The Parlour and the Streets*.[7] As jatras moved from the villages to cities, the jatra troupes started grandly calling themselves 'opera's, like Satyambar Opera or Ganesh Opera. 'This word "opera" was purely ornamental,' writes Makhanlal Natta, whose Natta Company never became Natta Opera. 'Some jatra owners just wanted to impress the English rulers of the time. A few even talked about building stages with balconies like in the Elizabethan theatre. Luckily, that idea went nowhere.'[8]

Jatra companies were clustered around Chitpur in North Kolkata. The big jatras would premiere in the markets around the area. City audiences would throng to see them, but the real VIPs were the nayeks or agents from all over the state who would check them out and decide which ones to pick up for their regional circuits. Chitpur remains the headquarters of modern jatra. 'So now an extremely metropolitan commercial nexus controls what is actually a traditional form. As far as I am aware, this is not true of any other traditional form,' says Ananda Lal.

Popular though it was, it was still no place for respectable women. The only women who acted in the Vidya–Sundar jatras were from the red-light area of Calcutta. But even they did not

---

Culture in Nineteenth-Century Calcutta (London: Seagull Books, 2019 [1989]), p. 116.

7 Banerjee, *The Parlour and the Streets*, p. 116.

8 Makhanlal Natta, *Rangamanchey Natta Company* (Kolkata: Dey's Publishing, 2014), p. 22.

venture out of the city. Jatra required a company to be on the road for several months at a stretch from the end of the monsoon. 'How could women be away from home and for that long?' writes Makhanlal Natta. 'They might get permission to be on the stage for a few hours a day for a few days of the week. Even that wasn't regarded with much favour. But to be away day and night for months on end in a Bohemian profession was out of the question.'[9] Also, out in the countryside, in an age before microphones, when jatras played to audiences of thousands in open fields, they needed actors whose voices could be heard by the last person in the last row. They needed men who could be women or purush-ranis, the male queens.

The First Ladies of Jatra

One of the earliest ranis or queens of jatra was Gopal Ude, a street vendor. As he walked down the streets crying 'Gandhar boleche champa kala chai' [Gandhar says we need ripe bananas], a rich businessman and music connoisseur was amazed. Not only was his voice sweet, but also he was singing in the classical raga Gandhar. He took Ude to a jatra troupe where he bowled everyone over, and then went on to become a sensation as Malini in the Vidya–Sundar jatras. Apparently, when he dressed as a woman, no one could tell he was a man. Eventually, Ude took over the troupe, brought in more female impersonators and trained them in a raunchy khemta dance which he had learnt from Keshey Dhopa (Keshey the Washerman). In no time, Gopal Ude's troupe and his dancing 'girls' with swaying hips and flashing thighs became the hottest ticket in town.

9 Natta, *Rangamanchey Natta Company*, p. 38.

Or so the story goes. Jatra is all about stories. Another story stars the sixteenth-century Hindu saint Chaitanya Mahaprabhu. It is said that Chaitanya showed his ecstatic love for the god Krishna by acting as Krishna's paramour Rukmini in the play *Rukmini-Haran* [The Abduction of Rukmini]—complete with saris, ornaments and bells round his ankles. He was so convincing, his disciple Chandra Sekhar writes, 'Nobody could make out that she is Master himself!'[10] That would make Chaitanya the earliest recorded purush-rani of jatra, a patron saint of female impersonators, as it were. Soon, jatras came with a 'sakhir dal', a chorus of young adolescent men who played women. It was a finishing school of sorts. The prettiest and most talented among them were groomed to become future purush-ranis.

If an element of suspension of disbelief was needed, that was par for the course. All of jatra was based on a healthy suspension of disbelief anyway. Jatra happened on open fields, on a stage exposed on all sides, with next to no props. It meant the man stabbed to death on stage would pick himself up and run off to the greenroom in full view of the audience. Or the hero and heroine, after tearfully promising to never see each other again in this lifetime, could collide on the gangway as they exited the stage.

Renowned jatra playwright Brajendra Kumar (Brajen) Dey writes, 'For ages, the palakars [jatra playwrights] have created dark new-moon nights over the arena, brought the foaming waves of the ocean and the crests of mountains to the view of their listeners—only by words—as they were spoken and enacted by the performers. Whoever needed the lighting technicians, the

10 Gargi, 'Jatra—Folk Theatre of India'.

tape recorders or the microphones?'[11] It was the speech, rising to a crescendo and then dropping to a stage whisper, that offset 'the garish costumes, crude make-up, exaggerated diction, sing-song delivery and the adolescent boys impersonating women'.[12] Bandyopadhyay adds that jatra actors needed a 'skill in playing with the body more to the tones and rhythms of the speech than the meaning or weight of particular words'.[13]

Theatre came with a stage, curtains, sets, sound and lighting. Jatra, at its purest, was just about actors and the audience. That meant, notes Bandyopadhyay, that jatra actors had to have a 'richer and more audible vocal range than stage actors, a greater capacity to hold poses and positions, and turn on the stage with the poses and positions to give all their viewers a fair view of the performances in its entirety.'[14] So when Phanibhushan Motilal as Nawab Siraj-ud-Daulah knelt to offer his crown to his treacherous general Mir Jafar in a scene filled with drama and pathos and some in the audience complained loudly they could not see because his back was to them, Motilal knew how to turn without breaking a beat and repeat the same movement for them.

In a world where the audience was ready to imagine a chair could be a throne, an execution block and a log of wood, it was perhaps not that much of a stretch to accept men as women either. Sometimes the imagination worked overtime. When Nirmal Rani, a female impersonator, stepped out into the dark

---

11 Brajendra Kumar Dey, 'Ballad of the *Palanatak*', *Rangavarta* 57 (September 1995), p. 28.

12 Ghosh, 'Jatra', p. 171.

13 Samik Bandyopadhyay, untitled article, *Rangavarta* 57 (September 1995), p. 1.

14 Bandyopadhyay, 'Theatre Traditional'.

to smoke a bidi before his next scene, he had to fend off drunk, lecherous villagers who mistook him for a real woman. On the other hand, when Oto Dutta's demon king Ravan grabbed jatra queen Babli Rani's Sita by the hair, the entire wig came off in his hands, revealing Sita's own distinctly male haircut. The audience was in splits, but the show went on.

At that time, even professional theatre had men playing women, some men adept at playing both genders. Sarat Ghosh played Jagat Singh in the swashbuckling play *Durgeshnandini*, arriving on stage on a live Arabian horse. But he started out in 1857 as the winsome princess Shakuntala, bedecked in golden jewellery. Ardhendu Sekhar Mustafi was famous for his luxuriant moustache but also for playing women like Sabitri in *Nil Darpan*.

Once, a conservative neighbour of the elite Tagore family in North Kolkata was aghast to see their women wandering around in the garden, in full view of the neighbours. Then he was assured that they weren't women at all: Jyotirindranath Tagore and his friends were acting as women in a house production and had stepped out for some fresh air. 'Rubbish,' said the indignant neighbour. At the same time, young Turks like the poet Michael Madhusudan Dutt insisted, 'Good theatre will not be possible unless we bring real women in.' To prove his point, he staged a play with actresses like Golapsundari and Elokesi, both from the red-light district.

Though he didn't realize it at the time, when Chapal Bhaduri came into jatra in the 1950s, the final countdown was about to begin for the male queens of jatra. Women were all over professional theatre. Jatra was the next frontier.

Paper Flowers and Moustachioed Queens

Men acting as women is hardly unusual around the world, from Greek and Roman times to the plays of Shakespearean England to Japanese Onnagata. In India, though, as Lal points out, 'the Natya Shashtra talks about *both* actors and actresses. At some point, the zenana and purdah systems changed that.' The public space became increasingly male, and men had to fill in for women on stage. They developed, writes Balwant Gargi, 'a highly stylised interpretation of women'.[15]

Jatra was not the only art form in India where men played women. Yakshagana in Karnataka, tamasha in Maharashtra, kathakali in Kerala, swang in Uttar Pradesh, naqqals in Punjab, bhawai in Rajasthan and Gujarat, shamang leela in Manipur—all these art forms had men playing women, sometimes with naturalism, sometimes as high camp. In some forms, like yakshagana, that's still the norm. Rural Bengal itself had other folk forms where men, often adolescents, played women—alkaap, domni, leto, manikpir, etc. Jatra, unlike many of these, was not limited to specific castes or groups. Occasionally, the female impersonators became bona-fide stars. Bal Gandharva was so celebrated that women in Maharashtra styled their saris after him. The government honoured him with a Padma Bhushan award and a postage stamp. Jaishankar Sundari of Gujarat was awarded a Padma Bhushan as well and had a theatre named after him in Ahmedabad. 'If they could get a Padma Bhushan, why not Chapal Bhaduri?' asks Rakesh Ghosh, who directed Chapal in several plays. 'He is no less deserving.'[16]

---

15 Gargi, 'Jatra—Folk Theatre of India'.

16 Rakesh Ghosh, interview with the author, 25 February 2025. All subsequent quotations from Ghosh are drawn from this interview.

'This is about power politics,' says Lal. 'Bal Gandharva and Jaishankar had a background in folk traditions but they were essentially urban. The Parsee theatre was clearly urban. The female impersonators in Bengal didn't come from that stratum of society.' Jatra's main audiences were outside the city. While the rich babus in Calcutta might hire a troupe for a night of high-jinks jatra, the cultural movers and shakers still considered it vulgar. They thought it beneath themselves to take up the baton for jatra, let alone for the men who had become its queens.

'In colonial Calcutta, the upper class thought that the sahibs were best in everything, whether it was literature or theatre,' says Lal. 'So they emulated the British. That meant proscenium theatre as opposed to open-air arena-style jatra. They thought theatre was modern and urban and jatra was outdated and rustic, full of dirt and vulgarity, something best avoided.' *Calcutta Review*, a nineteenth-century Anglo-Indian journal, calls jatras 'wretched from the commencement to the fifth act.' It finds the howling of jackals harmonious compared to the 'discordant voices' of the boys who acted as women. All in all, they were 'calculated to soil the mind and pollute the fancy.'[17]

Bangadarshan, a renowned Bengali journal from the same era, complains: 'Thanks to the present type of jatra, Krishna and Radha look like "goalas" [milkmen]; in the past, the qualities of a good poet made them appear as divinities.'[18] The jatra actors

---

17 Arpita Ghatak, 'Sacred to Secular: Jatra in Contemporary Bengal', *Research Scholar—IRJLE* 7(4) (2019): 84; https://www.researchscholar.co.in/downloads/13-dr.-arpita-ghatak.pdf (accessed 20 November 2025).

18 *Bangadarshan* (Kartik 1280 [1873]), quoted in Banerjee, *The Parlour and the Streets*, p. 180.

were acutely aware of the disdain. Phanibhushan Motilal laments: 'In the early days, when we went to perform in a village, we would only stay in a house at the end of the village, sometimes in the horse stables of the wealthy.'[19] That attitude never really changed, says Chapal. It meant he had to deal with a double social whammy—an effeminate man who worked in jatra.

However, jatra's grassroots appeal meant it was far more effective at conveying a message to the masses than the rarefied theatre houses of North Kolkata. For example, Mukunda Das was arrested in the 1930s by the British police for spreading revolutionary ideas through his jatra. But people still kept humming his songs with lines, like:

Chhilo dhaan gola bhora
Shwet eendoore korlo sara
[All those silos filled with rice
All eaten empty by white mice]

In patriotic jatras, the devil wore tight trousers and a jacket like the British sahibs while the righteous prince wore a dhoti. Brajen Dey said that, in the 1950s, his scripts were deliberately about nation building and Hindu–Muslim harmony. In other parts of India, political parties and theatre movements latched onto folk theatre as a way to spread their messages. 'Burrakatha, a rural oral storytelling form in Andhra became completely a platform for the Communist Party,' says Lal. 'But in Bengal, theatre groups like Bohurupee felt that Kolkata was their home and they didn't need to go into the villages.' Theatre star Utpal Dutt eventually started using jatra to push out political messages. He

19 Bandyopadhyay, 'Theatre Traditional'.

brought a certain spectacle and technical sophistication to jatra, even taking on themes like the war in Vietnam. But jatra, on the whole, remained the bumpkin country cousin. After Mamata Banerjee became chief minister of West Bengal in 2011, colourful jatra versions of her life story started doing the rounds.

In the 1980s and 90s, jatra went through an identity crisis. Commercial jatra had moved closer and closer to theatre, slowly abandoning the old open-on-all-sides stage. Jatra now had drop-scenes, lighting systems and orchestras, writes Sumanta Banerjee. Instead of evolving naturally with the times, jatra tropes were 'frozen into ridiculous anachronisms', the old folk music was vulgarized while 'the subtle humour and suggestiveness slip[ped] through the bhadralok [gentleman] imitator's fingers.'[20]

Jatra got little respect but it certainly had money. According to the *Economic Times*, in 1991, 80-odd groups in the Chitpur area of Kolkata did 'business worth Rs 20 crore a year, top-bracket groups like Natta Company notch up Rs 1 crore a piece'.[21] As the film industry and movie theatres reeled from the effects of video, more and more cinema actors jumped onto the jatra bandwagon, lured by the money on offer. The *Economic Times* article estimates a top star at that time could charge around Rs 15,000 per show and average 60-odd shows a year—a tidy sum. An article in the *Week* magazine in 2000 works out the maths: 'Jatra which runs for at least 100 nights guarantees a return of Rs 75 lakh and some might gross between 2–3 crore a year. On an average 5,000 people see a show and some might run

20 Banerjee, *The Parlour and the Streets*, p. 232.

21 Arunava Sinha, 'Jatra: Making Money from Melodrama', *Economic Times*, 4 August 1991, n.p.

for more than 100 nights. An average Bengal film can hardly cover its cost of around Rs 30 lakhs these days.'[22]

As movie stars flooded in, jatra became chintzy versions of films and television soaps. Makhanlal Natta laments: 'Most of the [film]stars have no feeling for jatra. They come to earn a hefty sum by lending their names. And the conditions they impose create hell for the jatra party.'[23] But jatra owners still wooed film stars, because in an age where television brought those stars to the living rooms of ordinary people, they hoped villagers would flock to the jatra to see their favourite matinee idols in the flesh. Unfortunately, the original jatra actors ended up playing second fiddle to the silver-screen stars. 'The medium and smaller actors in jatra [. . .] whose families have been into jatra for generations [. . .] are the ones who suffer the ultimate financial crunch,' rues writer Sunil Chowdhury.[24]

Of course all art forms must evolve. Lal points out that performance theorist Richard Schechner said one cannot preserve an art form like an antiquarian museum piece. If it's not evolving, it's more or less dead. Jatra's obituary has been written more than once. Even in the 1920s, purists were complaining that jatra had turned into a poor man's professional theatre of Kolkata, just a more mobile version. 'Jatra, in fact, has emerged and died out so many times, losing its own form every time, appearing in a new form altogether, retaining only a few basics like the theatre in the

22 Tapash Ganguly, 'It's Yatra Folks!' *The Week*, 13 February 2000, n.p.

23 Quoted in Ganguly, 'It's Yatra folks!'

24 Quoted in Kaberi Dutta, 'Jatra Jamboree', *Amrita Bazar Patrika*, 26 March 1994, n.p.

round, the musicality (though it has diminished progressively) and maybe a few acting techniques,' writes Bandyopadhyay.[25]

In the nineteenth century, jatra director Madan Master introduced the juri or double system in which four singers wearing turbans and long black tunics like olden-day lawyers would pop up from amid the audience and sing. The actor would sing one line and toss it to the juri who would then toss it to each other, playing with the melody, embellishing it with frills, using song to pass judgement on the happenings on stage, all of it going on for so long the actor could take a break, chew some paan and have a smoke. But the audience tired of this and started booing if it went on too long. By 1911, the juri was gone.

In its stead arrived the Bibek, the Conscience, offering a running moral commentary, underlining the to-be-or-not-to-be mental conflicts of the characters. The Bibek could be a mad fakir in a black robe, an old servant who spoke truth to power or a philosophical boatman. Brajen Dey turned Ravan's righteous brother Bibhishan into the Bibek in his Ramayana-based jatra *Swarna-Lanka*. At one time, Bibeks were some of the most highly paid jatra artistes, but gradually even they faded away.

But the demise of the jatra queens hit harder. Brajen Dey rues in an address to a literary conference: 'Those "queens" are no longer on the scene, and the only ones to sigh at their disappearance today are a few jatra lovers like myself.'[26] In an article for *Jugantar* newspaper in 1967, he despairs: 'The day the moustachioed queens were thrown onto the rubbish heap, from that day jatra started to go down the road to ajatra [ignominy].'[27]

---

25 Bandyopadhyay, 'Theatre Traditional'.

26 Dey, 'Ballad of the *Palanatak*', p. 26.

The 'ajatra' he alludes to is about a new kind of prurience that quickly infected jatra. Jatra had always had its wicked zamindars molesting damsels in distress, but at one time both roles were played by men. When women entered jatra, those scenes carried an extra charge as did the shimmying cabaret numbers. Dey writes: 'The lights would suddenly go off in the middle of a scene. A minute later, when the lights came on again, there would be the "raped" woman in a state of partial undress rearranging her clothes.'[28]

However, Lal points out, in the 'good old days', the young boys in the chorus were also routinely exploited. 'It's good that women have come to jatra, that they have some agency now,' says Lal. 'Many people think of female impersonation from a purist angle. They ask why can't we revive it. I think it's no longer necessary to, unless you want to do a museological piece for its own sake.'

But the purush-ranis were not just filling in for women, they brought an extra something to jatra, say aficionados. Dey claimed roles like Hairgopal Rani's Chikan Goylani, Chhabi Rani's Madira and Shatadal Rani's Tia would remain unsurpassed in the history of jatra. Natta Company's long-time manager Surya Kumar Dutta says in an interview: 'When we represent a lame or cross-eyed man, we do not import a crippled or cross-eyed man onto the stage. Theatrical enjoyment lies in the fact that an able-bodied man is limping and squinting. The natural thing is not the natural thing on stage. When a man acts as a woman, it is art!'[29]

---

27 Brajendra Kumar Dey, 'Jatray Nari', *Jugantar*, 29 September 1967, n.p.

28 Dey, 'Ballad of the *Palanatak*', p. 28.

29 Gargi, 'Jatra—Folk Theatre of India'.

It was challenging for sure. In jatra, actors performed night after night on an open stage. That means the audience had a 360-degree view. 'You had to be convincing as a woman from all sides. And your pitch and tone had to be consistent as well,' says Debojit Majumder, the principal researcher behind *Chena Kintu Ajana* [Known Strangers], a 2014 documentary about the lost queens of jatra.[30] In Sekhar Samaddar's play *Sundarbibir Pala*, the role of Heera Malini, the flower-girl go-between in the old Vidya–Sundar romance, is played by an ageing female impersonator rather than an actress. That role was written with Chapal in mind. Samaddar says, 'When a male actor plays a woman, he absorbs all facets of a woman, the gait, the body movement, the way she attracts a man. But there is also a natural masculinity. I wanted Heera Malini to have all that. Then she would be the complete package.'[31] Makhanlal Natta's anguish is palpable when he tells Majumder, his voice garbled by cancer: 'I miss the [purush-ranis] a lot but those days will not come back.'[32]

'Whether they were more skilled or less skilled than the women who replaced them is secondary,' says film director Kaushik Ganguly, who directed Chapal Bhaduri in several films, including the 2010 landmark film *Arekti Premer Golpo* [Just Another Love Story], one of the first explorations of alternative

---

30 Debojit Majumder, interview with the author, 16 November 2024. All subsequent quotations from Majumder are drawn from this interview.

31 Sekhar Samaddar, interview with the author, 17 April 2025. All subsequent quotations from Samaddar are drawn from this interview.

32 Dipankar Dutta (dir.) and Debojeet Majumdar (writ. and prod.), *Chena Kintu Ajaṇa* [Known Strangers], documentary film, 2014; available at: https://www.youtube.com/watch?v=f839_qQfbj8 (accessed 20 November 2025).

sexuality in mainstream Bengali cinema. 'Why would anyone want to keep watching the purush-ranis? It's the difference between real flowers and artificial flowers. This ultimately is a paper flower. It's only natural that people wanted real flowers.'[33]

Even Brajen Dey was not as opposed to women in jatra as he was made out to be, his son Tarun Dey argues in *Chena Kintu Ajana*. 'He wanted them to be able to act with dignity,' he says. 'So he said, why not let men continue doing these roles until women's security can be guaranteed?' But the discarded jatra queens could not help but feel spurned. In an article in *Jugantar*, Babli Rani complains, 'At one time, not even one night of jatra was possible without us. But now all the glory of jatra is attributed to the big male actors. What about us? Does jatra owe us nothing in our bad days?'[34]

Chapal Bhaduri too accepted—even welcomed—the arrival of women in jatra. He just thought there would still be a place for him alongside, perhaps in the role of a queen mother or the evil mother-in-law. For a while, there was. Until one day even those roles dried up.

Years later, watching him reinvent himself singing the songs of Sitala, the goddess of smallpox, Lal was struck by the poignancy of it all. 'Everything in his cultural past has vanished, the traditional jatra now replaced by "blow-hot" stripes, men enacting stylized femininity rejected by viewers for "real women".'[35] Now

33 Kaushik Ganguly, interview with the author, 18 February 2025. All subsequent quotations from Ganguly are drawn from this interview.

34 Prabhat Kumar Das, 'Jatragaaner Ranira', *Jugantar*, 29 August 1976, n.p.

35 Ananda Lal, 'Requiems for the Past', *The Telegraph*, 27 August 1999, n.p.

the jatra queen was playing goddess on the roadside in slums for a pittance. Even more ironic, says Lal, thanks to modern medicine, smallpox itself, of which Sitala was the goddess, had been eradicated.

Trans-formed?

Still, Chapal is luckier than most of his peers and those who came before him. He got to have a second act.

'I would not put Shatadal Rani and Chhabi Rani lower than Chapal Bhaduri,' says Majumder, who recounts the stories of over a dozen such male ranis in *Chena Kintu Ajana*. 'But who remembers them now? Who is documenting their lives? We filmed Janardan Rani for our documentary. I don't think he had done anything in the last 20–30 years.' The world of these ranis had vanished with them. No one had bothered to record their stories or keep track of them. Even finding their families was like a treasure hunt. 'We heard Babli Rani started a costume-rental business in Baranagar after his jatra life ended. We found a man who had such a business and asked if he had heard of Babli Rani. And he said, "He was my father!"' The stories, more often than not, were pitiful. One former queen, once lauded as the Elizabeth Taylor of jatra, stitched petticoats to make a living; another ran a small tea stall. One had committed suicide because he could not feed his family. At one time he was called the Jatra Lakshmi of Midnapore, the goddess with the touch of gold.

Majumder says the documentary was a labour of love because he knew time was running out. Most of the jatra ranis were dead. Among the few still around, Janardan Rani had chronic obstructive pulmonary disease. He lived in a small one-room flat with his family. When his daughter came to visit with her child, he slept under the bed. Sanjay Singha, the executive producer of *Chena Kintu Ajana*, says Janardan Rani was hesitant to even meet them. 'Some television channel had promised him money, got work out of him and then never paid him. He was afraid the same thing would happen again. He really needed money.'[36] Majumder adds, 'But there was also a deep sense of rejection. They felt they had given so much to jatra, but in the end they had been just thrown away.'

In Majumder's documentary, Chapal re-enacted some of his famous roles in full regalia. Janardan Rani, now stouter and far less feminine, chose to do it in his male persona. 'But once you put them on stage, their hunger, their poverty, their struggle, their financial condition, their health issues, all just vanished,' marvels Majumder. Satyabrata Roy, by then frail and fading, was hospitalized twice while they were shooting the film. 'The day before we did our last take with him, he had just got out of hospital,' remembers Majumder. 'He was so happy that day, talking and laughing even though his memory was fading. Next day he was dead. Perhaps he just stayed alive to tell us his story. It still gives me goosebumps.' Now Janardan Rani is gone as well.

Chapal's second act brought him into a world that had little exposure to jatra. After Naveen Kishore, publisher of Seagull Books, made the documentary *Performing the Goddess: The Chapal Bhaduri Story* (1999) and mounted exhibitions of his photographs of Chapal, a new generation, one that had never been to the jatra, discovered him.

Kishore himself discovered Chapal by chance. He had gone with Samik Bandyopadhyay to tape an interview with Chapal's

36 Sanjay Singha, interview with the author, 16 November 2024. All subsequent quotations from Singha are drawn from this interview.

sister, the redoubtable stage actress Ketaki Dutta. 'I have a memory of someone coming to serve us tea and biscuits, a man in a checked lungi, bending down and putting the cups and saucers before us,' recalls Kishore. 'But there was a familiarity to the gait, a rhythm to the way he walked. And on his feet were faint traces of red alta, the way women line their feet.'[37]

When Kishore discovered who Chapal was and learnt that he dressed up as Goddess Sitala for a living, he wanted to photograph him. He remembers the Sitala temple, the makeshift greenroom with its 150-watt bulb and the bustle of people getting ready. As he made chit-chat to put Chapal at ease, there came the moment when Chapal started to stuff his brassiere—the moment that comes up again and again when people talk about working with Chapal. 'His gaze changes. He becomes a stranger. I would not dare be familiar with him at that moment,' says Kaushik Ganguly. Sanjay Singha says that when they filmed the jatra scenes with Chapal, 'all the men would be sent outside as he put on his bra and blouse. I asked him why. We were both men after all. He said: you won't understand. You go outside.'

'There was a kind of shyness that threw me off balance,' says Kishore. 'He gets shy and I start feeling like a voyeur.' Perhaps it's that tension that made the photographs remarkable. Curator Gayatri Sinha heard about them and reached out to Kishore. He gave her five photographic prints and they sold for a tidy sum. The money went to Chapal, who at that time earned next to nothing playing Sitala. When Chapal approached Kishore later seeking a job—any job, even one that involved making tea and dusting books—Kishore was shocked. 'I knew so many artistes

---

37 Naveen Kishore, interview with the author, 26 November 2024. All subsequent quotations from Kishore are drawn from this interview.

like him, a cinematographer, a Chhau dancer, all still able mentally and physically to contribute in many ways, but incapable of writing a grant proposal. And I thought about making a talking-heads documentary. When a Bengali channel picked it up, that was more money in the kitty for him.'

Kishore was no jatra fan. 'Coming from theatre, I had a whole different sensibility of a certain kind of subtlety,' he says. 'Jatra was more like old Parsi theatre, lots of melodrama, everything exaggerated and over-the-top.' What transfixed him was not the acting per se but the process of transformation, 'the moment when the shyness sets in and the seriousness takes over. I was awestruck by that.'

Does Chapal Bhaduri become a woman at that moment? Or is it just a sister act of sorts? His own answers can appear contradictory. Sometimes he talks about it as just a technique whereby an actor focuses on a character. He rubbishes any notion that he might be a woman trapped in a man's body. And yet Ganguly remembers him talking about feeling a sense of unease and restlessness every month—likening it to the way a woman feels during her period.

Chapal sees no contradiction in his statements, even if gender politics in the world today would want him to choose one label and stick to it. But Chapal has no interest in making his life fit my labels. He is not shy about his love for another man and yet not invested even in the term gay. He never had any need for that term in order to live or love. Yet he is, says theatre director Rakesh Ghosh, possibly 'the first actor in India who was openly gay' though hardly anyone noted that.

In the 1990s–2000s, I edited *Trikone*, the world's oldest South Asian LGBTQ+ magazine. Those were the early days of the

South Asian queer movement, and the magazine, published from California, scrounged and scraped every bit of content that had both a queer touch and a South Asian connection, no matter how tenuous. Yet we never reached out to Chapal. I was born and raised in Kolkata, I spoke Bengali, but jatra and its last queen were somehow too foreign for me, too garishly unfamiliar.

Label Queen

Unlike Chapal Bhaduri, most of the other male jatra ranis chose to get married. But were some of them also queer? At this point, all we have are vague clues. In an interview with *Desh* magazine, female impersonator Satyabrata Roy says Chhabi Rani's fashion sense, hair styles and make-up would have been the envy of any female star, even though he was also a family man with children. 'But he was still rather effeminate,' says Roy. 'We would often tease him, saying it's hard to tell who is the woman here—you or your wife.'[38] In another article for *Jugantar*, jatra scholar Prabhat Das talks about two former jatra queens who share a room, cooking and keeping house together, but whether they were just roommates or more is unclear.[39]

Majumder says, given that most of the jatra queens were dead, he could hardly ask their families about their sexuality while making his documentary:

> I cannot say who was queer and who was not. But if I go by society's gender-assigned roles, there was considerable overlap with feminine roles. They did their housework

38 Quoted in Shirsho Bandyopadhyay, 'Beneputul', *Desh*, 9 May 1992, p. 30.

39 Das, 'Jatragaaner Ranira'.

themselves. They were very good at cutting vegetables. Many were very good at cooking. That's not to say everyone who cooks is gay. Janardan Rani was not effeminate at all. But he liked helping his wife take care of the household.

As a gay person himself, Majumder was curious about what made these jatra queens tick: 'Was there a thread of effeminacy in them that they developed? If so, how did they balance their family lives?' Jatra scholar Prabhat Das says in the documentary that these men could go from being a husband and father at home to being a newlywed bride on stage every night. 'They dealt with that duality on a daily basis,' says Das. 'It's amazing.'

Majumder says it would not be right to speculate about the sexuality of people long dead. At this point, it's hard to say even whether their femininity was innate or learnt, the result of years of acting as a woman on stage. In the afterword to the play *Sundarbibir Pala*, Malay Rakshit writes that while India has long had a concept of Ardhanarishwara, where the male and female reside in the same divine body, characters like Sundar Bibi and Ramanimohan in Sekhar Samaddar's plays—and indeed Chapal himself—do not neatly fit the label of 'third gender': 'Ramanimohan or Sundar Bibi are not of that nature at all. What Samaddar is exploring is how though they are born male, by continuously acting as women in their craft, they became feminine in body, mind and soul.' Ananda Lal, too, is wary of any Ardhanarishwara theory. 'This is the case of an actor who happens to be male taking on another role which happens to be female. It's not Ardhanarishwara—it's performance.'

'But I do feel for the very successful ones, there was some gender interplay, however subtle. And those who nurtured their feminine side, they were the ones who really reached the peak,' says Majumder. 'There was some trace of feminine gender ingrained somewhere, no matter what the sexuality was.' As Anuradha Ghosh describes the scenes of Chapal transforming himself in *Performing the Goddess* in an essay in the anthology *The Phobic and the Erotic*, 'we watch the body that is in negotiation between the male and the female.'[40]

Chapal himself makes little of any connection between his art and his sexuality. While acting is in his blood, he sees female impersonation as a vocation, something born out of necessity in tough times. His fluting voice and feminine mannerisms made him good at playing women, but he always takes pains to emphasize that he is effeminate, not female. Offstage he is very much a man, even if it's a man who feels no need to pass as heterosexual. In fact, Chapal reacts rather indignantly to being called transgender or hijra.

That becomes a flashpoint for his characters in both *Ramanimohan* and *Sundarbibir Pala*. In the latter, a character lashes out at Sundar Bibi, saying, 'Those who want to sell your personal story in a film will never value you as an artiste. Not even when the film is done. You will remain what you always were in their eyes—a eunuch, a hermaphrodite, a hijra.' When Sundar Bibi has a fight with Saraswati, a folk dancer in the play, he calls her a prostitute and she calls him a hijra. In *Ramanimohan*, his son spits the word out at him while Ramanimohan's wife covers

40 Anuradha Ghosh, 'Playing Woman, Playing Power: Performing the Goddess; a Reading of a Documentary on Chapal Bhaduri', in Brinda Bose and Subhabrata Bhattacharya (eds), *The Phobic and the Erotic: The Politics of Sexualities in Contemporary India* (London: Seagull Books, 2007), p. 482.

her ears in horror. 'Ramanimohan's female impersonation is seen as endangering patriarchy,' writes scholar Niladri R. Chatterjee.[41] It feminizes it and therefore emasculates it, destabilizing the very house that patriarchy built.

Samaddar says he did not want to get into gender politics at all in his plays. 'I wanted to look at the issue from an artistic point of view. And how being different leaves an artist vulnerable to abuse. If he is humiliated and insulted, that's abuse. But if someone tries to buy him for money, use him as a commodity, that's a kind of abuse too.'

Both Ramanimohan and Sundar Bibi are shown as family men. Sundar Bibi is married and has a son. Ramanimohan retorts that if he were truly a hijra, how could he have produced the very son who now calls him one? That line, Chapal says, always got resounding applause. But the jibe stings. Chapal says in an interview to Chatterjee: 'I am comfortable in my kurta-pyjama. I play women's parts. I have no wish to permanently become a woman, but I like becoming a woman occasionally, and then returning to being a man.'[42] As we began working on this book—still strangers, sizing each other up—one of the first things Chapal stated categorically was: 'I am not third gender. I am first gender.'

I remember being rather taken aback. At a time when transgender politics and the backlash to it are assuming global proportions, Chapal's vehement rejection of the word can feel somewhat

---

41 Niladri R. Chatterjee, 'Chapal Rani/Chapal Bhaduri: On and Off-Stage', in Tutun Mukherjee and Niladri R. Chatterjee (eds), *Nari Bhav: Androgyny and Female Impersonation in* India (New Delhi: Niyogi Books, 2016), p. 286.

42 Chatterjee, 'Chapal Rani/Chapal Bhaduri', p. 300.

disconcerting. Then again, this is about me trying to fit Chapal into the new vocabulary of Pride activism in India and beyond.

Director Rituparno Ghosh, who acted with Chapal as the filmmaker Abhiroop in *Arekti Premer Golpo*, says in an interview with the *Telegraph* that while both of their characters were queer, they were different. 'It is femininity in the case of Chapal Bhaduri but androgyny in the case of [Abhi]Roop. Chapal cannot wear ear studs which Roop can. This is Chapal's limit and he can't step out of it.' Ghosh goes on to expand on the difference between femininity and androgyny. 'A woman wears her femininity. An androgynous man, shifting between male and female, performs femininity.'[43]

Gender fluidity, androgyny, transness, gender dysphoria—these are all labels we impose on Chapal. But as I figured out over time, his connection with his audience is more primal. Films like *Arekti Premer Golpo*, says academic Kaustav Bakshi, locate the 'old theatrical practice of female impersonation within contemporary discourses of sexuality identity politics'. But the boy actors playing women on Elizabethan stage were a little different. Bakshi quotes Richard Cressy as saying they created a kind of 'androgyny and muted eroticism' and linked actors, dramatists and the audience in 'a sexually charged subculture of transgression'.[44] So Janardan Rani, a man who led a perfectly heterosexual life with

---

43 Reshmi Sengupta, 'The Third Sex', *The Telegraph*, 5 October 2009: https://www.telegraphindia.com/entertainment/the-third-sex/cid/582229 (accessed on 25 November 2025).

44 Kaustav Bakshi, 'Rituparno Ghosh, Performance Arts and a Queer Legacy: An Abiding Stardom', *South Asian History and Culture* 8(2) (2017): 292–93.

wife and children, says in *Chena Kintu Ajana* that a British man fell in love with him and wanted to marry him. 'But I couldn't give recognition to this love.' The love was not beyond the pale. He was perhaps even flattered by it, though he could not give it official recognition.

Rituparno, whom Bakshi calls Bengal's 'first queer icon', says: 'I consider myself privileged because of my gender-fluidity, the fact that I am in-between.' But he also says that society was not ready to go beyond lip service. 'When we were casting for the film, no one in Bombay or Calcutta agreed to play the bisexual character. Though all of them were gaga over Sean Penn [playing a gay character] in *Milk*!' He recalls an actor telling him he would have no qualms playing a murderer or a rapist 'because people wouldn't think he is either of the two.'[45]

In that world, Chapal showed his courage by carving out his own space. He isn't hiding behind any fig leaf, nor is he fazed by the growing complexity of gender politics. 'I would see him at colleges where people would throw wonderfully academically phrased questions at him,' says Kishore. 'He would speak directly in response and not try to be canny or clever. He is instinctively a storyteller.' And he knows how to tease his interlocutors as they try to pin him down with labels. When the *Hindustan Times* asks him if he would prefer tea or coffee, he says saucily, 'I am both man and woman. I can drink both.'[46]

---

45 Reshmi Sengupta, 'Be What You Want to Be: Rituparno Ghosh Speaks Out', *The Telegraph*, 8 August 2009: https://www.telegraphindia.com/-entertainment/be-what-you-want-to-be-rituparno-ghosh-speaks-out/cid/-607483 (accessed on 25 November 2025).

46 Dhrubo Jyoti, 'Chapal Rani, the Man Who Ruled Bengal's Jatra Stage as a Woman', *Hindustan Times*, 30 July 2018: https://www.hindustantimes.-

It's quintessentially Chapal Bhaduri, but in a world that is often cruel to those who don't fit their gender roles, the jatra stage surely afforded some protection to a girlish young man. It gave him a space to be who he was. 'Jatra, I believe, saved Chapal,' says Ganguly. 'Chapal Rani kept Chapal Bhaduri alive—the rani inside Chapal Bhaduri got some acknowledgement.'

Chapal himself has not studied queer theory. Nor is he aware of what happened at the Stonewall Inn in New York or on Castro Street in San Francisco. Even the anti-sodomy provision of the Indian Penal Code meant little to him. While speaking with to him, I realized he didn't even have a coming-out story, something we have been taught to believe every queer person must have.

What he has, though, is his own life story. That story became the second act of Chapal Rani. His first act had been about playing a woman as convincingly as possible. He had played queens, brothel madams, mad women and seductresses. The second act was invariably about playing a man who once acted as women. 'It was great that he could explore both genders,' says Lal. 'But he had portrayed such a diverse range of women.' As a man, though, most of his work in film and theatre was re-enacting, in some form, his own Chapal Bhaduri biography.

Reviewing one of his theatrical productions, Lal had observed that Chapal had 'acted much more naturally' as the husband and father than as the female impersonator in the play. There the ageing actor had 'looked tired, even exhausted,

---

com/art-and-culture/man-actress-goddess/story-3UGMWN1MtXyjshB1Tl5fHI.html (accessed 20 November 2025).

certainly not of the high quality that, in the drama, supposedly entrances the audience.'[47]

Yet the star factor remains. Samaddar remembers one performance of *Sundarbibir Pala* in Asansol, an industrial city in West Bengal, in front of an audience of over 600:

> Sometimes Chapal, because of his age, would forget his lines. Or lose his timing. But that night he was perfect. It was magical. He transcended the script. It's the moment of truth we live for in theatre. When other actors in the group would complain about him making mistakes, I would tell them, 'You don't know who you are talking about. Remember all these people are coming to see him, not you.'

Lonely Hearts

Chapal's last theatrical outing—before the Covid-19 pandemic put an end to them—was yet another iteration of the Chapal Bhaduri story, this time even more biographical, although the names were changed. *Upal Bhaadury: Tale of a Dead Star* was staged by Rakesh Ghosh. The play featured both Chapal and a younger actor, Ranjan Bose, also a female impersonator. Ghosh remembers Chapal watching Bose intently as the latter finished his make-up, the older star appraising the ingenue.

> Once Ranjan was done, Chapal-da said, 'Today your make-up wasn't quite right.' That upset Ranjan. Later I realized that also affected his acting. That's where

47 Ananda Lal, 'All for a Dying Art Form', *The Telegraph,* 10 June 2006: https://www.telegraphindia.com/west-bengal/all-for-a-dying-art-form/-cid/1538150 (accessed on 25 November 2025).

> Chapal-da fell back on his old jatra ways and scored a goal. In jatra, it was all about one-upmanship. That's how you got your applause. That applause determined everything from your pay to which piece of fish you got at lunch.

Later the director told Ranjan to turn the tables on Chapal by finishing his make-up first and telling Chapal that his wasn't quite right. He did so, and Chapal immediately retorted, 'I did my make-up poorly deliberately. I wanted to let you shine.'

It's a story about a diva but also about a man whose life found meaning on the stage. 'He is happiest when he paints his face and goes on stage. And gets paid for it, however modestly,' says Ghosh. But he feels that in the end the industry didn't do him justice. 'And the LGBT community just uses him to cut a ribbon or light a lamp.'

Ghosh himself identifies as queer. 'Chapal-da and I had an incredible inter-generational friendship,' he says. 'He was like a family friend, I dare say even family. We went on a trip to Benares together, me, my partner Ranjan, my mother and Ranjan's parents. I remember how at ease he was with the women, fixing Ranjan's mother's hair or the pleats of my mother's sari. I felt as if I was managing three elderly ladies on a trip.'

It was perhaps the closest Chapal ever came to having a queer family. Ghosh says Chapal is 'intensely romantic' and has fallen in love many times, though none of them ended well.

> In the heteronormative world, such things are commonplace. Stars fall in love, people gossip, affairs break up, marriages happen, marriages break up. It happened with Charlie Chaplin. It happened with Bengal's Uttam Kumar. So it must have happened with Chapal. But how openly could he talk about it? In the end, he was a

minority within a minority. Jatra was a minority art form, and he was a minority in it.

Yet Chapal did not choose the easy way out. His contemporaries chose marriage and domesticity. They had families and children who took care of them. 'Chapal sacrificed all that. He had the guts to live on his own terms. We have to salute that,' says Ghosh. 'He is a beacon and a pathbreaker. He showed young people you could be out and still have a position in society,' says Majumder. Yet none of it was done in order to be a pioneer. 'He is very brave and he is very matter-of-fact,' says Naveen Kishore.

Discussing Kishore's *Performing the Goddess*, Anuradha Ghosh notes that while Chapal is open about his relationship with a man, he also 'represents their relationship as a *man-woman* one, the woman being himself.' When the relationship ends, he 'adopts the stance of a rejected, wounded woman who suffers intensely yet wishes for his partner's well-being'.[48] That sounds rather like the noble long-suffering heroines of popular Bengali novels by Sarat Chandra Chattopadhyay, roles he had grown up seeing his mother play on stage. But when he plays Sitala, he becomes, says Ghosh, an empowered woman: 'We must remember that jatra primarily targets the rural audience and, in this given social context, a goddess—a devi—constitutes the only safe, therefore acceptable, model of female power.'

But despite that 'empowerment' coming as it does, after years of despair and utter desolation, a core of loneliness remains.

In many interviews, the word that keeps coming up when people describe Chapal is 'jovial'. And he is a raconteur par excellence. 'But there is an area of sadness and pain,' says

---

48 Ghosh, 'Playing Woman, Playing Power', pp. 481, 480.

Majumder. 'I think at some level he aspired to have someone who would love him. And for a while he had it but then it ended.'

Both Majumder and Ghosh remember Chapal weeping because he felt lonely. Chapal, like many of us, had wanted to belong.

Ghosh recalls an event at Jogesh Mime Academy in Kolkata where he was supposed to interview Chapal on stage. 'Ranjan and I reached a little late and found Chapal-da sitting on a chair crying his eyes out,' says Ghosh. There were two women sitting behind him. It turned out they were the daughters of the man who had once been the love of his life. He had not seen them in years, but they had come to meet him. They had told him that their father was now very ill. And though their love affair was long over, Chapal could not help his tears. 'But when he got on stage, he was once again the star, feeding us with the stories we wanted to hear. Off stage he was heartbroken and weeping. On stage he was Chapal Rani.'

Hall of Mirrors

I remembered Chapal telling me that same story about meeting the daughters of his former lover at that event. Except in his recounting, he left out one detail—his own tears.

It is a telling omission. Chapal who had known heartbreak and penury, who had dusted and arranged books in a library for a pittance, taken on utterly forgettable roles just for some money, does not ever want to become an object of pity.

Much of recent media coverage has tried to portray him as the forsaken actor spending his twilight years in an old-age home with not even his wigs and Benarasi saris for company. That loneliness is part of the script of much of his theatre work as well. In the introduction to *Sundarbibir Pala*, Samaddar says the character played by Chapal was inspired by Jiten Ghosh, a dancer in the domni tradition—a unique folk theatre originating from the Malda region in West Bengal—who had been reduced to selling lottery tickets in his old age. Samaddar says,

> I would wonder what their connection was to what we call the mainstream of society. The Jiten Ghosh who would drive people mad when he appeared as a woman, the Chapal Rani who would draw such crowds, they are now marginal in a society, almost alone. Who clings to whom to survive? Is art holding on to Jiten or Chapal, or are Chapal or Jiten holding on to art?

'I have seen his familial ups and downs, I know about his troubles, I have watched him move to the old-age home,' says Rakesh Ghosh. 'And sometimes I feel that the time I spent with him was time spent with my own destiny.' On the surface, Ghosh's reality is different from Chapal's. He has a life partner and a supportive family. He works in group theatre—a socially conscious alternative to more commerial theatre, which has greater respectability than jatra. 'But as a person who is part of the sexual minority, how much more secure are we really?' asks Ghosh. 'In India, the government will not recognize my partner. And in the world outside, Donald Trump refuses to accept alternative sexuality.'

As a gay man, that question nags me too. My queer vocabulary is different from Chapal's and I come from privilege that he never had. But, ultimately, we are both creatures of the fringe, uncertain about what security the future holds for us. I came to Chapal to learn about the history of jatra and the female impersonators who once ruled it. But I also got a master class in resilience. The hurt, the slights, the betrayals all remained. But as I spent time with him, I would notice how he had learnt to paper over these cracks. His story was about the phoenix rising from the ashes. Once a queen, always a queen. When he talked, Chapal Bhaduri was always ready for his close-up.

In an interview for the Bengali daily *Aajkaal*, Chapal said, 'I love to act because I do not like being alone.'[49] But today he is very much alone. Health issues confine him to his room. An attendant has to help him with his daily chores. It's a small room, filled up by his bed and steel almirahs, a room without much of a view, the windows opening onto the walls of the house next door. Sometimes he sounds dejected. 'The Chapal Rani story is over,' he says. But then when I show him an old photograph I have found, he lights up. He summons his attendant Chaitali over and says, 'Look at that picture. Can you recognize me?'

'You never saw me in my jatra days,' he would tell me sadly over and over again. 'One should not say this about oneself. But I looked beautiful. Now look at me. I am old and fat and I've lost my hair. If only you had seen me then.'

At first this lament for lost beauty amused me. It seemed the vanity of an ageing star. But over time I sensed the sadness was not that he had once been beautiful and was no longer that person. It was that no one could bear witness to that beauty any more. The great Bengali actress Suchitra Sen locked herself in seclusion in her later years. She wanted the world to remember her for the beauty she had once been, not the old woman she had become. No mother roles, no judging talent shows, no inaugurating exhibitions. She shunned the limelight with a ferocity that feels unimaginable in a world where every minor celebrity frets

---

49 Alokprasad Chattopadhyay, 'Aar Ekjon Chapal Rani Toiri Hobe?', *Aajkaal,* 13 April 2019, p. 10.

that ten minutes outside the limelight spells oblivion. At least in Sen's case, there were plenty of people around to bear witness to her luminous beauty. At a time when Uttam Kumar and Suchitra Sen were ruling cinema, Chapal Bhaduri was ruling jatra. But he no longer has anyone around who can attest to his beauty. He doesn't even have photographs from that time.

All he has are words. But I wondered, no matter what he said and what I wrote, whether Chapal Rani would feel truly seen. In *Sundarbibir Pala*, Sundar Haldar, who became famous as the female impersonator Sundar Bibi, asks that very question: 'Who is Sundar Haldar? What value does he have? If anyone will live on in the memories of people, it is Sundar Bibi.'

I came into the story knowing little about jatra, even less about Chapal Rani—and least of all about Chapal Bhaduri. As he told me his story over weeks and months, I realized he was not always the most reliable narrator. The World According to Chapal sometimes deviated from things he had himself said in earlier interviews.

In his memoir, Makhanlal Natta remembers his first encounter with Chapal thus:

> Chapal was a freelance artiste. He had heard of Natta Company's fame and wanted a chance to act with us. I said he will have to give a test. Chapal kind of crumpled upon hearing this. [. . .] Eventually we persuaded him to read a part. But he still seemed very shy and uncomfortable, practically unable to open his mouth. Finally, he recited the dialogue of *Padmavati*. It was a long piece, and by the time he finished, we were all overwhelmed. His way of talking, his facial expressions were all exceptional. But we also understood why he had seemed so shy as well. His

> enunciation and mannerisms were rather affected and girlish. That's why he was always diffident. He thought as soon as he opened his mouth, he would be teased and ridiculed, that he would become the target of jokes.[50]

Chapal's own recollection of that encounter was not exactly the same. But that is all right. This is *his* truth, and this is *his* story. Though in the end, this book, even if it is in his own words, is still about how *I* see Chapal Bhaduri. There is inevitably a gap.

At first I wanted to mind the gap, but as the book progressed, I was tempted to fill them with fictional interludes, imagining how other people might have viewed this remarkable person, people I might have interviewed had they been still around.

Chapal had once told me a story about trying to reach his mother through a planchette almost two decades after her death. He remembered a dim blue light in the room and everything going hazy, and then hearing his mother's voice in his ears. With time he had forgotten exactly what she had said, but he remembered that voice slowly dissolving into the darkness. 'People tell me it was my psychological issue, but I know what I heard,' he said. 'I was aware I was speaking, but it was not exactly me either.' The interludes in this book are the ghosts in this story. They exist somewhere between Chapal's reality and my imagination—and they too have stories to tell. It is up to the reader to decide how much to believe.

I had begun this project imagining Chapal Rani as an ageing jatra queen sitting in front of a mirror and talking into it. But slowly I understood there is no one mirror, that memory itself is

50 Natta, *Rangamanchey Natta Company*, p. 32.

a hall of mirrors. And none of the reflections are wholly true or untrue.

In the documentary *Chena Kintu Ajana*, Tarun Dey recalls his father Brajen Dey often saying that there came a moment when the great male queens saw themselves in the mirror and fell in love with the person in it. He felt that was the mysterious moment of transformation when the male actor became the female character.

When I went to ask Chapal about that, I realized that in the cramped little room of his old-age home, there is no space for a proper mirror. The only full-length mirror is on the wall outside, next to his door.

When I looked into it as I bade him goodbye, I saw not Chapal Bhaduri but myself.

BIBLIOGRAPHY

BAKSHI, Kaustav. 'Rituparno Ghosh, Performance Arts and a Queer Legacy: An Abiding Stardom'. *South Asian History and Culture* 8(2) (2017): 284–99.

BANDYOPADHYAY, Samik. 'Theatre Traditional'. *Hindustan Standard,* 28 October 1973.

BANDYOPADHYAY, Samik. Untitled article. *Rangavarta* 57 (September 1995): 1–4.

BANDYOPADHYAY, Shirsho. 'Beneputul'. *Desh*, 9 May 1992, pp. 28–31.

BANERJEE, Sumanta. *The Parlour and the Streets: Elite and Popular Culture in Nineteenth-Century Calcutta.* London: Seagull Books, 2019[1989].

CHATTERJEE, Niladri R. 'Chapal Rani/Chapal Bhaduri: On and Off-Stage', in Tutun Mukherjee and Niladri R. Chatterjee (eds), *Nari*

Bhav: *Androgyny and Female Impersonation in India*. New Delhi: Niyogi Books, 2016, pp. 283–301.

CHATTOPADHYAY, Alokprasad. 'Aar Ekjon Chapal Rani Toiri Hobe?' *Aajkaal*, 13 April 2019, p. 10.

CHOWDHURY, Sunil. 'Mukunda Das: Section 108'. *Dainik Statesman*, 11 June 2005.

DAS, Prabhat Kumar. 'Jatragaaner Ranira'. *Jugantar*, 29 August 1976.

DEY, Brajendra Kumar. 'Ballad of the *Palanatak*'. *Rangavarta* 57 (September 1995): 22–30.

DEY, Brajendra Kumar. 'Jatray Nari'. *Jugantar*, 29 September 1967.

DUTTA, Dipankar (dir.) and Debojeet Majumdar (writ. and prod.). *Chena Kintu Ajana* [Known Strangers]. Documentary film, 2014. Available at: https://www.youtube.com/watch?v=f839_qQfbj8 (accessed 20 November 2025).

DUTTA, Kaberi. 'Jatra Jamboree'. *Amrita Bazar Patrika*, 26 March 1994, n.p.

GANGULY, Tapash. 'It's Yatra Folks!' *The Week*, 13 February 2000, n.p.

GARGI, Balwant. 'Jatra—Folk Theatre of India', *Yakshagana*. Available at: https://yakshagana.com/jatra-folk-theater-of-india-by-balwant-gargi-continued/ (accessed 20 November 2025).

GHARAMI, Ashok Kumar. *Banglar Loknatya*: *Jatra*. Kolkata: Samakaler Jiyonkathi Prakashan, 2021.

GHATAK, Arpita. 'Sacred to Secular: Jatra in Contemporary Bengal'. *Research Scholar—IRJLE* 7(4) (2019): 83–88. Available at: https://www.researchscholar.co.in/downloads/13-dr.-arpita-ghatak.pdf (accessed 20 November 2025).

GHOSH, Anuradha. 'Playing Woman, Playing Power: Performing the Goddess; a Reading of a Documentary on Chapal Bhaduri', in Brinda Bose and Subhabrata Bhattacharya (eds), *The Phobic and the Erotic*: *The Politics of Sexualities in Contemporary India*. London: Seagull Books, 2007, pp. 477–82.

GHOSH, Kalyani. 'Jatra', in Ananda Lal (ed.), *The Oxford Companion to Indian Theatre*. New Delhi: Oxford University Press, 2004, pp. 171–73.

GHOSH, Kalyani. 'The Jatra: A Tradition in Discontinuity'. *Rangavarta* 57 (September 1995): 4–13.

ILF SAMANVAY. 'Chapal Bhaduri Unplugged: Legendary Female Performer of Jatra Theatre'. ILF Samanvay Translation Series, 20 April 2018. Available at: www.youtube.com/watch?v=hPSywJi_sio (accessed 24 November 2025).

JYOTI, Dhrubo. 'Chapal Rani, the Man Who Ruled Bengal's Jatra Stage as a Woman'. *Hindustan Times*, 30 July 2018. Available at: https://www.hindustantimes.com/art-and-culture/man-actress-goddess/story-3UGMWN1MtXyjshB1Tl5fHI.html (accessed 20 November 2025).

KISHORE, Naveen (dir.). *Performing the Goddess: The Chapal Bhaduri Story*. Documentary film, 1999.

KUNDU, Manjunendra (ed.). *Women Performers in Bengal and Bangladesh, Caught up in the Culture of South Asia (1795–2010s)*. New Delhi: Oxford University Press, 2023.

LAL, Ananda. 'All for a Dying Art Form'. *The Telegraph*, 10 June 2006: https://www.telegraphindia.com/west-bengal/all-for-a-dying-art-form/cid/1538150 (accessed on 25 November 2025).

LAL, Ananda. 'Requiems for the Past'. *The Telegraph*, 27 August 1999, n.p.

NATTA, Makhanlal. *Rangamanchey Natta Company*. Kolkata: Dey's Publishing, 2014.

SAMADDAR, Sekhar. *Sundar-Pibir Pala*. Kolkata: Lalmati Prakashan, 2018.

SENGUPTA, Reshmi. 'Be What You Want to Be: Rituparno Ghosh Speaks Out'. *The Telegraph*, 8 August 2009: https://www.telegraphindia.com/entertainment/be-what-you-want-to-be-rituparno-ghosh-speaks-out/cid/607483 (accessed on 25 November 2025).

SENGUPTA, Reshmi. 'The Third Sex'. *The Telegraph*, 5 October 2009: https://www.telegraphindia.com/entertainment/the-third-sex/cid/582229 (accessed on 25 November 2025).

SINHA, Arunava. 'Jatra: Making Money from Melodrama'. *Economic Times*, 4 August 1991, n.p.

Prologue

The year was 1974. Work was drying up. Then, suddenly, I got a call from Kamala Opera.

It was not a well-known company. I had once worked in famous Grade 1 theatre groups. This was more like a Grade 3 group, the kind where they didn't even give you a salary. You were just paid a daily wage after each show.

I was offered the role of the heroine's mother, an older woman, widowed, somewhat villainous. It was not a glamorous role by any means, but it was a meaty role and I grabbed it. Women were now commonplace even in jatras, the travelling-theatre companies. This play too had women in the cast—the heroine was a new actress. Men like me who had made a living playing women were finding it harder and harder to get roles. But I did not know how to do anything else. I was grateful to be offered any role.

One day, we had gone for a show at Peary Mohan College in Uttarpara, a town on the Hooghly River, just outside Kolkata. It was probably my sixth or seventh night with that play. I was delivering my lines when someone in the audience hurled a clay cup, the kind you have tea in, onto the stage. At first, I had no clue what was going on. I could not figure out what the problem was.

As people started shouting and screaming, it slowly dawned on me that I was the problem. The audience did not want to see me on stage—they wanted to see a real woman. There was a cinema actor in the audience that evening. He tried to calm the audience down, reason with them, tell them who I was.

But it was all in vain. They didn't care. They said, 'Chapal Rani might have been Chapal Rani at one time. But that was then. Now we want a real woman, bring us a real woman.' They didn't want to see a man play a woman on stage any more. Those days were over.

There had been many before me, like Chhabi Rani, Babli Rani and Rakhal Rani, who had made a name for themselves playing women on stage in jatras. We were so famous, we were all called Rani, or Queen.

It seemed like I was destined to be the last queen of jatra. The age of Chapal Rani was over.

There was nothing to be done. In desperation, the organizers asked one of the actresses in the troupe if she could step in and take over the role from me. It was going to be tough at such short notice and it wasn't a small part either. She said she would try her best. I explained what little I could to her. And that was it. There was nothing left for me to do. Once, audiences had worshipped me when I played Chand Bibi or Sultana Riziya or Queen Kaikeyi. Now I had to leave the theatre in shame, burning with humiliation, tears stinging my eyes.

They called me Chapal Rani, Queen of Jatra. But that was not an exit worthy of any queen.

I vowed I would never wear a sari again. I was 35 years old.

1
Childhood

Dancing Boy

August 1941.

India's most famous poet had died at his home in Kolkata.

As Rabindranath Tagore's funeral procession moved slowly down Central Avenue in the northern part of the city, winding its way to the cremation grounds, hundreds of thousands of people lined the route, desperately jostling and straining for one last glimpse as policemen struggled to control the surging crowd. Every rooftop, every balcony, every window was filled with people chanting, '*Jai Rabindranath-er jai, jai Biswakabi-r jai, Vande Mataram*'—hail Rabindranath, hail the great poet of this world, hail the motherland.

The body inched down the street, a flower-bedecked boat borne on a sea of humanity. Mourners tried to cool themselves with hand fans in the sweltering hot August afternoon, they threw garlands and flower petals from rooftops and balconies, they sang his songs, the melody rising up into the air, rolling over the streets like a tidal wave.

Anandolokey, mangalalokey birajo . . .

And

Jodi tor daak shuney keu na aashey . . .

I could hear them from our house on Balakhana Street. Our house was not on Central Avenue, but if you stood on the balcony on the second floor, between the houses and shops and past the old ice-cream factory, you could catch a glimpse of the main road. Now the ice-cream factory has become a bank, and a Radha–Krishna temple has sprung up on one side. Our old house still stands, a little worse for wear, but still there, a large red house with a shuttered balcony on the first floor and wet clothes and towels hanging from the balconies in front. That day, the roar of the people, the sound of drums and the voices raised in song could be heard clearly from that balcony.

As the music grew louder, I started to dance. I meant no disrespect. Whenever I heard music, my feet would automatically start to move.

All this was in my mother's memory, not mine. I was barely two years old.

The House on Dalimtala Lane

My name is Chapal Bhaduri. I was born on 29th July in the year 1939. Now I live in an old-age home.

I was the youngest in our family. I remember a photograph from when I was a little boy. In it, I am wearing a sweater and shorts. It was a black-and-white photograph but I recall it in colour. The sweater was blue. The pants were blue as well. I was wearing boots. And that face. As soon as you saw that face, you wanted to slap it, it is such a pampered-mother's-boy face, the eyes full of mischief.

I was a brat.

I had three older brothers. Much older. My eldest brother Kamalesh worked in some office whose name I don't remember any more. My middle brother Amalesh was an editor in films. My third brother Saralesh worked as a bus conductor for the state transport corporation. I was originally called Bhabesh but my mother preferred Chapalesh. It eventually became Chapal.

There were two sisters as well. Pratibha was the eldest, much older than I. Her daughter, my niece, and I were barely five years apart. Pratibha, named by none other than the great Rabindranath Tagore himself, was married but lived in our house. Sometimes her husband Pankaj came and stayed with us too. He is important to my story, but I will come to that later. Finally, there was Ketaki, whom I called Chhordi. She was five years older than me, and like my mother, she was an actress. She was nicknamed Chhoto or The Little One because my mother had hoped she would be her last child. But then I came along five years later.

I had another sister but I have only ever seen her on film—a flickering black-and-white image. Sagarika had been famous as a child actor. In 1936, Ma was touring with her theatre company across Dhaka, Rangpur, Sylhet in Assam and what is now Bangladesh. My sister, who was with her, fell sick from diphtheria, for which there was no medicine at that time. She died, but Ma still went on stage, leaving her dead daughter in the room. The audience marvelled at her mental strength, but Ma never got over that grief.

Another sister was born about six or seven years after me. I remember how pretty she was, with a head full of curls. She looked just like my father. We named her Lakshmi, but she lived only a few months. The day she died, Ma was supposed to shoot for a film. She didn't tell the director what had happened because she did not want the shoot to be cancelled on her account. But when she fainted on the set, everyone found out the truth. For my mother, Prabha Devi, star of stage, screen and radio, the show always had to go on.

So there were four of us brothers, two sisters, my mother and my father in that house. When my brother and sister got married, their families were added to the mix. In addition, there were four servants to help keep house. Someone's job was to sweep and clean while there was a cook for our daily meals. Another person helped raise me, a nanny of sorts. Someone else's main job seemed to be to accompany my father to the market.

It was a full house, our home at 13/1C Dalimtala Lane, the house where we moved to from the three-storeyed red house on Balakhana Street. Our new home was not far from the street where legendary actress Noti Binodini lived out her last days. Her house is still there, a small yellow two-storeyed affair with a very narrow balcony and a plaque out front bearing her name. It looks like a house a child might have drawn in art class. I never saw Binodini, but Ma would tell us stories about going to visit 'Binod-ma'.

The narrow streets of North Kolkata were full of mansions and palaces, with columns and arched windows, where Burma-teak doors led into great inner courtyards. Our street was nothing like that—it now has boxy apartment buildings all along it, noisy roadside temples, beauty parlours with neon signs alongside old-fashioned tea shops and a dry cleaner named Snow White. The city council has put up busts of great social reformers like Ishwachandra Vidyasagar and Raja Rammohun Roy and stuck some ornamental plants behind bamboo fences to create an illusion of little pavement gardens.

When we lived there, it was just cow sheds. The whole street smelled of cowdung or gobar, and that's why the area was named Goabagan. During the monsoons, when it rained torrentially, a smelly brown river of cow dung flowed down the street. Our house was set back from the street, off a narrow lane. It was a three-storey house but very cramped, squished onto just 14 chhataaks of land. In those days, we measured land in chhataaks and kathas, a chhataak being about 45 square feet. Now I feel rather suffocated when I go there. It seems to be without much light or air, hemmed in by buildings. But when I was little, it seemed big enough—three large rooms on the ground floor and a little bit of a courtyard. One room under the stairs, which was always pitch dark even in the middle of the day. That's where we kept all our heavy metal pots and pans. Another small room, to store the coal we used for cooking. When I was naughty, my brothers would threaten to lock me in that dark room.

On the first floor, one big room and two smaller ones. My father and my sisters lived in them. My brothers lived in the rooms on the top floor which also had a strip of a terrace where we would sometimes have sit-down feasts. At one time, one brother raised pigeons there. Ma would make pickles and put them out in the sun on that terrace. We never bought pickles from the store. Ma made them all at home. My favourite was the one where she took sour tamarind and sweet sugarcane jaggery, put it in little clay pots, tied the mouth tightly with string and then left it in the sun. Sweet yet tart, it tasted utterly delicious. Ma could pickle anything. Carrots, cauliflower, mangoes, even drumstick stalks.

PRABHA DEVI'S MIXED PICKLE

Take drumstick pieces and steam them till soft. Chop up cauliflowers and carrots into small pieces and steam. Stir them in a heated pan till completely dry.

Grind the following in a mortar and pestle (not a mixie) with a bit of vinegar—cumin seeds, ginger, garlic, chili powder, turmeric powder. Add oil to the pan, add the spice paste and stir fry it. Then sauté the vegetables. Add more vinegar if needed. Stir fry till well blended. Finally heat mustard oil (remember, you cannot do this with unheated oil) and pour it into a glass or ceramic jar. Add the vegetables and keep for a couple of days till the vegetables become soft and tart. We called it 'Madrasi pickle' though I have no idea why.

When I came to this old-age home, they first gave me a room on the roof, a room with a tin roof. I remember thinking: once we used the terrace to make pickles. Now it is my time to get pickled. My niece said: you cannot stay in this room—it might be all right in the winter but in the summer you will go mad.

Our house rent was 40 rupees per month. One day, a local contractor told Ma, 'You keep paying rent on this, Prabha-di. Why don't you buy it outright? I think you will get a good price.' So, in 1950, Ma bought the house for 14,000 rupees and then renovated it entirely. She made a room for herself downstairs and painted it in 'blue distemper' colour. In those days, you could get a kind of bulb called Philips Moonlight. It was a pale blue but emitted a really bright light. Ma loved those bulbs. Ma might not have been very educated but she had great taste. Every day, after she came back from the theatre, she loved to spray rosewater on her face. She had intricately embroidered Kashmiri shawls, and liked to get her saris from a weaver named Nandalal whose Dhaniakhali saris were all the rage in those days. She did up the house, and she did it all on her own money.

Aside from our large family, there were some people I didn't know who also lived in our house. I once asked Ma, 'Who are these people? They live here and eat our food day after day.' She said, 'These people were great actors at one time. Now their time is past. They are here for a bit. As soon as something comes up, they will leave. Why do you ask?'

'Just like that, I was curious,' I replied.

Ma grew grave. 'I am noticing you have a lot of curiosity about things, Tuku. (My nickname was Tuku. When my mother really wanted something from me she added another letter and called me Tuklu.) Too much curiosity is not good. You be careful.'

I must have been eleven or so at that time.

Another time, Ma could not find a silver coin. 'I had kept a coin here but it's gone. Have you seen it? I have asked everyone. Tuku, have you taken it?'

I acted innocent. Obviously, even at that age I could act. 'No, Ma. Why would I take it? Perhaps one of the servants did.'

'I am sure they did not.' She knew the servants in our house were entirely trustworthy. 'Tell me truthfully. Did you take it?'

'No.'

'Look into my eyes and tell me you didn't take it.'

'No, Ma. I didn't take it.'

Her face changed. 'Touch my feet and swear that you didn't take it.'

'I swear I didn't take that coin, Ma.'

'You are my child and yet you touched my feet and lied. Tell me, why did you take that coin?'

'I told you I did not.'

Ma did not say another word. But after a while she started to weep. At the sight of her tears, I could not take it any more. I threw myself at her feet and said, 'Ma, forgive me. Yes, I took that coin.'

'Why didn't you just admit it? Where is it?'

'I've spent it.'

'On what?'

'Sweets.'

'All right. Now swear that you will not lie again. Lies trap you in more lies. Lies and curiosity. You must avoid both.'

'What is curiosity?'

'Curiosity is when the door is closed and you stand outside trying to peep in and see what is going on, or listen to what the grown-ups are saying.'

The Greedy Boy

There was another lesson Ma taught me that I never forgot. It had to do with my greed.

I was always a greedy little boy. Because of her blood sugar, my mother was allowed only cream-cracker biscuits. One day, she complained: 'I eat just two biscuits a day—how come this tin becomes empty so quickly?'

'Perhaps the rats are eating them?' Baba said.

Ma shook her head and turned to me, 'Tuku, this is your doing. You could have just asked me. And tell me, why is all the butter disappearing too?'

'Cream-cracker biscuits with butter are just too delicious for words, Ma' I confessed.

I still remember that butter—Polson's salted butter.

We had mutton on Sunday and holidays. Two and a half kilos was bought for the household. In those days, there was no pressure cooker. The mutton was boiled in a big pot, then braised and sautéed with splashes of hot water and left to cook slowly on the 'shesh unoon', the last embers of the coal-fired stove. We would pile small pieces of coal into the stove, and the mutton would simmer and bubble for hours on low heat. An aluminium plate with raised edges was filled with water and placed on top of the pot. That water grew warm while the mutton cooked, and whenever the gravy in the curry reduced too much, you would add a splash of that warm water.

Thc smell from that simmering mutton curry filled the house like a delicious fog. In the afternoon, while everyone napped, I stole into the kitchen, gingerly removed the plate on top, used a spoon and fork to carefully extricate some meat and ate it with great relish. But then I didn't know where to throw the bones. Ma used to have a thick mattress on her bed with a couple of thin mattresses on top it and a white bedsheet on top of everything. She never used coloured bedsheets, only white ones. I carefully lifted the mattresses, stuffed the bones under them and then washed my hands and the fork and spoon and exited the scene of the crime.

In the late afternoon, as Ma got ready to go to the theatre, she told the maid, 'Check if the mutton is cooked. If so, take it off the stove.' Then she asked me, 'Do you want to taste a bit and see how it is?' I said, 'Oh no, no. If you've cooked it, it must be wonderful. There's no need to taste it.' And off we went to the theatre and I forgot all about those bones.

Every month, we used to drag the mattresses up to the roof and lay them out in the sun. The next time this was done, the bones were discovered.

'Why are there these bones under my mattress?' Ma screamed 'Right where I put my feet!' She was very superstitious and lived in fear that somebody would cast a spell of some kind on her. Now she was having a hysterical fit, certain that someone was using witchcraft and plotting her downfall.

Chhordi said, 'Let me see,' and took a closer look. 'These look like bones from our mutton curry. Look, they are still stained with turmeric.'

'How could bones from our curry get in my bed?' Ma was stumped, 'I serve you all with my own hands.'

My elder sister said, 'Hmm, I am sure this is Tuku's doing.'

As usual, I was all wide-eyed in my innocence. 'What's wrong, Ma?'

'What are these bones doing under my mattress?'

'Bones? What bones?'

'That's what I am wondering too.'

'Oh, those are mutton bones. How did they get here?'

'That's what I am asking you.'

'I don't know.'

Ma's eyes could bore into your soul.

'You must have stolen some mutton some day and were afraid I'd find out if you left the bones lying around! Tell me the truth. I won't hit you.'

I shamefacedly admitted I had.

'Why did you put the bones here?' She sighed. 'You could have just wrapped them in a piece of paper and thrown them onto the street. Don't do this again, love. Don't steal and eat.'

Sometimes there are things people tell you that just stay in your mind forever. From that day I gave up stealing.

Today I live in an old-age home in a room that's like a pigeon coop, a place where the fish curry tastes like water. And I remember all these things. Like the tiny fried shrimp I would have with a plate of hot rice and ghee and a side of fried potatoes before going to school. The way Ma made it, it tasted like heaven.

The baby of the family, I was quite the master at throwing tantrums. When it rained, I would refuse to go to school. Ma would be adamant. 'It does not matter if it's raining. You are going to school. You will go with an umbrella. And if there's no umbrella, you will get wet—but you will go.'

When I saw there was no persuading her, I changed my tune. 'I wanted to have ilish fish,' I whined. 'It's raining and I want ilish.'

'Don't be like that. You eat whatever has been made at home today.'

As I began to reluctantly get dressed, we heard the next-door maid calling out to my mother from our door.

'What's the matter?'

'We heard poor Tuku crying for ilish. As it happens, we are having some at home today. So Jona-mashi has sent him a piece. I'm sorry, she could not send enough for everyone, though.' Jona-aunty had a big family. She had seven children, so there was always some food to spare.

My mother was embarrassed, 'Have you gone mad? Don't you know that boy's greed? He is like a bottomless pit. If you give him an inch, there'll be no end to his demands.'

'Don't be silly. He is just a boy. Send the bowl back when you are done.'

Unashamed rascal that I was, I told Ma, 'Don't send that bowl back. It's very pretty. I want to keep it.'

Jona-mashi laughed when she heard that. 'Silly boy, that doesn't mean you will find ilish in that bowl every day.'

Ma's fish recipes were delicious as well.

PRABHA DEVI'S 'MACCHHI MULO' (FISHY RADISH)

Chop the white radish into thin strips, boil it and discard the water. Take the fatty belly of a rohu fish and boil with a pinch of turmeric and a bayleaf to remove the fishy smell. Discard the water. Remove the bones. Then fry it till its dry with ginger, garlic, ground cumin and the strips of radish. Ma named it Macchhi Mulo.

It tasted heavenly. Ma would say, 'If I even wash my hands and put that water in the pan, it will have its own special taste.' That was true. My sister would cook as would I but nothing ever had that special taste of Ma's cooking.

Oddly, greedy boy that I was, some of my earliest memories are of the devastating Bengal famine of 1943. I was very young, but they were such terrible days that I cannot forget them. People had nothing but rice and watery masoor dal to eat. Beggars would go from door to door, crying 'Ma, give us some phyan, please give us some phyan' (the starchy water left over from cooking rice). Women would come from the village, starving, all skin and bone, their eyes hollowed out, their clothes in rags, barely covering their shame.

Then the rationing started. Everything had to come from the ration shops—rice, sugar, wheat, flour, oil. Dalda or hydrogenated palm oil started then as well, I think. The tins had a picture of a tree on them. We called them tree-stamp Dalda. There was also Kusum Dalda. People do not remember these things any more. But I do, because I would go to fetch the rations. I remember gas lights in the streets, and how every morning the streets were washed and cleaned. Right behind our house were the municipal corporation's stables. I would hear the clip-clop of the horses going down the street as dawn broke over the city. None of that exists any more.

During the war, the sirens kept going off all the time. I can still hear them in my head. We would have to run and hide in a room downstairs, with cotton wool stuffed in our ears, till the All Clear sounded. Bombs fell on Hatibagan very close to where we lived. I had a little wax doll, a camel with a jockey. I was playing with it on the roof when the sirens sounded and Ma called me down. Later, I found the doll had melted. How I wept for my poor camel, but Ma just said, 'Good riddance.'

Escape to Srirangam

Finally, Independence came to India in 1947. But before that there were such terrible riots. I saw one man hold another by the throat and hack off his head off with a chopper on Sahitya Parishad Street. The head remained in the hacker's hand. The body jerked and twitched for a few moments, like a headless chicken. I have seen all this with my own eyes. I would raise the shutters of the window and peep through them. Everything still burns bright in my memory.

Ma though was a fearless woman. She would always carry a heavy silver box with her name, Prabha, inscribed on top. It had everything she needed to make her paan, her chief addiction. Sometimes I would wonder if she felt scared coming back alone, after dark, across the empty fields near our house. But she would scoff, 'Why should I be afraid? If anyone tries to do anything, I'll knock their eyes out with my silver box.'

But the woman who was ready to knock robbers cold with her silver paan box was terrified when the riots broke out. We were a Hindu family in a Muslim neighbourhood. There was a mosque right next to our house. It was so close, I could see them offer namaaz from my window. I even knew the azaan by heart. When the azaan sounded early in the morning, it felt kind of romantic. The mosque was so close, the maulvi would stand on its terrace and pass us all kinds of treats on special days. The maulvi told my mother, 'Ma, do not fear. If we both stand firm against the riots, no one can touch us.' But everything was in such chaos and the atmosphere so tense that Ma decided we had to leave and take shelter in my uncle's Srirangam Theatre. So she stuffed all her jewellery, her bankbooks, her important documents and her money into pillowcases and stitched them shut. Then she told us, 'Get hold of a stretcher, the kind they carry dead bodies on.' She spread a blanket on the bamboo stretcher and lay on it, clutching the stuffed pillowcases, as if she was very sick. She said, 'Let us go to Srirangam Theatre. The police station is right next to it. We'll be safe there. Don't make too much noise or cry or draw too much attention. If anyone asks what's happening, tell them our mother is sick, she is feeling very claustrophobic in the house and finding it hard to breathe. So we are going to Srirangam Theatre.'

Srirangam was barely a five-to-ten-minute walk from our house and right next to the Burtollah Police Station. The officer-in-charge, a Muslim man, was a friend of my uncle's. But Ma was terrified of walking with all her jewellery when the air was thick with stories of riots and carnage. It was hard to trust anyone in those overheated days. When we reached the theatre, we were hastily ushered in. Once we were safely inside, Ma sat bolt upright and cried, 'Hurry, tear open the pillows!' Now it feels funny, but at that time no one laughed.

Srirangam had been established by the great theatre actor Natyacharya Sisir Kumar Bhaduri. My father, Tara Kumar Bhaduri, was his younger brother.

I remember it well. Four steps from the pavement led into the building with two large rooms, one of which served as a booking counter and the other as an office. There was a wide passage between them lined with wooden benches. There the Bhaduri brothers and their friends would sometimes sit and chat over endless cups of hot milky tea. The passage opened out onto a beautiful garden filled with flowers which was my uncle Sisir Bhaduri's pride and joy. The audience would walk through this garden, past hedges of mehendi flowers, to reach the main auditorium. There was a huge oleander shrub and a night-blooming jasmine that smelt divine when it blossomed during the monsoon. It made for a magical walk into the auditorium. I used to steal plants from that garden for our own rooftop till one of my uncles caught me red-handed.

In the theatre compound was another house, which we called the 'inner house', where all the Bhaduri brothers had their own rooms, though Baba spent most of his time at our house. My uncle Sisir Bhaduri assigned a room to us on the ground floor. We stayed in Srirangam Theatre for several months. One day, my uncle removed the seats from the auditorium so that the military who had come to quell the riots could camp there. I do not think any other theatre did that.

But on Independence Day itself there was so much celebration. At midnight we were all listening to the radio. There were firecrackers going off everywhere. In the morning, all the shops, theatres, even people's homes were decorated with strings of little tricolours printed on paper. Children went to school and drew alpona patterns on the floor. People cooked up great feasts at home. After all, the country does not become independent every day.

Mother's Boy

The story of my childhood, though, is really a story about my mother. My mother was born in 1903. She was in a young women's theatre group run by a famous actress named Teenkori Dasi who once played Lady Macbeth on stage with the legendary playwright and director Girish Chandra Ghosh as Macbeth. Ma and the other girls would dance as sakhis or dancing girls in many plays and get paid 8 annas. When Sisir Kumar Bhaduri decided to re-mount the play *Alamgir*, he wanted a new face for the role of Rupkumari, a beautiful Rajput woman. The lead heroine Udipuri, the Kashmiri wife of Emperor Aurangzeb, was played by the actress Tarasundari. All the women from the sakhi group were sent to audition for the great Mr Bhaduri. Ma told me she was terrified, barely able to look up at him. Yet he chose her, he said, because of her voice and her eyes. Many great actresses of that time tittered at his choice, the great Sisir Bhaduri was losing his mind they said, Prabha was too tall, too dark, too uneducated to play Rupmati. But the audience loved her. They erupted in applause when they saw her on stage in *Alamgir*. There was a scene where she had to lift her veil with two fingers and gaze into the eyes of the prince. I have heard that Sisir Bhaduri did not like the way anyone did that scene until he cast Ma.

I cannot remember the first time I saw Ma on stage. Perhaps it was in the play *Rahgubir*. There was a scene in it where she has to feed poison to her own son. I can still remember her quivering lips, the bulging eyes filled with tears, but not a drop trickling down her face. She had just one line of dialogue when they handed her that vessel with the poison. 'Give.' Even now I can hear that in my head. It still makes me shiver.

There was another play where she played Mura, mother of King Chandragupta Maurya. In that, she dressed in a widow's white. There was a scene where King Nanda is trying to hunt down Chandragupta who has fled somewhere.

NANDA. Tell me, where is that Chandragupta?
MURA. I don't know, child.
NANDA. You don't know? Tell me, otherwise . . .
MURA (*voice rising*). Otherwise what? Otherwise you will kill me, Nanda? No, I cannot believe you can be so heartless. I am his mother. Alas, King Nanda, even if I knew it, I would not reveal it. Maharaj Nanda, what do you think? That a mother will push her son into the jaws of a tiger to save her own life? Alas, Mura, ignorant one. Do you not understand what it means to be a mother?

I have seen many actresses play that role, many of them big names. But no one could say that line, 'You do not understand what it means to be a mother' the way she did.

Years later, I remember reading Rajshekhar Basu's *Ramayana*. I read his description of Sita in exile—in a saffron sari with a red border, her hair cascading down, with the boys Luv and Kush hanging onto her. And it was as if I could see my mother. She had long hair, though it had thinned out towards the end of her life. Her lips were full, her nose shapely, she barely used any make-up, just a bindi made with a dab of sindoor. If there was one flaw, it was her addiction to chewing paan. That had ruined her teeth. She was not slim but full figured. Her arms, we would say, were like elephants' trunks. When she came out of the bath, her hair wet, her sari wrapped around her, she looked so lovely. When I close my eyes, I can still see her wet footprints on the floor.

The Theatre Bug

I would go to Srirangam Theatre all the time. At one time, it was called Natya Mandir. When my uncle Sisir Bhaduri took it on lease, he named it Srirangam. He built a revolving stage there. There was a piano right next to it where I would spread a small mat and sit next to the piano master and watch the greats even on house-full nights—my mother of course, Sisir Bhaduri, Ahindra Chowdhury, Rani Bala, Rathin Banerjee, Chhabi Biswas, Saraju Bala. I would watch mesmerised, whether I understood the play or not.

I remember Sisir Bhaduri as Chanakya in *Chandragupta*, tying his hair with his hands smeared with the blood of Nanda whom he has just slain. When Nanda humiliates him by dragging him by the tuft of his hair, Chanakya thunders, 'Enough, King

Nanda. This much and no further. Such an insult to a Brahman. Listen, all. A Kshatriya has told this Brahman to get out, but still there is no storm, there is no rain of fire, the world is not trembling.' Every hair in every pore would stand up when he uttered 'the world is not trembling'. He would leap from the stage and I would watch open mouthed. At that time, he was no young man. In *Raghuvir*, he was chained and shackled and there was a famous scene where he would break free. I remember the way he lay on stage, stricken with thirst and famished, in *Alamgir*. Once he was playing both Emperors Shah Jahan and Aurangzeb, father and son, at the same time. I can hardly believe that I have seen all this with my own eyes.

On the days there was no show, just one light would burn all day and night in the auditorium. It was quite eerie to see those dark empty seats in front and that one light burning. Some days my sister and I played chor–police, hide and seek, in the dark. On other days I would jump on that empty stage and act out bits of the plays I had seen.

One such day I suddenly smelt tobacco and realized my uncle Sisir Kumar Bhaduri was standing and watching in the dark, smoking his Burma cigar. He always smoked expensive cigars, while my father smoked cheap Charminar cigarettes which cost 6 paisa a packet. Another time, while we were staying at Srirangam during the riots, I was exploring the theatre on my own and happened to go past my uncle's room. He was lying in his easy chair, in his lungi and handloom-cotton kurta, with a book in one hand and his ever-present cigar in the other. I could see his feet from under the curtain. I tried to sneak away but he heard me and cried out, 'Who's there?' I was trapped. My heart started thudding. His voice sounded like a thunderclap. My stomach started to rumble. I felt like I needed to go to the toilet right away. He looked so stern with his thick black-rimmed spectacles.

'Come inside. Who are you?'

I said, 'Me.'

'Who is me?'

'I am Chapal, I live downstairs.'

'What downstairs?'

'Downstairs. With my mother.'

'Your mother?' Then his tone changed. He said, 'Oh, I know who you are. Prabha's son. What is your name?'

'Tuku.'

He laughed and said, 'Do you have a proper name?'

'Chapal Bhaduri,' I stammered. 'Do you want to know my father's name?'

He laughed and said, 'There is no need. I know you are Tara Kumar's son. Don't you study?'

'Oh yes, I do.'

'Well, then, why are you wandering around in the middle of the afternoon?'

'I was just exploring, seeing what was where.'

'You are wasting your time wandering around like this. You should be reading instead. Read story books. Even better, read your text books as if they are story books. That will help pass the time and exercise your brain as well. What do you like to study?'

'History.'

'Good. Then read history books. Can you recite a poem?'

'I can.'

'What poem can you recite?'

'*Panchabir* by Rabindranath Tagore.'

'Let's hear it. Don't be afraid.'

So I recited the poem.

He listened to the whole thing and said, 'Excellent. Your voice reminds me of your mother's. You must read Tagore's books. And when you are a little older, read Sarat Chandra Chattopadhyay and Bankim-babu and Dwijendralal Roy. You will learn a lot from the great writers. Do you understand what I am saying?'

I nodded mutely, too nervous to say anything.

'So what are you going to do now?'

'Go downstairs,' I said meekly.

'All right then, you can go.'

I fled.

He never came to our house on Dalimtala Lane even though it was close by, but I talked to him one other time. I was sitting by the stage in my usual spot near the piano, watching him act in a play. He recognized me and said, 'Why are you sitting here?'

My sister said, 'He's my little brother. He watches theatre every day.'

'Every day?' My uncle's eyebrows rose. 'You don't study?'

I replied, 'I do, I only come here in the evening.'

'But you should be studying in the evening. Anyway, watch if you like, but sit up in the box.' The auditorium had two levels, and on the upper level there were boxes as well. Ma forbade me to sit in the box, though. She said I needed to sit somewhere where she could keep her eyes on me even from the stage.

And she said, 'Don't go like this to the theatre every day. You should study instead.'

I replied 'I do study, but I like watching theatre.' I couldn't even pronounce theatre correctly. I would say 'theeataar'.

Then Ma said, 'No, you stay at home and study. Although if you love theatre so much, there's something you *can* do instead.'

At that time, gramophone companies would bring out 78 rpm records. My mother had acted in many radio plays which were called pala in those days. Oddly, that's the same word we used for jatra performances too. Every few months, Ma would get a letter asking her to come to the radio station to record a pala. These plays would air live on Friday nights from 7.45. There were no television serials then, so we would all wait, agog with excitement, to listen to the radio plays on Friday nights.

But Ma refused to get a radio at home.

I would beg her to get one. 'Everyone says Prabha Devi is so famous and makes so much money—but there isn't even a radio in her home. I have to go elsewhere to listen.'

'Why do you have to go anywhere?' She asked. 'You don't have to listen!'

'What are you saying? Just the other day you were acting for Dhaka Betaar Kendra. All the neighbours heard the performance on the radio. Everyone said how wonderfully you had acted.'

Ma had been given a gramophone as a gift by the gramophone company. She kept her beloved gramophone and those pala records in a room on the top floor of our house.

She told me, 'If you love theatre so much, then listen to one pala every afternoon.' Some of those palas extended over both sides of seven or eight records. I still remember those names—

Mirabai, *Shoroshi*, *Alamgir*, *Sheshraksha*, *Chirakumar Sabha* and so many more. Every afternoon, I would wind up the gramophone and listen to those records.

I didn't have that much enthusiasm for school. Geometry made my head hurt. English always made me want to go to the toilet. I liked Bengali, history and geography. I would get 75 on 100 in geography, 100 on 100 in Bengali, but 30 on 100 in English.

I liked school but sometimes I would come home for tiffin and not go back. Ma would say, 'Why are you lying in bed instead of going to school?' And I would reply, 'I ate too much. Now I can't go back.'

'Oh all right then, lie down,' she would say. I admit that I got a little too much love from my mother. I would lie in bed and lazily read a book.

My favourite author was Sarat Chandra Chattopadhyay, who could beautifully depict with such simple language how a family could break apart and then come back together. I did not know then that one day I would play Bipradas' mother in Sarat Chandra's *Bipradas*. I loved those books. All those characters—Bindu in *Bindur Chele*, Bijoya in *Datta*, Bankim Chandra Chattopadhyay's *Motibibi* and Rohini in *Bishbriksha*, and Rabindranath Tagore's Indumati in *Sheshraksha* . . . I did not understand them all as a child. I had to read them three or four times.

Ma herself was not very educated, but she would write poetry. She even showed her book of poems to the great Rabindranath. He named that collection *Gitayan*. He loved her very much because she acted in many of his plays. He designed the cover for that book. It had a baul folk singer strumming an ektara while a woman sits at his feet, looking up at him. Her face resembled my mother's. Rabindranath told Ma to use two of his tunes for two of the poems in her book. Ma recorded those songs. One went 'Nayan jhore hai' to the tune of his song from spring 'Rangiye diye jao'. I would listen to the records over and over again until Ma complained, 'Turn it off. I can't bear listening to it.' We had those books in the house for years until they started falling apart.

Ma also loved to watch English films. Baba told her, 'You can neither speak English nor read it. Why do you want to watch them?'

'You won't understand,' she'd say, 'I watch the way they act, the way they depict the character. That's enough for me. Language is no barrier when it comes to expression.' She would go to the morning shows on Sundays, 10 annas a show, and I would tag along. I remember some of them—*Caesar and Cleopatra*, *The Adventures of Robin Hood*. I loved Errol Flynn. He was so dashing. Ma's great idol was Greta Garbo.

But my absolute favourite thing was when Ma would say, 'Tuklu, help me with my part.' In those days, actors would have to keep entire parts memorised.

Ma would say, 'I will just say my part—you follow along. If I get stuck, then prompt me with the dialogue. Give me the cue.'

Once, she said something from her part, perhaps from a play like *Sita*, and I said, 'Why did you say that line like that?'

Her eyes went big. Her brows furrowed. Perhaps her theatre guru Sisir Bhaduri could do this to Prabha Devi, the queen of theatre, but I was a mere boy.

She said, 'What do you mean?'

'Why did you say it like that? You could also have said it like this,' I said, and showed her. My voice was girlish, not so different from hers.

My mother looked at me wonderingly.

'I learnt by watching you,' I said nervously, afraid I had offended her.

'Who *are* you?' she exclaimed. 'If you had been my daughter, what a great actress you might have been.'

Perhaps it was my girlish voice that made her say so. Perhaps it was the bits of her roles she saw me perform. Perhaps she was reminded of the unfulfilled potential of her dead daughter Sagarika. I never found out. But one day I did get my chance to act alongside her.

In 1945, Ma was acting in Sarat Chandra's *Bindur Chhele*. One afternoon, I was asleep at home while Ma was at the theatre. That day there was a double show. Suddenly someone poked me awake: 'Come with me. You have to act. Your mother is calling you.' I was perhaps six years old then. I reached Srirangam Theatre in a state of great excitement and found out that the little boy who played Amulya had not come. I was delirious with joy. All I could think was that like Ma and Chhordi, I would also say a 'part'. I was dressed up, my hair was tied in a knot and I was given a mud inkwell and a pen made of grass. Ma said, 'Just listen to me and do whatever I tell you.' The prompter Satya-babu said, 'Don't be nervous. Look at me and repeat whatever I say. And just open your eyes wide.'

But once I was on stage, it was like a sea of darkness out there. My little heart went pitter-patter. I was in a daze till Ma pinched me and said, 'Say, say: "You also come, Chhoto-ma."' I repeated the line like a parrot. It was just a small part in a small scene. In the next scene, Amulya is older and was played by Chhordi. The audience didn't even notice me, but for me it was a huge moment. I had stepped into the world of acting holding my mother's hand. I got five rupees as payment for that part. All the way home, I twirled that note in my hand, waving it like a flaming torch. I kept it carefully for a long, long time. It was my first earning as an actor.

The boy whose role I played eventually got better and came back to the theatre. But by then I had got a taste of being on stage. I was extremely upset when he returned, even though I couldn't deny him his part. He was the original actor, after all. I would go to watch the play, then come back home despondently and sit down to study.

The End of Childhood

But then Srirangam Theatre fell on hard times. Sisir Bhaduri had taken it on a 99-year lease. Now we say that it was the Sisir Age of theatre, but for many reasons the theatre was always beset with financial troubles. They were struggling to pay back loans. They could not pay the artistes properly. Finally, even Ma had to leave and start work in another theatre. That was heartbreaking for her. She had learnt her craft from Sisir Bhaduri. She was his disciple. She had wanted to be with him forever. But one day he told her, 'Prabha, see if you can get a chance somewhere else.'

So in 1949, Ma left Srirangam and went to Minerva, an old theatre on Beadon Street in North Kolkata where the likes of the great Girish Ghosh had acted. At the time, the famous actor Chhabi Biswas had taken Minerva Theatre on lease. Its playbill included shows such as Sachin Sengupta's *Dhatri Panna* and Tarashankar Bandyopadhyay's *Dui Purush*. Even my sister was there, doing child roles in plays like *Dhatri Panna* alongside Geeta Dey who became quite famous later. A little girl called Madhuri also acted in *Dhatri Panna* as a little boy named Kanak while I acted as little Uday. We became good friends. I would pull her pigtail and she would run complaining to her mother.

Sometimes she would come to our house with her mother who would beg Ma to find jobs for them because they were struggling to make ends meet. Ma talked to my uncle and managed to get her some work at Srirangam. Later Madhuri started acting more. She even did the Bengali version of *Snow White* at Minerva. Then she got into films and in the hands of Satyajit Ray became famous worldwide as Madhabi Mukherjee. But I knew her when we were little children, playing hide-and-seek in Chhabi Biswas' Minerva.

One day, Chhabi Biswas' money also ran out, and that board—we used to call theatres 'boards' in those days—went out of his hands. What was Ma to do? In 1950, she came to Rang Mahal Theatre. That does not even exist any more. There are only shops there now. Many of those great playhouses fell into disuse, decaying under lock and key, until one night a mysterious fire guts them. Then shopping complexes and apartment buildings rise out of the ashes. At that time, Rang Mahal's main business was to re-stage some of its old hits. Around then, my sister joined Star Theatre round the corner from our house. A famous actress named Purnima Devi, whom no one remembers any more, starred on Saturday and Sunday when they had double shows. But on Monday–Tuesday–Wednesday, when there were single shows, my sister played the heroine. In those days, because there was no TV, theatre drew good crowds even on weekdays.

In 1952, Ma was acting in *Shei Timirey* [That Night]. It was a play about women who were so tired of abusive husbands that they formed a Women Rising Committee, demanding equal rights for husbands and wives. Seven married women rented a house to run the organization. Ma played the maid, who also had left her husband, in that house. It was a comic part, and her performance had the audience rolling in the aisles. The play opened on Thursday, 6 November 1952. On Friday, Ma had a film shoot and then went to a small private meeting organized by a people's theatre group.

When she got home, she called me and said, 'I feel like having something sweet. Can you run down to Ramlal's shop and get me some kalakand?' Or perhaps it was rabdi. I cannot be sure any more.

She loved the sweets from Ramlal's shop, even though her blood sugar was high.

'I can't go anywhere now. It's late and I am ready for bed.'

'So what? Just go. It will only take minutes.'

'No, I can't. You just came that way, why didn't you get some yourself? I can't go now.'

The shop really was very close, especially if you knew your way around the interconnected alleys and lanes of North Kolkata. But I felt too lazy.

'Fine, be that way. If I die tomorrow, you'll be sorry.' Later, I heard that my eldest brother's friend, the one who married my youngest sister, got those sweets for her. He was probably trying to butter up his mother-in-law.

At 6.30 the next morning, Ma suddenly had breathing difficulties. We rushed to her room and found her gasping, struggling for breath. She kept trying to say something to us, and called for my sister and brothers. My youngest sister, whose baby was just ten months old, came running down from her room, her sari askew, her hair uncombed. My brother-in-law ran to get a doctor. Then Ma suddenly pushed my father aside, cried out sharply and fell back on the bed. It was all over, just like that, in less than ten minutes. When the doctor arrived, there was nothing he could do. We could not believe it. Ma had just had an offer for a Hindi film, though I do not remember what film it was. She had started Hindi lessons for it. The tutor, a man in his 30s who always wore a spotless white kurta, came as usual that morning. He had no idea what was going on. When he finally pushed his way in through the crowds, he was stunned. 'Maaji has gone? What a wonderful person she was,' he said, his eyes filled with tears.

Ma was only 48. She had no illness, no malady that we knew of. At most, her blood sugar might have been a little high. She was not supposed to eat sweets but she would eat them and say, 'I earn and I won't eat? And everyone else will eat? How can that be?'

Ma was laid out in a Santipuri sari with a red border, with red alta painted on her feet and sindoor in the parting of her hair and her favourite paan-jorda, her betel-nut leaves and chewing tobacco, in her hand. There were so many flowers you could barely see her face. They put a blanket with her own beautiful embroidery on her. Ma loved to sew. A Bihari boy named Bhikhu would bring her threads of many colours and Ma would use them to embroider beautiful patterns like peacocks and flowers. I asked her to make a mat for me once. She said she would make me one for my birthday and then embroidered bunch of roses on a mat with the words 'To Chapal from Ma'. It breaks my heart that I do not have it any more. She always made a fuss over me on my birthday. She would make payesh with milk and rice. I would get the choicest fish head. Ma would say, 'You eat like women. You like all these fish bones and fish heads.' At night, she would cook a mutton curry. Sometimes in the evening she would order prawn cutlets from a shop nearby. We didn't have birthday parties like you do now but all day the house would be in an uproar for Tuku's birthday, I would get new clothes and gifts. I remember my oldest brother giving me a pop-up book that I loved. Ma would give me 5 rupees as a present. But she was strict and did not approve of spoiling the children. One year, she decided to give me the Ramayan. I was upset. 'What will I do with the Ramayan? That's for old people.' Ma said, 'No, it's like poetry. You will enjoy reading it.' She got me the Valmiki Ramayan—a big book with a green cover and illustrations inside. I loved the pictures. One showed Taraka demoness and Ravan kidnapping Sita, the plate on which Sita had brought her offerings, fallen to the ground.

Once, I remember her sitting on the roof and sewing a mat while I sat next to her like a little monkey. The monsoons were over and the sky had changed colour as autumn approached. As she glanced up at the deep blue sky and the cotton-wool clouds, she told me, 'See that sky. I want to bring out that beauty in my mat.' A few days later, that mat was done and, indeed, that late afternoon sky was right there on the mat.

The only thing she never could manage to do was knit. Chhordi tried to teach her many times, but Ma would just end up rolling in laughter at her own plight. She did have a Singer sewing machine on which she would stitch my shirts and underpants with drawstrings and my father's undershirts. We were not poor, but she liked to sew. She would get longcloth and make pillowcases because she didn't like the thick ones you got in the market. Her bed was so big, she had to stitch her own bedsheets using a kind of cloth we called American cloth. I learnt how to spin the wheel on that machine. You had to get the speed just right. In 1950–51, she stitched an exquisite blanket using sarees she didn't wear any more. She would save the borders from the old saris and stitch them onto the blanket and then use it when she slept. That was the blanket Baba placed on her for that last journey after she died. 'Don't give that,' I cried. 'Ma spent so many days stitching that. How much she loved it. Let me keep it as a memory of my mother.' But no one listened to me. 'You be quiet. It's your mother's blanket. She loved it and so it should go with her.' The words of young children have no value. I got so many shawls over the years as gifts during felicitation ceremonies that I have long lost count. I've given most of them away to my nephews, the husbands of my nieces, even my grandnephews. But I still think about that blanket my mother had stitched with her own hands.

We took Ma's body to Srirangam Theatre first. It was swarming with people trying to get a last glimpse of her. Sisir Bhaduri came out from inside the theatre and stood silently beside her body. For a while he gazed at her face and then he shut his eyes and placed his hand on her forehead. There was a blackboard in the theatre. He took a piece of chalk and wrote on it 'Because of the death of the Queen of the Stage, the theatre will remain shut today. Tomorrow, there will be her memorial service.'

Once, the Bengal Theatre Academy had tried to give Ma the title of Natyadhishwari or Ruler of Theatre. She had rejected it, saying she required no titles, no adjectives. She was, simply, an actress, the disciple of Sisir Bhaduri. That was enough for her.

Years later, I saw a play called *Arshi* based on three great actresses of Bengali theatre—Noti Binodini, Prabha Devi and Tripti Mitra. The woman who played my mother had a great resemblance to her. But it upset me that they showed her reduced to terrible straits, practically needing to beg. Her cooking pot had cobwebs on it. I asked the actress 'Where did you read that my mother had to beg for help, that her cooking pots had cobwebs in them?' That might have been my fate, but it was not my mother's.

All theatres were shut the day my mother died. As I watched my mother burn, I felt as if all her roles were burning with her—Mura, Sita, Annapurna. It was all over in an hour and twenty minutes. We went home to an empty house. Her metal comb was still on her dressing table, strands of her hair stuck between its teeth. It smelt of her favourite hair oil—Lakshmivilas. There were two paans, neatly folded and ready to be eaten, in her paan box with her name *Prabha* written on top. Only she was not there.

A few years after Ma died, Rashbehari Sarkar took over Sisir Bhaduri's Srirangam Theatre. Everything my uncle had done to build Srirangam was wiped out. He was pretty much driven out of his own theatre as those who were once close to him became his enemies. That garden that was his pride and joy, the one from which I would steal plants, was ripped up. My uncle had to take shelter in the home of one of his brothers. At that time, the government tried to give him a Padma Shri award. But he refused it, saying: I do not want a Padma Shri—I want a national theatre. But that wish of his remained unfulfilled. On 30 June 1959, he too passed away.

Now there is a multistoreyed building complex where Srirangam once stood. The only thing that remains of my uncle is a statue of him, painted silver, right outside. A few buildings remain that hark back to those days: the Boys Own Library and Young Men's Institute with Free Reading Room set up in 1900 and the old Ramakrishna Vedanta Math, just a year older than me. Next to what used to be Srirangam is the Burtollah Police Station, which I remember from my childhood. Someone has painted brightly coloured murals on its walls, showing the street in its heyday with portraits of the great legends of theatre like Girish Ghosh and Noti Binodini. But who knows how many of the passers-by even know who they are.

I have tried to continue the acting tradition of Prabha Devi, as did my sister. But the regret remains. I still remember Ma's words: '*Tui jodi amaar chhele na hoye meye hoti, taholey ekdin boro abhinetri hote parti*'—if you were my daughter instead of my son, what a great actress you might have been.

Why she said 'daughter', I do not know.

All I know is she knew I had talent but she never got to see what I did with it. She never got to see me become Chapal Rani.

INTERLUDE

In Imagination

The Chorus Girl

You are writing the life of Chapal Bhaduri?

I find that funny. Not because he does not deserve a book. But because no one ever bothered to write a book about his mother, the great Prabha Devi. To know what makes Chapal Bhaduri Chapal Bhaduri, you have to know what made Prabha Devi Prabha Devi.

In those days, no one was interested in the life of actresses like us. I say us because we were like sisters, even though I never achieved even a quarter rupee of what she did. We started out together in Tinkori Dasi's group of chorus dancers. Prabha danced in the first row. I was in the back. No one remembers me. But she went places none of us ever imagined. Stage. Film. Radio. She was everywhere.

They thronged to watch her on stage, clap and shout, even send gifts. Someone sent her a gramophone. Someone gave her a radio. Some even called her Prabha Ma.

But I know what they said behind her back. There was only one thing they were interested in. How did someone so dark, so heavyset, catch the eye of the great Sisir Bhaduri? What spell did she cast with those big eyes? Did Prabha Devi come from the forbidden district?

It's not a question I choose to answer because there is no answer that can stop tongues from wagging. People have tongues.

Tongues will wag. Prabha told everyone who would listen that she came from a village in Bardhaman, that her mother came to Kolkata with her small children after her husband died, but that didn't stop the rumours.

Even her own family didn't spare her. That brother of hers, useless fool, told her never to darken the family home again. 'We know what you actresses really do,' he said. 'Just because you call some man your husband does not make him one. We know all about his other family. Once he is done with his games, you and those children of yours will be left to rot alone. Until you find some other man with another family who wants a bit of fun on the side. No, Prabha, we don't want you coming home. We don't want the neighbours peeping from behind the curtains to see that dancing girl from Tinkori Dasi's troupe.'

But she showed them, didn't she? Who among us bought their own house in Kolkata with their own money? Not just any house, a three-storey house just a stone's throw from where the great Noti Binodini lived. I have seen Binodini-ma with my own eyes, long after she left the theatre, sitting on her veranda in a plain cotton sari, gazing in the direction of Star Theatre, the theatre that was supposed to have been named after her until those treacherous bhadralok stabbed her in the back and betrayed her. They could buzz around her like bees all day and night but she was still a 'fallen' woman. How could those respectable folk go to a theatre named after her? I think it broke Binodini-ma's heart. They said her skin had turned white in patches. Sometimes she would wrap a shawl around her and sit quietly in the wings to watch some new play.

Anyway, I was telling you about Prabha's wastrel brother. When his own business failed, did that stop that man from coming to Prabha to ask for some money? You are rich, Prabha. You are famous. You have bought yourself a three-storey house. Won't you help your own brother?

She gave him two sweets and a tumbler of water and then told him never to come back again. Her husband said: Prabha, he's your brother after all, your flesh and blood. She said: what flesh and blood? My flesh and blood are those who live in this very house, I have no flesh and blood anywhere else. She was right about that. Even when she fell out with her oldest sons and they got themselves separate kitchens, the day she made her special kanta-chachchari with fish bones and fish oil, she would send them some. Once I said, 'What's the point of separate kitchens then?' and she laughed and said, 'Oh mukhpuri, you girl with the scalded tongue, don't worry your head about all this. Come and eat some of the kanta-chachchari instead with me.' That kanta-chachchari was divine. That rich taste still lingers in my mouth. No one could make kanta-chachchari like Prabha.

She got a lot of grief for turning her brother away. People said: her fame has gone to her head. Look at Prabha, she thinks she is better than her own family. What can you expect? You know where she is from, don't you?

But they didn't know and it doesn't matter any more. But when the day was done and the curtain had come down and she had gone home to 13/1C Dalimtala Lane and made herself a paan from that beautiful silver box she loved, when the city fell asleep, where did Prabha Devi go to in her head?

What did she dream of?

The answer might surprise you.

She didn't dream of the great roles she played on stage and there were many. Nor of the great Sisir Bhaduri, the king of theatre, who plucked her from obscurity, the man she called Baba. Or even of his brother, Tara Kumar, the man who became the father of her children.

She dreamt of Sagarika.

Sagarika—her lost child. She was carrying that child inside her when she came back on ship from that tour of America. That tour was a flop but she said there was at least one good thing that came out of it—the child. Sagarika, she who came from the ocean, though at home she was called Bula.

I remember that girl, that skin the colour of honey, the black curls on her head, the sparkling eyes just like her mother's.

Prabha had many children but she just knew, the way only a mother does, that Sagarika was the one who would carry her legacy. I thought so too. That child was a natural. The stage was in her blood. When she played young Yadav in *Praphulla* and Charan in *Pandit-mashai*, audiences said they had never seen a child act like that. Do you know, she even acted in the film version of *Pandit-mashai*? And on radio. At six, she had done theatre, film, radio—everything her mother had done. While other girls played ranna-bati with little toy pots and pans, she played the children from the great classics. While others learnt childish rhymes, she recited lines of dialogue.

And when she looked at you with those big eyes, everyone said, 'Mark my words, Prabha Devi's little girl will one day be bigger than Prabha Devi herself.' She was so talented, I told her mother, 'Prabha, put a spot of black kajal on her forehead. Protect her from the evil eye.'

Prabha laughed, 'Even the devil cannot bear to harm my Bula. Look at her. She is a little doll.'

Bula was tied to her mother's sari. Everywhere Prabha went, that child wanted to go. It was like the midwife had forgotten to cut the umbilical cord. In those days, touring theatres were all the rage. Sometimes when Prabha went on tour, she took along Bula as well.

I told her, 'Don't take the child. It's too much. Goodness knows what kind of places you will stay in. I hear it's all jungles and tea gardens with elephants and tigers.'

But Prabha never listened to anyone. I think she never felt safe if she could not keep an eye on that child. She was her future, the one who would carry the light. That's why she took her to Rangpur in Assam and that's where the child fell sick. The fever would not let up. She had trouble talking. Her breath was getting shallow. The sickness settled in her lungs. Prabha stayed up all night putting cold-water compresses on her burning forehead. Nothing worked. Later the doctor said it was diphtheria. There was no treatment then. It just took two days.

When she realized Bula was gone, Prabha let out a scream that chilled everyone to the bone. In those days, it was not unusual to lose children. My brother died as well when he was just five years old. Cholera. Smallpox. Malaria. Black fever. There was no shortage of ways.

Sagarika was not the only child Prabha lost. But Sagarika was different. In our fairy tales, we say there are special places where the princess' life spirit is hidden away. Sometimes it's in a pearl in the bottom of the ocean. Sometimes in a little locket in a golden box in a witch's treasure chest. If you steal it, the princess' life will flicker like a candle. Sagarika was Prabha's life spirit.

When Prabha showed her brother the door, I have heard her eyes were shimmering with tears, tears she would not let her brother see. But when Sagarika died, Prabha turned to stone.

My sister's sister-in-law Jaba lived in Rangpur then. She told me she saw that little body covered in flowers. She looked like a little princess who had fallen asleep. When they took her to be cremated, Jaba said it seemed half of Rangpur was walking alongside, weeping and crying 'Our little Charan is gone. Our little Charan has left us.' Only Prabha sat still, her eyes as dry as a midsummer afternoon.

That day they announced the show was cancelled. But it was their last night and Prabha said these people had come from far away to see her in Sita. How could she disappoint them?

That night she went on stage as usual. She had to be Prabha Devi, not Bula's mother. The audience could not hold back their tears but Prabha played her part as she did every day.

Jaba told me the people of Rangpur built a small marble memorial for Sagarika. I asked Prabha once if she wanted to go back to see it. She shook her head, 'Indu, when I think of Rangpur, I just remember the trees. Mango. Jackfruit. Jamun. Paniyal. Coconut. And sometimes I dream my Bula is running around among those trees. Running and laughing, laughing and running. When I wake up, the laughter breaks around me. I reach for her, but she runs away.'

Years later, I remember there was some other play she did where a small boy dies. One of her children, maybe Ketaki, played that boy. In one scene, the father comes to Prabha, holding the dead child in his arms. After a few nights, she told Sisir Bhaduri, 'Baba, I cannot bear this scene any more. I just cannot.' They dropped that scene from the play.

We are actresses. We spend all our lives weeping, laughing, loving but for lines written by other people. Our own stories remain locked up in us. Sometimes I think we even forget who we really are.

Prabha went on with her life. She had to. She had a family to look after. She had a house to run. She cooked, she cleaned, she supervised the maids, she managed the finances, she did everything. I would go to the house and see her squatting in the kitchen, her hands covered with fish scales but signing some contract for some play. She may have taken one of the famous Bhaduri brothers as a husband but Prabha didn't enjoy the luxuries of being a Bhaduri wife. Everything she built, she built on her own. I can say bluntly what others won't. Her husband lived in the house Prabha Devi bought and that is God's own truth.

But when Chapal came along, something changed in Prabha. That boy was different from the other sons. That boy watched her on stage with the same hungry eyes that Bula had. Sometimes when he talked, he sounded like a little girl, and I would see Prabha catch her breath as if she could not recognize her own son.

One day at the house, she beckoned me and, putting her finger to lips, asked me to be quiet. I was surprised. Prabha had a voice like a megaphone. When she hollered from the kitchen for the children—'Khokaaa, Tukuuu, Chhoto, Kamal, tea is ready, come down'—you could hear her all the way to Srirangam Theatre down the street. That day she led me to her room, the one where she kept her gramophone and records. As we peeped around the door, I saw Chapal standing alone in front of her big mirror. A little boy. With a cloth twisted round and round to make a bun, and a Kashmiri shawl draped over his shoulders, he was reciting from memory the lines from her plays. One play melting into the other and then into another. It was like watching a Prabha doll, the way he copied her laugh, the turn of her head, her walk, her eyes opening wide. Prabha whispered, 'Indu, where did this boy come from? He knows all my parts like the back of his hand. Only my parts. Never the hero's. Only mine.'

She shook her head, 'If he were my daughter, what a great actress he might have been.'

Neither of us said Bula's name but I know at that moment she was on both our minds.

Later I saw she had put a black kajal spot right behind Chapal's ear. He complained but she just laughed and held him close, 'That spot will keep you safe, Tuku, even when I am not here.'

We did not know that that day would come much too soon.

The day she died, that motherless boy came running to me and buried his face in my sari. As I held him close and felt his body shake, I promised him 'Just as I am mother to my two sons, from this day think of me as your mother too.'

Every theatre in theatre-para was closed. The newspapers the next day had pictures of the swarming crowds at Nimtala Burning Ghat. They say no one had mourned an actress this way since Binodini-ma died. But Binodini-ma had left the theatre many years before she died. She had written, 'I am alone in this world. I have nobody, no near and dear ones, no work, no faith, no reason to be. I just sit with my burden of pain and wait for death to come relieve me.' Prabha, on the other hand had acted till the day she died.

As I watched them take her away, I was thinking of the days when we were two-bit dancing girls with big dreams. Now the biggest stars of the day from Kanan Devi to Sunanda Devi were coming to put garlands on Prabha. It was an exit worthy of a queen, though it was an exit that happened much too early.

I remembered what she had told me that day as we watched Chapal play Prabha in her room on Dalimtala Lane. 'If he were my daughter, what a great actress he might have been.'

And then she looked at me and said: 'But he is not my daughter, Indu. He is my son. I don't know if this will be his blessing. Or his curse. Only time will tell.'

2
The Railways

School Days

When Ma died, it was as if the sky fell upon us.

I was a young boy still, a student at Town School in Shyampukur, in the heart of North Kolkata. School wasn't too far from home. Sometimes I took the tram, but whenever I spotted the conductor coming towards me to ask for the fare, I would quickly hop off. Often, I just walked to school because I knew all the short cuts through the alleyways and winding by-lanes. The school itself was on the main road where the old cinema halls with their grand facades stood a stone's throw from each other. I can still recite their names from memory, as if they were sisters in a family next door—Uttara, Minar, Sree, Chitra and the much younger Darpana. On Friday nights, when new films opened and the marquees were all lit up, the whole street felt electric, buzzing with excitement.

Most of those great single-screen cinemas have shut down, one by one. Some have been replaced by giant departmental stores, belching out gusts of cold air-conditioned air onto the street. Their names—CitiMart or Bazaar Kolkata—are so dull. They no longer sound like sisters. Some are just empty shells, padlocked and rotting away as they wait for their death sentence. Only Minar clings on somehow. Once upon a time, you could see the pavement beneath your feet, but now they are so packed with hawkers and shoppers haggling over cheap shoes, imitation jewellery and plastic knick-knacks that pedestrians prefer to walk on the road, darting between honking cars and buses and three-wheeler auto-rickshaws.

It's the old city, but the old buildings can barely be seen, wrapped up as they are now in billboards big and small, advertising gold-bordered Benarasi silks or brightly coloured suitcases. The one put up by Bikrampur Bastralaya declares 'we have no branches' and boasts that it's been selling saris for three generations, more than 70 years!

Seventy years is a long time. But I went to school in that neighbourhood even earlier. In those days, the biggest signboard belonged to the K. L. Dutta departmental store. That store sold everything, from saris and dhotis to oil and spices and fancy goods. K. L. Dutta and Kamalalaya Bastralaya were the shopping malls of that time. The signboard for K. L. Dutta was so big, it became a landmark in itself. You would use it to give people directions: 'Get off at Hatibagan crossing and turn left at the K. L. Dutta sign.'

All that is gone, but the Town School, set up in 1894, is there even now, its colonial architecture so strange beside the shiny KFC and Wow Momo outlets that have cropped up. Snack shops selling phuchka, chicken burgers and fruit juice crowd upon the gates of the school, whose sign still promises 'good education for very minimal cost'.

Those yellow walls painted with red geometric designs and the big bottle-green windows take me right back to my childhood, to daydreaming in the classroom, looking out and watching the clanking trams and double-decker buses go by. The city was never quiet except in the afternoon when a sleepy hush descended over the streets. I can almost feel our headmaster Purna-babu's hot breath on the back of my neck. 'What? You want to go out during tiffin break? I bet you want to line up for movie tickets, don't you? You think I don't know they've just released *Bhairab Mantra* at Minar? I'll show you *Bhairab Mantra*!'

The punishments Purna-babu came up with were legendary. He would take a pencil and jab it between your fingers with such force, tears would come to your eyes. Or yank you by the side-burns and slap you so hard you'd see stars. I got punished a lot especially in English class because I would mess up all the time with my grammar and spelling.

If I had spent one more year in school, I could have taken my matriculation examination, and that would have surely led to some kind of a good, stable government job. But no one thought about all that then, least of all me. Ma died and my schooling abruptly ground to a halt in Class 9. I had three elder brothers, all of them adults, all of them working, but they took no responsibility for my education. My eldest brother was very good in studies. As long as Ma was around, he pushed me to study as well. But after she passed away, somehow everyone forgot about me.

His, Hers and Theirs

There's a story behind that. My elder brothers were in fact my half-brothers. My mother had married twice. My two eldest brothers, Kamalesh and Amalesh, and my eldest sister, Pratibha, were the children of her first husband, Amaresh Sikdar. Mother had married him knowing full well that he had a wife and children. Amaresh

Sikdar married my mother all right but he never acknowledged her publicly as his wife. 'You're an actor,' he would tell her, 'you keep acting. As for us—let's just stay like this.' The stigma around women actors was that hard to shake off. But my mother wanted respect, respect she felt was due to her. In her own way, she was a very conventional god-fearing woman at heart. She wanted a proper home with a husband and children. In the end, they parted ways.

Ma joined Sisir Bhaduri's theatre company around 1917/18. That's where she met Tara Kumar Bhaduri, the man who would become my father. He was Sisir Bhaduri's younger brother, and he too had children, three of them, but he was a widower. Tara Kumar and Prabha Devi grew close and finally decided to get married. They had what you would call a love marriage these days.

The Bhaduri family, all six brothers, ran Srirangam Theatre together. Instead of hiring outsiders, they split up all the responsibilities among themselves. My father worked as receiver, which meant he was in charge of receiving money. In practical terms, though, it meant he had to do whatever was needed to keep the theatre running. One day he was the booking manager, another day the stage manager, yet another day he was in charge of the make-up room. Two other uncles acted while a third looked after the company's accounts. Father tried his hand at acting, but it was not really his thing. He was good-looking enough, so he would occasionally get a few roles, but they were bit parts, like a judge who shows up in the final scene, looks very magisterial, shouts 'Order, order' and then gravely pronounces the verdict.

Tara Kumar married Prabha Devi, but some of the Bhaduri clan never truly accepted her as part of the family. She was an actress, that too with children from a previous relationship. None of that sat well with the new in-laws. My father, on the other hand, took her children under his wing and accepted them as his own. Though parts of his family would go so far as to say *we* weren't real Bhaduris at all.

The Bhaduris had a big family home in Howrah, but we never went there. Instead, my father moved into the house my mother had bought in Kolkata.

Sikdar and Bhaduri—the conflict between these two surnames made life hell for us. Decades later, one of my cousins decided to sue me. By that time my parents were both long dead. I think what was at stake was some land that belonged to the Bhaduris. They wanted to make sure I didn't try and claim a share. One day, a court summons showed up in my name. Addressed to: Chapal Bhaduri, Father's Name: Unknown.

I could not imagine that after so many years I would have to fight a case to prove to the world that I was a Bhaduri. I have known a lot of humiliation in my life but this really stung. The newspapers smelt a juicy scandal and the reporters started calling me for a reaction . . . I had never seen the inside of a courtroom in my life but I decided that enough was enough, I needed to fight back. If they wanted to take a DNA test, I was ready for that too. I didn't care about the property, but I did care about my name.

My lawyer friend, Chanchal Banerjee, told me, 'You have been everywhere. You might as well have some experience of the courtroom as well.' We fought that case for almost three years. Every time there was a hearing, I would trudge all the way from my home in North Kolkata to Howrah across the river. It took a lot of time and a lot money but eventually they backed down. I remained Chapal Bhaduri, son of Tara Kumar Bhaduri.

My mother was not well educated and that was why she was treated like dirt by so many people, including some of her in-laws. People would say actresses like her came from the forbidden red-light areas. A man could marry as many times as he liked, but just because our mother had married twice, she was called all kinds of names.

Even her own brothers shunned her because she was an actress. I remember a man coming to Ma to ask for money and her turning him away. I was just a boy but I was struck by how much he looked like Ma—that same round face, those big eyes.

'Who is he?' I asked her.

'That is my elder brother, your uncle,' she said. 'But if you ever see him out on the street, do not speak to him. That man turned his back on me, his own sister, because he was ashamed that she was an actress. But now he has no shame about coming to that same sister and asking for money.'

Her eyes, I noticed, were glistening with tears. A few years later, I did in fact run into him on some street. When I told Ma, she said, 'Remember what I had told you. Even if he wants to speak to you, don't talk to him.'

That's how I learnt my mother had two brothers. Other children had a mama-bari, a house where their mother's family lived, where they went for summer holidays and were pampered by grandparents and uncles and aunts. I too had mamas, or maternal uncles, but I had no mama-bari—because they had all disowned my mother for being an actress.

Still, Ma put on a brave face and carried on with her life. Her favourite saying was '*Haathi chale bazaar, kutta bhauke hazaar*'—when the elephant goes to mart, a thousand dogs will bark. It was her way to cope with all the insults and indignities that had come her way. In time, I learnt to make it my mantra too.

The Household Help

After Ma died, we were in dire straits. Some cinema production houses still owed her money but we had to run from door to door to get what was due. Some of them, like the great actress Kanan Devi, paid up without even being asked, but others flatly refused.

At the time of her death, Ma had been working at Rang Mahal Theatre, but the plays there did not really have any roles for teenaged boys like me. There were a couple of other boys as well who had no work. Sumohan-babu, the manager, was a kindly man. He took pity on us: 'You boys have acted in our productions for so many years. You are like family. I know there aren't any roles for you right now but it's all right. We'll manage somehow. You just stay on, and at the end of the month, we'll give you a small salary, maybe 50 rupees. Only one condition—you have to attend all the shows.'

I still feel grateful for that act of kindness, though it never sat well with me to get money without doing real work. It reeked of charity and even as a boy it bothered me. So we carried on keeping a lookout for real work. Sometimes amateur-theatre groups would need a boy or two. It was usually when they had a show outside Kolkata, and their regular actresses could not travel with them. But those opportunities were few and far between.

Meanwhile, things were getting harder at home without Ma. Baba in his grief had started drinking heavily, and did not really have a job, just the bit parts in film and theatre every now and then. My older brothers had never wholeheartedly accepted Baba.

As long as Ma was around, they had kept their peace. The household ran on her earnings, after all. And it was she who had got them their jobs, even set them up with their separate kitchens after they got married. She knew they'd always had misgivings about Baba. While I might not have thought of my brothers as Sikdars, they probably thought of me as a Bhaduri. It had all worked somehow till she died. Then everything fell apart. Just like the country was torn apart by Partition, our little family also broke into two. I ended up in my sister Ketaki's portion.

Everyone had to pitch in however they could, but what could I do? I was just a boy. Other boys my age were going to school. I was squatting near the tap, scrubbing heavy pots and pans. I would pump water by hand from the tube-well and then carry it back home. I would drag heavy pitchers and buckets of water from the ground floor to the second floor. I washed everyone's clothes, then hung them out to dry. I soon became an expert at laundry work. I knew that you needed to wash trousers inside out, that you if did not pay special attention to the collars, you could never rid of the grime. As for myself: I barely had two sets of shirts and pyjamas. I'd wash one and wear the other.

Soon I was nothing more than the household help, bouncing around from one sister to another. One day I ate at my older sister's, another day at my younger sister's. At night, I rolled out a mattress, put a pillow on it and fell sleep, exhausted. Next day, at the crack of dawn, the whole routine started all over again. Not so long ago I would lie curled up in bed, waiting for my mother to call us each by name, to come down to the kitchen and have some tea. Her voice still rang in my ears. But those days were gone.

I became desperate to earn my own money.

Can You Dress Like a Girl?

At that time, my sister Ketaki was acting at Star Theatre. One day she said, 'Why don't you go and ask Chhorda—our brother who worked for the transport company—if he can find you some job, perhaps in the canteen?'

But it was my oldest brother-in-law Pankaj Niyogi who came to my rescue. I was 16, still young but flushed with adolescence. It's a bit embarrassing to say this about myself, but I was quite beautiful, tall with a full head of hair. Goodness knows where the photographs from those days have gone. My voice was very sweet as well. Whenever I heard Lata Mangeshkar singing on the radio, I would sing along. From my childhood, I'd had an air of girlishness about me. My brother-in-law had obviously spotted that.

'Do you want to work?' he asked me.

'Yes, Chhordi is saying I need to do something. But I don't know what work I can do.'

'*Tui meyechhele sajte parbi*?' I will never forget that line: can you dress like a girl?

And that is how my brother-in-law planted within me the seed of what I was to become.

'A girl?' I was taken aback. Even though I had girlish manners and a girlish voice and girlish everything, I thought of myself as a boy. How could a boy dress like a girl?

My brother-in-law worked in the engineering department of the Railways at Sealdah Station. He said, 'If you can dress up as a girl and act, I might be able to help you out. Our recreation club is staging *Alibaba*. Will you be able to play the part of Morjina, the slave girl?'

I was terribly confused. How could I play the part of a woman?

'But it happens all the time,' my brother-in-law explained. 'So many people do it. You have no idea how much money they make playing female parts. They are able to live off it and support their families as well. And most of them are practically illiterate. At least you have some schooling in you. But you have to decide if you want to do it.'

At that time, in jatra theatre, there were indeed many men who had become famous for playing women on stage—Chhabi Rani, Babli Rani, Nitai Rani and many others.

I went to ask Chhordi for her advice. She said, 'All I can say is that when someone is floundering in deep waters, then if he finds even a straw in front of him, he holds on to that.'

My brother-in-law said, 'If you can do it and they like you, then you might even get a job in the Railways.'

That sounded tempting. In those days, a job in the Railways was a golden job.

Still, I hesitated. 'How can I dress as a girl? What about all the stuff that a woman has?'

'You won't have to worry. They will dress you. All you have to do is sing and dance and say your lines.'

I knew how to do that already. In fact, I loved dance so much that Ma had arranged for a dance tutor for me after one of the theatre artistes noticed I had rhythm. The tutor was a student of the great Kathak dancer Gopi Kishan; she had even been to Mumbai to choreograph dances. The first time she tied those bells on my feet, they were so heavy I could barely lift my foot. But she really liked me. When she went to Benaras, she brought back an image of Lord Shiva for me. I still remember the bols, the recitations of rhythmic patterns. I know exactly when the tihai, the phrase repeated three times, was coming. I learnt for about three months. We had just started the bols when Ma died. Like many other things in my life, my dance lessons also came to an end.

But *Alibaba* was a different matter altogether. I had watched *Alibaba* so many times that I knew all the lines by heart. One of the great Morjinas I had seen had been played by Renubala, a friend of my mother's. There were several Renubalas in theatre. The one I speak of was called Renubala Sukh, because she had become famous for her performance as Sukh or Joy in the play *Atmadarshan*. After Ma died, she had held me close and said: 'Don't cry. I am still here. To me you are another son, just like my Subrata and Satya. Let me know If you ever need anything.' Subrata, Satya and I all played child roles and I called her Renu-ma. I knew she would help me with the part. So I told my brother-in-law I was willing to do it.

But first I had to go for an interview of sorts with Jyoti Kumar, the play's director, and Prabhat Ghosh who used to play the female roles. I was supposed to replace him because he was getting too old for these parts. He was not impressed by me at all, and didn't bother to hide his disdain: 'Oh, who is this? He is so skinny, his voice is so thin. How will he play Morjina?' At that time, my voice had not changed. Jyoti Kumar, on the other hand, simply asked me to sing Morijina's song, which I knew by heart thanks to Renu-ma. When I was done, he clapped and cried out, 'Wonderful! He's totally ready for the stage!' And just like that, I had the part.

I promptly ran to Renu-ma's. Her house is still there, in a lane near the old-age home where I live now. She told me not to worry and showed me the right sing-song intonation to use when Morjina says 'Baba Mustafa' as she guides the blindfolded tailor home. She taught me the dance steps, the compositions, the mannerisms, everything that had made her Morjina so famous.

I already knew a bit from sitting on my little mat near piano-master Ratan-babu's piano at Srirangam. I knew how women acted, how they raised their eyebrows, how they made their eyes big, how they conveyed love, how they showed fear. But that was just by observing. Renu-ma gave me my first official lesson in how to actually play a woman on stage. I will always remain in her debt.

Becoming Morjina

Rehearsals lasted only 16 days. Then, on the big day, I showed up at the Netaji Subhas Institute in Sealdah. There had hired a make-up man, Rati-da, quite a well-known one, in those days.

Rati-da looked me up and down and asked quite dismissively 'So what role are you playing?'

'Morjina,' I mumbled.

'Oh,' he said, a little taken aback. Then he said, 'Well you are young. You will look fine, I guess.'

He took some white powder and mixed it with some yellow, then added a bit of orange and made a paste while I followed along, trying to remember all the steps. Then he took a brush and slathered that paste on my face as if he was whitewashing a wall. There was no concept of pancake make up in those days. When the paste had dried, he dabbed some powder on my cheeks. When he was satisfied, he took a matchstick and drew my eyes and brows quite expertly. All that was left were the lips. He put a little colour on them, then used the tip of the matchstick to draw a fine line to emphasize the upper lip and make it a little more prominent. Then he stepped back, inspected his handiwork and hollered, 'This one is doing Morjina. Get him his outfits, Nirode.'

Nirode-da appeared with Morjina's shiny red-satin outfit. Of course, Morjina also needed breasts. But we didn't have falsies then, nor any concept of bras and bodices. Instead, there was a long ribbon with two small bundles of rags which they tied firmly around my chest.

Once that was done, Lalu-da, the hair-fit man appeared. In those days, we called hairdressers 'hair-fit men'. Lalu-da put a wig on me, and quickly tied up the long hair into plaits. Then he said, 'Now go, look at yourself in the big mirror over there.'

When I stood in front of the mirror, I could not recognize myself.

A pretty woman in loose Baghdadi pyjamas, a red shirt and a golden Irani waistcoat looked back at me. Her hair was tied in two thick plaits, and her jewellery gleamed golden. Someone explained that in Arabia, the maids wore gold while the queens wore diamonds. Morjina was a maid.

'Is this really me? Really? Or is this my sister?' I wondered, gaping at myself. A lot of young men had slowly come up, they were standing around me, staring. One of the older ones, he was perhaps 25 or 26, and quite handsome, came up to me: 'Everything looks beautiful'—and truly it did—'but there is one thing missing.'

'What?' I replied. 'I don't know what you mean.' At that time, I was quite naive and innocent.

He pulled out a red rose and offered it to me with a flourish.

'I can't take this,' I said, blushing. 'But you can pin it on me.' And that's exactly what he did while all the other boys whooped and whistled.

Then the drop screen went up. The clarinet, which was a must in jatras in those days, struck up the jaunty tune of Morjina's signature song 'Chhi chhi itna janjaal'. But I stood there utterly paralysed, peacock feathers in my hands, anklets on my feet, teetering in my heeled shoes. I took one step forward, one step back.

A man shoved me forward: 'Go on, enter! The scene is flowing by.' That was an odd phrase they would use: the scene is flowing by—as if it was a river. And so I stumbled onto the stage, head-first into my first female role.

The year was 1955, and I had no idea that role was going to change my life forever.

After the play was over, someone told my brother-in-law, 'What a complete package you've brought, Pankaj. He's totally ready. But will he be able to do big parts? He seems a little young and thin. Maybe a bit too tall as well.'

'He can try. Let's see what happens.'

Someone told me, 'Listen, next month, we have another play where we need someone for the girlfriend's role. Can you do it? You will have to sing and dance.'

I said, 'Yes.'

Later I asked my brother-in-law, 'But what about the money? They didn't give me any.'

'You can't get money here,' he scolded. 'This is a recreation club. But, as I said, if they like you, it might lead to something more lucrative.'

Seven days later I got a job at the Railways.

The Chain-Man

My designation was chain-man, salary 2.50 rupees a day, which came to about 75 rupees a month. My job was to measure the land with a steel chain. But I never actually measured anything. There was no question of going out in the sun. I had to protect my complexion for the stage, after all. That was my real job.

Every month there was a new play, because the Railways had so many departments and each had their own recreational club. And every time there was a dance scene, they would send for me.

Finally, I got a little fed up: 'Just dance, dance and dance? They are dressing me so beautifully but all I will do is dance? Never act?' Now that I had a taste of the stage, I had started to crave all those dramatic roles Ma had done—Annapurna, Sarama, Mandadori, Draupadi . . .

My roles were a little different. In those days, our plays had a 'drop'. It was like an intermission. After the first four scenes, a drop would fall and there would be a dance number. Then a few more scenes and then another drop and another dance number. The dance numbers were performed by me. I slowly acquired a taste for them. It's like when you first drink alcohol, you just have one sip. Then you have a little more and then some more. At the end some pass out, some don't. But you are well and truly addicted. This acting is a bit like drinking.

Jyoti Kumar, our director, had also once played female parts. I asked him if I could play Manorama in an upcoming production of Sarat Chandra's famous novel *Baikunther Will.*

'Manorama? You mean Gokul's wife?' He was sceptical. 'That's a villainous part. How will you manage that? There are others who can do it. Like Prabhat or Sudhanshu. You play Mamata instead, that friend of Maya's.'

He was right. Prabhat and Sudhanshu acted well and were good-looking to boot. But that incident finally made me decide that I needed to learn more about the nuts and bolts of acting. Otherwise I'd never go beyond the song-and-dance routines. I also needed to figure out how to do my own make-up. I had learnt a bit by watching Ma as she did hers. I knew some tricks, how to mix a little black with some red to get brown or blue and then add a little yellow for an exquisite turquoise.

One day, my friend Subrata, Renu-ma's son, said, 'Why don't you do your own make-up? You can do a better job than the make-up man.'

Subrata taught me some more tricks, like using some dark brown on the sides of the nose to make it look more sharp. Using the tip of a matchstick to draw a line around my upper lip to make them more full.

'What do I with my hair?' I asked.

'Your hair is quite long anyway. Just part it down the middle and brush it flat on both sides.'

There were two kinds of wigs at that time—full bust and half bust. The half bust you placed on your head, tied it in place from the back, then carefully blended your own hair into it. If you did it right, people couldn't make out where your own hair ended and the wig began. The full bust was, as the name suggests, a full wig, fully covering your own hair. The wigmakers—Farhad, Mehboob, Abdul—were all from the Chitpur area of Kolkata, near Nakhoda Masjid. You had to go and have your head measured by them, so that they could make your wig made to order. Now they are all gone. Like my hair. Now I have to wear a full bust, because I don't have so much hair any more. But when I was young, my hair was so long that I often didn't need a wig.

I learnt to do everything, from make-up to jewellery to wigs, and design everything according to the role I was playing. I think we who act, especially those of us who do female parts, need to know these things.

I used to work in the Railways under an officer named S. K. Bose. He had reached retirement age but was on a six-month extension. He was the main person in the construction department. There was also Sambhu-babu, the head clerk of the construction department. He played female parts too, sometimes. Of course, I had no idea how to do any of the work required in my actual job. For example, bricks would be stacked in the godown and I had to keep track of their number. There was a particular way to stack them. I didn't know any of this.

I went to Sambhu-babu. 'So many trucks filled with cement have come. They need to be stored in the godown. How do I do this inventory?'

He said, 'Each sack is a certain weight. Figure out how many tonnes of cement. Check the diameter of the iron rods coming in. Some will be one inch, some half inch, some quarter inch.'

Before long I had learnt what cubic feet meant . . . I learnt how to do what was needed. But I didn't really like any of it. So then I was moved to another job, in the dispatch department.

No matter where I was placed, I had permission to go anywhere, even to the head office, because I was S. K. Bose's chain-man.

The Road Not Taken

One day, S. K. Bose said, 'Go to Mughalbagan.'

'Mughalbagan?'

'It's near Narkeldanga. There are railway quarters coming up there. Five buildings, each four storeys. Go and check if the scaffolding is up.'

The word in Bengali for scaffolding is the same as the word for rent. I had no idea what rent S. K. Bose was talking about, but was too nervous to ask. I meekly left his room, and set off on my task.

When I returned, he said, 'So, is the scaffolding done? Should I go on an inspection?'

'Umm, yes' I stammered.

'Why are you stammering? Did you see the scaffolding or not?'

'Yes, yes, I saw,' I lied through my teeth.

Later, when he went to Mughalbagan, he threw a fit—the scaffolding was nowhere near done. 'Why did you tell my man the scaffolding was done?' he scolded the people on the site. Of course, they had no idea what he was talking about.

Then he turned to me. 'You said the scaffolding was done, Chapal?'

I just looked sheepish and shuffled on my feet.

'Do you even know what scaffolding means?'

I shamefacedly admitted that I did not.

'Why didn't you say so? Come with me to Beleghata.' He took me to a Beleghata neighbourhood where some construction was being underway and showed me what scaffolding meant.

Then he said, 'Climb up.'

I climbed up the bamboo scaffolding with a thudding heart. It was raining that day, and the bamboo poles were slippery.

'Check and see if the corners of the bricks on the third floor have been broken correctly.' In railway construction, the bricks would all have their corners broken off. Those bits were then powdered and mixed with some other stuff. And that's what's responsible for the rust-red brick colour across all the railway quarters.

That's how my boss taught me my work.

When it was time for S. K. Bose to leave after his six-month extension was up, he asked to see me. This created quite an uproar. S. K. Bose was an important man: Assistant Engineer (North).

My brother-in-law said, 'The saheb has asked to see you. Make sure you listen carefully, and do exactly as he says.'

'What is he going to say?'

'What do I know? All I am saying is whatever he says, try to agree. At least say: let me think about it and get back to you. Just don't say anything stupid.'

I nervously knocked on S. K. Bose's door.

'Sir, I am here.'

He could be tremendously irate, like the fiery sage Durbasha I had read about in our mythological stories.

'Who is it?' He asked. 'Oh Chapal. Come, sit.'

'It's OK, sir. I can stand.'

'No, no, sit down. Listen, I am leaving this office in a couple of days. I want to talk to you about something.'

I sat down.

'Listen, you are a good boy Chapal. I am very fond of you. You've paid attention to what I've asked of you. Whatever work you've done, you have done it with your whole heart. I want to do you a favour before I leave.'

'Favour?'

'I want to secure you a permanent job for you before I go. But it will be in another department.'

'Another department?'

'Yes. Do you remember the Beleghata workshop we went to? There's a job there. It will, however, mean that you get out of the shirt and pants you are wearing, put on shorts and a vest and beat iron. Do you think you can do it?'

I was in a fix. I tried to imagine myself in a vest and shorts, blowing on the bellows and hammering pieces of red-hot iron . . . To be honest, I could not see myself doing that kind of work at all. But I didn't know how to say that to his face.

S. K. Bose continued. 'You are quite clear-headed and quick to pick up things. That's why I thought of you. Think about it, and see if it's something you think you can manage.'

Then he looked me in the eye.

'If you are able to do this job right, you might go on to become a railway fitter or a foreman. Fitters and foremen are paid very well. There are a lot of perks to those jobs too. Sleep on it and let me know tomorrow. I am leaving the day after.'

When I came out of his room, all my colleagues gathered around me, wanting to know what SK-saheb had said. I'd suddenly become somebody important, perhaps even grown a tail!

I told them about the job he was offering me at the Beleghata workshop.

My friends were quite aghast. 'Arrey, no, no, you can't do all that. That's is not the job for a pretty boy like you. If you are in that workshop, hammering iron, covered in all that soot and dirt, what will happen to your good looks? And then how will you act? Don't even think about it.'

I hesitated. 'But he said this would secure my future. Someday, I might become a rail foreman, or fitter even.'

'Goodness knows how long that will take. Anyway, we are here for you, aren't we? Don't worry about anything.'

I naively believed them. Now I know better. To this day, whenever anyone says, 'We are here for you. Don't worry about anything,' I get nervous. How many times I have met people who told me, 'We are here for you.' But when push came to shove, no one was. Only a handful of people have truly stood by me during my bleakest days.

I discussed it with my family that night. Chhordi said, 'Are you sure you will be able to do that kind of work?' Scrubbing pots and pans was one thing, hammering iron another.

'I don't know,' I replied.

'Well, think about it carefully,' she said.

Then I went to my brother-in-law and said, 'I don't think I can do this job.'

My brother-in-law shook his head. 'People seldom get opportunities like this, Chapal. And here it's being offered to you on a silver platter and you are going to reject it? Have those friends of yours like Jiten and Nagen been advising you not to?'

'They are saying my acting career will be hurt. Right now, I work across many departments. Everyone knows me. So whenever a role comes up, they think of me.'

'Hmm,' my brother-in-law said. 'You are growing up. What are you now? 15 or 16? Think hard about the job. These roles won't last forever.'

I fell into a real quandary. I had been to the Beleghata workshop. I'd seen the work that went on there. I understood what I would have to do. But stuffing rags into my blouse and playing a woman on stage, acting and dancing and lapping up the audience's applause . . . I had tasted that adulation and I understood its draw. The love of an audience has a hypnotic power of its own. It's an addiction of sorts.

The next day, I went to S. K. Bose's office with my heart in my mouth.

'Sir,' I said hesitantly.

'Come, come sit down, Chapal. So what did you decide?'

'Sir, I cannot do this job. There is a problem.'

'What's the problem? Is there some objection at home?'

'No, the problem is from my end. You know, sir, I act in plays put on by the departments.'

'Yes, I know. But where's the problem? You can still do that while doing this job.'

'No, I won't be able to, sir. I don't think I can manage such hard labour.'

He sighed and said, 'Listen, let me tell you something. I am S. K. Bose, AEN–Special. I took a liking to you and that is why

I made this offer. But you are not willing to take it up. One day, you will regret it. Then you will think about what a terrible mistake you made today. You could have become a permanent employee of the Railways.'

He was right. There's a world of difference between permanent employees and temporary ones. When the Railways ration shop was shut down, the permanent employees who worked there needed to be given new jobs. So they were given ours, because we were not permanent. I still went to the office a couple of times, but my Railways 'career' sputtered to an end within a few months.

Sometimes I think about that day I turned down S. K. Bose's offer. If I had agreed to it, my life would have taken a completely different turn. When my jatra days were on a downward slide, and I felt nothing was working out, I remember thinking 'Did I really make a mistake that day? I am not sure where next month's rent will come from. I have to worry constantly about money. I have had to leave behind everything I once owned. Producers who once came begging to me to play a female part now tell me, "This year, we don't need your services."'

At that time, I would think about the life not lived. S. K. Bose had told me I could have become a foreman or a fitter. I would have gotten railway quarters. I would have a pension. Perhaps I would have married, been a father, raised a family.

But I would not then have been Chapal Rani.

INTERLUDE

In Imagination

The Niece

I am sorry if I sounded a little curt on the phone. The fact is my family was all right there when you called me.

I could not talk about Tuku-mama, I mean Chapal Bhaduri, with you in front of them. That's why I asked you to call me in the afternoon. That's when my husband is at office and the children at college. That's the only time I can really call my own. I am surprised you tracked me down and found my phone number. So, tell me, what would you like to know.

Chapal Bhaduri. It's years since I've heard that name, let alone laid eyes on him. How is he? I am his niece all right but I feel like I will disappoint you. I have very little to share about him.

You see, no one in my family knows we are even related. My mother was his eldest sister, half-sister to be exact, but she treated him as her own baby brother. I have heard that it was my father who got him his first job on stage, acting as Morjina in *Alibaba*. I have dim memories of the house on Dalimtala Lane where we all lived together when I was born. It was a house filled with the hubbub of people. I could run up and down the stairs, from one room to another, from one uncle to another aunt. But I really have nothing from that time, not even fading pictures in a family album.

I know my mother was an actress too when she was young and have heard she was not without talent either. But she gave it all up when she married my father. In society's eyes, she was always somehow tainted because she was the daughter of an actress. Everyone whispered that her real father was not the man who lived on Dalimtala Lane with her mother, the famous Prabha Devi. Her real father was another man, a Mr Sikdar, who was already married though he had set up a family with Prabha Devi as well.

My mother said she wanted me to have a normal life, one untouched by all those insinuations. So she found me a good husband, his family lived in another town, a family that had nothing to do with the world of stage and film and, more importantly, no interest in it either.

It was a solid middle-class family, not very wealthy but respectable. My husband had a good steady job. By then my grandmother Prabha Devi was dead, and the family had scattered to the winds. The house on Dalimtala Lane was sold off, and everyone moved out and set up their own homes in other parts of the city. That's when my mother wiped out every trace of her family history. She told no one about it, not even our neighbours.

Once and only once she took my sisters and me to the street where Srirangam Theatre had once stood. Sisir Bhaduri, the man who founded it, was dead by then. We walked down the street till we came to a very narrow lane near a small green mosque. Ma pointed at the lane and said it led to the house where they had all lived. 'Should we go see if it is still there?' I asked. But she said, 'No, that chapter is over. I don't want to meet anyone who might remember me. Let's go eat some Mughlai paratha at Ellora instead.'

Ma told no one our family story. She created a different one instead, something far less colourful. Prabha Devi, Sisir Bhaduri, Srirangam Theatre, Chapal Rani had no part in that new story. Now it feels strange to even think that my life was in some way connected to theirs. They are part of the cultural history of Bengal. I am just a housewife in a small town outside Kolkata. I cannot say I have done anything with my life other than cook and clean and raise my children. When I die, nobody will remember me other than my children

I remember Chhoto-mashi and Tuku-mama, Ketaki Dutta and Chapal Bhaduri, coming to my wedding. In fact, they were the ones who dressed me and did my make-up.

I remember Tuku-mama cocking his head and asking in that sweet voice, high as a flute, 'What do you think, Chhordi? Does she need a little more pink on the cheeks?'

'Not too much, Tuku. This is a wedding, not one of your jatras. Also the make-up must work with her red wedding sari.'

'That sari is very nice indeed. But I could have brought you something even more gorgeous from my own collection,' laughed Tuku-mama teasingly. 'Something actually meant for a queen.'

I giggled. Tuku-mama had not come in a sari. He was wearing a plain sunflower-yellow cotton kurta and crisp white pyjamas. But he still turned heads with his looks. He was quite tall and slim, with thick long hair. His big eyes and full lips could have been the envy of any woman. He laughed often and as coquettishly as any girl. And his skin was smoother than most women's, like butter, without a single hair on his arms and wrists.

'Don't laugh, silly girl,' he said patting my cheek. 'You should come one day and see my saris. I have saris from all over the country. Kanjeevaram, Benarasi, Muga silk, you name it. Everywhere I go, I pick up a sari.'

Some of our neighbours watched them, wide-eyed. Tuku-mama and Chhoto-mashi made for quite an exotic pair of birds in our very humdrum family.

'How do you know these people?' whispered Komola-mashi from two doors down, eyeing them curiously. 'Are they really your uncle and aunt?'

'Of course not,' I said hurriedly. 'They are like a neighbourhood uncle and aunt. Like you, in fact. They lived a few houses away from my mother when she was a girl. When they heard I was getting married, they insisted on doing my make-up.'

'Oh all right. Though I do think there's a bit of resemblance between you and him . . . the forehead and the mouth—'

'Oh really? You must be mistaken.'

'Anyway, I hope they don't make you look like some dancing queen. Or your in-laws will be in for quite a shock.'

I hoped Tuku-mama and Chhoto-mashi did not hear us. Ma had told them not to let on to anyone that we were related, that they were in fact her own brother and sister, related by blood and not by neighbourhood. She had made them promise, and they had, but she was stiff with fear that they would say something and burst the bubble of nondescript middle-class lives she had created for all of us.

'And for heaven's sake never mention them to your new in-laws,' she told me. 'We have nothing to do with the Bhaduris. I was always a Sikdar anyway.'

When my husband's family hosted a reception for our wedding, they asked my parents who we needed to invite from our side of the family. My mother did not include Tuku-mama and Chhoto-mashi. As neighbourhood uncle and aunty, they had no place in an event meant for the immediate blood family. It must have stung but I was helpless. But I confess I was also relieved. How do you explain Chapal Rani to people in whose eyes jatra is something only the lower classes enjoy? It was fine on stage . . . but inside the home, his womanliness made me feel a little awkward too. He was not like my other uncles. I could not imagine him sitting with my father-in-law and discussing the political news of the day.

Later, Ma heard from Chhoto-mashi that Tuku-mama had said it was a mistake for them to have come to the wedding. 'Why did you agree to go where you have to hide who you are?' he told Chhoto-mashi. 'We are not thieves or charlatans. We have nothing to be ashamed of. And we certainly are not nobodies. We come from the bloodline of Prabha Devi and Sisir Bhaduri.'

In the years that followed, I would sometimes see pictures of him in the papers, in jatra advertisements. I would wish they were in colour. Every time I came across one, I would save that page. With time it would become discoloured and brittle. Then I would throw it away, afraid someone would ask me about it.

Then one day he came to our town with a jatra. Perhaps it was *Chand Bibi* or *Sultana Riziya*. I forget now. It was a long time ago. I heard them going around on cycle rickshaws, announcing it through handheld loudspeakers on those little battery-powered PA systems and throwing handbills in the air. I picked up one when I went to the fish market.

That day as I chopped vegetables for lunch, I fantasized about sneaking out of the house at night to go see the play.

Of course, I did no such thing. I was a mother by then. My daughter was very young. My life revolved around my husband, my daughter and my in-laws. My husband was a good man. He was dutiful and kind. Sometimes he even took me out to see a film, but there was no question of a woman of our house going out on her own at night, that too to see a jatra, sitting shoulder to shoulder with all kinds of riff-raff.

Our maid was the one who went to see it. 'You should have seen that Chapal Rani, boudi,' she said as she mopped the floor. 'When he came on stage in that glittering white outfit, it was like the moon had fallen out of the sky right onto our stage in Lakshmikantapur. Everyone started cheering and chapping.'

'Tell me more about him,' I wanted to say. 'Could you tell he was actually a man?'

I had so many more questions, but my mother-in-law was in the same room, and I did not want to show too much interest in a jatra queen in front of her. So I bit my tongue. At night, I lay in bed and wondered what it would have been like to go see him. Would he have recognized me? Would he remember how he had done my make-up when I was getting married? I am sure he did not even know this was the town where I lived. Would he tell me stories about his mother, the great actress Prabha Devi, the grandmother I did not remember and whose name had been erased from my family history? I can't imagine that in his busy life, touring all over the state, he had the time to think about me or remember dressing me for my wedding. But I remember every detail of that day, what he wore, what he said, the lilt of his voice. Chhoto-mashi was well known as an actor but Tuku-mama felt more glamorous to me, a bird of paradise.

I saw Chhoto-mashi or Ketaki Dutta once on stage. By then my mother-in-law was dead. We had gone to Kolkata for a few days. I told my husband I wanted to see a play, and he took me to see *Barbadhu* though he was himself not much interested in theatre.

Chhoto-mashi took my breath away. She was such a powerful actor, and what a bold role. After it was over, my husband said, 'Happy? Let us go get a cup of tea somewhere.' 'I dared not tell him that it had been my aunt on stage. After all, she'd played a prostitute, the 'outside wife'. Who knows what he would have thought of me. I wished I could have gone to the green room and said hello. I could have told my husband she was my neighbourhood aunt who had come to my wedding . . . Perhaps my husband would not have minded knowing the truth . . . and Chhoto-mashi would have put the past aside and hugged me . . . Now it's too late. The lie has become the truth and we are its prisoners.

My mother had wiped clean her past. I once asked her why. She said she wanted to free me and my sisters from the burden of being the children of the stage. Those stories, she always said, have happy endings only on stage, never in real life.

I don't know if that is true. My life, while ordinary, has been happy enough. I really have nothing to complain about. But I hope you can tell Tuku-mama I am sorry it has been this way. Please give him my regards and my pranams. I will always be his fan, even from far away.

3

The Amateur

The Theatre Club

My Railways chapter was over. But I had been bitten well and truly by the acting bug.

Pankaj Niyogi, my brother-in-law, the one who had pushed me to play Morjina on stage, understood the itch.

'Do you know Darjipara Natya Parishad? It's an amateur-theatre club run by Raghunath Sen, one of the brothers of the Sen Mahasay sweetshop family. Raghu-babu is crazy about theatre. They need men to play female roles. One of my friends plays the violin for them. Why don't you talk to him? They might have something for you.'

Saroj-da, the violinist, took one look at me and said, 'Oh, you are Pankaj's brother-in-law? I heard you work for the Railways and act in their plays.'

'I did, but now that train has left the station,' I replied cockily. 'I don't have that job any more.'

'Oh well, why don't you act for our club then?'

Amateur-theatre clubs were all the rage in Kolkata and beyond. Practically every neighbourhood had one. Mitali Sangha or Bhratri Sangha . . . they were all named more or less along those lines. Sometimes they set up a stage right in the middle of a neighbourhood, sometimes they hired a hall to mount their productions. You could make 75 rupees a night by acting for them. When the recreation clubs at big companies staged plays, they paid better, 100–150 rupees, and conveyance even for rehearsals. Banks paid the best—almost 200 rupees plus conveyance. A princely sum at that time.

Women acted in these plays, and some managed to run their households with the money they earned. At that time, both men and women played the female roles in amateur theatre, although the pay was different. If women got 100 rupees, the men may have got 60 or 70. But women like my Chhordi or Geeta Dey were getting busier and busier and hiking their rates too. So the three of us boys—Chapal, Subrata and Satya—found ourselves in fairly good demand to play heroines, secondary heroines and dancers.

There was a well-oiled system in place to hire us. The theatre clubs would approach costume companies like B. Brothers and D. Brothers who served as go-betweens. The costume companies would make the bookings and take a commission as well. Though women were acting on stage already, audiences still accepted men in female roles. They might have teased us a bit sometimes but our challenge was to make them forget after a while that they were watching a man on stage.

Darjipara Natya Parishad would try and get a famous artiste to star in their productions. They would stage their plays at some of the old mansions—all famous addresses like the Shobhabazar Rajbari with its huge colonnaded nat-mandap courtyard, or Haralal Chand Mallik's grand house in Bagbazar or Motichand Sil's mansion. There was not much money in it for the actors but there certainly was prestige. Darjipara Natya Parishad, unlike some other amateur clubs, didn't work with women at all.

One of their favourite playwrights was Phani-babu. In those days, the world of jatra had two Phani-babus. Playwright Phanibhushan Mukhopadhyay, who was honoured with the title Bidyabinode. And actor Phanibhushan Motilal. To tell them apart, Bidyabinode was called Boro Phani-babu or Phani the Elder, and Motilal was Chhoto Phani-babu or Phani the Younger.

Boro Phani-babu from Howrah's Ramrajatala, was a well-educated and cultured man. The son of a jatra actor, he made jatras more contemporary. He took on the usual mythological and historical subjects like Bhagyadevi (Goddess of Fate) and Kalidasa but also more 'hot' topics, like the indigo plantation workers rising against the British. He was quite a versatile actor too, slipping into all kinds of roles from the upright father to the cunning servant with equal ease.

Phanibhushan Motilal aka Chhoto Phani-babu, who lived in Behala, was a small thin bald man with a powerful voice. He had once played women but successfully switched to playing the hero. Even in his 60s, he would play young heroes, though the role he was most famous for was Siraj-ud-Daulah, the last nawab of Bengal. He was phenomenally popular. Once, when he failed to show up for a performance, the enraged audience set the stage on fire.

At that time, Boro Phani-babu was elderly and his star was fading. I was young and didn't understand the plight of an artiste whose fortunes were on the decline. That I understood only too well much later. Boro Phani-babu had written a play called *Muchir Chhele* [The Cobbler's Son] about the evils of caste.

Darjipara Natya Parishad decided to stage that same play under the name of *Bhakta Ruidas*. I was given the part of the goddess who would come to the king in disguise and sing.

Darjipara Natya Parishad had no shortage of money thanks to their flourishing sweetshop business. So their productions were always a grand affair. I had a splendid costume with a magnificent crown. Originally, I was supposed to play the courtesan Lakshmiheera but the director said, 'No, Chapal must play the goddess. Have you seen his eyes? Nobody else has eyes like that. And he sings so beautifully too.' Subal was picked for the other part. Poor Subal didn't want to play a woman, but they coaxed him into it somehow.

Rehearsals would go on till 10.30–11 at night. One night, I saw a big car pull up to the door.

'Whose car is that?' I asked Panda, another actor who also played female roles.

'Oh, that's Raghu-babu's car,' Panda replied.

'Who's come? Someone important?'

'No, no. That brings food from their factory. The stuff that was extra or somehow a little defective, maybe misshapen—all that comes to the house. It gets used up as snacks at home.'

The next day I caught hold of Raghu-babu. 'I heard all the extra food comes to the house. Can't we also get a taste?'

'Of course you can,' he replied. 'Tell you what. Come to our factory one day. And eat to your heart's content.'

But the sweets came to me by a different twist of fate.

Boro Phani-babu had written a script about the famous playwright Kalidas. In that play, I played Goddess Saraswati. There was a scene where a girl with wild unkempt hair crawls up to the plate of offerings put out for the goddess and gobbles up the sweets. She is of course the goddess herself, just in disguise.

Those sweets, for the stage, were made from some cheap sugar paste.

Raghu-babu was aghast.

'If Tuku eats this sugar paste every day, his voice will be ruined. And he has several songs in this play, difficult songs based on ragas. I don't want him to choke on these. The sweets will come from our factory henceforth. They need to be of good quality.'

'But it will have to be made up to look like offerings to the goddess,' said someone.

'That's my problem,' replied Raghu-babu.

The next day, he said, 'Tell me what you think of the offerings today. I've had it made specially for you—soft sandesh, mashed with jaggery.'

'Specially for me?' I teased him, 'Oh hush! I'm going to have to tell your wife!'

'What! Don't you remember I gave you the mirror I got at my wedding?'

I said, 'Indeed. That just proves my point. Which man gives another man his wedding mirror?'

He laughed uproariously, 'Well, now you must sing even better.'

There was a story behind that mirror. Once I had forgotten to bring my own. As soon as I mentioned it, Raghu-babu flew into a tizzy, then rushed someone over to his house and had a hand mirror brought over.

'Keep this in your make-up box,' he told me. 'You don't have to buy one. But don't lose it. This mirror isn't just any mirror. There are sentimental memories tied up in it.'

'What memory, Raghu-babu?'

'It's a mirror from my wedding night. Take good care of it.'

They were wonderful people, Raghu-babu and his brother. I felt I was part of a family.

Some of those productions were tremendously elaborate. I remember performances at the Shobhabazar Rajbari. As soon as you entered, there was an enormous courtyard, entirely covered by a carpet. The carpet in turn was covered by spotless white sheets. There'd be cushions everywhere for the guests to lean against. Attendants would spray rose water. Everyone sat on the ground. We would stand in the middle and act while a live orchestra provided the music. There could be seven violinists playing all at once. Nowadays you get at best one miserable violin whining away.

I think I acted in some four or five plays for Darjipara Natya Parishad, for two years from 1956. They were all female roles. I was not Chapal Rani yet. Even then, I never wanted to play the male roles though I was certainly happy to suggest good-looking actors for them.

'Why don't you give the role to so-and-so instead of that actor?' I would say, recommending an actor whom I found rather handsome.

The director would say doubtfully 'But he isn't a very good actor.'

'What does that matter?' I would shrug. 'He looks like a hero. That's all that is important.'

Of course I had my own agenda. I would get to act opposite them, there would be scenes of intimacy, some romance and songs. That much contact was enough to keep me happy. I enjoyed it and I dare say the men liked it too, whether or not they admitted it openly. But it was only on stage. As soon as the make-up came off, we were back to being who we were.

There was a lot of prestige associated with those Darjipara productions, but no money. They were not a professional group. This was a hobby for them. But I took comfort in the fact that at least I was acting instead of just sitting around.

We made good money when we got calls to take our shows out of the city and into the countryside. In the villages, they would build a stage in a field by laying down boards and hammering them into place. They would make curtains out of saris, and organize Petromax lights. But they also needed actors, and, more importantly, actresses. The few women who worked the amateur-theatre circuit in Kolkata rarely wanted to travel to some faraway village. And even if they did, they charged a hefty premium.

So the village clubs would contact the costume companies who would in turn contact us and fix a rate. The village club would rehearse the play with substitutes, but ask us to be there three days before the show for final rehearsals. We would give a counter offer: one day of final rehearsals. Finally, we would agree on two days. They would then send the script with an advance maybe of 20–30 rupees and the train fare. When we showed up, sometimes they would put us up in a mud hut with a thatched roof, sometimes a proper brick house, perhaps some officer's quarters. We would rehearse all morning till lunch, then again all evening till 10, sometimes three times a day. In those days, even if we got paid 120 rupees plus train fare, that was a lot of money.

There was something rather lovely about acting out in the country—the thatched huts, the water that came from an old-fashioned well, the fish at lunch that had been freshly caught from the pond. In the afternoon, a stupor would descend as the village dozed, the lazy stillness punctuated perhaps by the loud coos of a koel bird. I would marvel at my good fortune. We were not very well educated, but somehow God had shown us a path to make ends meet by acting.

The Fatra People of Jatra

Sometime during 1957 we had gone to Deoghar, where the religious guru Anukul Thakur had his ashram. We were going to stage *Samrat Ashok* [Emperor Ashoka]. A professional jatra group called Nath Company had also come there.

One night, two men came to see me after our play. One was a small plump man, very friendly. He came up to me and said, 'I want to talk to you.'

'And who are you?' I replied

'I am Kanailal Das,' he said. 'I play female parts in Nath Company under the name of Banaphool. Come and see our production tonight. Mahendra Gupta will be in it.'

Mahendra Gupta was a big name in those days, both as actor and director. The other person with Banaphool also acted in female roles. Everyone called him Chhoto Khoka but he acted under the name of Kanan, because that was the era of the singing star Kanan Devi in films.

That night, after our performance, I went to meet Banaphool and Kanan. That was the first time I saw a jatra company's dressing room. There was straw everywhere on the floor, and a big sheet of tarpaulin spread on top, for people to sit on. Some people sat on huge metal trunks. Saris, tunics, wigs hung from a clothesline. Mahendra Gupta, as the star, had his own chair.

'How do you find it, Chapal?' Kanai asked.

'It looks impressive,' I replied.

'Chapal, do not waste your talent in amateur theatre. Join a professional jatra company. I can try and find something for you. I've heard that Chhabi Rani is leaving Natta Company. They want a fresh face. Should I try and see if they are interested?'

I had no idea who Chhabi Rani was or Natta Company for that matter.

'It's a very big troupe,' Kanai told me. 'It's a good professional company. And they pay very well too.'

'I see. Well, let me speak to my father and see what he has to say,' I replied.

Father was not too happy.

'I don't really approve of the fact that you act in these female roles in the first place,' he grumbled. 'And now you are saying you want to do jatra!'

Our family came from theatre. People like my father looked down on jatra as low class. There was a saying: '*Jatra korey fatra lokey*'—those who do jatra are rubbish people . It got no respect among Kolkata's culturati. Even I had not been to the jatras growing up. But outside the city, in the countryside of East Pakistan and North Bengal, in the tea gardens and collieries, people loved jatra. My uncle Sisir Bhaduri recognized that. He once said that it was in the world of jatra that you could see the real power of acting, and every actor needed to study it. I have heard that even the great actors and playwrights like Girish Ghosh would go to watch jatra. But the stigma remained. Jatra was where washed-up actors ended up. Once, an actor told me he worked in Srirangam plays for a long time. 'And then what happened?' I asked. 'What else? I grew old. I needed to survive. I had a family. So I joined the jatra. Now I work with Ganesh Opera.'

I never finished school. But most of the actors in jatra had studied even less. Many came straight from the villages. Country bumpkins, in the way they carried themselves, the way they talked. They usually wore dhotis and a silky 'linen' kurta, the colour of fresh ghee. And they all wore their hair long. If any middle-class boy's hair grew a bit too long, his elders would smirk and say, 'Go, get a haircut. Why are you wearing your hair like some two-bit jatrawala?' Now in an age when superstar actors go around with pony tails, that memory makes me chuckle.

People really looked down on the jatra. Many years later, I was taking the train to a performance in Kharagpur. A very distinguished looking man, probably in his 50s, struck up a conversation with me. We exchanged pleasantries and I asked him what he did. He said he worked with a big production house and had his own business as well. Then he asked me what I did. I said I worked in jatra. The man did not say another word to me for the rest of the journey.

So it was no surprise that Baba was less than happy when I told him I wanted to act in jatra.

He said, 'You'll be constantly away from home, perhaps seven or eight months a year, going here and there. The season is long, from the months of Ashwin in the autumn to Jaisthya in the summer. Why don't you look for something else to do? Leave this life and try to find something more respectable. Don't forget what family you come from.'

'I understand, Baba, but I can't just rest on the family fame. I had to get into this because that's all I could do, given the little bit of education I have. I know a lot of people pick up bad habits during the jatra life, being constantly on the road, away from family. But I promise you, I won't be like that.'

Eventually, he relented. 'All right, do it if you wish to. But keep yourself under control.' He meant I should not pick up bad habits like alcohol.

In July 1958, Kanai took me to meet Surya Dutta, the manager of Natta Company Jatra Party. Their office was in an old mansion on Hatkhola Street in North Kolkata, facing the river, next to the Circular Railway line. Natta Company has shut down now but you can still see that massive red-brick mansion if you come down the river on a steamer. The house peeps out from behind the trees like some forgotten fort. Though when you get close, you see it is rundown and dilapidated. The terrace juts into the sky, the weeds growing in the cracks are slowly becoming trees themselves.

The neighbourhood was busy then too, but it is far more congested now. All along the rail tracks is an unbroken line of ramshackle huts and shanties patched together with canvas and tarpaulin. People sit on the rail lines in their lungis and nighties, chopping wood, stripping bamboo poles, sorting old papers and discarded bottles. Life happens on those tracks. Big trucks come by to pick up piles of papers and bottles and men carrying overstuffed sacks on their heads trudge across the tracks, shouting at people to get out of their way. The river flows placidly in front as it had in my time, but the promenade is lined with little temples now, built to honour all kinds of gods and goddesses, from Shiva to Ganga herself. Barbers have set up little makeshift salons to shear the heads of those who come to do the last rites on the river bank. And all along the way, propped up next to the little temples, or resting in the shade of the big flame-of-the-forest trees, are large and small images of Goddess Sitala, astride her donkey, still dressed in red sari and golden crown but slowly disintegrating in the rain and sun. The goddess of smallpox, she's never immersed in the river like the other gods and goddesses. She's left to return to the elements on her own. I could never have predicted it then but in time Sitala would become a big part of my own story.

Doll House

Putulbari—or Doll House—stood out among all the other big mansions in the neighbourhood, not only because it was massive but also because it had sculptures of dolls all along its roof, like sentinels keeping guard. You could see them right from the river. There was a story that the owner's daughter had been obsessed with dolls but then died in a freak accident. There were rumours that the mansion was haunted. Some say by the daughter, some say by a courtesan supposedly murdered there, or by freedom fighters slaughtered by the British. No one really knows, and I never saw any ghosts . . . Most of those dolls have fallen off one by one, though a couple are still standing . . .

You entered Putulbari not from the river but from a narrow side street. The entrance itself is so dark and forbidding even in the middle of the day that it's not hard to believe the ghostly rumours. The red brick has greyed over time, thanks to the harsh sun and monsoon rain, but the architecture is somehow holding firm, stony bearded faces peering out from the arches over the doors around the central courtyard. The tenants' washing hangs from its windows and wrought-iron-grilled balconies. In one room, a pile of old iron trunks gather dust, all that's left of the fabled jatra company. A chunk of plaster has peeled off the grey wall and the bricks underneath lie exposed. Above it, in faded red letters, you can still see the words: 'Natta Company Jatra Party'. And under it, in bright yellow, 'Office Upstairs'. But there is no office anywhere any more. The only sign of life is a little pot with a tulsi plant on the veranda, the very veranda where I would stand and listen to the sound of the train whenever I felt sad. Somebody still waters that plant, perhaps the ghosts of Putulbari.

Ever since I have known it, Putulbari has been occupied by a host of tenants. Some had a room, some took up almost an entire floor. There was a factory on the ground floor that made vests and cardboard boxes. I remember a musty warehouse filled with junk which smelt of something old and secret. Natta Company was spread out over the upper floors. The women who lived below would tell me, 'We hear you act the part of queens. Why don't you show us something?' I would laugh and say, 'Come to the rehearsal.' They never did.

We climbed up four flights of creaking wooden steps to the main office. I saw rows of beds laid out in a room, each with its own pillows, neatly folded blankets and mosquito nets. It looked like a hospital or an army barrack. Kanai said it was where the actors stayed. Mostly from the villages, they lived here as if in a hostel while they rehearsed the plays.

On the top floor sat the man we had come to meet. Makhanlal Natta was the proprietor of Natta Company but Surya Dutta was the one who managed it. He was the life and soul of Natta Company. He was already quite elderly, and had been managing the company since Makhanlal Natta's father's time. Makhan-babu called him Surya-mama or Surya-uncle. He had started out learning tabla from Makhan-babu's grandfather. He didn't have much education by way of books and degrees but he knew the ins and outs of jatra. Unfortunately, he was rather dubious upon seeing me: '*O Banaphool, tumi kaare aancho*? *E korbe Chhabir part*? *Eto roga*.' (Whom have you brought, Banaphool? He will play Chhabi's roles? So skinny.) Even though he had lived in Kolkata for years, you could hear the lilt of East Bengal in his speech.

'Just listen to him. His voice is very sweet.'

'Hmm, let's hear a few lines of dialogue.'

He listened to me and shook his head. 'His voice is sweet but too thin and soft. Jatra acting is high melodrama. It's at a high register. How will he manage it? He looks pretty but I really don't know if he can pull it off. But let Makhan come. He's gone to see a football match. Why don't you all sit down and have a cup of tea and wait?'

Makhanlal Natta's grandfather Baikuntha Natta had started this jatra company in 1869. They were from Barisal in what is now Bangladesh. Jatra companies were split into two groups in Kolkata: Kolkata companies based out of the Chitpur area; and 'outside' groups like Natta Company, regarded thus because they had come from places like Barisal, even though their offices were also in Kolkata. Makhanlal Natta was one of the few jatra proprietors who was very well educated and could even speak in English. In his free time, he would read the poetry of Rabindranath Tagore. A very good student, he had come to Kolkata to study science. He wanted to become a teacher but he had taken over the jatra company after his father's sudden death.

Eventually, Makhan-babu showed up, a lean, bespectacled man with a neat moustache—a small man but with quite a personality. He was dressed in a fine cotton kurta, his white dhoti immaculately creased. That was his uniform. Later in life, he switched to white khadi and wore nothing but that. 'Who's this, Banaphool?' he asked as soon as he saw me.

'Sir, this is the boy I was thinking could replace Chhabi-da. But Surya-babu is not sure he can pull it off.'

Makhan-babu looked at me thoughtfully. 'See, Surya-mama,' he said. 'Isn't there something about his face that reminds you of Chhabi Rani?'

He inspected me like one would inspect a bride.

'Walk up and down,' he said.

I did.

'Move your hands and legs.'

I obeyed.

'Show me the calves of your legs.'

I lifted up my pyjama legs obediently.

'Say a few lines.'

Then he pronounced his verdict.

'Take him, Surya-mama. Make him into another Chhabi Rani. His pronunciation is very good, much better than Chhabi Rani's. His looks are good. His voice is very sweet too although a little too soft. We will have to work on that. But I think there is potential here.'

Surya-babu was still doubtful. He thought it was taking too much of a risk. 'Remember, he will be coming in Chhabi's place. The audiences are used to Chhabi. Those are big shoes to fill.'

At that time, I didn't understand the significance of those words: 'Chhabi's place'. Chhabi Rani was Natta Company's star asset, a legendary name in jatra, the reigning queen of female impersonators. He was suddenly leaving Natta Company that season because Ganesh Opera had offered him a hefty pay hike. That's why they were desperately looking for someone else. Makhan-babu had been very insulted that Chhabi Rani was leaving his company. He had told Surya-babu, 'We will show him. Find me another Chhabi Rani.' I had no idea about any of this behind-the-scenes drama. I was just elated that I might finally get paid for acting.

'Come, follow me,' said Makhan-babu. He took me to huge room with large black and white floor tiles, like a chessboard. There was a picture of the gods Krishna and Radha on the wall. Later, I discovered that those gods were worshipped every day. The origins of the company lay in a group called Machrang Baikuntha Sangeet Samaj, which would travel by boat all over what is now Bangladesh, singing devotional Krishna songs. Because it had been started by Baikuntha Natta, people called it Natta Company.

'We are at heart a Radha–Krishna troupe,' said Makhan-babu. I dutifully bowed to the picture.

'But don't think that just because we are Krishna devotees, we are all pious vegetarians. We are hard-core Bangals from Barisal too. We can't think of eating rice without fish,' he chuckled.

Then he took a silver coin and placed it in front of the Radha–Krishna image.

'Sit down,' he instructed. 'Ask Krishna and Radha for their blessings so that you might act well, bring a good name to both yourself and the company. Promise to listen to your elders.' Then he told me to take the coin and keep it with me. It was symbolic, a way of saying that I was now bound to them. There was no formal contract but Radha–Krishna had been our witness.

I kept that coin for many years.

I said, 'Can I leave?'

'Wait, we must talk salary.'

I sat back down.

'Look, you are absolutely new. You will have to make a name for yourself. You will have to work hard and we will have to work hard as well to make something out of you. For now, your salary will be 100 rupees a month. And another rupee for tea and snacks on the days when we cannot provide food.'

With a 100-rupee salary, you did not get a formal contract. For that you had to wait to reach 300 rupees. Without a contract, they could get rid of you at any time. But I was unaware of all that. All I knew was that I had landed an acting job with a salary. I was over the moon.

Once my salary was finalized, I went to Raghu-babu and said, 'Raghu-babu, I cannot act with your group any more. I am joining a professional group.'

'You will leave?' he was crestfallen. 'Then our Darjipara Natya Parishad will also sink. How will it function without you?'

'What can I do?' I said. 'I need the money. I really have no other option.'

'That's true, that's true. I am very sad to hear this but I understand your situation. But why don't you discuss this with Boro Phani-babu?'

'Well, that will not solve my financial problem.'

'I understand, but you should talk to him. He has a lot of experience in the world of jatra.'

When I told Phani-babu, he nodded thoughtfully, 'Good for you, but will you be able to manage? A professional troupe is very exhausting. I know that well. I was with Ganesh Opera for years. Which group are you joining?'

'Natta Company.'

'Hmm, I heard Chhabi's just left Natta and come back to Ganesh. Are you joining in his place?'

'Yes.'

'Well, you should do what you think is right. But be warned, they will finish you.'

'What do you mean, sir? You make them sound like murderers.'

'They will take everything you have and then spit you out. You will be stuck there for 10–11 years, because they won't let you go easily. And if you draw the crowds, maybe they will keep you even longer. Eventually, they will suck you dry. But what can you do? Everyone needs money.'

The Change Artiste

I joined Natta Company as a 'change artiste' in place of Chhabi Rani on a salary of 100 rupees in 1958. At that time, Chhabi Rani must have been making 750–800 rupees. At 100 rupees, I was a bargain for the company. The irony is that, years later, when I had to go on leave from Natta Company, Chhabi Rani came back as a change artiste to replace me.

I didn't know it then, but I was stepping into a long and rich tradition of female impersonators in jatra. There used to be a great female impersonator known as Rakhal Rani. In his place came Phani Bhattacharya who became famous for his mother roles. Then Chhabi Rani came in his place. And, finally, I.

Right away they handed me about eight or nine roles that Chhabi Rani had made famous. Like Anjana in *Raja Devidas*, Kohinoor in *Kohinoor*, Jharna in *Satyashrayee*. Parts in jatra were denoted by numbers. One part might be 350, another 550. It meant the number of lines associated with that part. I had to memorize all those parts. That was hard enough but harder was facing the constant comparisons to Chhabi Rani. People who would come to book shows would say, 'If your troupe has Chhabi Rani, then and only then will we make a booking, otherwise not.'

I was about 17, Chhabi Rani must have been 35. Audience members would say, 'Oh Chapal looks nice, sings beautifully too, but he is no Chhabi Rani.' My blood would boil, but what could I do? I was stuck with his parts. It was like eating his leftovers.

In a jatra called *Pratishodh* [Revenge], Chhabi Rani had a scene where he dresses the bride and performs a baran, welcoming a new bride into the house with ritual and ceremony. It was a very emotional scene. The hero is marrying a young woman whose face has been scarred by smallpox. His brother is opposed to the match as is his mother. Only his brother's wife supports him. She's the one who goes to the girl, dresses her as befits a new bride in a Benarasi sari and welcomes her home with the baran sequence. It was a mega scene and lasted at least 20–25 minutes, but the audience never got restless. Everywhere we did *Pratishodh*, I would hear the same complaint: 'You performed the part of the sister-in-law so well, we felt you were our own sister-in-law. But no one can do the baran scene like Chhabi Rani. We would watch speechlessly when Chhabi Rani did the baran.'

That comment was like a bedbug, chasing me from performance to performance. I had never seen Chhabi Rani do that scene. I had no idea what was missing. When I was given the part, I was warned 'This baran scene is very important. You are going to have to master it well.' But what did I know of wedding rituals? I was just a boy of 16.

Surya-babu told the others, 'Chapal's a boy, he's new. We must all help him. All of you who were on stage in that scene, tell Chapal what Chhabi used to do. As long as he does a couple of those things, it should be fine.' But no one helped. Instead, they said, 'How will a couple of things be enough? That scene goes on for 20 long minutes.'

Someone else who also did female parts sneered, 'You're doing female roles and you've never done a baran before?'

'Only women do baran,' I retorted sharply. 'Am I a girl? I just play female roles on stage.'

Eventually, a few people told me about a couple of rituals. I spoke to others outside the world of jatra and learnt the basic steps—how to hold the paan leaf, how to touch the new bride on her head with it, what to place on the tray, how many times to rotate the tray laden with offerings and auspicious items. I learnt it in the end, but no one held my hand through it all or even offered encouragement. All they said was, 'Yes, yes, it's all right—but not as good as Chhabi Rani.'

Chhabi Rani was legend. People called him the Elizabeth Taylor of jatra. I was no one. My name wasn't even on the posters. Harigopal Das was Natta's main singer for female roles, the gaaiye or 'singing' female. Even his name would be on the poster, but not mine.

Meanwhile, Chhabi Rani was unhappy that I had replaced him. He went around telling people, 'That Natta Company has brought some amateur boy to replace me. Some dancing boy. They will never get bookings.'

At the Tiljala Tinworkers workshop in Kolkata, the organizers demanded their advance back when they heard Chhabi Rani was no longer in the cast. Makhan-babu pleaded 'Yes, I have brought a new boy. Please, first watch his acting and then judge him.'

They were equally adamant. 'What acting are you talking about? We have seen Chhabi Rani in this very role. How will this raw lad do justice to it?'

'But you have not seen him yet,' implored Makhan-babu.' Why don't you see him perform? If you still feel the same way after that, then you don't have to make any payment to me.'

Then he told me, 'I have placed a lot of faith in you, Chapal. Don't let me down.'

He was incensed with Chhabi Rani: 'Chhabi Rani has been with us from my father's time. He left the group and then came back. And now he is stabbing us in the back like this, instigating people to cancel bookings!'

Surya-babu teased me in his lilting East Bengal accent. 'Have you heard what Chhabi Rani is saying? You're going to have to be really superb to shut him up. There is a scene where your character has to break her bangles. You watch out. That was Chhabi Rani's big scene. Do that scene extra well. You must top him.'

'No, no, don't scare the boy,' Makhan-babu interjected. 'I am sure he will be fine.' Makhan-babu was my great champion and mentor. He knew I was a total novice and he taught me all he knew. He said, 'Look, you have no work all day. Rehearsals are in the evening. Every day, after lunch, you sit down with a script and read it. That way you will learn the part and understand the characters as well.'

I can say without hesitation that Makhanlal Natta made me Chapal Rani.

And Surya-babu taught me all he could about acting. He showed me how to sit straight like a queen, how to stand commandingly on the stage, how to lift my chin up just so to look regal but with a whiff of hauteur, how to convey emotions using my hands. He trained me morning till night, teaching me dialogue throw and helping me expand my vocal range. In *Raja Devidas*, there was a scene where I had to laugh after killing my husband. 'But I don't know how to laugh!' I said worriedly. 'I will teach you,' Surya-babu reassured me. I didn't know you could break a laugh down like that, step by step. That's why I called him Gurumoshai or teacher. Once, I touched his feet and asked for his blessings. One of the actors exclaimed 'What are you doing, Chapal?'

'What do you mean?' I replied. 'He is my guru.'

'Well you are the son of a Brahman. They are Duttas from Barisal, goodness knows what kind of Dutta, what caste,' he shuddered, 'Now I worry about you touching me onstage as well.'

'Fine,' I replied. 'I'll turn my back to you when I deliver my dialogues. But I cannot turn my back on my gurumoshai.'

The first time I faced the audience in one of Chhabi Rani's roles was nerve-wracking. As I went on, I could hear a murmur run from one end of the audience to the other. It was a like low rumbling thunder. It was only when I started to act that the whispering finally subsided.

There was a very dramatic scene in that play. I am pregnant and my father, king of Bhusna, comes to take me back to his palace.

KING. Come with me. Your child will be born on the soil of Bhusna.

PRINCESS. No, Father. I will not leave my in-laws. My child will be born right here, not on the soil of Bhusna.

KING. What insolence is this! Insulting your own father in front of your father-in-law!

PRINCESS. Insult? What insult? Father, what is there left to insult? The day you went and accepted a sweet paan from the hands of the Nawab, you lost all my respect. It's only because you are my father that I am restraining myself. (*My voice would rise to a crescendo.*) Otherwise I would cut you to pieces and throw you into the river.

As soon as I would say these lines, the house would erupt in applause. Those who envied me sneered and said, 'Oh look what this boy is doing for claps.' Those who supported me said, 'Good for him. Chhabi-da would never get any claps for this scene.' Applause was the lifeblood of jatra performers. I learnt that quickly.

There is a postscript to the story of Chhabi Rani. In 1974, after my professional jatra career had more or less ended, I was acting in the religious guru Omkarnath Thakur's ashram where women were not allowed to perform. There I was the director as well as actor. Once, we staged a play about Krishna, his foster mother Yashoda, his real mother Devaki and his paramour Radha. Chhabi Rani, then long past his heyday, came to me then and said, 'Chapal, will you give me a part?'

I told him, 'Maybe you can do Devaki's part.'

He looked at me. 'You will play Yashoda of course because Omkarnath Thakur himself has selected you. Subrata will play Radha. Devaki has so little to do. Just a couple of scenes.'

'Yes, but that's all I can offer you,' I said. At that time, nobody could cross me. My decision was the final word when it came to the production.

'All right, I will do it,' he replied resignedly.

Chhabi Rani always liked to dress up. When I saw the pink and gold Benarasi saree he had selected for Devaki, I put my foot down.

'Are you really going to wear that sari? Can't you see what I am wearing as Yashoda? A plain white silk saree with a red border, red blouse, simple gold ornaments—bangles on my wrists, a necklace and earrings, my hair open. How can Devaki be dressed like this?'

'Oh, you think I cannot wear this?'

'No. You've chosen a pink Benarasi. You cannot wear this. Take it off. You have to wear something simple. It's a mother role and you should be dressed like a mother. Omkarnath Thakur will not be happy if he sees you like this. I am not letting you get on stage in this saree.'

This had happened to me earlier. Omkarnath Thakur had made me change my saree to fit a mother's role. I was so upset. Everyone was gorgeously dressed and I had to wear a white saree.

'What are you smiling about?' I grumbled at my friend Subratra who was grinning mischievously. 'You all can wear what you like. I have to wear white!'

Chhabi-da could do nothing. He grudgingly changed his saree.

But that all happened much later. Much water had flowed under the bridge by then. In those first days in jatra, I had to struggle to find a place for myself. But Chhabi Rani was my senior. At the end of the day, I did respect him even though he badmouthed me when I was a nobody.

On the Road

Jatra life was hard work for a novice like me. The show started at 3 p.m. and went on for four hours. Then we packed everything into a truck and went off to another town and did it all over again late into the night. The next day I could hardly move. Someone in the company told Makhan-babu, 'Oh Makhan, who is this heroine you've got us? After one day's performance, he is wilting like a bunch of spinach. Do you think he'll be able to act tonight?'

I hurriedly said, 'Why not? If I rest a little bit now, I'll be fine.'

All I knew was that I had earned about 12 or 13 rupees including my food allowance by doing three shows. That felt like a lot to me.

Slowly but steadily I built a name for myself. I was young, I was pretty, I had a melodious voice. I would go to a shop to buy a toothbrush and the shopkeeper would say, 'Aren't you Chapal Bhaduri? Weren't you in the jatra last night?'

Some of the older artistes could not stomach that. That's when I understood there was something called 'kick out' in jatra parlance. I would be on stage and never get to say my lines because the other actor would say his part but not give me my cue. I would stand there like an idiot and people in the audience would snicker, thinking I was a newbie who had forgotten his lines.

I complained to Harigopal, who was the heroine. 'Why didn't you say all your lines? I had so much dialogue after that. I was supposed to exit the stage first and then you were supposed to exit. But you exited before me and left me hanging.'

Harigopal got into a huff, 'I am not answerable to you. You go complain to the boss.'

Surya-babu heard everything and told Harigopal, 'This was not fair, Harigopal.'

Harigopal threw a tantrum and said, 'I've been insulted. I won't work from tomorrow.'

Everyone was aghast. He was the singing star. How would we function without him? Makhan-babu played peacemaker. 'Whatever has happened has happened. Let it be. Harigopal, don't do these things any more. Chapal is new. He doesn't know his left from his right, his front from his back. We have to teach him. And I am determined that I will make him another Chhabi Rani one day.'

Harigopal calmed down a bit but he never got over his jealousy. He once said, 'This one has just conquered hearts by showing off his looks. Can he show off his acting skill like me?'

By that time I was a little more confident about myself. I shot back: 'If by acting you mean screaming, then I cannot screech my lungs out like you. No woman talks like that. Even when you are trying to show romance, you sound like you are quarrelling.'

'This is how it's done in jatra,' he told me. 'Don't be over-smart. Don't try to teach me.'

'Well, try something else. A little more natural.'

But I too had a lot to learn about my place in this new world.

When we went out of Kolkata, we would have to travel by truck. We would leave at night, the trucks loaded with boxes filled with our costumes, every artiste's bedding tied firmly with rope, mosquito nets, pillows. Sometimes there would be two trucks because they were so many of us, cast, crew and musicians.

The first time I travelled at night, I was terrified. It was windy and I was afraid the truck would topple over at any moment. There were two seats beside the driver, but those were reserved for the hero and the heroine. They would not clamber up onto the bed of the truck like the rest of us.

I was horrified. 'How am I going to climb up there?'

'This is how we travel,' I was told. 'We go by truck. You get up quickly, there's no time to waste.'

'But what if the truck turns belly up? It's so overloaded.'

'It won't. Don't worry. These trucks are used to this. All the jatra companies around here use these trucks. This is how we get to places. And sometimes we'll have to go to places where trucks cannot reach, perhaps it's five miles in the interior. Then we'll have to unload everything from the truck and pile it onto a bullock cart. And on the way back, we will again come five miles by bullock cart, then load the truck and go to the next destination.'

The class division continued even in the bed of the truck. The main actors after the hero and heroine got the prime spots in the middle. I was absolutely new, lowest in the pecking order. They gave me a seat right on the edge. I was terrified, sure I would fall any minute. Thankfully there were a few artistes who felt a bit kindly towards me.

One of them said, 'Oh, poor Chapal is scared. Don't seat him at the edge. Seat him in the middle.'

And we set off racing down the Grand Trunk Road in the dead of night. Those journeys seemed endless, but after a few months I got used to it. In a few years, the trucks gave way to buses. But there too the hero and heroine sat near the driver where it was the most spacious. The next in line got the seats usually reserved for the ladies. I was too new to merit a spot even there. I got one of those split seats.

I complained that it was uncomfortable.

Makhan-babu took pity on me.

He said, 'Chapal might be new but he works hard. He needs some comfort too. We cannot deprive him just because his pay is still low.' I was assigned a double seat by the window close to the door. The bedding was stacked next to it so I could at least put my feet up.

I did have to hear some snide remarks for this little perk.

'We have never seen the boss being so indulgent to anyone else. This Chapal seems to have worked some special magic here.'

Everything, from your privileges to your dignity was determined by your pay grade.

For Whom the Bell Metal Tolls

I remember the first time I sat down for lunch with the jatra company. We had gone to a colliery in Ballavpur, near Raniganj. In those days, we got a lot of bookings in collieries and tea gardens. We had reached the Ballavpur colliery before lunch.

When I came down after my bath, Padma Thakur, the cook, took one look at me and said, 'Oh it's the new queen. The one who has come in place of Chhabi Rani. Not bad looking.'

'Where should I sit?' I asked demurely.

'There,' he pointed. 'See that mattress.' There was a long jute mat laid out on the floor for everyone to sit on.

'Oh, there isn't any separate mat?' I asked.

'Separate mats? No, no, you won't get all that now. Perhaps later.'

I gingerly sat down on the edge of the mat. Padma Thakur brought a cheap enamel plate heaped with rice, and plonked it down in front of me, 'Make a well in the rice, I'll pour the dal into it.'

I was aghast. 'An enamel plate!' I exclaimed. 'I've never eaten off such a plate in my life!' My idea of enamel plates was that tuberculosis patients ate off them in hospitals. Here I was an actor, replacement for the famous Chhabi Rani and I was being served lunch on a common low-end enamel plate?!

The cook raised his eyebrow sarcastically, 'And how much do you get paid, son?'

'That's not important,' I said haughtily. 'I have come in place of Chhabi Rani.'

'That's true,' said Padma Thakur. 'But let me tell you, you are no Rani, not yet. You might eat from bell-metal plates at home. But in a jatra company, you have to first earn 300 rupees and then and only then can you get a bell-metal plate. Anyone who makes less than 300 doesn't get one. By the way, you'll get rice, dal, mashed potato and one piece of fish. Don't ask for anything else.'

There was nothing fried to accompany the dal. That you only got when you reached the 200-rupee pay grade. Once you reached 300, you got the bell-metal plates and bowls and water in a bell-metal tumbler. And, most excitingly, you got two or three types of fried items and two pieces of fish. You could even get some stir-fried bitters or a shukto as a first course if you wanted.

There was nothing I could do. Padma Thakur had already served the rice. I couldn't reject it. Rice once served cannot be put back into the pot.

Somehow, I finished my lunch that day.

The next day, I found a nearby farm with banana plants. I asked one of the villagers if he could lop off a leaf for me.

The man recognized me from the performance, 'Aren't you with the jatra company? I saw you yesterday. Why do you need a banana leaf? Don't they give you plates?'

'They do, but I have a problem. Please, just give me a leaf.' The man cut off one off and handed it to me.

When I went to eat brandishing the leaf, everyone stared. Some people even choked on their food.

'What's the matter?' I asked Padma Thakur. 'Is everything a little too spicy today? Why is everyone spluttering?'

'They are choking looking at you!' the cook chortled.

'Me? Have I grown a tail?'

'No, it's the banana leaf you're waving about.'

I was unapologetic. 'I will spread this banana leaf on the enamel plate. Then you can serve me my rice on the leaf. I am still going to use your enamel plate because I am only a 100-rupee artiste, after all. But I will eat off the banana leaf. Look, I've even washed it nicely.'

The other artistes began to whisper. Later, I heard they complained to the proprietor about my airs and fancy ways.

But at that moment Padma Thakur looked at me and smiled, 'Fine. Put that banana leaf on your plate.' Then he shook his head and told the rest of the company, 'This one has brains. Mark my words. This one will go far. One day he will surpass even Chhabi Rani.'

I got the bell-metal plate finally. And I got it within three years.

INTERLUDE

In Imagination

The Ghost of Putulbari

Putulbari. The House of Dolls. Once called 'a perfect example of Calcutta rococo' by some white man. There's not much left of the dolls, though. I just might be the last one. But I was not always made of plaster and stucco. I was real once.

I was the pretty one in our family. Why just our family? I was the prettiest girl in the whole neighbourhood. Everyone said I would marry a prince. Every morning, my mother would take the skin off the milk and rub it on my face. The smell would make me want to vomit. But she said it was for my own good.

It did me no good at all. The only man it impressed was that pimp who lived down the lane. We didn't know he was a pimp. All we knew was that he worked for some bigwig babu in the shipping business. He had such airs, as though he was a lord-sahib himself with his pencil-thin moustache and the attar he sprayed on every evening. He once got me some perfume in a little glass bottle. It was so pretty, shaped like a woman. He said it had come from France in one of his employer's ships. Even after the perfume was gone, I kept the bottle in a box with my earrings and necklaces.

Do you know I work in a palace? he told me. And on its roof are statues shaped like these women. One day, I will take you to see it.

He would tell me more, stories of balls and parties where champagne flowed and men smoked cigars and people talked about racehorses and theatres with names like Sans Souci. Let me take you to Putulbari and you will see, he said. They have the grandest parties, with dancers from Lahore and the air smelling of rosewater. Even the English come to eat, drink and make merry when the ships arrive laden with all the goods from Europe. It smells like England, all lavender and rose, when they unload those crates. You will see the who's who of Calcutta there and who knows which zamindar's son will take a shine to you. Your fortune will be made.

I was an ordinary girl from an ordinary family in a lane off another lane in North Kolkata. My father taught Bengali and Sanskrit in a small school. When we took the rickshaw past some streets, my mother would say: pull down the curtain, don't look at the women in those houses. They are fallen women.

What did I know of life?

I believed that man and everything he told me. If you find the right man, you can live in a mansion on Chowringhee and wake up every day at 10 and drink fresh pomegranate juice. Come with me and I'll show you the big soiree at Putulbari, he told me.

One day, I stole out of the house, I who had never been anywhere on my own. He took me to Putulbari all right. Huge pillars held up the top two floors and in the middle was a magnificent courtyard. Gods and goddesses from mythological stories perched on top of the columns. But it was no palace, just a warehouse for crates and boxes that had come by ship. Room after room was filled with them. His boss lived upstairs, a fat man with pomade in his hair, reeking of paan. There was no party with chandeliers and horse-drawn carriages and dancing girls from Lucknow. I was the party. And more girls like me brought from all corners of the city and far-away villages.

After you went to Putulbari, there was no going back home again. When I understood that, I ran up to that roof and looked out at the Ganga flowing past. The pimp came up behind me, 'Look, I can take you somewhere where you'll be safe. There's a woman who can give you a home. You can make money.' I knew what he was talking about. 'Trust me' he said with a wink. 'I'll come visit you. Regularly.' I slapped him as hard as I could. As he lunged at me, I jumped.

Later, I had my revenge. One day, as he was leaving the building, one of the statues on the roof toppled off the edge. We didn't kill him, oh no. That would be too quick for someone who made so many girls suffer. We just made sure he'd never walk again. He spent the rest of his life crawling, like the worm he was.

Some thought the statues were the guardian angels of Putulbari. Far from it. We were its Nemeses and our prey were the men who visited. We would watch and wait, and catch them when they were at their most vulnerable. Perhaps one was drunk. Or another's mistress had left him. Or he'd lost a packet at the races. Or his business was failing. That's when we would strike.

Slowly, the great brick house lost its glory. Moss covered the gods and goddesses on the old columns. The river silted and the ships stopped coming. The man with the pomade hair who owned it died, the girls said of syphilis. The house was split up into smaller and smaller pieces. This house is haunted, people began to say, although we never showed ourselves to anyone. Still, no one wanted to live there, only those who could not afford to go anywhere else. Even they avoided the roof after dark. Some said the old wooden stairs creaked mysteriously at night. Some said they heard women cry, anklets tinkle . . . although, really, we had stopped crying a long time ago.

Then a jatra company moved in on the top floor. We watched the men come from the villages, roll out their bedding and sleep on the floor, as though on a railway platform. They were harmless people, scared of the big city. There was no fun in destroying their lives. Though, yes, it was fun to watch them rehearse their plays about kings and queens and gods and goddesses.

Then one day a boy came to join Natta Company Jatra Party. He was tall and slim with a full head of hair, and when he sang he sounded like an angel. For a minute I remembered the girl I had once been, sitting in a room in North Kolkata with my little bottle of French perfume. This boy, like me, knew nothing of the ways of the world. His name was Chapal.

He was shy. If anyone shouted at him, his face would crumple and his big eyes would shimmer with tears. Every day, he'd open a big iron chest, take out pages and pages of scripts and read them, rocking back and forth, as if he was still in school, learning the lines by heart. Sometimes when he was happy—or when he was sad—he'd sing, and I could hear him from the roof. And every time I thought it was a young girl by the window, singing to her lost lover.

One day, I heard a lot of shouting. The boy kept forgetting his lines and someone kept telling him he was a failure, that his mind was elsewhere, that he would flop on stage. The more that man shouted, the more flustered the boy got, the more he stumbled over his lines. The other actors started to laugh, relieved they weren't the target of the drama master's temper. When Chapal started to sniffle, the master got angrier: 'Stop being such a ninny. Get out and don't show your face till you know the part by heart.' One lout said, 'But he can't help being a ninny. He's just a girl, isn't he? Haven't you seen those hijras? The ones that clap their hands and swing their hips, and pretend they're more women than real women?'

Chapal turned and ran from the room, his face bright red.

I found him standing on the veranda, looking down at the rail tracks that ran below us. His cheeks were stained with tears. Night had fallen. The lights had come on in the city but here it was still dark. Just beyond the tracks was the river. We could see the lights of Howrah railway station across the water, glimmering in the darkness.

I knew what he was thinking because I had been there myself. He was looking down at the tracks that ran past Putulbari. He could hear the goods train drawing closer . . . It would have been so easy to float down like a feather from that roof and end all the pain right then right there. I could feel my sister Nemeses prick up their ears as they watched him. After a long time, another man, another prey, another game. 'Come, join us,' they started to whisper. 'Come, be free.'

I saw Chapal hesitate . . . The sound of the train's whistle grew louder.

Come join us, my sisters whispered again, their voices hypnotic, pushing him to the edge. For the first time I could not join them.

Finally, I could stay silent no more. Stop, I told them. He is not one of them. He is different. He doesn't deserve this fate. The sisters hissed and flapped angrily but the spell was broken. Chapal stepped back from the brink. The train whooshed and clattered away into the distance. The darkness settled back down and the river flowed on, unperturbed, its waves splashing quietly against the embankment.

Someone shouted: 'Chapal? Where are you? Are you up on the roof? You know no one's allowed to go there.'

'Don't hide in the dark,' shouted the owner of the jatra company. 'Or the ghosts of Putulbari will get you.'

In time, my sister ghosts left Putulbari one by one for other haunts, leaving me alone here. The last putul-ghost of Putulbari. Meanwhile, Chapal, became a big star though I never saw him after he left Natta Company. With every passing year, the house sagged a little further, a little more plaster peeled off the walls. Every time a train rumbled past, the cracks in the wall grew bigger. Someone built a public urinal across the street not far from the main door, and now the smell of piss mixes with the smell of cooking fires and river sewage. Natta Company remained on the top floor, but it was a shadow of its old self. The old man died. All that's left is faded letters on a wall—Natta Company Jatra Party, Office Upstairs—and an arrow pointing nowhere. Locks hang from most of the doors and pigeons flutter angrily whenever anyone comes up the old stairs. But the old bricks that formed the arches and columns of Putulbari still hold firm, like a tough old aunt who refuses to die.

A few months ago, a car pulled up in the middle of the day. The sun was high in the sky, and it was hot and the street was busy with trucks and cars and the cries of children running along the tracks while their mothers sorted piles of discarded bottles.

Three people got out of the car. One had a big camera and started taking pictures of the house and the lonely doll on its roof. Another made notes in his writing pad. I paid them no heed, people like that come here all the time. But there was an old man with them, in kurta and pyjama, a bespectacled old man with thinning hair who had trouble walking. As he pointed to the house and said something, something about his voice suddenly reminded me of Chapal.

And I laughed to myself. The old man's voice was high and sweet but surely it could not be Chapal. Chapal Bhaduri had the waist of a dancer. His hair was long and thick. This shuffling old man with a belly pushing out of his kurta was no Chapal Bhaduri. You can't fool me that easily.

I knew Chapal Bhaduri. Once I was his guardian angel.

4
The Queen

The Singing Milkmaid

Chand Bibi changed everything.

Until then, Harigopal Rani had been the apple of Natta Company's eye—their singing-dancing superstar.

But Harigopal couldn't stand me. He made it his goal in life to ensure that I didn't get any singing parts.

One year, Natta mounted a production called *Lohar Jaal* [The Iron Web]. There was only one singing role, but it was that of Chikan Goylani, a woman who sold milk from house to house. Chikan Goylani was a woman past her prime, who constantly rued her lost youth. Hardly the kind of glamorous role Harigopal was used to.

'A milkmaid's part?' Harigopal was aghast.

I tried to reassure him. 'But it's such a good role. You weren't here the day they did the reading. It comes with crackling dialogue and catchy songs. You even get a scene with Surya-babu himself. Imagine how excited everyone will be to see the pairing of two jatra legends—Harigopal and Surya Dutta.' Surya-babu knew how to dance, at one point he had taught choreography to us actors. In *Lohar Jaal*, he was playing the role of Nilmani

Ghatak, an old man in love with a winsome younger maid who leads him around by the nose. Chikan and Nilmani had a parody song-and-dance routine together: 'O Jeebon Kanhaiya'.

But Harigopal was sceptical, unsure whether to trust me. 'Hmm, just because you've got a little education in your belly, you think you understand everything.'

'No, no, not at all. All I'm saying is you should just try once and see.'

He finally took on the role, albeit reluctantly.

'I am a singing star, a top-class heroine,' he complained to anyone who would listen. 'How can I do this nonsense ha-ha-hee-hee comic role?'

'It's a really good role,' Makhan-babu cajoled. 'Give it your best and see how it works out.'

'Well, then, I'll dress the way I want,' pouted Harigopal, 'I'll wear the sari on my bare body—no blouse.'

Now, Harigopal didn't really have soft feminine curves. He was on the manly side. But Makhan-babu was desperate, so he agreed to his demands.

Slightly mollified, Harigopal went off to the market and got himself a huge aluminium pot which he painted to look like a clay pot, and then wrote on it in big white letters: '*Chikan Goylanir Doi*'—Chikan milkmaid's yoghurt.

Then he came to me. 'Chapal, I have a problem. How do you think I should carry this on my head?'

'The way anyone carries anything on their head,' I replied.

'No, no. It will fall off as I move around the stage. And everyone will laugh at me. As it is everyone laughs at whatever I say in this stupid role.'

'That's a huge compliment, Harigopal-da. You have no idea how difficult a comic role can be.' Only the greatest of artistes can pull it off. Like Charlie Chaplin. Excuse my impertinence but I know you don't read much or watch too many films. If you did, you would understand what I am trying to tell you. I can't do comedy myself. If you can nail this part, mark my words, the rest of us in the cast will be left in the dust by your Chikan Goylani.'

He thought for a bit, letting my words sink in. 'Hmmm, but how do I attach this pot to my hair?'

'I am sure you can figure out a way.'

He finally did. He made a hole in his pot and inserted a wire through it which he attached to his wig and then covered it with rags so it didn't scratch his scalp. He sat and worked on it all afternoon, in the sweltering heat. People asked him to bathe and eat his lunch but Harigopal, absorbed in his project, paid no attention to anyone.

Eventually he came to me, beaming with pride: 'Look, it doesn't wobble.' That pot was indeed as steady as a rock.

He called his dresser. 'O Biru, bring me that black-bordered sari that Chikon Goylani wears.'

He wore the sari bare-bodied over his pyjamas, planted the wig with the pot on his head, and struck a saucy pose with a hand on one hip.

'So, what do you think?'

'You look amazing!'

'Now, what will happen if I strike up my song and Suryababu starts dancing with me, holding his umbrella?'

'It will be a sensation,' I told him. 'You watch and see. Everyone will be raving about the two of you this evening. You will be quite the hit pair.'

And that's exactly what happened. Everyone was on tenterhooks, thinking the pot would fall. But it didn't. The audience was amazed at how Harigopal ran onstage with the pot on his head and his hands on his hips. He put his heart and soul into the performance that night. As he swayed his hips and danced with Surya-babu, the entire audience was on its feet, whistling and hooting and clapping. They brought the house down.

I too had a great role in that play with a lot of action and fiery dialogue. But I have to admit that it was a challenge to come onto the stage after Chikan Goylani.

After that, wherever we went, all we would hear was Chikan Goylani and Chikan Goylani. The audience would rave about him, and Harigopal was over the moon.

'See Harigopal-da, when you put your mind to it, you can really bring life to any role,' I told him. 'That pot proved to be the game-changer. And you know the best part? You figured it out by yourself.'

Harigopal finally warmed up to me. He even began to tease me: 'Look, Chapal, I am getting more famous than you.' And I would say, 'Hmm, I am getting a bit of a name too.' It was all good-natured joshing.

He started to act with new energy, but time was not on his side. He was growing old and his looks were fading. It was harder and harder for him to play the kind of roles he had become well known for. I was younger, my voice was naturally feminine and my looks and style, whether it was the way I dressed or the way I acted, felt more modern and contemporary to the audience. Harigopal increasingly came across as old-fashioned.

In cinema, it was then the age of legendary beauty Suchitra Sen. I copied her look, her hair, the way she draped her sari and wore her jewellery. I figured out that the way she styled her side-burns helped highlight her cheekbones in photographs. I tried to do the same. She used to wear high-collar blouses called air-hostess collars. I wore them as well. In the film *Ekti Raat*, she had pearl earrings that were like a bunch of grapes. I went to New Market in Kolkata and got myself a pair that looked just like them.

I even met her once. Chhordi had taken me to the studio where Suchitra Sen was shooting for the film *Indrani*. I realized how much the camera loved her. In person, without make-up, she looked lovely, but nowhere close to the dazzling beauty we saw on screen. Still, I was so intimidated by seeing her face to face that I did not have the courage to tell her that I tried to imitate her looks onstage. Later, my sister told me to stop doing so. It was too modern a look for jatra, she told me. I should preserve the spirit of jatra, she said, and she was right.

Anyway, Harigopal saw the writing on the wall. In 1964, he hung up his dancing shoes and left Natta Company.

A Book Heroine

I was doing well at Natta but I was chafing from only playing Chhabi Rani's hand-me-downs over and over again.

One day, Brajendra Kumar Dey, the playwright who had written some of Natta Company's biggest hits, told Makhan-babu, 'Tell Chapal to pay more attention to his acting. Since we have taken him on and he's risen so fast in these last few years, I'm thinking the time has come for me to write a play centred on him.'

That play was *Chand Bibi*. The year was 1964.

I was elated. I had seen Ma act as Chand Bibi on stage. But that was in her later years. Kshirodaprosad Bidyabinode had written the original play. Chand Bibi was the fiery regent of Bijapur sultanate who rode into battle to defend her kingdom against the armies of the Mughal emperor Akbar in the sixteenth century. In Bidyabinode's version, she is 50 years old, with a son named Ibrahim and a grandson named Bahadur. Brajen-babu kept me in mind and made his Chand Bibi younger, a widow of indeterminate age. He tweaked the other relationships as well: Ibrahim became her brother, Bahadur became her nephew, someone whom she had installed on the throne of Ahmednagar while she appointed herself as regent.

I could see myself as this Chand Bibi. I was tall, my voice was sweet yet powerful, as befitted a queen. In jatra parlance, I was well suited for what they called a 'book heroine'.

I immediately started designing all of Chand Bibi's costumes in my head. Makhan-babu showed me the usual outfits for warrior princesses that Natta Company had in its stock—spangled dresses made of heavy velvet.

'No, no, this won't do,' I exclaimed, dismissing them all. 'I want to wear what the real Chand Bibi might have worn.'

Surya-babu acquiesced.

I went off to New Market to find a jeweller who would make me gem-studded earrings. The funny thing is, I've never had my ears pierced despite playing women for so many years. I've always used clip-on earrings. In those days, you could get clip-on versions of almost everything, whether earrings or nose rings. And what I could not find, I would get shipped from Madras or Bombay, thanks to a shop in Kolkata who would happily source them for me. Now clip-ons are harder to find because everyone, man or woman, is getting their ears pierced. Luckily, my earring-wearing days are over.

The main outfit for Chand Bibi was a dazzling white peshwaj, a short form-fitting waistcoat with gold brocade which I wore over a heavy satiny-white kurta. And diamond bangles with a long diamond necklace. The diamonds were actually glass, but they sparkled like real gems. At that time, they knew how to make imitation versions of everything—glass that looked like diamonds or lustrous pearls made out of wax and grains of rice. New Market was like an Alibaba's cave for costume jewellery—you could get everything you wanted.

The highlight of the costume was a diamond-studded crescent moon with a long feather attached to my turban. I went all over the city looking for the perfect crescent and eventually found it in a hole-in-the-wall shop in Bagri Market near Nakhoda Masjid in the crowded Muslim heart of the city, filled with stalls grilling beef kebabs and biryani shops and tailors. My moon was a little bigger than the crescent moon on Lord Shiva's head. But how it glittered! It was so resplendent, I had no need for a crown.

The blouse was custom-made for me by my favourite tailor Qasim who had a shop behind New Market. They were master tailors, the kind you cannot find any more. I didn't have to wear my artificial breasts when I went to give my measurements. They could just look at me and figure out the blouse size, such was their skill. They were great craftsmen, as were the wigmakers like

Mehboob, Farhad, Abdul, all of whom also had shops near Nakhoda Masjid. My sister used them as well. I loved the wig she used in the play *Anthony Kabiyal*, so I told Farhad, 'Please make me one as well.' By then, Farhad was a legend among wigmakers.

He said, 'These are very expensive. Will your Natta Company spend that much money?'

'They will. I will tell Makhan-babu,' I said confidently. 'Take my measurements.' He made me a beautiful wig, exactly like a young woman's hair—with a middle part and waves on the side.

In the war scenes, Chand Bibi wore full leather armour. The breastplate was tied at the back with laces, the front had rows of silver discs while the arm and leg guards had patterns on them that looked like a filigree of iron. It made for a stunning ensemble when Chand Bibi strode onto the stage in full battle regalia.

There was one other outfit, the 'Arabian' one, and it was a black burkha. I purchased the black silk and Qasim cut it for me so that it flared like one of those classic gentlemen's black umbrellas. The niqab or veil was made of sheer black georgette. When I cocked my head, the audience could see my eyes. Three outfits, each striking in its own way, and I had to change quickly from one to another.

Chand Bibi opened in Kolkata at S. C. Allen Market in North Kolkata. That market still exists, though now it's been painted blue and white. In the middle of the market are concrete slabs where sellers set up mounds of vegetables or chop squawking chickens and big silvery fish on huge curved bontis. In the morning, the hubbub is deafening and the place is awash in blood and fish scales and feathers. Little shops line the sides, selling all kinds of household goods, from sachets of detergent to brooms made of dried grass, loofahs made of gourds and shopping bags made from recycled sacks. That was our theatre. And the storage room, that was where we female performers did our make-up. Amid sacks of produce, we sat in the corner and transformed ourselves into queens and princesses. As Chand Bibi strode onto the stage, out of the corner of my eye I could see big jute sacks of potatoes and onions, piled in a corner, ready for next day's business. Even though the 'stage' had been washed and swept, it seemed to still smell of the day's market, as if years of fish and vegetables and dried spices had seeped into the concrete itself.

Even now it is a busy street . . . so many old houses, their rickety balconies overlooking the noise and bustle . . . late-night biryani restaurants cheek by jowl with little pharmacies, brightly coloured temples and grimy tea shops where an aluminium kettle seems to be always on the boil. Night is when these streets truly came alive. It was a red-light area then, and even now, if you go in the evening, clusters of sex workers, lipsticked and powdered, in tight salwars or nylon saris, stand in front of the paan and cigarette stores, trying to tempt passers-by with their charms. You can't walk there without someone approaching you and offering girls (or even boys) in a low voice 'Why don't you come and check them out at least? Not very expensive, for 500 rupees you can get fuck, suck, everything. Come with me. There's no charge for looking. Take a look, and maybe come back another day.'

We would open at ten, or even later, after the market had shut down. On jatra nights, sometimes the market's night shift would be cancelled. The entire neighbourhood, vegetable vendors, fishmongers, rickshaw pullers, whores, pimps and their clients would show up. In those days, you could book Natta

Company for the princely sum of 750–800 rupees a night. By the mid-'70s, after its *Noti Binodini* became a huge hit, the same Natta Company could command 30,000–40,000 rupees. But it did not come easy. Makhan-babu put a lot of blood, sweat and tears into building the company.

My fame was spreading. Until then, my name had appeared only on the handbills that were distributed before a performance: Chapal. Nothing more. But for *Chand Bibi*, Natta Company took out advertisements in Bengali newspapers that included the line: 'A new look, a new attire—Chapal Rani as Chand Bibi. Come and see.' There were large handbills as well that carried the names of all the actors.

I was overwhelmed with excitement when I first saw my name in big letters. I rushed to show it to my sister Ketaki.

'Oh that's wonderful!' she replied. 'But why do they say Chapal Rani? They could have just said Chapal Bhaduri. After all, we are Bhaduris, aren't we?'

'That's because I'm playing a female part. A queen, a rani.'

'Ha! I thought the age of kings and queens was over. Aren't we a democracy now? Anyway, in our world of theatre, there are no kings and queens. Then again, I don't understand how your jatra works.'

There was always a little friction between the two worlds—theatre and jatra. Chhordi saw me act in jatra when I was playing Riziya Sultana. She had come with the actor Shekhar Chatterjee.

He came over to meet me after the show, 'Who designed your outfit? Whose idea was it?'

'Mine,' I replied.

Riziya had four wigs and outfit changes, sometimes within the space of five minutes. 'What about that scene in the prison cell? It looked like you'd shaved your legs for it. Have you?'

'Oh no, no. I was wearing skin-coloured inners. You can get leggings which are skin coloured. I found these black panties too, that just cover your private parts. And I wore a fine net skirt on top of that with a gold brocade border. How did it look?'

'My God! I almost felt like I should kidnap you then and there.'

'What nonsense!' Chhordi interjected, 'This is my little brother. You can't flirt with him like that, Shekhar! Stop it!'

The Moon Rises

The night that *Chand Bibi* opened, I had an unexpected visitor.

'Where is this Chapal Rani I hear so much about?' a voice called out outside the dressing room aka the onion-storage closet.

Someone ushered the man inside. I had just finished dressing. He was an old man, perhaps in his 60s, with a round belly and round glasses.

When he saw me, he stopped short and raised his eyebrows.

'Oh, this is the famous Chapal Rani? Hmm, yes, this all looks very modern. I must say your outfit looks rather splendid. In our days, we just wore whatever was given to us but yes, we certainly could act up a storm.'

'And who are you?' I asked.

'I am Haripada Bayen,' he said. I understood immediately. At one time, he had been Haripada Rani, renowned for his female roles in plays like *Badshah Alamgir* and *Raja Harishchandra*. His voice was still thin and feminine but no one could imagine now that he had once been famous for playing lissome women onstage.

'Indeed, I have heard of you and your fame,' I replied politely.

'That's why I came all this way to take a look at you,' he said a bit condescendingly. 'Do you know that at one time I played this very character? Chand Bibi of Ahmednagar. And not too shabbily either. I became quite famous for this role. Mind you, you certainly look the part. Named after the moon and looking like the moon indeed. But I hope you can do justice to the role. Don't let me down now.'

A little miffed, I said haughtily 'Why would I let you down? I am not here to uphold your sainted reputation or sully it. I will just act the way I have always acted on stage. And to be perfectly honest, I don't really care what you think. It does not affect me a whit. And I don't think the audience cares either.'

'What!' He stared at me, utterly flabbergasted. He had not expected such a snippy response. Looking back, I have to admit a lot of that was my ego talking. Those billboards were clearly going to my head.

I didn't meet Haripada Rani ever again, but the performance that night created quite a sensation. There was a scene where one character asks another what Chand Bibi looks like. He replies, 'I cannot tell her age exactly. But she looks like a ball of fire.' I really think Brajen Day wrote that line with me in mind. The white outfit encrusted with glittering diamonds indeed made Chand Bibi look like a white-hot ball of fire on stage. During the war scenes, people burst into applause as soon as I strode onto the stage, looking every inch the warrior princess in my suit of armour.

When Chand Bibi comes in full battledress to meet Murad Khan, the Mughal prince, he thunders 'Who are you? Are you Chand Sultana?' She replies 'Are you Murad Khan?' Then they salaam each other across the stage. It was always a thrilling moment. The audience lapped it up.

My co-star Arun Dasgupta devised that scene. It was such a swashbuckling role. Now as I sit here battling arthritis, it's hard to imagine that once I did swordplay on stage night after night.

The owner of that market was a man named Dhruba Das, a rakishly handsome man. He had a bit of reputation for being a regular at the brothels in the area. He almost went berserk at the sight of me as Chand Bibi, and wanted to give me a prize as a token of appreciation. He showed up waving a crisp 100-rupee note.

'I want to give this to you as a gift,' he announced. Giving gifts was not uncommon but in 1964 a hundred rupees was good money.

'Well, why not? Just announce on stage that you want to reward Chapal-babu for his performance at Chand Bibi. This is your market anyway,' I said airily.

He seemed hesitant.

'What's the matter? Is there a problem?' I asked.

'No, I mean this money . . . how should I give it?' he trailed off a bit sheepishly.

'Give it the way everyone else does.'

'No, I mean where and how should I give it?'

'You can put it in my hands. Or pin it on me like the others do.'

'You mean, pin it on with a safety pin?'

'Why not?'

'But where?'

'You can pin it however you like. And wherever you like.'

The man was a bit of a rascal. He gestured towards my chest: 'How about if I pin it right there?'

'On my breasts?' I replied coolly. 'Yes, of course, if that's what you want. They are fake anyway.' I had sponge inserts for my breasts; foam had not yet hit the market.

I think he was a little crushed by my matter-of-factness. He quickly backtracked: 'No, no, it's all right, I'll just pin it to your tunic.'

I calmly took the money, then turned and handed it to someone standing beside me: 'Here's some money from Dhrubababu. Please, order sweets for everyone.' In those days, a rosogolla cost perhaps 2 annas. There were 16 annas to a rupee. 100 rupees meant a lot of rosogolla.

Now I think I treated that money rather too nonchalantly. I should have accorded it more respect. After all, it was money I had earned with my hard work. But I never learnt to save. I spent it all on myself and on others around me. I didn't think enough about a future when that money would stop rolling in.

When I stepped into jatra, I earned a salary of 100 rupees. A year later it became 175. Then it rose to 350. By 1962, I was making 600. In 1963, it went up another 100. When I made *Chand Bibi*, I hit 1,000. And it was still on its way up.

Teaching the Teacher

Chand Bibi raised Natta Company to new heights. As it did me and my name. Someone from one of the Chitpur jatra companies apparently said, 'I can't believe it's that same Chapal. Why, at one time, he could barely talk!' I retorted. 'Tell them, when we come out of our mothers' wombs, none of us know how to talk. We learn how to do that from our mothers. These plays I am doing, they are like my mother. The playwright is like my father. They are teaching me to find my voice.'

Chand Bibi was also the first time I questioned the playwright. I was finding a new confidence in myself, something I did not know I possessed.

There was a scene where Emperor Akbar's son Murad wants to buy Nandini, a white elephant, for 4,000 gold ashrafi coins. Chand Bibi buys the elephant instead, for herself, for 20,000 gold ashrafi. An insulted Murad sends a messenger to Chand Bibi to say he wants that elephant, come what may, even if it costs him 20,000 gold ashrafi. Otherwise he will not hesitate to attack Chand Bibi's kingdom. She is equally adamant that she will not give it up.

> MESSENGER. Is that your last word then? You will not give up Nandini?
>
> CHAND BIBI. No! I will not give up Nandini. I do not care who is upset by that. Listen carefully to me: go and tell your lord Murad that the moon in the sky might slink away in fear but Chand Bibi, this moon from Ahmednagar, does not know the meaning of fear.

A dramatic line like that should have elicited tremendous applause. Yet, somehow, it always fell flat. That bothered me. In jatra, a performer's worth is measured in applause. We did not wait to hear what critics wrote about us in newspaper reviews, because we got no reviews. For us, the feedback was always instantaneous. I thought a lot about that line and then had an idea about what to do to give it a bit more punch. But when I shared my idea with Surya-babu, he shot me down: 'No one can change the dialogues without consulting with Brajen-babu first. He is the playwright, after all.'

We called Brajen-babu Mastermoshai or Teacher-Sir because he was so learned. He had a degree in economics but was so fluent in English that he had been hired as an English teacher in Faridpur. When the jatra was staged in Ichhapur where he lived, I got my chance. When he came to see the play, I met him and explained the situation, 'Sir, I want to change that line a bit.'

He looked at me with great surprise, 'I am the playwright and you want to change my play?' I will never forget that look he gave me.

I hurriedly said, 'Nothing will change sir, the meaning will stay the same. I just want to change the language.'

'What exactly do you want to do?'

'After delivering the rest of the dialogue in Bengali, if I suddenly switch to Urdu, that won't go against the character. Or change the meaning. But I believe it will change the impact of the line.'

'Hmm, let's hear it.'

'I'll say the first part exactly the way you have written it. Then I will say, "Listen to one more thing, Mansabdar Dharam Singh, go tell your lord Subedar Murad, *aasman ka chand dhal sakte hain, lekin Ahmednagar-ki chand hamesha hi Chand rahegi*"—The moon in the sky might wane, but the moon of Ahmednagar will always remain this Chand. I think saying that line in Urdu instead of Bengali will give it more punch because the story is set in Mughal times.'

He mulled it over and said, 'Fine, try it tonight.'

I did—and the theatre just spontaneously burst out in applause. As soon as that scene ended, Brajen-babu came up to me and embraced me. That was the greatest reward I could have received as a young actor. It was very generous of Brajen-babu. I was just a young cocky actor but he let me try it my way. If he had said no, I would not have dared to go against him. Not every playwright would have been so magnanimous. After that, I always said that line in Urdu. And the audience never failed to applaud. How did I know to tweak that line? I have no idea. What can I say? Acting runs in my blood.

That wasn't the only change we made. That play also starred Phani Rani, one of the great female impersonators of the time. She played a Rajput woman, the mother of Chand Bibi's general, Nandan Singh. People thought she was a widow, but she always wore red, like a married woman. That was because she had been married to a Rajput chieftain but he turned out to be a traitor. When she discovered his treachery, in a fit of rage she pushed him off the ramparts of their fort. But he survived. So she ran away, and finally took shelter in Chand Bibi's kingdom where she continued to dress in red. Chand Bibi called her Chachi, or aunt.

In one scene, I tell her, 'Chachi, commanded by their emperor, the Mughals are marching towards our Ahmednagar to fight. Now is the time for us to go to war and thrust our daggers into their hearts, not caring that we might be wrestling with death itself.' I would say that line and exit, but there would be no reaction. In the scenes before us, the male actors would get a huge round of applause, but our scene would fall totally flat. So one day we changed it slightly. In the end, instead of me speaking those lines, we wondered what it would be like if both of us spoke them together.

'Now is the time for us to go to war, to wrestle with death and thrust our daggers into their hearts,' we said in unison, and froze. The lights went off, the stage was dark. And the audience went absolutely wild. The air felt electric, crackling with tension. Even we felt hot, as if we were on fire.

The ranis won the day.

Sharp Knives and Sharper Tongues

Chand Bibi was memorable for another reason. An accident happened during *Chand Bibi*. We were performing somewhere outside Kolkata. We had gone by bus. A lot of jatra people liked to drink, mostly local liquor because it was cheap and easily available. They often asked me to join them. But I always demurred: 'Don't ask me to do all this. But if you have some good paan-jarda, then let me know.' Betel-nut and chewing tobacco were my only vices.

That day, under that blazing sun, the actor who played a villainous character named Pir Mohammad had a bit too much to drink and started misbehaving in the middle of the road. Passers-by began to stop and stare, and be nasty: 'Look at these fellows. At night, they act on stage but during the day they're drunk out of their minds. They're all like this, these jatra actors, all low-lifes.'

That stung. I told the actor, 'What kind of person are you? Don't you have any self-respect?'

But he was beyond listening. He slurred 'Who's talking to me?'

'It's me, Chapal.'

'Oh, the queen. The queen has come. What is the queen saying?'

'Why do you drink that dog piss if you can't tolerate it?' I said hotly.

'Are you calling me a drunk?'

'Yes, I am.'

'OK, I'm drunk if you say so. But I'll show you who's who tonight.'

'Fine! Let's see what you can do. I know exactly what you're capable of.'

In the play, after Pir Mohammad commits an act of treachery Chand Bibi, as regent, summons him to appear before her. As she asks where he is, he sneaks up from behind and plunges a knife into her breast. It was a special knife with a spring—in truth, the blade retracted but from afar it looked like it was entering Chand Bibi's heart. As he stabs me, I try to grab him by the hair and then I collapse dramatically onto the stage.

All the props that were needed, or requisitions as we called them, would be laid out in the correct order, one after the other, so the actors could grab them on the way to the scene. That night, instead of the prop knife, for some reason there was a real one. So when Pir Mohammad stabbed me, there was blood everywhere. My blood.

Utter chaos erupted.

After that, that actor could not be found anywhere.

By the time he was found, we were all aboard the bus, ready to leave. He was brought before me, almost like a re-enactment of the fateful scene from the play.

He was in tears. All his bravado had drained out of him. 'Chapal-da, please forgive me. It was a terrible mistake.'

'What were you thinking? When you said you would show me tonight, is that what was in your mind? What would have happened if that knife had gone in an inch deeper?'

He fell at my feet. I pulled him up: 'Don't touch my feet. Just don't drink like that any more. If you must drink, drink after the show is over, and in your own room, not like that on the open road, in full view of everybody.'

'I promise, Chapal-da. Please say that you forgive me.'

What could I do but forgive him? Come to think of it, he was rather good-looking. But I have to say he did obey me. He would still drink but at night, in his room, after the show had ended. Now he too is dead. But if I touch my chest, right below my neck, I can still feel the scar.

The fame of Chand Bibi went to my head. My feet were barely touching the ground, thanks to all the adulation. One day, we had gone to perform in the old historic town of Bardhaman. We were still travelling by bus. We had stopped somewhere for breakfast. I did not feel like getting off, so I asked someone to bring me some yogurt and a couple of sweets, not too many. After all, I had to maintain my figure.

Someone came up to me and said tentatively, 'Chapal-da? Can I say something?'

I raised my eyebrows: 'Who are you?'

'Umm . . . it's me.'

'Who?'

'Tonight we are performing *Chand Bibi*. And I have a scene with you.'

'Which part are you playing?'

'Pir Muhammad.'

'Oh yes. Kartik has gone home. You must be filling in. Let me take a look at you. Yes, you will do fine. What do you need?'

'I was just worried about that last scene where you have to grab me by the hair and I have to escape from your grasp and plunge a knife into you. I was wondering . . . if we could go over the choreography of the scene . . . so I understand it properly.'

My tone became icy. 'Listen, young man. Let me tell you something. Our bus is standing in the middle of the road because people are getting breakfast. You think this is the right place to discuss your part? With me? You should have talked to the director about what needs to be done. How dare you come up to me like this? What impertinence! Have you even looked at your own face in the mirror?'

To be frank, he was not bad looking, though he had some acne scars on his cheeks. But I was on a roll.

'How much do you earn that you think you can just walk up to me to go over your part? And that too here in the middle of the road?'

Once, when I had turned my nose up at a cheap enamel plate in the dining hall, Padma Thakur had sneered, 'How much do you get paid, son?'

I didn't realize it then but I was tossing Padma Thakur's words back at that poor young man. Taken aback, he didn't know what to say.

Eventually, I said disdainfully, 'Come to me right before the show starts. And I'll tell you whatever you need to know. Go away now, don't disturb me while I am eating.'

He slunk away, red-faced. But someone noticed our little exchange—Surya-babu. At that time, he said nothing at all.

But later, he came up to me and said softly, 'Chapal, why don't you have some non-spicy curry today? It's quite good.'

'No, no, I don't like that stuff,' I replied. 'It's too bland and plain.'

'Chapal, don't eat too much spicy food,' Surya-babu said gently. 'I think too much spice has made your tongue a little too sharp.'

When I still did not understand what he was getting at, he said, 'You need to watch your tongue, Chapal. I saw how you behaved with that boy yesterday. Do you think that was right?'

Then he told me a story about Tara Bhattacharya, the great actor who had become famous by playing the venerable saint Ramprasad. He was so extraordinary in that part that, at the end of the performances, the audience would throng around him to get his blessings as if he was the real saint. But he would shoo them away angrily, as if touching them would somehow sully him, such was his arrogance. One day, in the middle of his performance, the song died in his throat. No sound would emerge any more. His life fell apart.

Surya-babu said, 'Chapal, listen. Once you told me that even though people loved your performance, your name was never on the posters, no one announced it on the loudspeaker. But now with *Chand Bibi*, your name is everywhere. Are you happy?'

'Yes, it makes me very happy.'

'Do you find you can work now with extra enthusiasm?'

'Of course.'

'Then why did you speak to that new boy like that?'

'How could I discuss our parts in the middle of the road like that? Was that the time or place?'

'You could have explained that to him. Son, such arrogance does not behove you. *Diye dhon dekhey mon, kere nitey kotokhon*—seeing the wealth given, the mind is captivated, but how long till it is taken away? It's true that people love you for your performances, Chapal. But they will remember you for your behaviour long after you are gone. You must learn to shed your arrogance and treat others with the respect they deserve as fellow human beings. It may feel like I am scolding you today, but think of it as my blessing.'

I was mortified. Later that evening, I sought that boy out, sat him down and went through the scene with him. He was nervous about exactly how to stab me, afraid he might push the knife too hard and hurt me. I told him not to worry about it. All the while I remembered how once I had been a junior artiste and so many big stars had treated me with utter disdain. It made me cringe that I had been doing the same to this poor boy.

Surya-babu had been right when he told me, 'Treat everyone with respect.'

When *Chand Bibi* opened, I was still Chapal Bhaduri. That play made me Chapal Rani. Actually, that was just my name on the posters. In the jatra world, no one called me Chapal Rani. They simply called me Rani or Queen. Rani. Rani. Rani.

After a performance at Patna University, a student asked me for an autograph. I signed Chapal Bhaduri. Then, underneath, I wrote in brackets: (Rani).

INTERLUDE

An Excerpt

Sultana Riziya by Brajendra Kumar Dey

Riziya enters

RIZIYA. No. (*She looks at everyone one by one*)

MAHMUD. Why, Mother?

RIZIYA. The mullahs will shout at the top of their lungs that Islam has gone to the dogs. The maulvis will pull out the Sharia, the Hindu pandits will show us the Manu Samhita—everyone will decree fatwas that a woman's place is in the kitchen, not in the royal court. Amir Osman will cover his face in shame and say he would rather hang himself to death before accepting a woman's rule.

OSMAN. Queen . . .

RIZIYA. Purandar Rai, however, will give his all to make sure royalty gets its due.

Purandar bows low.

RIZIYA. But Sultan Altuniya, Ikhtiaruddin, Itigeen and Behram will all speak in one voice and say that a woman should serve a man. She can never rule over hundreds of intellectuals, thousands of soldiers and hundreds of thousands of able-bodied men. Isn't that true, Sultan?

ALTUNIYA. Why are you saying these things?

RIZIYA. Am I wrong, Amir Osman?

OSMAN. I was only saying . . .

RIZIYA. It looks like Purandar Rai is drowning in his dilemma. Has your sister been weeping copiously to you? Has she been throwing herself at you, sobbing?

PURANDAR. Please don't misunderstand me, Queen. I was merely saying . . .

RIZIYA. Mamud Khan, I have received my weapons training at your hands. My father was responsible for my birth, but you were responsible for my training. You know my talents better than I do. Still, I am requesting you, forget this dream. Install Bahram Khan on the throne. I will be the first to salute him.

OSMAN. My Queen, you are very . . .

RIZIYA. Noble, sir . . .

OSMAN. I had come to say—

RIZIYA. Precisely this.

OSMAN. If Prince Behram does not sit on the throne, the mullahs and maulvis will be very upset. Otherwise, as you well know, if it was left to me . . .

RIZIYA. There's no end to the esteem you hold me in? That I know of course, Amir Osman

MAHMUD. That is not possible, Mother. I will take this throne and throw it into the Yamuna river but none other than you will sit on it.

ALTUNIYA. Ruknuddin's throne belongs by right to his young son.

PURANDAR. Why? Because he is your relative's son? After installing a disabled child on the throne, who will be the real ruler? You? Or Begum Shahturkan?

ALTUNIYA. Be silent, Hindu.

RIZIYA. Why, Sultan? The Sultan of Bhatinda gets to poke his nose into the affairs of the Delhi sultanate but the mansabdar, the leader of the imperial army, can't say anything? Do Hindus not have the right to speak in a Muslim kingdom? My friend, that age has ended with the death of Ruknuddin. If you have eyes, look, see the new age is dawning in the east. Look at its light breaking. If you have ears, listen well. This world is not for Hindus or Muslims or Buddhists or Christians—it's for humans. God created humans.

MAHMUD. That is why I want you on the throne of Delhi, Mother.

RIZIYA. No one will accept a woman's rule.

MAHMUD. He who does not, will die.

OSMAN. Will it not be a grievous sin to put someone else on a throne that legitimately belongs to the young prince?

MAHMUD. I will take that sin upon myself.

RIZIYA. The subjects will rise against the crown, Commander.

ALTUNIYA. They already have.

PURANDAR. Even if they don't want to, you will not spare them, I am sure.

MAHMUD. Let the rebels remember that Mahmud Khan isn't dead yet.

PURANDAR. You keep that in mind as well.

RIZIYA. Why are you being so stubborn, Commander? I am an immature woman, what do I have in me that will let me rule over an entire sultanate?

MAHMUD. An elephant does not know the strength it possesses. That's why the mahout gets away with goading it.

RIZIYA. Commander, you are like a father to me. I can tell you things I would be too ashamed to tell anyone. Even if you have not seen it with your own eyes, I am sure you have heard it all. My very body feels dirty and polluted. What shame is this. Even if he is a step-brother, he is still my elder brother. What a cursed life I have that my own brother should . . .

PURANDAR. This is not your shame, Queen. It's his. He has gone to the grave carrying its burden. Please do not dwell on the past any more.

MAHMUD. Go mother. And prepare yourself. In three days, I will install you as Sultana Riziya in front of everybody.

ALL. But—

MAHMUD. Still but? Amir Osman, Altuniya, Purandar. Is this your last word? You will not agree to my proposal?

PURANDAR. I am like your son, Commander. Do not misunderstand me. But I find it hard to bring myself to agree.

ALTUNIYA. The father's throne rightfully belongs to the son.

OSMAN. As long as the prince is alive, the citizens will accept the rule of no one else.

RIZIYA. If your wishes reflect the wishes of the people, I declare that I do not want the throne of Delhi.

MAHMUD. The one who understood the wishes of his subjects to a tee, the one who could make a king into a fakir and a fakir into king just like that, see what that man, the late emperor Altamash had decreed. (*Shows a scroll*)

PURANDAR. The emperor's own signature. (*Bows low*)

ALTUNIYA. Please see what he has written, Amir Osman.

OSMAN. After my death my throne should be inherited by—

RIZIYA. My daughter Riziya. My beloved gracious father, may your wishes be fulfilled. (*Kneels and kisses the scroll*)

MAHMUD. I was in Persia when he died. All of you took advantage of that and installed Ruknuddin on the throne. Today, I will rectify that mistake. He who wishes can stand by me. He who does not can stand apart. But do not resist. If you do, I will tear you to pieces. So think carefully. (*Exits*)

PURANDAR. Please accept my good wishes, Princess. I will felicitate you first in the royal court. May God bless you. (*Exits*)

OSMAN. If this was the emperor's wish, then that is the end of the matter. If anyone opposes this, I myself will . . .

RIZIYA. Cut off his head? I know that.

OSMAN. I am sure you do. Your father was my . . .

RIZIYA. Bosom friend. After the father, have you made friends with the son, Behram?

OSMAN. Oh, the shame of it. Is he even a man?

RIZIYA. Sultan Osman.

OSMAN. But I spoke on his behalf for a reason. I cannot bear anyone's tears. Well, Princess, once you are on the throne send this old rascal to Mecca as soon as you can. Anyway, what's to fear when we are all here? All right, let me take your leave. (*To himself*) Let the whole ship go down. (*Exits*)

ALTUNIYA. How does the person who holds their father's wishes in such high esteem insult me like that, Riziya? What kind of judgement is that?

RIZIYA. How does the person who will have to prostrate himself on the floor and salute me dare to call me by my name? What kind of judgement is that?

ALTUNIYA. Now the princess can get remove me from my post. But I will not take this insult lying down.

RIZIYA. No one has the power to show respect to the person who seeks out disrespect. And the tigress has no need to see which jackal is roaring from which hole in the ground.

ALTUNIYA. So much arrogance is not good, Princess. Mark my words. One day, that proud head will be rolling at my feet. Or I am no son of a Muslim.

RIZIYA. That neck will break but that head will never bow before you, Altuniya. (*Prepares to exit*)

ALTUNIYA. A woman, even if she is the queen of Delhi, is still a man's servant.

RIZIYA. Sultan-sahib, it seems one pair of shoes has been of no use to you. On your way out, please take another pair.

ALTUNIYA. Princess

RIZIYA. Salaam. (*Exits*)

ALTUNIYA. Altuniya forgets nothing, woman. One day you will regret this. That day I will be in the judge's chair and you will be at my feet in chains.

5
The Natta Years

A Day of Strange Events

The 25th of October, 1960. It was a day of strange events.

I was in Garbeta in Medinipur that day, a small town on the banks of the Shilabati river, several hours by train from Kolkata. Natta Company was staging *Lohar Jaal*.

I was sitting in the make-up room, getting ready for the show. As always, Biru, the dresser, had arranged all the props I needed in a box in front of me. I took a look at them, then held up a key and said, 'Biru, why have you given me this key? We use this one in *Pratishodh,* not *Lohar Jaal*. Have you forgotten that we are doing *Lohar Jaal* tonight?'

Biru clicked his tongue: 'Oho, I'm so sorry. I don't know what I was thinking. Don't tell the boss, please.'

I shook my head and put back that key. I remember it well. It was an iron key.

There was a meeting that day about another play. There had been some cuts and edits to it and everyone was summoned so they would know the changes. I was feeling very restless and found it hard to sit still and listen. I told Brajen-babu, 'Have any of my lines been cut?'

He said, 'No, your lines are fine. You don't need to sit in if you do not feel like it.'

I said, 'Good. It's past 10.30 already. I need to go to the toilet, bathe and have my lunch by noon.' In those days, we didn't have bathrooms attached to our quarters. We had to go out into the fields. I had an assistant, Sona, who did female roles occasionally but also ran errands for me and did odd jobs. Sona and I went out to the fields, but the stray dogs just would not leave me alone. They kept coming at me and barking while I was trying to do my business.

'What's going on, Sona?' I said irritably. 'Why do these dogs keep coming towards me? They are behaving very strangely. Chase them away, please.'

After I was done with my toilet, I bathed and went to have lunch. By then I was a star and my menu had been upgraded. Now I was entitled to rice, a dollop of ghee and fried fish or a spicy fish curry. I was careful about how much rice I ate, though, because I needed to watch my figure.

As soon as I sat down to lunch, Padma Thakur bustled over. 'Oh Rani, you are here? You don't want me to take your food to your room?'

'No, just serve me here. And Sona, why don't you have your lunch with me now?' I made sure Sona got some small perks every now and then.

Padma served the rice. I had a mouthful and crinkled my nose.

'Is this rice fresh, Padma-da? Or is it yesterday's? It feels a bit watery to me.'

'What are you saying, Rani? It's absolutely fresh!'

'You try some, Sona.' I said. He did, and looked at me puzzled. 'It seems fine to me, Chapal-da. I don't know what's wrong.'

'No, no, it's watery,' I insisted. 'Anyway, forget it. I don't need it. Where's the fish? I'll just have that.'

But as soon as I tried to eat the fish, that too smelt funny to me. 'What's wrong with you, Padma-da? You usually cook fish curry so well. Today, it smells. You take a bite, Sona.'

Sona tasted it and looked even more confused. 'But it's very good, Chapal-da. It's so tasty, you could make a full meal out of just the gravy and some rice. What don't you like about it?'

'I don't know, it's not tasting right to me.'

I got up and left.

When I sat down to get ready for the show that night, a new problem arose: I felt there was a dark tinge to my make-up. I was convinced the dressers had taken water from the tube-well instead of the pond. I always insisted on using pond water because I thought tube-well water had too much iron and that affected the colour of the make-up.

'You got water from the tube well, didn't you?' I asked accusingly.

'Of course not. We got it from the pond when we went to take a bath,' the dresser replied.

'Don't try to pull a fast one on me. I can tell. What do you think, Sona?'

'But Chapal-da, you look fine. Absolutely tip-top.'

The show at least went off all right. At midnight, I went to the dining room for my usual roti with some vegetables. I tended to avoid eating fish at night.

Suddenly, someone told the cook, 'Oh Padma, Makhan-babu has come. Quickly make some rotis for the boss. He might have dinner.'

I was a bit puzzled. As far as I knew, Makhan-babu was supposed to go up north to Cooch Behar. Why had he suddenly come to Garbeta instead? Makhan-babu walked into the dining room and came towards me.

'Chapal, have you had your dinner already?'

'Yes, Makhan-babu, but why are you here? Weren't you supposed to go to Cooch Behar?'

'Yes, yes, but I don't know if I can make it in the next few days. How are you, Padma?'

'Babu, what would you like for dinner? Shall I fix you something?'

'Nothing, nothing. Just give me a couple of sweets. You don't have to make anything now. I've eaten.' Then he turned to me: 'Which way is your room?'

I pointed towards it.

'All right,' he said, 'I'll go with you.'

One of the other team members asked worriedly 'Where will you sleep, Makhan-babu? All the rooms are occupied.'

'Don't worry,' he said. 'I'll sleep in Chapal's room tonight.'

I swallowed nervously. I might have become a bit of a star but for the owner of the troupe to room with an ordinary artiste, that too one who did female roles, felt a little awkward. But I didn't know how to say that.

'But where will you sleep?' I stuttered. 'Where will I sleep?'

'Don't worry about me. Let me ask someone to get a couple of extra blankets. We'll manage. You can use one as a mattress.'

I hurriedly tried to change the sheets. He said, 'Don't fuss. It's just one night. Just give me your slippers, I need to go to the toilet.' I felt it was all very peculiar—the owner of the company wearing my leather slippers, sleeping in my bed. But I kept quiet, and soon we both fell asleep.

The next morning, after we woke up, I said, 'I am going to go and get some tea.'

'No,' he said. 'You sit down. I'll organize that.'

But when he came back, he didn't have the tea with him. 'Oh, where's the tea?' I asked.

'It's coming,' he replied.

Then I saw, one by one, all the company members trooping into my little room, and slowly beginning to stand or sit around me. There was a man named Jibon in our group. He could do all kinds of roles from kings to serfs because he knew all the parts. If we were ever in a pinch, we would say, 'Oh Jibon-da, help. So-and-so hasn't come today. Please do this role.' We called him 'Gol Aloo' (Round Potato) because potatoes are so versatile, you can use them in almost any recipe. Jibon-da came and sat next to me and gently rubbed my back.

'Why are you doing that?' I said irritably. 'I don't like it when people touch me. It makes me uncomfortable.'

'Listen, I need to tell you something,' he said slowly.

'What?'

'Nirmal, you tell him.'

'No, no, Jibon, you tell him.'

'What's going on? Why are you all behaving so weirdly? Is this a jatra?'

'Listen, Chapal, let me tell you something. People, you know, must . . . '

As soon as he started talking, something clicked in me. Perhaps that is what they mean by sixth sense. 'Has something happened to my father?' I asked.

'Yes, Chapal. Yesterday at 10.30 in the morning, your father . . .' He didn't have to say any more. I understood everything.

The last time I had seen my father was a week before. I was about to leave for Garbeta. The car had arrived for me. (I was now travelling by car, not on the back of a truck any more.) A neighbour had got into an argument with me. We had thrown onto the street the banana leaves we'd used for a meal and the street dogs had scattered them everywhere. The woman was complaining about that, and I was giving back as good as I got when my father stopped me: 'Don't lose your temper like this. Don't create trouble before leaving. Look, your car has come, you'd better be on your way.'

That was the last thing my father told me.

I stared at Jibon for a few seconds, and then slapped that poor man. I used to read the Bhagavad Gita every day. I threw the book away. I tore off my sacred thread and screamed, 'I need to leave right now. I can't act any more.'

'Of course you must go,' said Makhan-babu soothingly. 'That is why I have come. To take you to Kolkata. You will go with me.'

'Right away.'

'We can't go right away. We have to wait for the train,' he said. 'I will take you myself. But first, come with me.'

He took me to the pond. I saw he had made all the arrangements, brought everything I needed for the bereavement rituals. He had the cook prepare hobishyi, rice and dal and potatoes boiled together, the food we eat during the mourning period.

As I came back to Kolkata by train, the strange events of that day kept replaying in my head. When a family member dies, we are supposed to touch iron. We go to the crematorium where stray dogs roam. We eat pre-cooked watery rice. We eat no fish or meat or food cooked with oil. We wear no leather. We sleep on the floor.

I still have no explanation for that strange day.

But I remain ever grateful to Makhan-babu. At that time, our family was not well off. But Makhan-babu stood like a rock beside us, paying for my father's funeral. Makhanlal Natta was not just the owner of the troupe. He was family.

But in every family come rifts and misunderstandings. We had ours as well. Though that came later.

The World in My Grasp

I had become a star. After *Chand Bibi*, there was no stopping me.

Life was a whirl. We were on the road all the time—Bardhaman to Durgapur, Durgapur to Raniganj, Raniganj to Asansol, criss-crossing the state. The colliery towns were always good business. We would have bookings for five or six days in one place sometimes.

Then a tour of North Bengal—Alipurduar, Siliguri, New Jalpaiguri, Cooch Behar, Mathabhanga, Dinhata. At that time, the Farakka bridge had not been built across the Ganga. We would have to take a train from Kolkata to Shaktigarh Ghat and then run across the sand banks with all our luggage and baggage to the opposite side, to Monihari Ghat, where another train would be waiting to take us to New Jalpaiguri in North Bengal.

The first time we got there, I didn't know what to do. Everyone just heaved their trunks and bedding onto their heads and started running across the sand. There were no porters around, just a lot of soldiers. I was sitting there flabbergasted, looking about me, unsure. Surya-babu saw me and said, 'Chapal, what are you doing, sitting there like that?'

'Nobody's told me what to do,' I replied. 'Nobody's called me.'

'Who is going to call you, Chapal? Come on, come with me.' He hollered at someone to take my bedding and baggage. Then he turned to me, 'Listen my boy, this is a jatra company. Nobody will call you, nobody cares. You might think these are your friends but every man is for himself here. Remember this advice I am giving you, standing on this sand bank, under this open sky. Smile at everyone, be polite to everyone, but don't get too intimate with anyone. Remember that.'

I remembered that lesson all my life.

A season in North Bengal would go on for two to two and half months. Then we could come back down south to Howrah and Hooghly and Bardhaman. After Diwali, we would return to Kolkata and have a few days off. By spring, business would slacken. The Kolkata troupes would pay 75 per cent salary, so we called them shikibaad groups, 'a quarter short'. But Natta Company didn't do that.

I was just so happy to be able to eat my fill three times a day. After years of struggle, that itself felt like an achievement.

We would travel to all kinds of towns, big and small. In some places, the green room was the room used to store potatoes, the walls covered in yellow dust. Sometimes we did not have a proper house to stay in and would set up camp near a stream or a small waterfall. Someone would dig up the soil and slap together a small makeshift mud stove on which we could cook rice and dal, boil some eggs and potatoes, fry them with turmeric and chilli paste and rustle up a quick curry. There was a kind of pleasure in sitting by the dusty roadside, eating a mound of steaming rice and that piping-hot, spicy red egg curry off banana leaves. If there was a sudden storm, our banana-leaf plates went flying and we'd scramble after them, laughing and cursing. We would spread a mattress on a field right after the paddy had been harvested and sit on that. The ground would be lumpy and uneven, but if I complained, someone would immediately say, 'Where did you come from? Chhabi Rani would never say something like this!'

Those comparisons never stopped. When the jatra company started providing the bigger stars with cars to go to the shows, tongues started wagging. 'Oh Chhabi Ran never got a car. He just took the bus and the local train. How did Chapal get a car so quickly? How did he become equal to a hero like Arun Dasgupta so fast?'

After a few years, I stopped eating at the little roadside eateries. Instead, I would ask for fresh rosogollas (with a little extra syrup, because I had a bit of a sweet tooth) and yoghurt, and I would mix them with my private stash of puffed rice. I didn't like eating the greasy food that had been sitting around for hours at some wayside restaurant. But people would look at me askance for even that. 'Look at Chapal. Too fancy to eat with the rest of us.'

Sometimes we went to a pice hotel, homely places where you could have as much rice as you wanted, with a simple fish curry and vegetables. Then I would take along the labourers who worked for us for a meal as well. They were the ones doing back-breaking work—loading and unloading the heavy metal trunks in which we carried all our costumes and props. Even that would not go unnoticed. Someone would raise an eyebrow and sneer 'Look at him. A few years ago, he was just a dancing boy because his family had no money. And now he's throwing money around. Wonder how he managed to get a raise.'

I did it not because I wanted to show off but because I learnt it from my mother. Every year, before the big Durga Puja festival, she would buy stacks of clothes from Kamala Stores and make sure everyone who worked at the theatre, not just the shift workers but also their wives and children, got something new.

By 1963, I was getting somewhat famous. I was even doing jatra on the radio. They would trim our three-hour-long scripts down to an hour and then ask us to record them. I could play fiery parts as well as softer roles. I enjoyed both. I didn't need glycerine to make my eyes well up with tears. The only thing I could not do, which my mother had been very good at, was comedy. I tried once during my amateur days but realized soon enough that it was not easy to do physical comedy like Charlie Chaplin.

Those were good days for Natta Company. Even the old Chhabi Rani roles suddenly found new life. In *Sonar Bharat* [Golden India], about the twelfth-century Rajput kings Prithviraj Chauhan and Jaichand, I played Purnima, wife of Jaichand, while Arun Dasgupta played Prithivraj. When Chhabi Rani had acted as Purnima, the jatra had never quite clicked. But now

Brajen-babu rewrote the play to centre it on Purnima, and it worked magnificently.

There were new plays too. Like *Bilwamangal*. In the original play, Girish Ghosh had written Chintamoni as a woman of ill repute, a prostitute. But in Brajen-babu's version she is a Brahman housewife whom Bilwamangal abducts. But he does not touch her. Even though he is a drunkard and a man of loose morals, he senses that she is his wife from a previous life. So he sends her back to her husband. But society will no longer accept her, she is now tainted in their eyes. So she returns to Bilwamangal. In the play, I played Chintamoni while Arun Dasgupta played Bilwamangal, and it was a massive hit.

Purnima, Chand Bibi, Chintamoni—the world seemed to be in my grasp. The only problem was that I was quite tall—5-foot-10. And in women's clothes I looked taller. Makhan-babu tried to find tall strapping men to act opposite me. Tapan Kumar was very good looking. Swapankumar was not handsome but manly, as was Shekhar Ganguly. Nabakumar Banerjee who played Ram was just like an artist's rendition of the prince—beautiful eyes, straight nose and fair skin that was painted blue for the production. And I remember Mathura Mohan Biswas from my amateur days—a tall slim man with a perfectly shaped nose and lips.

But my staple heroes were Arun Dasgupta, Shekhar Ganguly and Manoj Kumar. Arun was not that handsome, and not that tall either, we stood head to head as a couple, but he was a consummate actor. Shekhar was tall and good-looking, with strong, muscular arms—just perfect for a romantic hero. I could easily rest my head on his chest. When he started acting as Chintamoni instead of Arun Dasgupta, the love scenes suddenly had a lot more sizzle.

But it was just on stage, entirely make-believe. I was in fact great friends with his wife, Chhaya. I had acted with her in an amateur company. They became like family to me. Even though he knew me for decades, Shekhar always used the formal 'aapni' when talking to me. When I asked him why, he said, 'That is my respect for you. The fame you earned so quickly as Chapal Rani in professional jatra is an inspiration. It took me a long time to get that respect. In fact, I am still fighting for it.' He got it too in the end, with jatras like *Gangaputra Bhishma* [Bhishma, Son of Ganga] that created a sensation.

The great theatre actress Tripti Mitra once came to see us in a jatra festival at Biswarupa theatre. She said she really wanted to see how men performed as women on stage. After the performance, she came and hugged me, 'What have you done? If you keep performing so well, we won't have any livelihood left.'

I felt like fortune was finally favouring me.

Things Fall Apart

But what I did not realize then that the flip side of success was envy.

In 1964, we had gone to Dooars, the floodplains that lead to the hills in North Bengal. We had six days of shows scheduled in a town called Haldibari. The first day was supposed to be *Bilwamangal*. But it rained incessantly, the stage was ruined, there were pools of mud everywhere. As a result, the performance was cancelled. The next day, it was bright and sunny. They announced that *Bilwamangal* would be staged with Arun Dasgupta and me in the lead. But in the afternoon the storm clouds gathered, the rains started and soon the stage area was flooded again and the performancc was cancelled yet again. The people who had booked the show grumbled that *Bilwamangal* was ill-starred and told us to choose something else.

At that time, four of us actors, Arun Dasgupta, Shekhar Ganguly, Manoj Kumar and I would share a room. We called it a fleet—a large room, with four beds in four corners, with mosquito nets.

We had become very close friends, or so I thought. We would buy chicken and I would cook a curry. After the show, we would heat it up and eat dinner together and chat about this and that. Country chicken was lean and tasty, unlike the bland fat broiler chickens we got in the city. Sometimes in the jungles of North Bengal we would even get jungle fowl—a much tougher, gamier meat.

The next day, Arun-da stayed back in the room while the rest of us went to the market to have some tea. On the way back, we heard the announcement on a loudspeaker 'Tonight at 6, instead of *Bilwamangal*, come and see *Sonar Bharat* with Arun Dasgupta, Chapal Rani, Shekhar Ganguly and Manoj Kumar.'

I was happy. In *Sonar Bharat*, I played the mother, Purnima. Shekhar played the son, Rupchand. Both our parts were juicy ones. The audience always cheered loudly for our duo.

Manoj shook his head and said, 'Oh no! Arun-da will be pissed.' Arun Dasgupta always complained that his role in that play as Prithivraj was not flashy enough, that Purnima and Rupchand stole all the thunder. When we returned to the room, I said, 'Arun-da, have you heard the news?'

'What news?'

'The play has changed.'

'What do you mean the play has changed?'

'They are saying *Bilwamangal* is bad luck. So they will do *Sonar Bharat* today. And *Chand Bibi* tomorrow.'

If Arun Dasgupta was the leading light when it came to *Bilwamangal*, I was the star when it came to *Chand Bibi*.

I was teasing, I really had no ulterior motive. To my astonishment, Arun-da started shouting at me, calling me names, insinuating disgusting things: 'Of course, they did, you are their darling after all!' He thought I had orchestrated the whole switch with Shekhar because I was very popular with the booking agents in North Bengal.

Makhan-babu said, 'Forget it, Arun is upset because he wants more money. And I can't pay him what he wants. I have a troupe to run, after all. I think he will probably go to another group next season. This is all drama leading up to that.'

But that was the end of our friendship. Arun-da and I still acted together in all the plays that had made us famous. The audience never understood that in reality there was nothing between us any more, not even friendship. Everything was acting.

Once, someone asked me to introduce him to them. I said, 'I cannot. We have had a falling out.'

'Falling out? With Arun Dasgupta?'

'Yes, we don't talk. We see each other but don't speak to each other. We turn our faces away.'

'Then how do you do those love scenes together? Such intimate passionate scenes!'

'That's called acting. That's what we are paid to do.'

Soon that story took a more vicious turn. Arun Dasgupta called a Natta Company meeting with Surya-babu and Makhan-babu without informing any of us who acted in the female roles.

Arun-da said that times were changing, that Natta Company needed to bring in women if it did not want to be left in the dust by the other companies. Makhan-babu and Surya-babu balked at the idea because their company had always had men playing women. But Arun-da managed to talk Makhan-babu into it, though Surya-babu said he would leave the company if such a thing came to pass.

We who played women were told it was just going to be an experiment, and though we would not act for a few shows, nothing would happen to us.

But I didn't want to get paid for sitting around. I said bluntly, 'I can't stay here and suffer this kind of humiliation. I will go somewhere else.' And I went and signed on with Nabaranjan Opera. Sonali Goswami joined Natta Company in my place. All the women who joined Natta Company came through Arun Dasgupta. That was his great coup. But the experiment flopped resoundingly. Within one month, all the bookings were cancelled. The women quit, as did Arun-da himself, and Natta Company came running back to us, pleading with us to save the day.

But by then I had signed on to Nabaranjan Opera. They had even given me an advance. The manager refused to let me go. But the owner of the company, Jibankrishna Das, told his manager, 'Let Chapal go. We can take Bina Ghosh in his place. Our company already has stars like Swapankumar and Jyotsna Dutta. We'll be fine. Chapal was the heart of Natta. They will sink without him. As the owner of one troupe, I can't let another fellow owner suffer like that.' With that, he tore up my contract.

When I went to return the advance, he refused to take it back. 'If you ever come back to us, I'll pay another thousand rupees on top of that,' he told me with a smile. I understood that day what it meant to be a true gentleman.

Years later, I heard someone shouting 'Chapal, Chapal' as I was walking down the street. I turned and saw it was Arun Dasgupta. I was stunned. 'You are talking to me?' I said.

'Why not? Oh, are you still holding on to that old grudge?'

'Well, we have both held on to it for at least four years now, haven't we?' I replied. 'You never even phoned me once.'

The Mother of All Roles

I returned to Natta Company where Brajen-babu had written a new play called *Mayur Singhasan* [The Peacock Throne], based on the story of the Mughal emperor Shah Jahan. I played the wife of his son Aurangzeb, a Hindu woman named Rukmini who becomes Rahmat-un-Nisa. That play didn't click. Natta Company started to struggle.

But my great unfulfilled desire was to play a bride. I told Brajen-babu, 'I really want to play a bride. With full bridal make-up.'

'All right,' said Brajen-babu. 'I will write the role of a bride for you. But not a Bengali bride. A Rajputani bride. And you can dress to the hilt.'

Then he came up with *Chitor Lakshmi*, set in the fortress town of Chittor in Rajasthan. I would play the Rajasthani bride Kamalmir. Excitedly, I started planning the costumes and jewellery. I looked up outfits and ordered a red skirt. It was different from the Chand Bibi–type parts where I would have to thunder, 'I am Chand Bibi.' This was a coy bride, a Rajasthani belle, a kind of character I rarely got to play onstage.

Suddenly, one day, Makhan-babu said, 'Chapal, we have a problem.'

'What?'

'The problem is with the part of Lakshmibai.'

'What can I do about that? It's not my role.'

'See, there are five of you women in the company. You, Harigopal, Phani, Shukhoranjan and Nemai.'

'We are not women, we are men.'

'Whatever. Five of you, five female characters. If you play Kamalmir, who will play Lakshmi?'

Lakshmi was the queen mother of Chittor.

Makhan-babu sighed and said, 'I am sorry, but you will have to play the queen mother.'

I was aghast. 'Me? I am so young. Why do I have to play the mother?'

'Well, you played the mother in *Lohar Jaal*.'

'That was the fourth wife. This one is a mother with a grown son.'

We argued back and forth but to no avail.

'Look Chapal, everyone has a role. Phani has a part. Nemai is playing the Chittor Goddess. If you are to play Kamal, what will Harigopal play? Harigopal has never played a mother on stage. He won't be able to manage it. He has a slim figure. He's used to singing roles. You can pull off both mother and coy young girl. You are so much more versatile. Only you can do the mother justice.' He laid on the flattery.

I protested loudly. 'This is not fair. How can I play Sujit-babu's mother? I just joined the company not so long ago. And he's a veteran. And why should I leave the heroine's role? I was the one who asked Brajen-babu for it.'

'Even Brajen-babu says we have to do it this way.'

I had to give in finally, but I still tried to wrest what I could out of it.

'But I won't wear these costumes that you have.'

'Oh, what do you want to wear?'

'I have seen how my mother played a widowed Rajputani in *Dhatri Panna*. I want a skirt of very fine white cloth. It can't look like a petticoat. It must be pleated and billow when I spin in it. And a full sleeved white blouse with a white veil. I'll have to get some white in my hair.'

'You dress however you like. Just play Lakshmi.'

And that was that. Ultimately, the role of Lakshmi ended up being the best received role in the production. But I still felt sad that I didn't get to play a bride.

I complained to Brajen-babu: 'Now that I've had to play Sujit-babu's mother onstage, who will accept me in other kinds of roles?'

'Don't you worry,' he told me. 'You will play a different kind of mother, one that will create a sensation. Just see what I am writing next for you.'

'Whose mother?'

'Kaikeyi, Lord Ram's stepmother.'

The play was *Bharat Biday* [Farewell to Bharat]. That's a role I can never forget. It was based on the Ramayan, but Brajen-babu had entirely reimagined the epic. I played Queen Kaikeyi. In the story we are used to, she is the villain of the piece. She forces her husband, King Dasharath, to send his eldest son, Prince Ram, into exile for 14 years, so that her own son, Bharat, can ascend to the throne. But in this version, Kaikeyi loves Ram as much as, if not more than, her own son.

But she becomes the victim of circumstances. Sage Vishwamitra needs Ram to go to war against evil forces for 14 years. He asks King Dasharath first, but Dasharath refuses. Furious, Vishwamitra goes to Kaikeyi and reminds her that when the king's body was covered with sores, she had nursed him and cleaned his pus and blood. For that he had promised to grant her two boons. Vishwamitra tells Kaikeyi the time has come to ask for those boons.

KAIKEYI. Do you want these two boons?

VISHWAMITRA. Yes.

KAIKEYI. Then as the heavens, earth and underworld are my witnesses, I swear Great Sage Vishwamitra, that I, as the wife of King Dasharath, will fulfil the desires that he could not. Tell me, what boons do you wish for me?

VISHWAMITRA. The first boon will end the great celebrations and fanfare happening throughout the kingdom to mark the rajabhishek, the royal consecration of Prince Ram. That must be stopped. Instead, there will be a rajabhishek of your son Bharat.

Kaikeyi laughs hysterically.

KAIKEYI. What are you saying? You are a man of such learning. Bharat is a mere boy. What does he know of warcraft? How much experience has he of statecraft? Does he even know how to sit on a throne and tend to his subjects? How can you say that the king should announce his consecration and not Ram's?

VISHWAMITRA. There is more. This is merely my first request. And do not forget, Queen Kaikeyi, that you have promised to fulfil my desires. You have given your word.

KAIKEYI. What is the second boon you want from me?

VISHWAMITRA. That for 14 years, Ram will go into exile in the forest.

KAIKEYI (*screams*). No! What are you saying? I have raised Ram from when he was a baby. I have nursed him, fed him the milk from my breast. How will I send my beloved Ram into exile for 14 years?

VISHWAMITRA. You must. The forces of evil are rising. I need to marshal the Aryan forces against them. And I need Ram and only Ram for that. Tell me whether you will ask for these boons from King Dasharath.

KAIKEYI. No. I cannot. If I ask for this, the heavens will break over the king. Who knows if he will even survive the shock. I cannot ask for this. I cannot. Please ask me for some other boon, anything else, Great Sage.

VISHWAMITRA. You have given your word to Great Sage Vishwamitra. Do you not know who he is?

KAIKEYI. I know the Great Sage Vishwamitra. But perhaps you do not know the Great Queen Kaikeyi. O Great Sage, you have sat in some remote caves and worshipped God. I have lived in this busy world and worshipped my husband. You cannot harm even my little finger. With just a grain of the sindoor from the

parting in my hair I can turn you into a heap of ash.
But I will not do that. Ask me for something else.

But it is to no avail. What has to be will be. She tells Vishwamitra that because of this cruel boon he was demanding of her, the world would forever think that stepmothers are heartless. He reassures her that one day the world will come to know of her sacrifice but for now she will have to act that way.

VISHWAMITRA. You will have to bear this for 14 years. When Ram goes into exile, you must not shed one tear. If you weep, Ram and King Dasharath will understand this was an all act.

KAIKEYI. How can I? Can a mother ever stop her tears?

But he is unmoved. On the night before Ram leaves, Kaikeyi keeps vigil.

KAIKEYI. O cursed night, sleep on. Dawn, do not break. O Sun, do not rise, may you never wake. At first light Ram will leave for the forest. All Ayodhya will be wrapped in darkness. May that black day never come.

Kaikeyi adored Ram. When the four princes came home with four brides, she wanted to be the one who welcomed Ram and Sita home by doing the baran ceremony to welcome him. She pleaded with Ram's own mother Kaushalya to go away and let her welcome Ram home. And Kaushalya laughingly agreed: 'All right, you are more Ram's mother than me. You do the baran for him.'

That allowed me to finally settle a long outstanding grievance. I had never forgotten how I had been told that I could not do the baran scene like Chhabi Rani. That had rankled for years.

I even told Brajen-babu, 'I want you to write a play that's tailored for me.'

'You mean one where you will be in the title role?' he asked.

'That would be wonderful,' I said. 'But whether I have the title role or not, I have one and only one request. That role must come with a baran sequence. And it cannot be some ordinary baran sequence. It has to be regal, it needs to be gorgeous. It must be the mother of all barans.'

He was astounded. 'What are you saying? You are going to tell me what to write and what not to write!' He was a renowned playwright, an expert in history, the headmaster of a high school and I was a nobody.

I hurriedly said, 'No, no, I don't have the temerity to do that. People keep bringing up Chhabi Rani's famous baran scene. I need to show them Chapal Rani can do it too.'

Finally, I had my baran sequence. A baran set in a palace, no less. We wrapped the trays in foil so that they looked like silver. Then we placed all kinds of things on them—saris, fruits, clay lamps with their wicks doused in ghee. I planned it all down to the last detail. We didn't use a match to light the lamp. We did it the way they must have done thousands of years ago—with a flaming torch.

Chhabi Rani's famous baran sequence had lasted 20 minutes. I made sure mine lasted at least 30, sometimes 40. The whole play was about three hours long. Some days, if we were in a rush, I was told to cut it short—but that scene became famous.

In it, I would greet Sita and say, 'Child, I am Ram's mother too. And now your mother as well. Raise your head and look at me.'

At that moment there would be a thunderclap. I told the musicians the exact moment it needed to happen. I would raise the lamp and exhale sharply so that it would go out without the audience understanding how it had happened. At that moment, the thunder would rumble, there would be dramatic music, Kaikeyi would shudder and Sita would gasp in horror at the ill omen and fall into Kaikeyi's arms while Ram gazed into her eyes. It was always a moment of high drama and entirely choreographed by me.

The audience just loved that scene. I told Makhan-babu, 'Now call everyone and show them what a baran scene looks like. Ask them if Chhabi Rani's famous baran scene in *Pratishodh* can stand next to Chapal Rani's baran scene in *Bharat Biday*.'

That role was a powerhouse. Kaikeyi would be in a black sari and a black blouse, her hair cascading down, the red sindoor in the parting of her hair burning bright. It was so arduous that in the summer I would be soaked in sweat. So I had another identical outfit that I could immediately change into.

In the final scene, when Ram, Lakshman and Sita leave the palace to go into exile, King Dasharath and Queen Kausalya are weeping and beating their chests. An angry Lakshman calls Kaikeyi a witch, not a mother. And I face the audience—one eye filled with tears, the other eye blazing fire and hold these two duelling expressions until Ram, Lakshman and Sita depart. It was exhausting and it left me drained every time.

Finally, I would be alone on the stage—no music, just the sound of one lonely violin. Kaikeyi, utterly dishevelled, sits clutching the royal robes Ram, Lakshman and Sita had left behind when they went into exile. Kaikeyi feels them, smells them, holds them close and finally screams 'Oh my Ram, oh my Sita.'

At that moment, the three conspirators—Vishwamitra, the wicked maid Manthara and Kumati enter.

VISHWAMITRA. What is this, Kaikeyi? Do I see tears in your eyes?

KAIKEYI (*laughs*). What tears, O Sage? I am laughing. See I am laughing. These are tears of joy. But why did Sita go? She is a foolish girl. Why did she go into exile as well? I had not asked her to go.'

Once I lost my voice. I didn't know how I would scream 'Ram, Ram' hysterically. Panchu Pal, our great clarionet player, came to my rescue. 'Don't worry, Chapal,' he told me. 'You just say Ra—, I'll manage the rest with my clarionet.' He matched his clarionet so well to my voice that the audience never understood what we had done.

What a role it was. My lips had to say one thing, but my eyes had to convey something completely different. And I had to depict that conflict that raged inside her mind through my expression. That role gave me so much fame that, when the script was published, Brajen-babu dedicated it to me and Phani Bhattacharya who played the role of the wicked maid Manthara.

Of course, some complained about the way Brajen-babu had reinterpreted Kaikeyi's character. But that might have been the greatest role I ever did in my jatra career, even more extraordinary than Chand Bibi.

The Dancing Girl and the Old Monkey

When I had started at Natta Company, I was a complete greenhorn. *Chand Bibi, Bilwamangal, Mayur Singhasan* and *Bharat Biday / Mahiyasi Kaikeyi* had raised me to unimaginable heights. I learnt a lot at Natta Company—it made me Chapal Rani.

But, eventually, we fell out.

It happened with *Sultana Riziya*. By then Shekhar Chatterjee, our leading actor, had left Natta after being wooed by other companies. Makhan-babu reorganized the troupe. He took loans to make it even more big-budget. He lured in some big names of the day and got them to sign on—Purnendu Sekhar Bandyopadhyay, Sujit Pathak and Manoj Kumar.

But the new actors like Sujit Pathak didn't want to play the big roles in all the productions. They found it too exhausting. In *Bharat Biday*, Sujit refused to play Bharat. He just wanted to play a side role of a charioteer. Purnendu Sekhhar also turned down the villain's role in *Chand Bibi*, opting to play the elephant keeper who had only two scenes.

These big artists wanted a starring role in a couple of productions and take it easy during the others. As a result, Manoj and I had to work like dogs to make up for them. Finally, I too decided I had had enough. I told Makhan-babu, 'I won't play Rukmini in *Mayur Singhasan* any more. I want to play Nadira.' The whole play rested on Rukmini's shoulders while Nadira had only three scenes. Makhan-babu said curtly, 'Do what you feel is best. But if the troupe goes down, none of you will be spared.'

The new play of the season was *Sultana Riziya* and I was excited about that. By now, I who had started at 100 rupees was earning 6,000 rupees a month. In 1965, that was a lot of money. I was very much in demand, my looks were at their peak. I would behave like a diva too. I was arrogant, demanding this and that. I went to Madras and bought jewellery. The ornaments from Madras, golden or studded with gems, were famous for looking very realistic and were used in many films, especially mythological ones.

When Brajen-babu was writing *Riziya*, I made a demand. 'Don't make Riziya appear in the very first scene. Have her enter in the third.'

Brajen-babu raised his eyebrows. 'I am the playwright. This is my play. And you are telling me when my heroine should appear!'

'No, no,' I said hurriedly. 'I was just thinking that if you show her from the very beginning, there won't be any element of surprise. The audience needs that.' He looked at me thoughtfully and said nothing. But when the play was done, I saw that Sultana Riziya made her entrance in the fourth scene.

I worked hard on that role. At first, Riziya hates being a woman. She dresses like a man in pyjamas and kurta, ties her hair in a bun like a Sikh man. Slowly, her feminine side emerges when she falls in love with Yakub, an Abyssinian man. The role actually required four wigs. People could not keep their eyes off me when I stepped on stage in the feminine outfits.

There was a scene where Yakub has been thrown into prison and Riziya comes to meet him. I would wear a skin-coloured body suit under my outfit, my hair wavy and feminine. And on top of that a very sheer net outfit. It was as if she was nude underneath it. I wish I had that photograph still. Riziya wants to seduce him but Yakub rejects her.

YAKUB. I do not want to see you like this

RIZIYA. Then how do you want to see me? Did you not say you wanted to marry me?

YAKUB. That was to come close to you.

RIZIYA. Then everything you told me in the palace was a lie. Fine. I am going to appoint you a guard of my horses. You will come every day with a horse. And I will put my foot on your hand and climb on top of the horse and go for a ride.

The jatra version had deviated a lot from the play to make it more audience-friendly. In the novel and the play by Baradaprasanna Guha Ray, Riziya is shown as hating men. She spent her time with the women of the harem. In fact, the novel had very little by way of romance though she is always meant to marry Altumiya. But in the jatra version, they needed more romance. That upset some purists. Such changes were common. When *Alibaba*, the first play I ever did, became a Hindi film, it was nothing like the story in Arabian Nights. In that, Morjina was a slave girl, Alibaba was her master, married to Fatema and Hossein was their son. In the film, Alibaba and Morjina were shown as lovers!

At one production of *Riziya* outside Kolkata, an elderly man came to meet me. He remembered an old production with the famous actress Tarasundari. That Riziya was nothing like this Riziya. The elderly man came to the dressing room after the show: 'I enjoyed the production but the Riziya character was not quite right.' I asked why. He said, 'I remember Tarasundari's Riziya. Tarasundari was Riziya and Riziya was Tarasundari. This Riziya was more of a dancing girl—a Riziyabai.' Everyone burst out laughing except me. I felt like someone had smeared cow dung all over my face. In retrospect, I feel perhaps I should not have done Riziya. Some roles just carry the indelible stamp of some artists. Riziya was one such role for Tarasundari.

At that time, stung, I said, 'Do you think that Riziya has lost her dignity because of the way she has been reimagined? Or do you think there was something lacking in my performance?'

The man replied, 'No, no, I don't blame you at all. You did what you could with what you had been given. But what kind of Riziya was this?'

My mood was off. The big-name stars were not pulling their weight. Actors kept changing, so the group was not gelling and we were struggling to connect with the audience. It all came to a head in Medinipur. The first night was *Bharat Biday*. That went off well. The next night was *Sultana Riziya*. That was a flop. On the third night we staged *Chand Bibi*. Everyone acted terribly. On top of that, Surya-babu, despite my protestations, had shoved in a singing scene with a boy who messed up his lines. The more I tried to cover up, the more flustered he got. The audience started booing and jeering. We somehow finished that show. But I lost my temper and told Surya-babu, 'Instead of sitting there like a block of stone, like some old Shiva idol, why not teach the actors to act?' Those words, uttered in a moment of frustration, would come back to haunt me.

After a production of *Sultana Riziya* in the steel town of Jamshedpur, all Natta Company shows were stopped. Sujit Pathak was sent packing. Makhan-babu summoned me, said he needed to have an urgent talk about the company.

As soon as I got there, Makhan-babu started rattling out one complaint after another against me. He said I was not cooperating with the group and deliberately acting poorly. I tried to protest but he paid me no heed. 'You are a traitor,' he said. 'An elderly gentleman came to meet you to try and teach you something but you insulted him!' I tried to explain that someone was filling his ears with poison but by then he was past listening. He said I had even made a learned man like Brajen Dey look like a fool in front of the public. Then he showed me a letter Brajen-babu had allegedly written: 'I could never imagine that Chapal could become so arrogant. I wrote the play *Riziya* centred on him, and he goes around criticizing it everywhere, telling audience members openly that this Riziya is not the old Riziya. I have learnt a bitter lesson. I will no longer write a woman-centric play after this. Chapal did not give me my due respect.'

I had done no such thing. Later, Brajen-babu's son Tarun told me, 'Let bygones be bygones, I don't think my father could have ever have written a letter like that.' Tarun truly felt that. He always treated me with great respect, he even invited me to his daughter's wedding.

'But I never said any such thing to Brajen-babu,' I protested to Makhan-babu.

'You must have. On top of that you called Surya-mama an old monkey.'

'Monkey! Shame on me. How can I use a word like that about the man from whom I have learnt my acting? I told him: you are sitting like an impassive Shiva idol in this green room and not looking at what's happening on stage—who is working hard and who is cutting corners and letting us all down.'

'You are lying. Everyone heard what you said.'

I realized there was nothing I could do. There was a conspiracy at work against me. Actors like Arun Dasgupta who did not want men to act in female roles any more had been leading the charge against me already. Those who had resented me in my early days were now even more envious of my name and fame. They thought I had risen too fast and wanted to clip my wings. They had found their chance.

'What do I need to do?' I asked.

Makhan-babu silently handed me a piece of paper. It was a new contract.

'27th of November 1967. I, Chapal Bhaduri, promise that from today I will act with good intent, and the manager and owner will evaluate my performances. If they think the performance is not up to par, I will be taken off during the course of the performance itself. A junior actress will replace me on stage, and I will sit in the audience and watch the play.'

I read the contract and said softly, 'This is not a contract. Only a fool would sign this. And only those who want to drive someone out based on the lies of others would draw up a contract like this. You will rip my costumes off me, and I will have to sit there and watch someone else act in them. This is just meant to insult me, nothing else. I am not signing this. Goodbye.'

'Fine. Don't sign. But you must return all the money you got as an advance. You must return it within three hours.'

I went to Nabaranjan Opera and promised I would work for them the next season and asked for an advance. In three hours, I rustled up 6,000 rupees and gave it to Makhan-babu and severed my connections with Natta Company, people I had considered family for over a decade.

I left with my head held high. But after I got home, I was so upset I came down with fever and diarrhoea. For days I lived on cans of chicken soup from New Market and bread and apples.

I ate so many apples, I think I stank of apples. It felt like I had torn out a part of myself.

As soon as I left Natta, Arun Dasgupta brought in his favourite actresses, like Shonali Dasgupta and Shanta Dasgupta. But wherever they went, they faced angry audiences who wanted to know: 'Where is our Phani-babu? Where is our Rani, Chapal Rani? Where is Harigopal?' Booking agents stopped paying up. At his wits' end, Arun-babu persuaded Makhan-babu to split Natta Company into two troupes. Natta 1 would only have women playing female roles. Natta 2 would have men playing those roles. But it was all in vain. None of the experiments worked. Eventually, Natta 1 shut down and Natta 2 dropped the 2 from its name. By then, I was already at Nabaranjan Opera.

When I had completed almost 10 years at Natta Company, I remember Makhan-babu telling me, 'This is indeed huge, that you've been with one group for so long.'

'You know what I wish,' I replied. 'I wish to be with this company all my life. Now I play heroines. When I am old, I will play crones. But I will be with Natta Company.'

Surya-babu smiled and repeated his favourite adage: '*Diye dhon dekhe mon, kerey nitey kotokhon*. Everything is fleeting. Don't fool yourself into thinking life will go according to your wishes all the time. It does not take long for everything to change.'

'Why are you saying this?' I asked.

'One day you will understand,' he replied.

Now I did.

I had started at 100 rupees a month. I ended my run at Natta at 6,000. I spent money like there was no tomorrow—on jewellery, clothes, beauty products. I thought nothing of putting down an advance of 1,000 rupees, a lot of money in those days, for a Benarasi sari. I thought I was a hot commodity.

When I had first joined Natta Company, I was clueless about the jatra world. They took care of every little thing, even telling me what tram to take from my house and how much the rickshaw would cost.

'What do you do in the afternoon?' Makhan-babu had asked me.

'Nothing much.'

'Rehearsals start at 4 or 5. Do you think you can come earlier?'

'For what?'

'See that big iron trunk over there. All the scripts are stored inside. Every day, take out a new one and read it like a story book. Start with *Raja Devidas*. Read it for a couple of days and only after that memorize your lines. You need to get up to speed quickly.'

That's what I would do. I would go there after lunch and spend all afternoon reading and practising, perfecting my enunciation. Reading all those scripts helped me get a sense of the characters much better than most did. I understood the context. I could then think a lot more about how to make my characters come to life.

Sometimes it was hard to manage lunch early at home and get to Natta Company on time. When he heard that, Makhan-babu said, 'Tell people at home not to worry. You will eat with us.'

At that time, his mother was still alive. She loved me dearly. I can still recall the catfish stew she would make with fresh green cilantro.

Surya-babu, Makhan-babu and Brajen-babu—they made me what I am. Makhan-babu steeped me in the world of jatra. Surya-babu taught me so much. He corrected my pronunciation. He showed me how to walk on stage, how to gesture like a queen. And Brajen-babu wrote entire characters with me in mind. I was lucky. I got their love and affection. I would have been nothing without them.

Even when I was struggling in my career, I never forgot what Surya-babu told me. 'Don't cheat on your performance ever, Chapal. Those foundations, upon which our stage is built, never cut corners there, never give it less than your all. Or you will fall through the cracks. Our jatra is our Goddess Lakshmi. Our audience is our Goddess Lakshmi. Never insult the Goddess. If despite that anyone cheats on his performance, then he is the son of a whore.'

Not long ago I was acting on stage, but my body was just not holding up. Then I remembered his words, and as God is my witness, I gave it my all.

The True Gentleman

We had a bitter parting but I can never deny Natta Company any more than I can deny my own parents. I have eaten their salt. That was where I learnt my craft. They were family to me. I never thought of it as a company. Unlike other people, I never bothered to sign and take my salary. They just gave it to me. Our trust in each other was unshakeable.

Once, when we were touring Assam, I was entranced by the fabrics I found—tussar, garad and endi silk. I marvelled at their softness. Makhan-babu overheard me praising them. When we were leaving, he got me a length of endi silk and said, 'Make a kurta for yourself with this after you return to Kolkata.'

One year, for my birthday, Makhan-babu gave me a watch. It was an Omega Tissart, a very expensive watch though I did not understand its value when he gave it to me. One day, I was going somewhere by train, and it had stopped for a long time at Tinsukia station. There was a watch engraver there and I had him inscribe my name on the back—C. Bhaduri. Years later, I presented the watch to the husband of my youngest niece. I told him he could cover the inscription with some design but he said he would let it be.

He joked later 'You made a big mistake giving me that watch.'

'Why?' I asked.

'Did you know it was a gold watch?' he said.

'You come from a family of gold merchants. No wonder you recognized its worth,' I joked but it might have been the best present I ever got.

Years after I left Natta, one day I was walking towards my sister's house when I heard someone shouting my name. I turned and saw Makhan-babu in a car. He had just picked up sweets from the famous Nakur sweet shop in North Kolkata.

'Chapal, come, come, get into the car. It's been so long. How are you doing? How is work?'

'I am sure you know everything. You must hear about it over the grapevine. I am not doing too badly. Anyway, after all these years . . .'

'Oh, forget about that. What's happened has happened.'

I got into the car. He insisted on turning it around, going back to the sweetshop and buying more sweets for me.

'There is no need to do all this,' I protested.

'Sweets are not about need. Sweets are for pleasure,' he laughed. 'Listen, Chapal, if you ever need anything, if you ever have a problem, don't hesitate to get in touch with me.'

'I am fine,' I said. 'I am working, I am getting paid. What else do I need?'

'The salaries must be lower, though.'

'That's true, but what can one do?'

'Don't forget, I am always there for you.'

He dropped me near my sister's house though he did not come inside. Perhaps he too felt awkward, remembering the bitterness of our parting.

Years later, Makhan-babu got cancer. Half his tongue had to be removed. When I heard that, I really wanted to see him. Years had passed, we had both gone our own ways and I was not sure he would want to see me any more. I knew a young man who worked in Natta Company also respected me immensely. I told him, 'Will you take me to see Makhan-babu?'

He said, 'But he can barely talk any more. It's hard to understand him, his speech is so garbled.'

I said, 'That's all right. Just tell him that Chapal Bhaduri wants to see you. And see what he says.'

I was told that he jumped up and said with gestures and garbled words, 'Bring him at once.'

So I went. So many memories were tied up with that house. Sometimes when I messed up during rehearsal and got scolded by Surya-babu, I would sulk in the dark in a corner of the veranda. Trains would pass below me and I would wonder if I should jump under the wheels of one, but then I'd pull myself back. All those memories came flooding back as I walked up the old wooden stairs to Makhan-babu.

He just sat there looking at me for a while. He looked frail and elderly. His hair had turned white. He had a scratchy white beard as well. But he still wore his simple starched khadi kurta.

I said softly, 'Can you recognize me? It's Chapal.'

His words were slurred but his joy was unmistakable. He told the young man who had escorted me, 'Chapal didn't just work here. He lived here. This was his home. In the afternoon, he would sit with Surya-mama and read all the parts and learn everything he could. And his cooking. I can't begin to tell you how much he has cooked for me.'

'Would you like me to make something for you again?' I said. Makhan-babu just smiled.

I have known many owners of many jatra companies but there was only one Makhanlal Natta.

He was a true gentleman.

INTERLUDE

In Imagination

The Other Rani

Chapal Rani, Chapal Rani, Chapal Rani.

Sometimes I think none of us other Ranis ever existed. You people have made him the queen of all queens.

But if there was Chapal Rani, there was also Bibhuti Rani and Upen Rani and Rakhal Rani and Babli Rani. And so many others. Who sings their stories?

You call Chapal Rani the last queen of jatra. But what about Kanchan Rani who took on his roles when Chapal stormed out of Natta? Did you know that when the script of *Sultana Riziya* was published, the playwright dedicated it to 'Natta Company's Rising Star—Kanchan'? Poor Kanchan, he didn't last long though. Last I heard, he was driving a cycle rickshaw somewhere.

I know Chapal started out as Morjina. But when Babli Rani danced as Morjina at the Sobhabazar Rajbari in Kolkata, the zamindar stood up and shouted 'Encore' as soon as he finished his first number. So of course he had to do it again. Then the babu said, 'Encore' again. And again and again. They could not stage the play at all that night. Babli Rani just kept dancing to that 'Chhi chhi itna janjaal' song till dawn broke.

Chapal might have had a rebirth playing the goddess Sitala on street corners, but when Jatin Rani played Manasa, the goddess who protects us from snake bites, one man grabbed him by the ankles and wailed, 'You've already taken my two sons. I have only one son left. Please don't take him away from me.' He refused to believe this was just an actor.

I am sure Chapal has told you about how superstar Uttam Kumar was bowled over by him when he played Michael Madhusudan's mother on stage. How could a man show such maternal feelings on stage? Well, I can tell you, no one could beat Phani Rani when it came to playing mothers. Phani was a little short and stout, not much to look at, but when he played a bereaved mother, there wasn't a dry eye in the house. The actor Bikash Roy was so impressed with Phani Rani's Annapurna that he sent the most famous actresses of the day, Kanan Devi and Molina Devi, to watch the play. 'You should go and learn something from Phani Rani,' he told them. As for Uttam, once he mistook Satadal Rani for a woman when he saw him in *Chandimangal*. He and Bikash Roy laid a bet about whether it was a man or a woman and Uttam lost. I wonder what the wager was.

But when it came to sheer variety, I would say Kshitish Rani was hard to beat. One day Kshitish Rani was the queen, another day he would be the queen's maid. And he would play both with such flair. I remember once he was the dancer who had to seduce and kill a man named Katlu Khan. My goodness, all the men in the audience stopped breathing when Khitish Rani did his seduction number. He would have put any of your Bollywood item dancers to shame. The Raja from Gauripur in Assam was so impressed, he gave Kshitish a gold medal. I have seen it myself.

Chapal was good-looking all right but there was a reason why Chhabi Rani was called the Elizabeth Taylor of jatra. That oval face, the beautiful fair skin, those big eyes. Yet when he was not dressed as a woman, you might think Shyamapada Roy, son of a postmaster, was a serious-minded Bengali schoolteacher in his crisp white dhoti-kurta and glasses. Once, Chhabi played a widow on stage, in a simple white sari, bare-bodied, with no blouse or inner wear. Now that was truly sensational! That was the stuff of legends. There are so many such stories that will die with me for no one cares about the lost ranis of jatra. When Sudarshan Rani came on stage as a Ceylonese princess in Mymensingh, there was a stampede and a group of men kidnapped him. The jatra had to stop till he was returned.

Don't think I have anything against Chapal. Why should I? While other ranis faded away, he managed to reinvent himself and become some kind of icon. Good for him. He was lucky that way. He had a second inning of sorts. The rest of us just ended up on the scrap heap. One day I went to work and was told: 'You don't need to come from tomorrow. We have hired an actress.' The Elizabeth Taylor of jatra would sit next to a railway station stitching petticoats for pennies. Are you surprised they didn't want to talk about the old days any more? The hurt runs deep.

They called us queen but we came to jatra because we thought it was a way out of poverty. We played women to put food on the table. Most of us had little to no education. With the money we earned, we helped our parents. We raised our own families. But in the end, when jatra threw us out, we slid right back into poverty. We got fame, adulation, gold medals but not much else. You can't cook fame, can you? The luckier ones, like Upen or Khitish, became managers of some troupe or other. It wasn't as glamorous as being a rani but it at least kept the kitchen fire going.

Rakhal Rani had a whole brood of children. But in the end, he had to melt all his medals to make some money. When that ran out, he sold peanuts on the riverfront to make ends meet.

You might think I sound resentful about Chapal Rani but you are mistaken. I am not. I am just saying weren't there other ranis who were just as deserving of a second chance? Sure, he might have had a little more schooling in him than most of us. But only a little bit more. But, as they say, in the land of the blind, the one-eyed man gets to be king. I think he was a little proud of all that Sisir Bhaduri theatre blood in him. Sisir Bhaduri might have been the Emperor of Theatre, but our audience didn't care two hoots about that. To them, Chapal Rani was a jatra queen like the rest of us. No more and no less. Why do you all do nostalgic profiles of him while the rest of us are forgotten? Do you know that the Swapankumar–Satadal Rani duo was so famous that people called them the Uttam–Suchitra of jatra? Satadal's pictures once sold for 35 rupees a piece. Who remembers Satadal now? But Swapankumar is still remembered as the King of Jatra.

I wasn't half bad, even if I say so myself. I got my start in the sakhir dal, the troupe of dancing boys that accompanied a jatra. I was quite young when I started. I had not even grown a moustache. But I could sing and dance. One of the managers noticed I had some talent and helped groom me. Yes, I had to flirt a bit and be sweet to him but as they say: to get a little, you have to give a little.

I have some old pictures saved in this album. Can you tell that's me in that sari? I remember that sari very well. It was a very beautiful yellow. I had a full set of emerald jewellery that went with it—emerald head piece, necklace with locket and wrist bands. And look at this one. I am dancing in a Mughal court here. And here I am in a social drama about a woman who has been raped by some goons and wreaks revenge. Actually, I was one of the first really modern ranis. Babli Rani and I were the ones who did the first proper socials when jatra started moving away from Ramayan-Mahabharat and history. Once, when we were performing in a village, the women wanted me to teach them how to wear a sari the modern way and do make-up. Now that was flattering!

All that is over now. No one will take a second look at me. I don't show this album to my grandchildren. My son says they won't understand it and will be very confused that their grandfather passed as a woman. He used to be very embarrassed about it when he was a boy. His friends in school would tease him that his father was a jatrawala, that his father wore saris on stage. I would tell him: don't pay attention to them, this is an art like any other, and I have to give it all my dedication.

My wife did not mind. Sometimes she even went to see the jatra. But we never discussed my work. And I didn't model myself on her either. We didn't copy women. The best among us somehow absorbed what it meant to be a woman. I was a husband and father at home and a new bride on stage. And to me it didn't feel odd at all to go from one to the other.

I think Chapal should have also got married. We all knew about his gentleman lover. I've seen him once. He was very manly. Gentlemen admirers weren't uncommon in our world. I had my share too. Men would send me expensive gifts—French perfumes, Danish biscuits, English soaps. Some of us ranis had regular admirers, sometimes more than one. I knew someone who named his special male friends by the days of the week—there was Mr Monday and Mr Wednesday and Mr Alternate Thursday. Others had special friends in different towns, like a Siliguri friend and a Durgapur friend. When the jatra reached that town, we always knew so-and-so rani would not be rooming with the rest of us.

We spent so many weeks and months on the road, it was natural for us to develop some feelings for each other. Sometimes the nights were cold and lonely, and after we had a bit of drink to warm us up, one thing would lead to another. But there was no need to talk about it. Everyone knew that so-and-so boy from the sakhir dal was the special friend of so-and-so star. Some of the heroes had an understanding with some of the ranis or the dancing boys. It was an arrangement of sorts but not something you flaunted like a medal from the Raja of Gauripur.

I never understood why Chapal felt the need to hang all his dirty laundry out to dry. And that too so late in life. I mean, he is a jatra actor, not one of these activists one sees on TV these days, waving rainbow flags. Me? I don't believe in those terms like gay and lesbian. If I identify as anything now, it's as a married man.

It's not like Chapal's gentleman friend didn't get married and raise a family. What did Chapal gain by standing by his man? In the end, blood is thicker than water. When that man threw him out, he had to go back to his own sister, didn't he? At least, if he had married and had his own family, he would have had that in his old age. Fat lot of good all his devotion did him. And who knows if he was as devoted to that one man as he claimed to be? He had many admirers sniffing around him. He could flirt up a storm when he wanted to. In his youth, he was quite the looker, that I will readily admit.

But people don't realize that looks fade. They think their beauty will last forever. That these men will buzz around them like honeybees even when they are 50 and 60 and 70. But men are opportunists. In the end, they will go crawling back to wife and children with their tails between their legs. I always knew that. That's why, no matter what little fun and games I have had with some of my gentleman admirers, I never let it get in the way of my family life. I can proudly say there was never any other woman in my life other than my wife.

There was one gentleman who was really besotted with me. He would follow me from town to town. He would book hotel rooms for me. He would ask me to dress as a woman even when we were together in private and write me love letters. I can't say it wasn't exciting and flattering. But both of us knew that it was just a game, that one day it would end. And it did. It hurt for a while but then I got used to it. I burnt all the letters.

This is Bengal, not London or America. Our societies are different. Our values are different. I tried to tell Chapal this once when we met at some jatra festival the government had organized. And you should have seen how snippy he got with me.

'I don't care what you think,' he told me. 'I am not going to apologize for my life. Or hide in the shadows, living some lie with a wife and children. It's not like I have done anything that's a crime.'

As if I was doing something that was a crime! I mean, look at me, I am a very respectable person. I married, had two children, got them both married. I have done my duty, haven't I? Is that a crime? Meanwhile, he lives in an old-age home.

At least I have my own house, even if it's a 90-minute train ride from Kolkata. No one in my neighbourhood knows I was once a rani but that's OK. My daughter-in-law takes care of me. My son is there when I need to go to the doctor. I am fortunate.

Chhabi Rani, for all that beauty, had nothing in his old age. He would stitch petticoats and sell them in the market, never telling anyone who he was. Phani Rani was such a great actor that when he played a villainous role, people would throw their shoes at him. Yes he couldn't afford his blood-pressure medicines at the end. Haripada Rani was so famous for his roles in *Badshah Alamgir* and *Saiba*. He had such a golden touch, they would call him Jatra Lakshmi. In the end, he didn't have enough money to take care of his family. His wife and son found him hanging from a tree one morning. He had tried several times before but failed. Once, he threw himself into the river with a pot tied around his neck, but a fisherman saved him. Another time, he tried to hang himself from a bamboo pole but it broke. This time he succeeded. So much for the glamorous life of the jatra ranis. That Kanchan did the right thing, leaving jatra to drive a cycle rickshaw. Pulling a rickshaw, selling vegetables, running a tea shop, all that was better than the life of a jatra rani if you ask me. I realized that too but by then it was much too late for me.

Now there is no one I can talk to about that life any more. For a while, I would keep in touch with some of the other ranis I had known. We would get together for a cup of tea and talk about the old times. We would tease each other about the admirers we had had. Now it's funny to think how we fought over them, stabbed each other in the back, competed for their attention. Called each other names. Now most of us are gone or too old to meet up. Our knees hurt. Some have high blood pressure, some have high blood sugar . . . Even my wife is gone. There is no one to talk to about the life I'd once led. But then my daughter-in-law brings me my morning cup of tea and I count my blessings.

Are you done looking at that album? You can take it if you like. I really have no need for it any more. That grandson of mine is very inquisitive, always poking around my cupboard. I am always nervous he will stumble upon it. I'll just keep this one picture if I may. It will remind me of the old days. Sometimes even I can hardly believe it was real.

Maybe when I am long gone my grandson will find it. He will surely not recognize me. Perhaps he will think it's some woman his grandfather once loved in secret.

He won't be entirely wrong.

6

The Post-Natta Years

The Mother

I was nervous. The year was 1968. I had just left Natta Company in high dudgeon and joined Nabaranjan Opera. But I was not sure if I could live up to the name and fame I had earned at Natta. Natta had made me a star. Could I shine as bright without it?

The first role Nabaranjan handed me was Jahnavi, mother of poet Michael Madhusudan Dutt. Swapankumar, the proprietor, was a legend in the world of jatra, and a very arrogant man. When I started rehearsing for the part, he said, 'Not like that. This is not Natta Company. This is a jatra troupe from Kolkata.' Swapankumar thought of Natta as somewhat provincial, peddling melodrama for less sophisticated audiences. Nabaranjan was based out of the Chitpur neighbourhood in North Kolkata, the city's jatra heartland.

Jatra offices lined both sides of a busy thoroughfare, down which trams trundled all day. The trams have stopped along that route now. But the booking offices still line the street, for jatra companies with names like Agnibeena Opera, Sandhyadeep Opera, Agragami Opera. Despite those grand operatic names, they're just small, brightly painted storefronts tucked between lithography stores, book binders and print shops. The more successful companies might have a dusty cabinet filled with trophies and cups. Most have little more than a desk and a few plastic chairs under a row of framed gods and goddesses adorned with tinsel garlands, the kind that festoon Christmas trees.

Garishly Technicolor posters of the latest productions line the walls and hang crookedly from trees and lampposts outside, advertising the season's latest jatras, their bright reds, shiny golds and neon blues lurid against the faded old buildings along the street. The jatra names are flowery, and written out in elaborate Bengali curlicues—*Srimati Rajkumari Bhalobashar Bhikhari* [Miss Rajkumari, Beggar for Love], *Gharer Lakshmi Parer Bou* [Goddess at Home, Wife on Loan], *Shantir Sansarey Shakunir Pasha* [The Vulture's Gambit in the Fine Family], *Aamar Jeebon Protishodher Bigyapan* [This Life of Mine, an Advert for Revenge Most Vile], *Kajallatay Kaalkeute* [Cobra in the Kohl Container] . . .

Head shots of the stars jostle with each other on the posters—leering men in sunglasses pointing guns, wild-eyed women brandishing swords, weeping mothers in red-bordered white saris, brides bedecked in red and gold and buxom seductresses flashing their cleavage in tight sleeveless dresses. Now there is no shortage of women in jatra, and their names are splashed on the posters too—Madam Aparajita, Miss Arati, Miss Priyanka, alongside 'super singing star Abhiraj'. Some vestiges of the old world remain, like Diamond Library, a bookstore that specialized in jatra scripts. Their flyers tell us to read jatra plays and save our culture. But most of the companies I worked with and knew are long gone. And most of the scripts I'd worked with are out of print as well. Even Diamond Library, established in the 1870s, no longer stocks them.

My first play with Nabaranjan Opera was *Michael Madhusudan*.

Michael Madhusudan Dutt had a life that was just filled with drama. Lover of Byron's poetry, he was the man who brought blank verse and sonnets into Bengali. A convert to Christianity, he was disinherited by his father for his rebellious ways. The Bengali establishment didn't know what to make of the tempestuous young genius who had a married a woman of European descent. Many great actors have played him on stage and on screen, including Sisir Bhaduri, and also Ahindra Chaudhuri and Utpal Dutt. Our director Swapankumar was playing Michael. I was playing Michael's mother Jahnavi, driven out of her mind by the bitter fight between father and son. At first, she is like any well-to-do nineteenth-century housewife. I dressed in a white sari with a red border and a white blouse, simple gold jewellery and the white shankha and red pola bangles that married Hindu women wear. Then, everything starts to fall apart as she slowly goes mad with grief for her son. Dark circles appear below her eyes, she stops caring about the way she dresses, wanders about in a torn sari. It was not a glamorous role but one that any actor would relish.

Bina Ghosh, a big star of the stage, had made the role famous.

Swapankumar told me to think deeply about the character and figure out how to put my own stamp on it instead of trying to copy Bina. Though young, I didn't mind playing the mother's role. Perhaps because I had lost my own mother so young, I found solace in mother roles.

I added my own touches. There is a scene where Jahnavi, half-mad, recites a line from an old nursery rhyme about the moon. Bina Ghosh would drag those lines out. I decided to sing them like a lullaby as I exited the stage. I had to show her heart breaking when her husband disowns their son but only through my facial expression, without speaking a word. In those days, as a wife, she could not go against her husband. As father and son fight and tempers rise, she keeps looking from one to the other, back and forth, back and forth, conveying her turmoil just through her eyes.

In another scene, a tear has to trickle down my face but only from one eye. At first, I could not manage it. Tears would come out of both eyes. 'I cannot do this,' I told the director.

'You need to figure it out,' he said, 'We will support you in every possible way. I have asked the light person to focus on you, so the audience can see your full face.'

'I will try, but it might take a while.'

'You need to do this, Chapal. Keep practising at home. I cannot tell you how to. You need to figure it out for yourself.'

I finally figured it out, but it was so stressful I almost had a nervous breakdown.

The dialogues by Bidhayak Bhattacharya were magnificent.

JAHNAVI. O Madhu, I am your mother. I want nothing from you, my son. Nothing. I just want a little peace, I beg of you.

MADHUSUDAN (*springing up in bed in his own house*). Ma, Ma.

HENRIETTA (*his wife*). What's the matter, darling?

MADHUSUDAN. I saw flames everywhere, and in the middle of them, my mother calling out to me—Madhu, Madhu.

Those scenes would give me goosebumps. The audience loved them, so Swapankumar was happy. *Michael Madhusudan* became a huge hit. He toured with it for four years straight, one year with Bina Ghosh and three years with me. We even staged it in the huge stadium in Cuttack.

In 1970 or '71, we staged it in Kolkata, at the famous Rabindra Sadan theatre.

There were VIP guests that night—Uttam Kumar, superstar of Bengali cinema, and his leading lady, Supriya Devi. They had come as Swapankumar's special guests. Swapankumar was the king of jatra and Uttam Kumar was the king of movies. Uttam was a mega star, he couldn't walk into the theatre without being mobbed. So he drove up to the back entrance in a car with tinted windows and stood quietly in the wings. The jatra had already started by the time he arrived.

My character had just three or four scenes. I was done within an hour and a half. When my part was over, Uttam Kumar said he wanted to meet the person who had acted as Jahnavi.

The manager took me to him. He was still standing by the wings. By then I had removed my make-up and costume and was in ordinary clothes, white rayon pants and a short-sleeved shirt. Uttam Kumar looked annoyed and said, 'Not him, I want to meet the actress who played the mother.'

That person who had brought me to him said, 'This is Chapal. He played the mother. He is Ketaki Dutta's younger brother. He has made quite a name for himself in the world of jatra.'

'Yes,' I said, 'I played Jahnavi.'

Uttam stared at me for a minute in surprise and then embraced me tightly. My heart was racing. My head was spinning. I felt I couldn't breathe. This was the chest on which the legendary actresses of Bengal, Suchitra Sen, Sabitiri Chatterjee, Supriya Devi, had all rested their heads in famous romantic scenes. Supriya Devi was standing right next to him. And yet it was I who was in Uttam Kumar's arms! I could not believe it was true!

I suddenly remembered a conversation from many years ago. My mother had started doing a lot of work in films. Sometimes, after coming back from work, she would sit on her big bed with its pristine white sheets and chat about her day with my father. Precocious as I was, I would sit there between them, shamelessly eavesdropping. One day, my mother said, 'There is this new boy who's come into films. I see in him what the actor Durgadas Banerjee also has. Glamour. Charisma. His real name is Arun but he calls himself Uttam. I think he will go far.' My mother clearly had a good eye when it came to actors. Like a jeweller, she knew how to how to tell a real jewel from a fake one.

Then Uttam Kumar looked into my eyes and said, 'Are you married?'

'No,' I replied.

He stared at me in amazement.

'You are unmarried?'

'Yes.'

'So you are neither a father nor a mother. How then did you evoke such maternal feeling, such tenderness? How? That heart-wrenching scream "Madhu"?' he looked into my eyes, holding my face in his hands.

I looked back at him and repeated my mother's favourite line: '*Aami ja noyi ta hòyei ami obhinoy korchi*'—I have to become what I am not, that's called acting.

'What can I give you?' Uttam asked me. 'Tell me, what you would like?'

'Nothing, just your blessings so that I might act even better.'

I have no photograph of that night, no autograph. All I can say is I will never receive a greater award for my acting.

But there was a fallout. Someone told Swapankumar that Uttam Kumar had been standing in the wings and talking to me instead of watching his performance. Swapankumar was annoyed, but couldn't tell me anything directly. Instead, he started shouting at everyone else: 'I heard some people took Uttam Kumar to the wings while the show was on. I won't tolerate such behaviour in my troupe.'

'Forgive me. I was the one who was talking to him,' I said. 'It was probably just three minutes, maybe less. We just stood and talked. You can do whatever you want. If you want to beat me with your slippers, please do. If you want to throw me out of the troupe, that's your right. After all, this is your troupe.'

Later, Swapankumar calmed down, 'I hope you are not angry with me.'

I had to be very careful not to ruffle feathers. At one point, Nabaranjan Opera wanted to tour North Bengal. Swapankumar may have been the King of Jatra, but his troupe had never really toured North Bengal before. I, on the other hand, was a veteran of those parts from my days with Natta Company.

When we reached Siliguri, I was shocked. 'O Haren-da,' I told one of the organizers. 'What have you done?'

'What are you talking about, Chapal?'

'Look at these festoons. Remove them at once.' We used to call those big banners festoons.

'Why? What's wrong?'

'See what's written on them. "Our famous Chapal Rani is now acting in Nabaranjan Opera's *Michael Madhusudan* as his mother Jahnavi. The great Swapankumar will play Michael." My name is above Swapankumar's! Get those banners down at once before Swapankumar arrives. He might take great offence and leave immediately.'

And rightly so. After all, he was a great actor. I have learnt a lot from him as well.

Haren-da was unmoved. 'Why? You are Chapal Rani.'

'Do not say that. He is a superstar, the king of jatra.'

'But he has never come to North Bengal. Everyone knows you all the way from here to upper Assam to lower Assam, whether Hamiltonganj or Dibrugarh.'

'No, please do not do this. Please keep this request of mine.'

'How will we announce you, then?'

'First Swapankumar's name. Then mine.'

'All right, we will announce his name first. Then everyone else's and finally we will say "And Chapal Rani".'

I had devoted friends like these everywhere. I can call them fans, I can call them admirers. I have heard many dirty insinuations about them as well. All I can say is they might have been enamoured of my looks but they were also equally enamoured of my craft. There was nothing dirty in their admiration for me.

Changing Jatra

By then, women were in all the jatra companies except Natta, the last holdout. Even Nabaranjan had its own heroine—Namita Chatterjee. But I still got my roles, old or young. Sometimes I was Madhusudan's mother. Sometimes I was the devious queen of Gaud, widowed but still youthful, ready to use her beauty to get her way. Jatra was full of young women, but there was still a shortage when it came to actors who could play the mother roles.

And once, just once, I even got to be a man on the jatra stage.

In *Raktalekha* [Written in Blood], I was playing the zamindar's wife, Nibhanani. The play was based on a film and had a dual role for the hero—two brothers, Bishu and Nishu. The problem was they had two scenes together. That was possible in film, but we were in a fix, wondering how to pull it off on stage. We looked far and wide for someone who looked like Swapankumar, but in vain. Eventually, I had to put on men's clothing and three-inch heels and become Bishu for those two scenes. They adjusted the lighting, so that people couldn't tell it was me and not Swapankumar. It was my one and only time playing a man on the jatra stage. A picture survives of me in that role, in a suit and sunglasses, a hat perched on my head. What no one can tell is that, underneath that male drag, I was dressed as a woman. It had to be that way because I needed to change from male to female in less than five minutes.

I had to tell Farhad, the hairdresser, that I needed a special wig for Nibhanani.

'What kind?'

'A hairpiece with a bun, something I can put on and take off very easily. It can't require spirit gum or something like that to keep it in place.'

I could take it off and turn into Bishu, and in the next moment, put it back on, wrap a sari around myself and become Nibhanani, the zamindar's wife.

I had worked for 10 years at a stretch for Natta. But times were changing. I moved from troupe to troupe the way football players change teams. That had become the norm of the jatra world. After Nabaranjan, I went to Satyambar Opera in 1970. I was there for about two years.

Satyambar Opera was an old company—over 110 years old. Bandana Devi used to play the mother roles for them. When she left, they asked me to come in her place. By then, the lead heroines were all being played by women.

That was not the only big change. When I started with Natta Company, jatra took place in open fields. The stage or the ashor was just a raised wooden platform, maybe two or three feet high, with a sloping ramp that led to a makeshift green room. Sometimes it had a silk curtain with the company's name on it. The ramp was not just for entry or exit. It was an extension of the stage. It could serve as the street, the way to the temple, the main road. The weeping heroine could stumble down it. The comic fool could stagger on it. Armies marched up it. And if the jatra came with a Bibek or Conscience, he might stand on that gangway and warn the characters of their folly. As one character exited, another would enter. They would cross like passers-by on the street, almost as if handing off the scene to each other.

The Petromax lights were often fastened to four poles on four corners of the ashor. Props were minimal. If there was a chair on stage, it filled in for the king's throne and the jailer's chair and a prisoner's seat and whatever else was needed. In *Mayur Singhasan*, every time Emperor Shah Jahan came on stage, we threw a piece of red velvet with a brocade border on a wooden chair and it promptly became the fabled Peacock Throne. Sometimes there were two chairs, and we used them to orient ourselves. One was front right, one was front left. If there were other props, often the actors themselves would bring them in as well as take them away.

There were no mics. That was one of the reasons men played the part of women. Audiences of ten to fifteen thousand could show up to see a jatra in an open field. The actors' voices had to carry to the last person in shows that went on for hours. Few women had voices powerful enough for that. Later, in some venues, we had mics at each end and a catcher on top. But, mostly, we just had to make do with our voices. So we learnt how to do volume control. We could scream our lungs out, but we also knew how to do romantic scenes in low voices but that could still be heard in the last row. Everything had to be over the top, lit up by those Petromax lights, and yet nothing could seem outlandishly comical.

When Shekhar and I acted in *Chintamoni*, we had some very romantic scenes together. I had to lay my head on his chest and look into his eyes. But I have seen that scene later, when a mic would dangle like an eggplant between the hero and the heroine and utterly ruin the romance. I found hanging mics unbearable. They would be raised or lowered depending on the actor's height. I would be in an intimate scene, my head resting on the hero's chest and suddenly the hero would turn his head and a microphone would materialize like a third wheel.

More importantly, I felt the dangling mics ruined the actors' concentration. They ended up paying more attention to running back and forth between the mics than to the emotion of the moment.

The acting styles also changed. When I started out, people would complain that my style was too natural and that jatra needed to be played at a higher pitch. During my early days at Natta Company, Sujit Pathak was playing the emperor and I had a small but important part as Jaharat-un-nissa. He showed me how he thought I should do it.

I listened politely and then said, 'But I will do it my way.'

Surya-babu was listening and he warned me: 'All right, but make sure it fits the jatra style.'

In one scene, Jaharat has invited her brother over for a feast for her young son Latif's birthday.

JAHARAT. O bhaijaan, you have arrived. Come, come. Please be seated. What good fortune. You have come to you sister's home after so long. Why have you not come before? I am always on your side, my brother. I have never been on my husband's side in these matters. Please sit. Let me send some sherbet with Latif. Then we can proceed to the feast.

But the emperor does not know that the sherbet the boy is carrying is laced with poison.

LATIF. Uncle, O Uncle, Mother has sent this drink. Please have some.

EMPEROR (*caresses Latif*). O my sweet nephew. How wonderful to see you. You must have some too. You drink first, then I will.

Latif takes a sip.

LATIF. O Mother, my throat is burning. O Mother, what is happening?

Latif collapses.

JAHARAT (*rushes in*). Latif, what is happening. Latif did you finish your task? Your ta—?'

I said I would not finish that last word. I would only say ta— instead of task.

Sujit Pathak complained 'No, you sound like you are doing cinema. Jatra is different.'

'I plead guilty. But I want to bring some of cinema to jatra as well. Tell me how you think your mother or wife would say those lines?'

'Are you talking about sounding natural?'

'Yes'

'Forget that. Jatra is seen by the riffraff. Jatra is all about the unnatural.'

'I cannot accept that. I cannot say those lines like that.'

He repeated the lines almost at a screech, then said, 'If you do it like that, you will surely get a round of applause.'

'This kind of unnatural delivery just to get some applause! I want to get my applause by talking naturally.'

'That will never happen.'

'Why not? I can and I will. In this very play.'

'But if you don't raise it to that pitch, I can't pick up the cue from you and do my bit.'

'You can just pick up from my "ta—" and finish the word.'

EMPEROR. Task, yes, the task is done, Sister, the task is done. Shame on you. Is this what you had invited me for?

Emperor exits. The boy's father, Farrukhsiyar, enters.

FARRUKHSIYAR. What has happened? Why is Latif lying like that? Jaharat, what has happened?

Jaharat sits as if turned to stone.

FARRUKHSIYAR (*feels Latif's pulse*). What is this? He is dead. Tell me, who has killed my Latif? Tell me, who?

Jaharat is silent.

Farrukhsiyar picks up Jaharat and shakes her. (Shantigopal, who used to play Farrukhsiyar, was thankfully a strapping man. Otherwise he could not have lifted me up like that.)

JAHARAT (*choking*). M-m-m-me.

Farrukhsiyar drops Jaharat with a thud. (He would drop me hard and it would hurt but there was a joy in that too, for in that moment he truly was my husband and I was the wife.)

We got our applause, and I had done it my way. After that, Natta Company's acting style changed. It stopped being so exaggerated. Now, everything has changed again. The old historical plays have given way to social melodramas. Perhaps it's because the old playwrights are no longer there either. Playwrights like Brajen Dey were learned men who knew their history. They are long gone.

Jatra Changing

When I began, the concert party or musicians would line up on both sides, at a slightly lower level than the actors. The musicians would set up—a harmonium on each side, the tuba, the cornet, the clarionet, violin, flute, tablas and dholaks, cymbals, bells and the three-cornered 'triangle' that you played with a stick. You needed all that for the 'jatra sound'.

Someone would hold a gong up to his ear and strike it so hard, we could feel it reverberate in our hearts. As the orchestra started tuning their instruments, we in the green room would pick up the pace and the crowd would know that was the cue to start settling down. The show was about to begin. The playbill, if there was one, was nothing but a thin cheaply printed piece of paper listing the characters and scenes. The audience would sit on the ground, on sheets of tarpaulin. The 'VIP' seats were simply folding chairs. When the 'second bell' rang out, the tempo of the music would rise, the drums would get into a frenzy, and as the music reached its climax, someone might shout 'Raja! Raja!' 'Who calls? Who dares disturb me thus?' And so the jatra would begin.

That old heritage is long lost. The sakhir dal, the chorus of young boys who would sing in the background, is long gone. That had also served as a kind of training pool for future ranis. When that was axed, that talent pool dried up. The Bibek-er gaan, the song of Conscience, is gone. The old playwrights are gone, the old directors too. The very style of acting has changed. No one became another Shekhar Ganguly or an Arun Dasgupta. Bela Sarkar was an excellent actress as was Bina Dasgupta. But they were few and far between. Even in our time, some cinema actors like Jahar Ganguly and Tulsi Chakrabarty did jatra but those were amateur shows. Then film stars started flooding in because there was money to be made. Some could sing, some could not, some could dance, some could not. Troupe owners wanted to cash in on their name and glamour, so they offered them big money. Soon, television actors followed. The real jatra actors were pushed aside. People complained that this jatra didn't feel like jatra any more. It was like watching bad cinema on stage. But the film stars kept coming. Now jatra feels like an old mansion, ruined but with a tacky coat of new paint, clinging to the memory of glory days.

For historical plays, you need actors with a certain stage presence and physique. In real life, a warrior like Prithviraj Chauhan might have been short and fat. But on screen you need someone who looks manly, like the Bollywood star Akshay Kumar. Nowadays, in jatra, I see actors and actresses who don't take care of themselves . . . the women squeezed into obscene outfits. We too had cabaret scenes but they had class. We were fully covered, except for a slit at the end so we could show our legs.

But I cannot just blame jatra. Once, my mother discovered that in one of her plays they had added a dancer who performed in a bra and skirt, making obscene gestures while the audience whistled loudly.

'The stage is my temple,' Ma told the stage manager. 'I cannot let it be sullied like this.'

The stage manager said, 'What can I do? This is what the audience wants.'

Ma said, 'Well, in the case I can't come from tomorrow. Please find someone else to replace me.'

I think the last decent jatra I saw was called the *Ram Rahimer Ma* [Mother of Ram and Rahim]. Ruma Dasgupta directed it.

She had once acted with Natta Company, so she had some of that rigorous training. By then, jatra had crossed all limits in its desperation to please audiences. Bela Sarkar told me that she had to sometimes jump into the fire pit not once but thrice when she played the mythological character Amba. The audience would demand it.

In my day, the musicians set the mood. Drums would rumble to warn of ominous times. Trumpeters would blow to signal war. Thunderclaps would underscore a dramatic moment as the lamps blew out. The flute player would gently bring us back to earth. Now, even the musicians are gone. When I first saw jatras begin with the sound of a Casio keyboard instead of a clarionet, I wanted to weep.

At Natta Company, they would sing Radha-Govinda devotional songs for half an hour to the accompaniment of drums and cymbals before we got ready to go on stage. The very air would bc saturated with that music and devotion. I knew they did it because they were Krishna devotees.

At first, I was not interested in it.

Surya-babu told me, 'Whether you sing or not, listen to the kirtan songs.'

'But why?'

'Why? See these big stars, they stay up late. Not one comes for the kirtan. They come in right before their scene, put on their make-up and go on stage, Afterwards, they eat, drink, gossip and fall asleep. But if you listen to these songs, the melody will enter your very being. If you sing with them for half an hour, your vocal cords will grow warm and open up. It will help you on stage. If the melody is already in your head, you will be able to hit the right notes more easily. While you are doing your make-up, keep your ears open. Note the scale where it ends, so you can pick up from it as you enter.'

Surya-babu might not have had much of a bookish education but I learnt so much from him.

When the theatre actor Utpal Dutt came into jatra, he modernized it. Originally, we would enter and exit through the same gangway. Dutt set up different passages for entry and exit. That sped up scene changes considerably. He changed how we used lighting too. When I started, there were no electric lights in jatra. We performed by the light of Petromax and hurricane lanterns. When electric lights arrived, they would be placed in sets of three on each side with a big light in the centre. After that, lights became more sophisticated and directors like Dutt showed how they could be used for special effects.

In *Louho Kopat* [The Iron Door], for example, we showed the passage of time from daybreak to the dead of night just through light and sound. At Satyambar, my first big production was based on the tragedy of the 1919 massacre at Jallianwala Bagh, Amritsar, where British troops killed a crowd of protesters gathered in a park that had only one narrow exit. Historians say anywhere between 379 and 1,500 people died that day. And at least 1,200 were injured.

We needed to show the scale of that tragedy, but we didn't have hundreds of people on stage. Utpal Dutt used lighting to make it seem like Jallianwala Bagh was teeming with people. He used sound to give the impression of many rifles firing. As the guns rang out, it seemed as if the people in the compound were running helter-skelter to escape the gunfire, but it was all done through lighting.

I had to play Mahinder Kaur, a Punjabi lady, wife of subedar Arjun Singh. I had only four scenes. I wore a salwar suit like Punjabi ladies wear, tied my hair in a tight bun. It was not a glamorous role, so I used very little make-up, just drew my eyebrows lightly, added a touch of eyeliner, no lipstick, no blush. Once we were in Jamshedpur, and I was standing outside, getting some fresh air, when a man came and told me, 'Maa-ji—Mother—why are you standing outside? You should go in.' He thought I really was a middle-aged Punjabi woman!

Audiences were also becoming more demanding. We needed to do special effects on stage to satisfy them. When my mother acted in *Chand Bibi* on stage, it was famous for a scene where the character Joshibai comes on stage on a horse. The first few days, the actress would ride onto the stage on a real horse. Instead of being awestruck, the audience would start laughing as the stage would shake, the sets would tilt and almost fall over. After a few days, the company dispensed with the horse.

But one always looked for new ways to entertain and amaze the audience. In *Plabon* [The Flood], I played a Muslim girl who falls in love with a Hindu boy. She kills her father, then surrenders. Towards the end, she steps up to the gallows crying 'Allah hu Akbar', a cloth is put over her head, the azaan sounds—and she is hanged. Her body writhes and twists and falls out of sight . . . into a passage below the stage that took me straight to the green room. We had come a long way from the old jatra days where the dead body would get up and walk off the stage!

In *Sipahi Bidroho* [Sepoy Mutiny], a jatra based on the 1857 War of Indepen-dence, I played a mother. It was based somewhat on Maxim Gorky's *Mother*, a role I have done as well. Except this mother had half her face burnt by fire, and was left with one eye bulging. So we used a dab of spirit gum to keep one eye closed, and cut a ping-pong ball to make it resemble an eyeball and stuck it on that eye. Then I used make-up to suggest that the skin on half the face was burned and scarred. It looked gorily realistic in the end. Though I did have to put my poor eye through a lot of torture every time.

Shekhar Ganguly was the director for many of those plays. He would point out everyone's mistakes and give them suggestions on how to do better. But he never told me anything. One day, I asked him to give me some feedback as well. He smiled: 'We go back a long way as actors. Why, in the old days, we even went to the fields together to do our toilet. I can't teach you acting. Even women have a lot to learn from your acting. To me, you are a great artiste.'

I stood there staring at him, astonished. At a time when my star was fading, I didn't expect to hear something like that from him. I have kept his words close to my heart.

In 1972, I went to Bangladesh with Satyambar Opera. The 1971 war of liberation had just ended. Bangladesh was a brand-new country. It was a beautiful country. I remember drinking coconut water everywhere. Big green coconuts, just a few paisa each. I brought back an exquisite sari—the creamy colour of magnolia flowers with a broad golden border. But amid all the beauty, the signs of the war were still everywhere, even in an old schoolhouse where we put up. The wall was pockmarked with bullet holes. There were rusty stains on it. Those are blood stains, they told me. 'This is nothing,' a student said. 'We saw all this with our own eyes, the killings, the torture. We can never forget those days.'

When we came back, the season ended and with it my contract. The company owner said, 'We are taking Bandana Devi back this season. There won't be any roles for you. Please try elsewhere.'

I went home.

Sex and Seduction

I had no earnings any more. I was just sitting at home, all alone, waiting for someone to call me. I had not imagined I would end up like this. Even when women started joining jatra, I thought they would play the young heroines while I would get the mother roles. But suddenly I found that there was no room for me any more in the world of jatra.

The groups that would have me were growing progressively smaller. Arya Opera. Kamala Opera. Tarak Opera. Calcutta Opera. My candle that had been burning so brightly was spluttering to an end.

One day, I heard that jatra actor Dilip Das was looking for me. I knew him well, and I knew he was very fond of me. I decided I would do whatever it was he had in mind for me and for whatever money he offered. Times were getting desperate, and I couldn't be too picky.

Dilip told me he had taken Arya Opera on lease. He said he had two scripts on hand, and there were two roles in them for which he had me, and only me, in mind. He liked to call me Queen.

'Everyone says Chapal Rani is finished. You show them that's not true, Queen,' he declared grandly. He was perhaps a little drunk that day but I like to think that he really meant what he said. But he said he could only afford to pay modestly, not more than 600 rupees. I acquiesced. I didn't have much choice.

But the roles were indeed exciting. In *Nihoto Golap* [The Murdered Rose], I had to play the landlady of a brothel. By day a very respectable woman, part of genteel society in South Kolkata, going in her car to take a dip in the holy waters of the Ganga. By night a dragon lady, extracting money from the girls in her North Kolkata brothel. If anyone didn't pay up, she unleashed her ruffians on them.

Dilip said he would take me somewhere to research that role. That somewhere was a brothel in the red-light area of Sonagachi.

'Why are you taking me there?' I asked.

'Don't worry. Trust me. We have acted in these areas anyway. What's the problem going into their homes?'

We went to Nanda Rani's flat. Infamous in that area in those days.

'You stay here four or five hours,' Dilip instructed me. 'Talk to the woman who's the landlady here. Pay attention to the girls. See what they do all day, how they get ready. But pay special attention to the landlady.'

To my surprise, the women there were thrilled to meet me. They clustered around me, clucking like excited chickens.

'My goodness. Didn't you come to perform Chand Bibi here? Please, come to my room. Please, sit with us.'

It turned out they had seen me as Chand Bibi when I had performed at Allen Market which is right near the entrance to Sonagachi.

'We have to take good care of you,' one woman said, 'Dilip-da told us to make sure you got everything you needed.' Clearly, Dilip was well known to them!

'Please,' said another, 'have something sweet.'

'No, no,' yet another admonished her, 'I don't think he will do that.'

'Why would I not?' I was taken aback.

'No, I mean . . . ' the woman hesitated, 'will you eat in our establishment?'

'Why won't I?'

'Well . . . you do know who we are, what we do for a living . . . '

'I know, and I have no problem with any of it. You are like my sisters. Treat me as your brother. And which brother says no to sweets at his sister's home?'

'Are you sure?'

'I am. Just try me.'

They got the sweets. And I ate them all.

I really had no problem eating with sex workers at a brothel. Religion, caste, profession—none of these matter to me. As far as I am concerned, everyone is a human being trying to get by in this world. At one of the Kolkata jatra companies, I knew a very good singer named Bhakta Mullick. I once asked him which Mullick family he was from since I knew many of them from all over Kolkata. He flushed but didn't say anything. Later, he pulled me aside: 'Please don't call me out like that. We are Muslim Maliks. I hope that doesn't bother you?'

'Why should it bother me?' I was astonished. 'We are all humans.'

Bhakta must have had another name, a Muslim one, but because he got famous for singing songs of devotion or bhakti, everyone called him Bhakta Malik. He went along and kept his religion discreetly out of sight. Perhaps it was an issue for some people, but none of it mattered to me. Once you are on the stage, there's really no Hindu–Muslim–Christian–sweeper–tanner. We are all playing a part.

The madam of the establishment eventually showed up.

'So, who do we have here? What do you need?'

'Dilip has written a character like you. I am going to play her. So he sent me here and told me I need to watch you while you work.'

She laughed: 'That Dilip is a rascal. He wants to hang our dirty laundry out in public for everyone to see!'

But she sat me down and explained how the system worked.

'I do have a local tough who keeps an eye on the girls and on the pimp. He gives me all the intel. If I get to know the girl is lying, I have to turn the screws on her. She denies it and then does all kinds of drama. I have heard every sob story known to man. They need to send money home. The mother is dying, or the father has cancer, or the sister needs to get married . . . There's always some emergency. But I can't let that melt my heart. I know it sounds inhumane, but what can I do? This is my business. You cannot run it with a soft heart. But then, when they really need help, I am the one they come to.'

Then she paused and summoned one of the girls. The actor in me picked up on that tone of her voice. I knew immediately that my character would copy not only her looks but also that sharp commanding tone. Half of acting is about observing.

I still remember my look in that role of Tarini landlady—the black-bordered sari with a green blouse, the nose stud, the gold bangles, a slender necklace, diamond earrings and a streak of white on one side of my neatly parted hair. Nothing flashy, nothing over-the-top, a lady of great dignity but also utterly ruthless.

GIRL. No, no. I didn't have a client last night.

TARINI. No? But I was told that you did. And that he stayed all night.

GIRL. That's not true.

TARINI. Is that so? Jhumman!

(*Jhumman, the tough, enters holding a chain.*)

She says there was no one in her room last night. Just check it out, will you? Take her to her room. Bolt it from inside.

Jhumman starts dragging the girl away.

GIRL. No, no, no! Please, no.

TARINI. Go on, tell me, who was with you last night?

GIRL. Here take the money.

TARINI. How much did you make?

GIRL. 400 rupees.

TARINI. Keep 100 for yourself. Hand over 300.

The other role Das wanted me for was Kuti Bibi in *Louho Kopat*. That was a juicy role too, but entirely different. While Tarini was a steely high-society matriarch, Kuti Bibi was a sultry peasant woman. Manju Dey had played her on screen. Kuti Bibi had just one scene in the play but what a scene it was—it lasted a full 40 minutes and showed an entire day passing. The scene opened when it was dawn, the roosters were crowing and the stage glowed red in the light of the rising sun. By the end of the scene, it was late at night, the world was asleep, and the stage was lit only by the ghostly light of the moon. I used very little make-up for that role, and wore a simple, slightly frayed printed sari. My appearance was dishevelled . . . But there was an earthy sexiness about Kuti Bibi. Luckily, I was still young enough to pull it off. Kuti Bibi would wear the sari a little high, so you could see her silver anklets. Her husband, Fakir, kept her dolled up but could not satisfy her sexual desire. So he began to use her charms to entice young men to the house, and then tempted them with promises of get-rich schemes. Kuti Bibi would spread out her mattress, sit with them and entertain them. At some point, Fakir would mix drugs in her food to make her fall asleep. Then he would tell the young man to come along, help him dig up the treasure. But in truth he would kill the young man and steal all his belongings. Kuti Bibi did not know about the murders, though she suspected Fakir was up to no good.

KUTI. Oh, you godforsaken Fakir. You pay me no attention. Look at the state of my sari. You have no idea what kind of dirty comments I have to hear all the time, the kind of looks I get.

FAKIR. Don't worry, Kuti. Just you wait. Today, our money will be doubled.

KUTI. Again? Which sucker did you trap this time? I am telling you: I will warn him this time.

FAKIR. Just you wait and see. A young man called Hossain will come today.

KUTI. And what does he look like?

FAKIR. So handsome you can't even imagine. If he was your husband, you'd be such a splendid couple.

KUTI. What are you saying? You are my husband, my khasam. How can you say such things? When will he come?

FAKIR. Any moment now.

KUTI. Ah yes, the sun is high in the sky now.

Hossain enters.

KUTI (*to herself*). My goodness, he is really handsome. This is no ordinary chicken. This is a robust jungle fowl! (*To Hossain*) Who are you, young man?

HOSSAIN. I just met your husband. He told me he knew a way to double my money,

KUTI. I see.

They stare at each other.

FAKIR. Hmmm. What now, woman? You seem to be getting a little excited at the sight of this handsome young man.

KUTI. Well, what can I do, husband? Look at this torn sari I have. I can hardly cover myself properly any more.

FAKIR. Look, I have brought you a new sari. A beautiful sari.

KUTI. Oh, it is beautiful indeed. I love this dark-blue colour.

FAKIR. Wear this sari tonight when you serve Hossain dinner. Talk to him. Soften him up. Do whatever you need to. Just make sure he does not run away.

Fakir exits.

At some point, Hossain and Kuti are alone. She is wearing the new sari and looks radiantly beautiful.

KUTI. How was dinner? Did you like your rice and chicken?

HOSSAIN. The chicken was tasty. But a little spicy, Bibi, a little too spicy.

KUTI. Why are you calling me Bibi? I am not your wife. Fakir is my husband.

HOSSAIN. How are you with that man? You should come with me.

KUTI. Why? Are you propositioning me? I am not going anywhere. Lie down here and rest.

Later Kuti unrolls the mattress and lies down. By now it's dark. The stage is lit by only a dim blue light to suggest a moonlit night.

KUTI. Lie a little away from me.

HOSSAIN. Why, my dear? Why should I lie at a distance? Put your head on my arm over here.

KUTI. For shame. What will people say? Move aside.

Kuti turns to the side.

FAKIR (*watching from afar*). Enjoy, enjoy while you can. It's going to be all over for you in a little bit.

KUTI (*yawns*). How sleepy I am.

Kuti falls asleep. Fakir enters.

FAKIR (*in a whisper*). Hossain, come, come. We need to go double your money now. Give me your money.

Both exit, leaving Kuti Bibi sleeping alone in the moonlight. An owl hoots.

Kuti turns over and reaches out to touch Hossain.

KUTI (*sleepily*). Hossain-miya, where are you? Come to me, dear. (*Kuti opens her eyes.*) What happened? Where is Hossain? Where did he go? Did that Fakir take him somewhere?

A white spotlight focuses on her eyes.

In the next scene, we see Fakir filling a hole with earth, stamping the ground with his feet.

KUTI. You didn't listen to me did you, Fakir? You killed that handsome young man, didn't you? How could you, you scoundrel? Wait. I will expose you to the world. I am going to the police.

FAKIR. Stop. Kuti Bibi. Don't go. Don't go.

Kuti exits.

Those roles got me a lot of acclaim, perhaps a little too much. Men would scream from the audience 'Kuti Bibi, Kuti Bibi, don't worry. Hossain might be dead but we are still around. We are there for you.'

When Arya Opera's leading lady, Madhusree Devi, heard them shouting, she went through the roof. She was already annoyed that the posters for both productions featured my name above hers. She was the leading lady, after all. On top of that, she was in a relationship with Dilip Das himself.

'How dare you give Chapal-da the part of Kuti Bibi? And Tarini landlady? While I just get to play that Nepali woman and wear these baggy clothes.'

Dilip protested 'But you are very beautiful, that's why I gave you those parts. You really suit the role of Kanchi.'

But we all knew it was a far less meaty role.

'In any case,' Dilip said soothingly, 'Chapal as Kuti Bibi has only one scene.'

'So what? I could have done that scene.'

Then Dilip slipped up and said something he should not have: 'You couldn't have acted like that.'

Immediately, all hell broke loose.

'How dare you? What are you insinuating?'

'I am sorry but can you pull off a Tarini the way Queen does? With white in your hair, yet exuding so much sexiness? Can you?'

Madhusree got even angrier and began insulting me up and down.

Dilip turned to me apologetically: 'Chapal-da, I hope you aren't offended.'

I said I was not. He was like a brother to me. I had known him for years. But I knew my time was up. Madhusree was Dilip's lover, after all. When push came to shove, I would get the shove.

And they were not able to pay on time either. One day, I was told that there was a show somewhere that night and I needed to be there.

I said, 'I can't go.'

'Why not?'

'You have not paid me a penny. First clear my dues from the last one and a half months. Come and pay me and then ask me to go somewhere.'

No one came, and I didn't go either.

I quit Arya Opera, or perhaps they called to say they didn't need me any more. Either way, it was over.

'What about my things, my costumes, ornaments, wigs?' I asked.

'We incurred heavy losses because of you. You aren't getting any of that back,' they said flatly.

I argued but they did not return anything—my make-up kit, my wigs, an aluminium suitcase filled with gold-plated silver jewellery, my saris . . . I was upset then but it does not matter any longer. They are of no use to anyone any more, and there is no one I can give them to. Those days of men who played women on stage are over.

Curtain

When I had played Chand Bibi, I commanded a salary of 6,000 rupees. Then it started to drop. First, I was told I would be paid half that. I had no choice but to accept. By 1972, it had gone down to 250 rupees. By 1973, I had no work.

Then, suddenly, I got a call from Ambika Opera. Four friends had got together to start that company sometime in the 1950s. Amiya, Madhu, Bimal and Kaliyadaman—thus Ambika. They were upfront with me. An actress was leaving the company with two months left in the season. They desperately needed someone to fill in for her in two jatras. In one jatra, I would have to play Mother Earth. In the other, *Aami Siraj* [I, Siraj], a historical character, Ghaseti Begum of Bengal.

But before I formally signed on, the manager showed up in a tizzy one day. There was a show that night and the actress had quit. Fortunately, I am one of those people who can just listen to lines and somehow memorize them. When I went on stage as Mother Earth, in an orange silk sari with a red border and a red blouse, my hair open, everyone was amazed. At one point, I had

45 continuous lines of dialogue. I broke it up into five parts—and each part was met with resounding cheers. In seven days, I memorized all my lines. It was a swelteringly hot summer, but I managed to do 78 shows in two months.

It was gruelling, but in my heart of hearts I was relieved. I had done a lot for Ambika in their time of need. When the next season started, I was sure they would remember that. But it didn't turn out that way. They said in the new season women would play all the female roles—both the heroines and the mother roles. They offered to keep me as a sort of back-up option, the actor in reserve. 'You can learn all the parts and be ready. In case one of the women calls in sick or something, you can fill in for them. But, obviously, we cannot pay you what we did last season.'

'Can I get a job as a manager?' I asked in desperation. I knew Kshitish Rani who used to do female parts too. When those roles dried up, he became the manager for Nabaranjan Opera. As an actor, we already knew the industry and the booking agents well. While it was not a glamorous job, it was at least some kind of employment, it kept body and soul together.

But they would not hear of it.

'Oh, you won't be able to manage that kind of work.'

'Why not?' I said. 'People know me well all over North Bengal. Put me in charge of your North Bengal bookings.'

'We don't think you'll be able to do that kind of hard work.'

I rattled off the names of actors who had done it.

'No, no, you won't be able to.'

'That is not true,' I protested. 'When I stepped into Chhabi Rani's shoes, people said I wouldn't be able to do it. But I showed them. I made myself into Chapal Rani.'

But they were unmoved.

'Once you came to me and begged and pleaded. Without an actress, your troupe was about to shut shop. I learnt my lines almost overnight and saved you. I had hoped that you would be grateful enough to keep me on in the new season. But now I've learnt that the world of jatra is filled with ingrates.'

'How dare you say that?'

'I am saying it. What are you going to do? I have never double-crossed anyone in my life. That is not in my nature. But you stabbed me in the back. Once, your Amiya-babu cajoled me into joining your company. Where is he now? Let me tell you, your troupe won't last too long.'

And it did not. Within two years it broke up, but that did not change my fate.

In 1974, I got the call from Kamala Opera and that led to the fateful night when someone threw a clay cup at me on the stage. I had always thought of the audience as my Goddess Lakshmi. It has given me so much. But it has also thrown clay cups at me. It stung, but I could not complain because the times had indeed moved on. I had become a misfit on that stage.

That day, I left the theatre and went back home. I lived by myself in a little room in Bagbazar, in North Kolkata. The rent was only 70 rupees per month. I felt I could somehow manage at least for a bit. I didn't need much—just some rice and boiled vegetables and dal to get by.

I tried to leave the theatre with my head high. But when I came back to my room, and shut the door, I broke down and wept. Almost at once I realized how pointless it was. I was sitting there, alone, crying my eyes out. There was no one to even console me. Life had to go on. I got up, I needed to figure out something to eat. I got some sweets from the little shop across the street, ate them, drank some water, prayed to my gods and went to bed.

That was it. My career in jatra was over just like that.

Figure 1. Chapal Bhaduri (*left*) and the author in front of the house on Ananda Prasad Street (earlier Balakhana Street) in which Chapal was born.

Figure 2 (TOP LEFT). A recent picture of the house on Dalimtala Lane where Chapal grew up.

Figure 3 (TOP RIGHT). The house on Girish Chandra Avenue in which Chapal lived with his elder sister Ketaki Dutta.

Figure 4 (BOTTOM). The street outside the old-age home where Chapal now lives.

Figure 5 (FACING PAGE, TOP). Town School on Bidhan Sarani where Chapal studied.

Figure 6 (FACING PAGE, BOTTOM LEFT). The house of Noti Binodini off Bidhan Sarani.

Figure 7 (FACING PAGE, BOTTOM RIGHT). A statue of Sisir Kumar Bhaduri that stands before the site of the former Srirangam Theatre, now replaced by a modern residential apartment building on Raja Rajkrishna Street.

ESTD
1894
TOWN SCHOOL

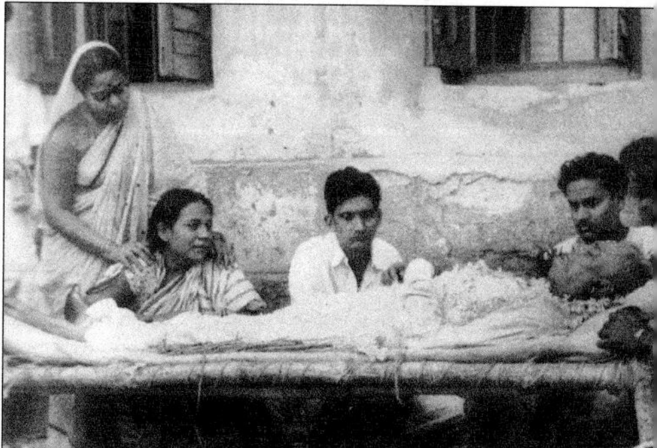

(CLOCKWISE FROM TOP LEFT)

Figure 8. Prabha Devi, Chapal's mother.

Figure 9. Prabha Devi (*left*) with her young daughter Sagarika on her lap in the film *Annapurnar Mandir* (1936).

Figure 10. Sisir Kumar Bhaduri (*second from left*) and Chapal's father Tara Kumar Bhaduri (*extreme right*) in the play *Sita*.

Figure 11. Ketaki Dutta (*second from left*) and Saralesh Bhaduri (*third from left*), Chapal's sister and brother respectively, among others, beside the body of their father, Tara Kumar Bhaduri.

Figure 12. Sisir Kumar Bhaduri (*left*) and Prabha Devi (*right*) in the play *Reetimoto Natok*.

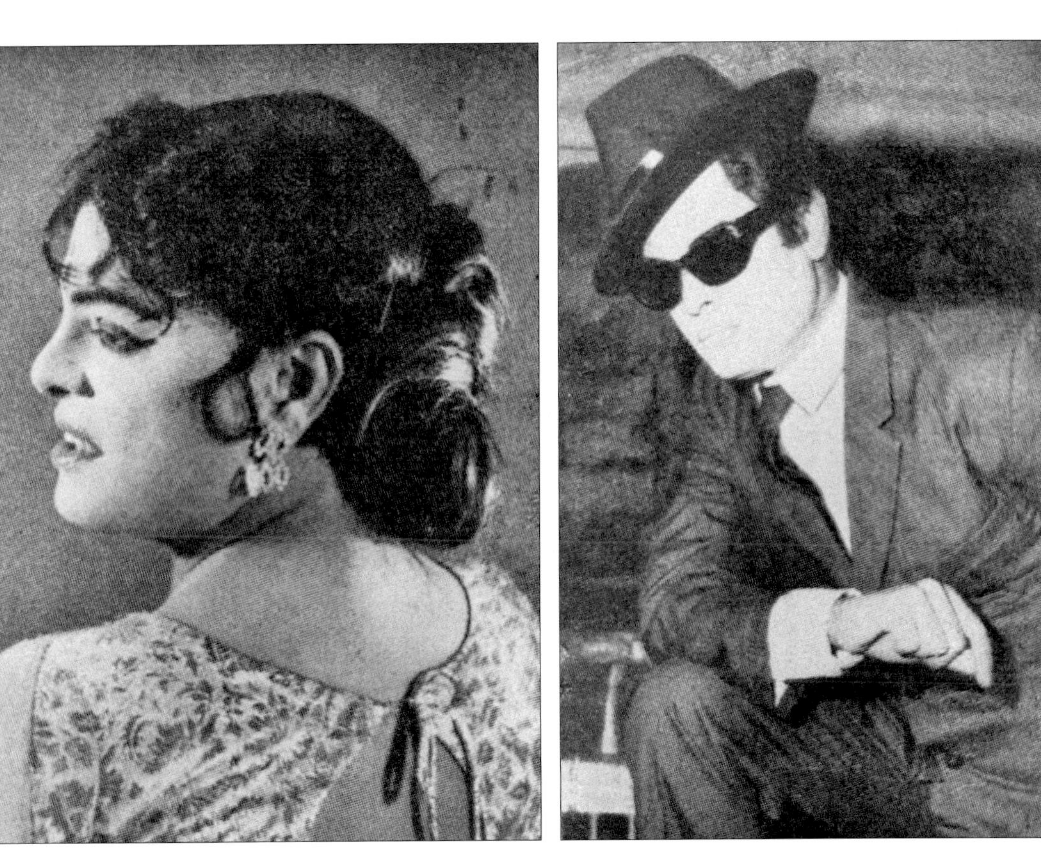

Figure 13 (LEFT). Chapal playing a female role (Anjana) in *Raja Devidas*.

Figure 14 (RIGHT). Chapal playing a rare male role (Bishu) in *Raktalekha*.

Figures 15–17 (ABOVE). Other 'queens' of the jatra stage: Chhabi Rani, Janardan Rani and Babli Rani.

Figure 18 (LEFT). Chapal Rani in an unidentified jatra role.

Figures 19–20 (TOP). Sunil Kumar Maiti; as Satadal Rani in *Chandimangal*.

Figures 21–22 (BOTTOM). Rakhal Chandra Das; as Rakhal Rani playing Kubeni in *Bangabeer*.

Figure 23 (ABOVE). Chapal without make-up (*c.*1960s).

Figures 24–25 (FACING PAGE, TOP AND MIDDLE). Chapal on the balcony of Putulbari, North Kolkata, 1998.

Figure 26 (FACING PAGE, BOTTOM). Makhanlal Natta (*left*) of Natta Company with Chapal in Putulbari, 1998.

Figure 27 (BELOW). The roof of Putulbari, 2025.

Figures 28–29 (FACING PAGE, TOP). Outside and inside Putulbari, 2025. The statuary on the top survives, although the first-floor balcony was bricked up sometime after 1998.

Figure 30 (FACING PAGE, BOTTOM). Bengali sign inside Putulbari: 'Natta Company Jatra Party—Office Upstairs'.

উপরে অফিস

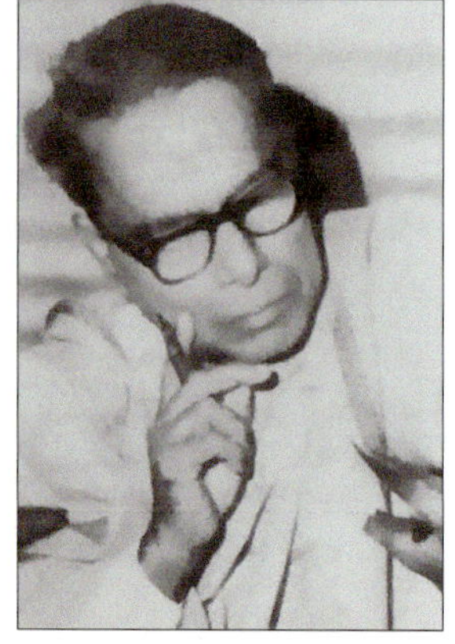

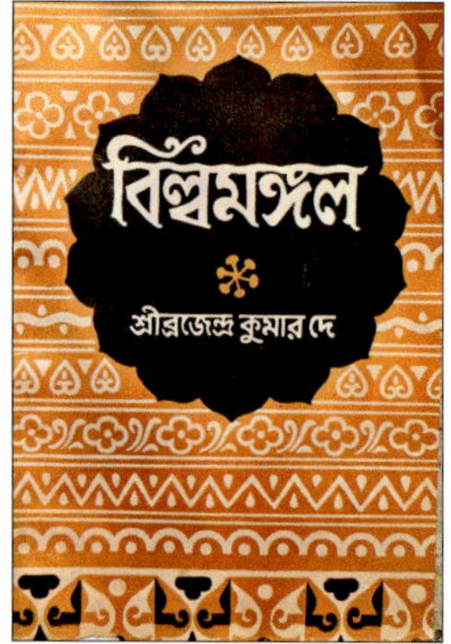

Figure 31 (TOP LEFT). Surya Kumar Dutta, long-time manager of Natta Company.

Figure 32 (TOP RIGHT). Brajendra Kumar Dey, prolific writer of jatras.

Figures 33–34 (MIDDLE). Covers of the jatra scripts *(from left) Bharat Biday* and *Bilwa-mangal*, both written by Dey.

Figures 35–36 (BOTTOM). The jatra neighbourhood of Chitpur in North Kolkata, including the Diamond Library bookstore on Rabindra Sarani, which still sells jatra scripts.

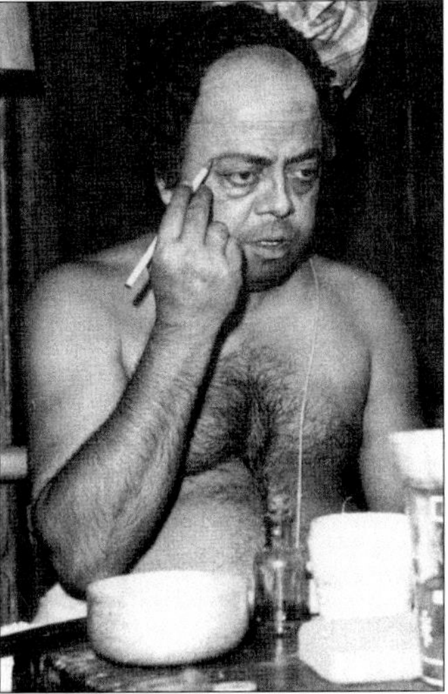

Figures 37–39 (ABOVE). Chapal's male co-stars on the jatra stage (*from left*): Swapankumar, the King of Jatra; Arun Dasgupta, applying make-up for the Natta Company production *Vidyasagar*; and Shekhar Ganguly.

Figure 40 (LEFT). A Bengali newspaper advertisement for Nabaranjan Opera's *Michael Madhusudan*, starring Swapankumar along with Chapal Rani.

নব রঞ্জন অপেরা

প্রোপ্রাইটার—শ্রীজীবনকৃষ্ণ দাস

১১৭, রবীন্দ্র সরণী, কলিঃ—৬ ফোন নং ৫৫-৭৮৬২

মধুসংলাপী বিধায়ক ভট্টাচার্য রচিত ও জনপ্রিয় নট স্বপনকুমার পরিচালিত

যাত্রা জগতে বিজয়-বৈজয়ন্তী নাটক

মাইকেল মধুসূদন

বিধায়কবাবুর রাষ্ট্র বিপ্লব — সুর : অমিয় ভট্টাচার্য

সত্যপ্রকাশের নূতন প্রভাত — সুর : অজিত বোস (বাদু)

ব্রজেনবাবুর নেকড়ের থাবা

আনন্দময়ের দেব-গিরী

শ্রেঃ—স্বপনকুমার

অনিল রায়, মধু মল্লিক, মোহন চ্যাটার্জি, প্রণয় কুমার, রবিন চক্রঃ, মুকুন্দ ঘোষ, অমূল্য বোস, মহেন্দ্র ব্যানার্জি, দুলাল সিকদার, প্রফুল্ল দে, কানাই হালদার, মুকুল দে, গোপাল ব্যানার্জি।

শ্রেষ্ঠ নারী চরিত্রাভিনেতা চপল রাণী ও রূপালী

বিনয়-কণ্ঠী নমিতা চ্যাটার্জী ও তিলোত্তমা

উদীয়মান সঙ্গীত-সুধাকর সুধীর ধাড়া

নৃত্য-গীতে—বাংলার বুলবুল মীরা গুপ্তা

ব্রাঞ্চ অফিস—হিন্দ মেডিক্যাল স্টোর্স (ফোন—আসানসোল ২৭২৬)

পরিচালক শ্রীশম্ভুনাথ ঘোষ

কোলিয়ারী তত্ত্বাবধায়ক শ্রীঅভয়পদ ঘোষ

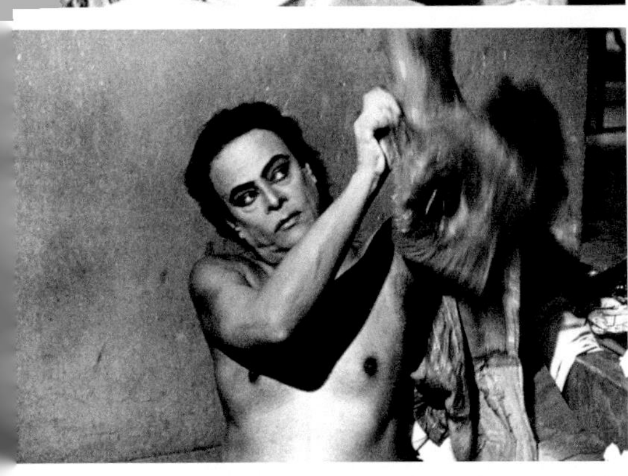

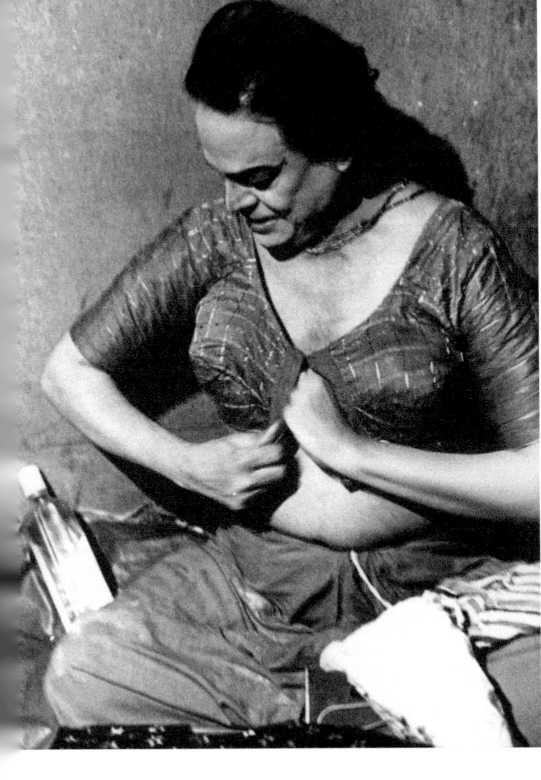

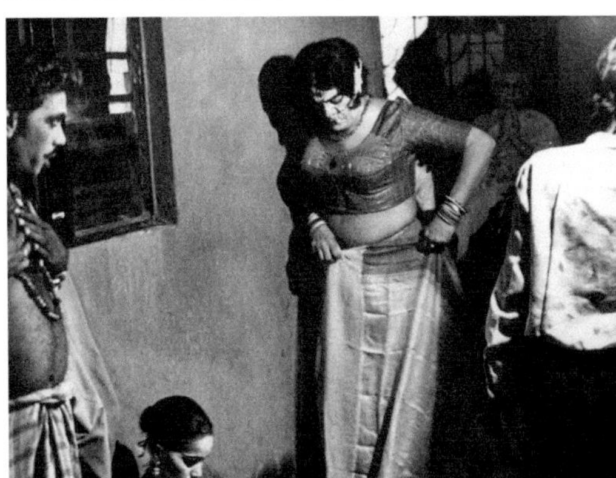

Figures 41–51 (FACING PAGE, ABOVE AND OVERLEAF). Chapal transforms into and performs Goddess Sitala at the Taltala Sitala Mandir in Central Kolkata; a photo essay by Naveen Kishore (1998).

Figures 52–55 (ABOVE, CLOCKWISE FROM TOP LEFT). Chapal with his elder sister, actress Ketaki Dutta; Scenes from the play *Nijabhumey* (1998), in which Chapal acted alongside Dutta.

Figure 56 (BELOW). A report by Sunandini Banerjee in the *Statesman* about Chapal's trip to Canada in 2001.

Total impersonator

CF/416

14.5.2002 The Statesman, Calcutta

Talking and translating, explaining and storytelling... the Vancouver workshops with *jatra* performer Chapal Bhaduri was not all theatre, says **Sunandini Banerjee**

THERE we were. In Vancouver. None of us had been so far away from home. Ever. I was excited. Uncertain. Without my luggage. He was excited. Uncertain. Without the ability to speak the English language. Chapal Bhaduri and I. Invited by the Roundhouse Community Centre, Vancouver to perform his *Ekmukhi Sitala* as part of the opening show of Dialogue with India, organised by the Hoopoe Curatorial of Montreal. Which was to be followed by a week-long workshop conducted by Chapal*da*, where I would be required to frantically translate questions to and from the artists and performers who wished to join.

The first couple of days we would arrive at the Roundhouse and spend long evenings rehearsing with the musicians, who juggled with the demands of *jatra* and wrote down and rewrote cues and hand movements and delicate wiggles of the eyebrows which could denote anything from anger to divine retribution, and hence, needed to be accompanied by suitable music. Chapal*da* charmed them with his solo rendition of the Sitala story, the creation and ultimate installation of the goddess in the Hindu pantheon. However, they only spoke Hindi and English, and he spoke very little Hindi. So I would sit on the sidelines, ferrying cups of coffee to and fro, explaining, translating, pacifying, scolding, and praying fervently that the performance would be a success.

That over, Chapal*da* and I spent the next morning not flushed with success at the unexpected attendance at his show nor at the felicitations and congratulations which I translated for his benefit till late into the night. We were worried. Never having workshopped before, Chapal*da* was nervous on the first day of the workshops. What would be asked of him? Would the participants find him interesting enough to return? I bravely reassured him, knowing the first session would have to be captivating enough to make them think signing up was not a wasted effort. Hence, I would have to talk and tell and recollect and share.

There were about six Canadian women the first afternoon. A motley crew of playwrights, actors, dancers and theatre persons. They had all watched the performance and this sparked off a series of questions about his art – that of female impersonation and of *jatra*. What did the word "*puja*" mean? Where does Sitala figure in the Hindu pantheon, what is the implication of a religion so peopled with "female" gods? And why does Chapal*da* himself play a goddess? Chapal*da* talked about his life, his childhood, his actor mother and how he grew up watching her act and spending hours in the green rooms, before and after her performances. He spoke of how he came to acting, again purely to survive, after a relative mentioned fairly casually that he would make a good woman on stage. Then followed training in song and dance. He spoke of how he learnt to fine tune his characters and get under their skin. He would try and read up more about the women he would have to play and think about the way they should talk, walk or cry. He spoke of what it meant to be a homosexual and to have "come out" with the fact. I was, in turn, asked what it meant to be a Bengali, and Indian. What was India?

Chapalda as Sitala; At the workshop with other performers

The second day the group watched the documentary on Chapal*da* called *Performing the Goddess* and more questions surfaced. Experiences of being women in different cultures, different lands, and different backgrounds were shared. How was *jatra* different from ordinary proscenium theatre? What were the economics of the situation? What does it mean to be a part of a joint family? Why was the family unit breaking up. What did it mean to be an actor in Canada? What did it mean to be a Chinese performance artist in Canada? How difficult was it to find funding? Where does one have to compromise to simply survive as an artist? The reason I am highlighting these questions is that instead of being a pure theatre workshop what it ended up being was a kind of multicultural interchange where we began to see much more than acting take place.

We made friends, all of us. Perhaps it was not all theatre. We were getting to know one another and discovering the qualities of life in places all over the globe, and realising that despite all our differences, we were startlingly similar. And Chapal*da*, effortlessly sliding in and out of his male and female personas, fit in with a great deal of candour and ease. He was, there, in those workshop sessions, precisely who he wanted to be. Chapal Bhaduri. Female impersonator. No apologies. And I was talking and translating and explaining and storytelling and lifetelling by doing what I do best. Rushing in where angels fear to tread. No apologies from me either.

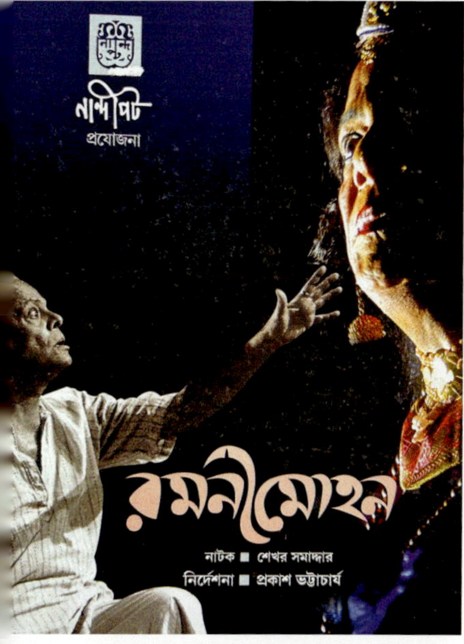

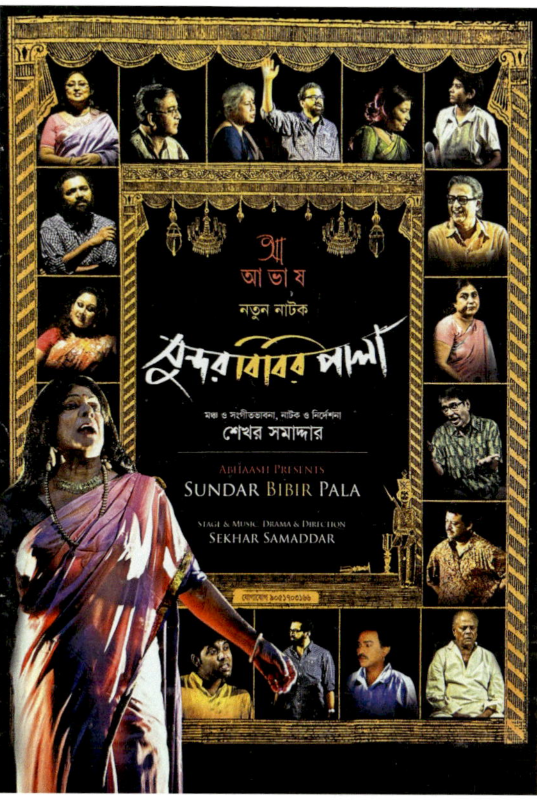

Figures 57–60 (LEFT, FROM TOP). Playbill for *Ramanimohan* (2006) and scenes from the play featured in it.

Figure 61 (ABOVE). Playbill for *Sundarbibir Pala* (2012).

Figures 62–64. Make-up session and scenes from the documentary *Chena Kintu Ajana* (2014) in which Chapal recreates some of his iconic jatra roles.

Figures 65–68 (FACING PAGE AND BELOW). A photo shoot for designer Parama Ghosh (2023).

Figure 69 (OVERLEAF). Chapal on the strand by the river Hugli in front of Putulbari in North Calcutta, November 2022.

INTERLUDE

In Imagination

The Hero

Night had fallen.

We had veered off the main highway to a rutted road that led us past paddy fields and ponds into the forest. The headlights of our car picked out only bushes and trees on either side. The road was becoming increasingly potholed and rough. There was no sign of human habitation anywhere, only darkness that pressed in on us from all around.

We had a jatra show at 11 that night in a village nearby. My heroine, Bina, and I were on our way in our own car. She was in full princess regalia, covered head to toe in gold jewellery. Our driver was getting increasingly nervous as the road went deeper and deeper into the forest. There was no sign of a village anywhere, not a glimmer of light.

'Are you sure we are going the right way?' he asked.

'This is the road the manager told me to take. At least I think so,' I said, but my doubts were growing too. I imagined wolves and leopards watching us from the bushes. We had gone too far to turn back. Bina was starting to have palpitations, convinced we were going to be eaten by tigers or whatever ghosts and monsters lived in the trees. I could only hear the hum of cicadas. In the silence of the night, it sounded almost ominous, like the approach of an angry mob.

Suddenly, I saw the flickering glow of a lantern. There was a little mud hut in a clearing in the middle of nowhere. I didn't question what a hut was doing in the middle of a forest. Like a drowning man clutching at a straw, I got out of the car and started shouting: 'Anyone home?' A dark burly man with a big moustache emerged, his hairy chest glistening with sweat. He was wearing a dhoti and carrying a lantern.

'What are you doing here so late?'

'I think we are lost. We are trying to go to Battala village.'

'But this road does not go there. And don't you know, this jungle is infested with dacoits?'

'Oh my God, please help us and guide us to the right road. I have a lady with me in the car.'

'But I am the dacoit!' If this had been a jatra, he would have now laughed ha-ha-ha and the audience would have laughed with him. In real life, all my blood seemed to leave my body. I was convinced this was the end. Then the man lifted the lantern to my face: 'Wait. Aren't you the one they call the Jatra King?'

'You know me?' I was amazed.

'I have seen so many of your jatras,' he replied.

That night, he sent his teenaged son to be our guide, to lead us on foot. We left the car and driver with him while his son escorted us out of the jungle and onto the main road and further along until we could see the lights of the jatra stage and hear the music. Then he saluted us and vanished into the darkness. As we stumbled into the dressing room, the manager heaved a sigh of relief. But after I told him about our adventure, he turned pale.

'Few people come out of that jungle unscathed,' he said. 'No one goes there after dark. It's a den of bandits and robbers.'

Next morning, we took a jeep and went back into the jungle. In daylight, it didn't look threatening—just many shades of green and filled with the chirping of birds.

We found the hut but no trace of the dacoit. The car was untouched. The driver said the man even served him a meal at night—a couple of rotis and some dal and vegetables.

Is this my story? Or some other jatra king's? It doesn't matter. I tell you this story to show what jatra fame was like. This story should have become the stuff of legends. But no one knows about it because we never got any respect from city folks. When I started acting, my mother lied to my relatives and said I worked in a colliery. Even that was more respectable.

You people talk about Uttam Kumar, the superstar of Bengali films. They still write books about him. How many people write books about Swapankumar, the emperor of jatra, the man who was my idol? Did you know, when anyone tried to hire him, he would hand them 32 pages of conditions? Such as: a new car and chauffeur for a whole year. The car had to go all the way to his green room, no matter where he was doing his jatra. And: no travelling anywhere by boat, because he had a phobia about boats and water.

Show managers from the Sundarbans in South Bengal came to his dressing room once and protested. 'Sir, we hear you won't travel anywhere by boat. But our villages are all on little islands in the delta. Will the people of Sundarbans be deprived of the great Swapankumar? Won't they get to see him?' As he removed his make-up, Swapankumar calmly replied, 'Why shouldn't they? If they fly him there, they will certainly get to see him.' They actually got a minister to sanction a runway in the Sundarbans. Swapankumar flew there in a Fokker Friendship plane for his show. Can Uttam Kumar top that?

At one time, he was in such demand that producers would line up outside his door to get him to join their company. He would say: 'All right, write all the names on chits of paper, put them in this box, blindfold me and I'll pick one up. And that'll be the company I'll join this season.' It didn't matter which company he was part of. He knew his fans would follow him from wherever he went.

But you genteel folk thought of us jatra types as lowly, so you didn't give us the time of day. *Jatra kore fatra lok, naatok kore bhadralok*—Riff-raff people do jatra, respectable people do theatre. But had you seen Swapankumar's style? I have seen Swapankumar act for seven minutes straight with a lit cigarette in the corner of his mouth. Every night, night after night. He never faltered. As for his sex appeal, it wasn't just jatra actresses running after him because they hoped he'd be their ticket to stardom. I can't name names, but once, when he was staying at someone's house while on the road, not one but three of the women of the house snuck into his bedchamber in the same night, one after the other. He satisfied them all.

I was no Swapankumar, but I had my fans too. It wasn't just the women. Men slipped me notes as well. Certainly, some of the ranis of jatra were more than happy to warm my bed while we were on the road. Sometimes, I indulged them. It was just time-pass. They were mostly homos, anyway. That's why I can't understand why you people give them so much importance now. They were such a small part of the jatra story, a footnote really. They had their day because at that time women did not act in jatra. That chapter is closed now.

The story of jatra continues, though. My fight has always been to keep jatra alive and thriving. Old timers like Chapal Rani will say jatra is not what it used to be. Of course not. If it did not change with the times, it would be dead. Jatra started, they say, in the days of the mystic saint Chaitanya Mahaprabhu. He apparently dressed as Rukmini—sari, blouse and all—and the jatras went on all night long. Then they used to have the adventures of Prince Sundar and Princess Vidya, stories of romance, murder and thrills. Religion, mythology, love, freedom fighters—jatra kept changing with the times because art must mirror the times we live in.

Sometimes they staged jatras for babus in their grand mansions, where they sprayed the audience with rose water. Sometimes it was for villagers or people who lived in slums in the city and needed nothing more than a bit of song and dance and bawdy jokes.

The only constant was change. Less poetry, more prose. More theatre, fewer songs. Less god-goddess mythology, more social issues.

Jatra had to become more modern. I did my bit. When I joined jatra, the directors were hardly directors. They were nothing better than motion masters. They just taught you to move on the stage, how to stand, how to deliver dialogue. Everything was over the top and melodramatic. 'Show us some art,' the audience would shout. And the big stars would strike postures before exiting the stage like a magician showing tricks and everyone would cheer.

I tried to bring in a more natural style. I had done a bit of theatre. When I wanted to bring that kind of direction to jatra, everyone said that would be the end of jatra. When Swapankumar did *Michael Madhusudan*, everyone said it was doomed. A jatra about a poet, that too with half-breed wives, who was going to watch that? No sword fights, no suspense, no comedy, just Swapankumar reciting reams of poetry! How would that ever work in jatra? But it created a sensation. I think I saw it seven times. Even in the collieries they wanted Michael. And Chapal Rani as Michael's mother.

When films came along, jatra changed too. If Uttam Kumar had a hit with *Stree*, we would have *Stree* the jatra next season. If next year he did *Sannyasi Raja*, we would turn that into a jatra. But it wasn't just a copy. Sometimes I dare say the jatra was more true to the real novel than the film. So who says the golden age of jatra ended with the Chapal Ranis? Jatra has always been there, our greatest folk art.

People would laugh and ridicule us for being too melodramatic. But the point was always to shock, dazzle, startle. I have come on stage with a severed head dripping blood. Or seen a jatra open with someone firing a gun. Or bringing on a live camel. Three to four thousand people in an open field won't settle down like good schoolchildren without something big, a bit of a bang, to shock them. I think we men had to work harder than the ranis who had all their make-up and costumes. We can be thin, sallow, bald men, but when we get on that stage, we have to have the weight of kings. And then if the audience doesn't clap, we might as well be servants.

I remember this fine actor who would strike his forehead with his hand in a dramatic scene. Usually when he cried '*This* head of mine' and hit his forehead, everyone clapped. One night, nothing happened. Desperate, he struck his head again. And again. He punched his head hard. But nothing worked. It was just not his night. Later, I saw he had a black bruise on his forehead, poor chap. The blood had congealed. We needed those claps. Without those claps, our rates would not go up.

Chapal Rani was the queen of claps until one day they didn't want him any more. That's the law of the jungle, and the law of jatra, whether you are king or queen. I still remember when the jatra company was booking shows for me, and someone told the manager, 'Not him. We don't want to see that old man play the prince. We want fresh blood.' It seemed just the other day I had been the fresh blood when someone said, 'We want to see that boy as Siraj-ud-Daulah. We hear he's very good. We don't want the old Siraj from last season.' That was the end of the actor who had played Siraj-ud-Daulah for 10 or 15 years before me. I certainly didn't shed tears for him. I was over the moon. So when my turn came to be replaced, what right did I have to cry foul? We might play kings on stage but ultimately the audience is king. Remember, they come on cycles and bullock carts from miles away. They spread little mats on hard ground, over the stubble of freshly harvested paddy, and sit there for hours in the cold just to watch us. Why should they settle for second-rate, an old king, a fake queen with her blouse stuffed with rags?

Other things were lost too, not just the ranis. When I was young, all jatras had a Bibek or Conscience. Since the early 1900s. The Bibek could appear anywhere—inside the king's bedchamber or on the battlefield. He was the one who voiced what the audience was thinking. He could put questions to kings. He could be anyone—the old faithful family servant, the Hindu servant of a Muslim badshah or a beggar saint. But he was the voice of unvarnished truth. Some actors were famous only for playing Bibek. They earned as much as the hero and the rani. But then people got tired of them. Audiences thought they slowed the action down. Companies did not want to shell out money for them. So Bibeks disappeared from the script and the stage. Who cried for them? Who wrote their obituary? Did you?

It surprises me to see you shed such tears over those homos who played ranis. Maybe they were not all homos, but I think the most successful ones were. Sometimes in those love scenes when the 'heroine' would lock eyes with me, I knew it wasn't all acting. I won't deny that occasionally my heart fluttered too. But then, when I held them close and those rag stuffed breasts poked at me, the illusion shattered into smithereens. Though one thing I must admit: Chapal Rani maintained his figure. His skin had a glow. He knew he had to hold onto the appearance of youth.

But holding on to respect is another matter. Then, again, we never really had that. I've heard one of our biggest stars, Phani Motilal, would demand taxi fare from his producers but then take buses everywhere, so he could pocket the balance. When Swapankumar acted, he not only demanded the best hotel room and imported cosmetics but also a full feast every night—jumbo prawns, hilsa from the Padma river, tengra fish swollen with roe, a whole roast chicken. And what did he eat in the end? Plain chicken soup. The rest was his haq, his right. He had to exert it or they would quickly forget what he was entitled to.

All kinds of actors get Padma Shri and Padma Bhushan awards from the government. We don't even get a pension. We get a scarf and a scroll from some state drama group if we are lucky. Yet it's because of jatra that hundreds and thousands of villages know the poetry of Michael Madhusudan Dutt.

At least here you are doing stories about Chapal Rani in an old-age home. I hear he has turned his jatra into some kind of stage show that people buy tickets to see. He has done plays where he just plays himself—a man who was once a woman on stage. But we never got even that. Once I was out, I was out. No one was interested. Chapal had documentaries made about him where he even talks about being a homo. What is the world coming to? Yesterday he was making us cry by playing the saintly Sita on stage, the mother of all virtues. And today he's flaunting his homosex! People will hang out any dirty laundry they can just to get media attention. I am sorry but I cannot do that.

The downfall of jatra happened not because the Chapal Ranis were kicked out. It happened because jatra was always the stepchild. No one cared for it. The government never nurtured it. My sons didn't go into jatra. They wanted a profession that made real money. Their wives want real diamonds, not the glass jewellery Chapal Rani wore.

Once, I was in a jatra based on a very famous Bengali novel. In that, the zamindar is married to a beautiful woman whom he adores. But he has an evil house physician who drugs the woman and then rapes her. The book never describes it but we slowly figure out what happened. When we staged that jatra, someone came and told me, 'That was a good jatra, good acting but why didn't you show the rape? That would have made it more exciting for the audience, no?'

'Some things are more horrifying when left to the imagination, are they not?' I replied.

'Then why put in on your posters?' The man was indignant. 'I saw that only and came.'

Then I saw: the posters had a woman, half-dressed, screaming, her sari falling off her shoulder, while a man clawed at her. It was a complete lie, false advertising. I left soon after.

Some days when I sit with my glass of whisky, some of my old lines come back to me. Once I could play with the audience like a cat plays with a mouse, milking my lines, slowing them, speeding them up till I could hear them clap. I knew how to raise my voice and drop it for maximum effect and still be heard by the last person in the last row. And when I close my eyes, I can see the man I was, the smooth skin, the unlined face, the jet-black beard fixed by spirit gum, the sword at my waist, the brocade on my waistcoat . . . Chapal Rani was not the only one with beauty. The men had it too, though we might have been shy to talk about it. Otherwise, why would thousands fall in love with us every night?

Night after night, I stood on that open stage in an empty field. A sea of people in front, to my left, to my right and behind me. I knew that when I said, 'I love you' to Chapal Rani, I was really talking to them. And I knew they would love me back.

In my dreams, I can still hear them clapping.

7

A Woman in a Man's World (and Vice Versa)

A Beauty Regimen

No society magazine ever asked me to write down my beauty tips, the way they ask film heroines. If they did, it would go something like this.

SKIN CARE

Massage hands and feet daily with cream or olive oil. Among lotions, I prefer Cuticura and Nivea. In powders, my go-to product is Doreena talcum powder. It was my mother's favourite as well along with her Max Factor products. But for your skin, I think the best treatment is a little pure mustard oil right before your bath.

FACE CARE

Massage night cream carefully into the face, around the eyes and nose, right down to the neck. Be patient and do not rush. Next morning, wash the face with cold water, then soak a handkerchief in warm water and carefully scrub the face to get the cream off. Finally, wash the face with a good soap. This whole process can take up to 10–15 minutes.

HAIR CARE

My standard hair oils were Lakshmivilas or Jabakusum. Alas, now my hair has grown very thin and no oil can change that.

But the real change happens inside me as I do my make-up.

Picture this.

I am sitting at the dressing table, my mind focused on my role. The moment I put on the petticoat, something begins to shift inside me. When I fix the breasts to my chest, I start feeling strange—half of me is still Chapal Bhaduri but the other half has become Chapal Rani. As I put on the rest of the outfit, piece by piece, the blouse, the sari, the necklace, the bangles, Chapal Bhaduri starts to recede and Chapal Rani comes to life. The lips are the last touch. When they are done and my wig is fixed, it's hard to think of myself as a man any more. If that thought even crosses my mind, I will never be able to do justice to the role.

Physically, everything about me remains male, yet I am also female in that moment. What I have below my waist no longer matters. I am no longer a man, not even a man who dresses as a woman. I forget that I was a man when I sat down at that dressing table. Now I feel shy to even look at men, but I can understand full well from their gaze what they are trying to say, what they want, what they desire. And I like it. Of course I like it. I liked it that very first time when I dressed as Morjina and that boy gave me a rose. I remember the electric current that went through me as if it was yesterday.

Becoming a woman, even if it's just on stage, definitely had an effect on me. I swear, at that time, for three or four days every month, I would feel ill the way women do when they have their periods. For a few days, I would be weak and listless, and then I would be consumed by an intense sexual hunger. The men around me would feel incandescent, creatures made of fire. And if I could not satisfy the hunger raging inside me, I would feel agitated and physically ill. Luckily, as long as I was in a relationship with my friend, he could take care of my needs. Even now, in my 80s, I feel desire burning inside me but I have learnt to control it better.

An Element of Secrecy

When I worked at Nabaranjan Opera, they would hang a curtain in the middle of the dressing room. The men dressed on one side, the women on the other. I would dress with the women but they complained that made them uncomfortable.

Kshitish, the manager, had once also acted in female roles as Kshitish Rani. I told him, 'Please do something. I can't dress in peace with them constantly complaining. Should I dress with the men instead?'

Kshitish went to the hero and proprietor, Swapankumar. Swapankumar asked him, 'So where does Chapal dress and do his make-up?'

'There is one room for the women, one for you and one for the other men. We have put Chapal in the room with the other men now because the women are not comfortable with him changing in their dressing room.'

'Hmm, I can understand their concern. But we can't let Chapal dress with the other men either,' said Swapankumar.

'There is an element of secrecy that is part of the transformation from a man into a woman. Preserving that is vital. If Chapal dresses as a woman in front of all these men, then the whole beauty of it will be ruined. He needs his privacy. I have an idea. My dressing room is large enough. Why not make some space for him there?'

He turned to me: 'Do you have any problem with that?'

I knew no one would dare to overrule the great Swapankumar. 'Of course not. But you are the director. On top of that, you are a big star and our leading man,' I mumbled. 'You really think I should use your room?'

'It's no problem at all. The room is very big. You can easily use one corner. I've been in this business long enough. At one time, my heroines were all men. Like Shatadal Rani and even Kshitish here. These women are new, they don't know that world. Don't mind them. As long as you have no objection, we can share my dressing room.'

'I have no objections. I just worry it will be an inconvenience. So many people come to meet you. I will be in the way.'

'Oh, screw all that. Maintaining the secrecy of your transformation is much more important.'

From then on, I always used Swapankumar's dressing room, though I had to hear many dirty insinuations but such is the world of jatra. I realized that Swapankumar really understood what it meant to turn Chapal Bhaduri into Chapal Rani. It was so much more than a simple costume change.

Yet it was all an act. At the end when I took it all off, I was back to being Chapal Bhaduri.

Off stage, I never wanted to wear women's clothes. I was perfectly content to wear kurtas and pyjamas or even trousers and suits if needed. On my birthdays, I would love to dress up in silk kurtas that gleamed like pearls and tight churidar pyjamas. I would wear gold rings, my gold watch, maybe a chain around my neck and host dinners at home. But I would never wear a sari or any of the jewellery that I wore for my roles on stage. The thought never occurred to me.

There was only one occasion when I wore a female costume that was not part of my character on stage. We had gone to Assam, and I saw the wraparound silk outfits that women wear there. I had not seen them before and was enchanted.

'What are these?' I asked the shopkeeper.

'Mekhola,' he said.

'How do you wear them? Is it like a sari?'

'Not really. Would you like one? Please take one.'

He offered me a beautiful green mekhla with black embroidery but I hesitated.

'What will I do with it?'

'We know you have a show of *Raja Devidas* in Jorhat tonight. We would be honoured if you wear it on stage. We are planning to go to see the jatra tonight anyway.'

'But how can I change my outfit? I already have my outfits for the play.'

'You are playing a princess. This will work perfectly. We will even come and help you wear it.'

When I told Makhan-babu and Surya-babu, they burst out laughing. Surya-babu said, 'No, no we can't suddenly have an Assamese outfit pop up in the middle of our play. Our play is not set in Assam.'

'Oh, let it be,' chuckled Makhan-babu. 'They are so excited about dressing Chapal, let them do it.' He thought it was good sport.

So I did *Devidas* that night in an Assamese mekhola. I have to admit it didn't really suit the role, but I wore it nonetheless and got away with it.

But I never wore saris in public and never wished to either.

Clothes Make the Woman

Imagine me standing in front of a mirror. I am Kohinoor, the adopted daughter of Badshah Shah Alam.

'Tell me, mirror,' I say. 'Who is more beautiful? You or I?'

It takes a lot of work to turn Chapal Bhaduri into a beautiful princess like Kohinoor. Hair, make-up, clothes, breasts, voice.

My Kohinoor outfit was rather elaborate. The base was black but it had heavy brocade zari embroidery, done with threads in many iridescent shades—green, blue, pink, white and golden. They were all intertwined in such a way that every time I moved, the entire dress shimmered. A line of fake 'Nagin' stones was embedded into the border at the bottom. It was stunning as an outfit but so murderously heavy that I could barely manage to do one or two scenes in it.

Chhabi Rani had designed the outfit. As a change artist for him, I inherited both the outfits and the roles meant for him. It took a while for me to get outfits that were wholly mine.

One day, Surya-babu suddenly said, 'Come early tomorrow. We have to get your outfits cut.'

'Outfits cut! What on earth is that?'

Off we went together through the narrow, crowded streets of Burrabazar, one of the oldest markets in Central Kolkata. Once the yarn and textile market in British times, home to cloth merchants with ties to Dhaka, Murshidabad and Cossimbazar, it's still the biggest market in India. At one time you could get everything there, from English broadcloth to spices from Ceylon to crockery from China. It is still bustling, crowded, overwhelming, a warren of pattis or neighbourhoods with names like Dhotipatti, Fancypatti, Chinipatti, each specializing in one kind of goods.

Surya-babu led me to a textile shop and told the shop owner, 'This is notun rani, the new queen. He's come in Chhabi's place. Cut a blouse for him.'

The material was thick, shiny velvet.

'I have to wear these heavy velvet blouses?' I protested. 'I am going to look so fat. Why don't we get something a little finer?'

'No, no, in jatra your outfits must be a little flashy, a little shiny, a little heavy. You have to dazzle the audience after all. Otherwise what's the point?'

The tailor measured out, or as they called it, 'cut' a velvet blouse and a velvet skirt. I didn't like them, but as a newbie artiste I didn't have much say in the matter.

Over time, as I got more confident, I started designing my own outfits. Then I could research them to my heart's content. I took the picture of a Rajasthani village woman to the tailor and asked him to make me that kind of a skirt and blouse. I studied little details, like how Marwari women veiled themselves vs how Punjabi women wore their dupatta. I didn't just have elaborate costumes for the sake of it. In jatra, speed was essential. In *Riziya*, I needed to change from one outfit to another in a matter of minutes. Even the women were astounded at how fast I could do it, but I designed the outfits that way.

And it helped that I had a tailor who understood me well.

Like Qasim had his own shop in a narrow lane near New Market. There was also Ghiasuddin in the Metiabruz area, Kolkata's mini-Lucknow where a deposed Nawab once lived out his exile. Ghiasuddin was my sister's go-to man for her outfits. Those tailors, and the best ones were Muslim, could customize our clothes so that our outfits stood out from the rest. Most jatra outfits came wholesale from Sindurpatti in Burrabazar. Shops like the one belonging to Panchkori Chattopadhyay had become a one-stop shop for many jatra troupes. You could get outfits for everyone there—kings, queens, dancing girls, soldiers, gods, goddesses.

In *Durgeshnandini* [Daughter of the Feudal Lord], the jatra based on Bankim Chandra Chattopadhyay's novel, I was playing Bimala, wife of Birendra Singha, a feudal lord. Hers is a mature kind of beauty while the other character, Tilottoma, daughter of Birendra Singha, is younger and more conventionally pretty. I chose Bimala's outfit with great care—a green chiffon-georgette sari with a golden border and a blouse of such sheer fabric that you could see the lines of my black brassiere through it.

'Why are you dressing up so much for this role?' someone in the group sneered, 'It's not exactly a mother role, but Bimala isn't some young woman either.'

'So how should I dress?'

'I don't know. But do you think all that make-up, that kind of outfit suits your character?'

'Did you know that Bimala was so seductive that when she danced for the rebel Pathan leader Katlu Khan, he was completely besotted? That's how she stabs him to death to avenge her husband's murder! Have you even read the novel? If you had, you would see how Bankim Chandra described Bimala's looks. He said she had the beauty of the setting sun.'

I didn't just memorize the lines that were given to me. I read the novels, the plays on which those roles were based. To be a true actor, you have to know these things. And if need be, you have to go beyond what's written on paper. As I did for *Sonar Bharat*.

The year I broke my hand and could not act, Chhabi Rani came back to Natta Company as my change artiste. At that time, his stock was on the decline, though he still had his good looks. He played Purnima, wife of Jaichand, a rival of Rajput king Prithviraj Chauhan. But his role made no impact on the audience even though it was a very poignant role.

In the play, Purnima goes mad after Jaichand dies and wanders dazedly around the battlefield, looking for him. She spots Muhammad Ghori, the Afghan invader.

PURNIMA. Who are you? Who? Are you a ghost? Or a demon?

GHORI. I am no ghost or demon. I am Mohammad Ghori. Who are you?

PURNIMA. I am King Jaichand's queen, his head queen. How dare you address me with such familiarity? Do you know who he is?

GHORI (*scoffs*). I won't know Jaichand? I am the one who slew him.

PURNIMA. Ha-ha, he thinks he killed Jaichand. What a fool!

Ghori grabs her by the hair and strikes her.

PURNIMA. What? You kicked me? Me?

Ghori draws his sword to kill her. Qutbuddin Aibak, a general of Ghori, enters and holds Ghori back.

AIBAK. What are you doing, my sultan? Do you know who she is? She is King Jaichand's wife.

PURNIMA (*to Aibak*). Who are you? You saved my life?

AIBAK. Yes, Mother. Let me help you up. Don't worry. You have nothing to fear.

PURNIMA. You called me Mother. Mother. Since you called me Mother, I must bless you. But how can I bless you? What do I have any more? (*Rises to leave, then stops.*) Wait. Let me see. (*She scribbles on the ground, like an old-time astrologer drawing a chart about the future.*) What did you say your name was?

AIBAK. Qutbuddin Aibak.

PURNIMA. I tell you, Qutbuddin Aibak, centuries will come and go but your name will not perish. No one will forget the name of Qutbuddin Aibak—no one.

Qutbuddin Aibak, of course, goes on to establish the Delhi Sultanate and commission the Qutb Minar in Delhi.

People usually play mad people by babbling and shrieking. I played Purnima differently. Every day, on my way to the Natta Company office, I used to see a mad woman sitting on the street near the Hatkhola post office, scribbling in the dirt. Sometimes she would pause and look up at the sky, wipe away whatever she had written and then scribble some more. It was as if she was calculating something, doing arithmetic in her head. I would feel sorry for her, but I also thought, 'Ah-ha, that's something I can use.' I used the madwoman of Hatkhola in my interpretation of Purnima. The actor who played Ghori would be annoyed by the length of time I took in this scene with all my scribbling. But I was adamant. This was my last scene in the play, and I was determined to do it my way.

When I did Purnima, no one cared about Prithivraj or Sanjukta, the hero and heroine of the play. Everyone only talked about Purnima.

The Art of Make-Up

Make-up is a big part of the transformation to a woman. But you have to make sure it suits your character. A goddess' eyes are different from that of a princess. An ordinary woman cannot look overly made up. An aged woman cannot highlight her lips too much. You should always be able to tell the bad girl from the good girl by her lips and her eyes. The bad girl's lips were always full and luscious, the good girl's less so. The fallen woman had one kind of lips, the queen another, the goddess something else. By the end of *Bharat Biday*, Queen Kaikeyi had almost no lipstick at all because she had to look utterly devastated.

When I started in jatra, make-up tools were so primitive. All we had were some pastes—safeda was white, a yellow called purée, and a dull red paste called metey sindoor. You had to mix all these with water to get a shade called gala, and figure out a recipe that worked for your role. Then you brushed that onto your face.

We whittled a small stick to a sharp point. That's what we used to apply kajal to the eyes.

There were no fake eyelashes. So we took black soot, mixed it with molten wax and made a paste out of it. Then we took a special pointed little brush, heated it over a candle and gently applied that paste to our eyes. It was dangerous, but it did make our eyes look large and beautiful. That was important. This was not theatre where your make-up can show up well under the stage lights. In jatra, all we had were Petromax lamps.

One time, I wasn't paying attention. As I was doing my eyes, my wig caught fire from the candle. Luckily, our bus driver noticed, jumped up and put his arms around me and valiantly tried to put out the flames. His act of chivalry didn't go down too well with his wife, though. She had already been complaining that he was staring at me a bit too much. So when he grabbed me, she became hysterical. I wasn't too upset—he was quite hunky.

Later, when I sometimes had a make-up man with me, I would teach him little tricks. Here's how to draw the eyes so they would look bigger, like the Goddess Durga. How to mix a brown and red colour and use that to highlight the cheeks. After you apply powder, brush it gently with some water, then put on the pancake make-up. It will look brighter. Once everything is done, dab the face with a swab of cotton wool soaked in glycerine. That makes it a little 'glazy'. These are all tricks of the trade.

But I never let anyone touch my lips. I did my lips at the end. They always had to be done by me.

Once, though, I was in an utter fix. In 1969, Nabaranjan Opera put on *Notun Probhat* [New Dawn]. Swapankumar came to me and said, 'Chapal, there isn't really any part for you in this production. Most of the characters are young modern women and our actresses are playing them. But there is one role that's a possibility. It's Paribano, wife of a poor Muslim farmer, mother of a six-year-old boy. It's a good role, even though it doesn't have many lines.'

'I'll do whatever you tell me,' I said.

But there was a problem.

Swapankumar said, 'You can't use heavy make-up. Or elaborate costumes.'

'But how can I pull this off without make-up? After all, I need to shave every day. There's a dark tinge to my chin now. I will need to mask that.'

Swapankumar shrugged, 'I have full faith in you. Figure out something and show women that you can go head to head with them.'

I was confounded. A woman could have pulled it off easily. But how could a man do this without heavy make-up? I went to my sister, Chhordi, for help.

She was amused by my predicament.

'What kind of clothes has your Swapankumar said that a poor Muslim farmer's wife should wear?'

'A torn blouse, a torn sari. My hair does not need to be anything special.'

'Wear a black blouse,' she said. 'I have one. Use that. Tear it a bit in front and a bit in the back so you can see a bit of skin. You are fair. It will look good against the black. And a torn sari.'

'And what about my make-up? What should I do about that?'

'Use Number 9.' Number 9 was a reddish colour, like brick. 'Put a little coconut oil on your face, no Vaseline, then use a bit of that Number 9 and blend it in well. Don't use powder. But dab your face with a puff, so that the oiliness is gone and the skin seems smooth, no any dark patches. Do your hair up in a loose bun and wear a silver nose ring.'

I added black glass bangles. Later I swapped them out for plastic because I was afraid they might break on stage. I could wear women's bangles because I knew how to bend my wrist and slide them on.

After I played the poor Muslim farmer's wife, everyone was stunned. Swapankumar's wife, the lead heroine, said, 'Why were you not born a woman?'

When she said that, my mother's face flashed before my eyes.

The Change Artiste

In the beginning, I needed others to do everything for me, from hair to make-up. Slowly, I learnt what worked for me and what did not. Soon, I could do it all myself. It took me just 25 minutes to dress for *Chand Bibi*. *Sultana Riziya* took a little longer. Most roles would take even less, 10 or 15 minutes. Then I would sit and gossip with the other actors as they did their make-up.

Once, we had a show in Rishra, an old industrial township on the bank of the Hooghly, an hour from Kolkata. In those days, you had to cross a rail line to get there. If you were unlucky, you could be stuck for a while at the level crossing.

Our show was on a field next to the railway tracks. That day, Natta Company was staging *Sonar Bharat*. The performance was scheduled from 5 p.m., right after the factories in that area had closed down for the day. It would go on till 8 at night.

Makhan-babu and I reached the level crossing in our car and found the gate was shut. But we were not too worried. It was just about 4.45, and the show was not to begin until 5. Yet I could hear the strains of very familiar music coming from the field.

'Can you hear the music?' I asked Makhan-babu. 'That sounds like Panchu-da's clarionet.' Panchu Pal, the clarionet player, was a staple of the jatra scene at the time.

'Just open the car door,' I told Makhan-babu.

'What are you going to do?' He was shocked. 'Are you going to run across the tracks?'

I sprinted across the tracks, rushed to the tent—and I found they were already on the second scene! I was scheduled to make my entrance in the fourth, in full costume and make-up as a Rajasthani princess.

Soon Makhan-babu got there too and was in a tizzy.

'How could you all start like this? You knew Chapal had not even arrived.'

'People thought it would get too late if we started at 5. So we had to start an hour earlier,' the manager said.

'And you just did?'

'Don't get into all this back and forth now,' I told Makhan-babu. I turned to the dresser and said, 'Just give my peshwaj jacket.' I was already wearing my Rajasthani pyjamas.

I held my arms out and said, 'Put my blouse on.' He did.

'Hair.' They put on the wig.

I quickly drew my eyebrows, smudged my eyes with some eye-liner on my fingers, draped the veil around me like a Rajasthani princess and walked onto the stage. No one realized I had barely made it, but I made my scene.

Hair Line

Now for hair. I remember clearly the first time I did my own hair. The play was called *Keranir Jibon* [The Life of a Clerk]. It showed the life of a very ordinary family. We would light a mud stove on stage, the mother would roll out rotis, the elder daughter would cook them on the coal-fired stove. I played that elder daughter, a widow who had come back to her brother's family after her husband's death.

Until then, my friend Subrata always did my hair. One night, he could not travel with me because he had a show elsewhere.

'Oh no,' I said. 'Then who will do my hair?'

'But I've taught you how to,' he said.

'Will I be able to do it on my own?'

'Here, let me show you again.'

After that, I had no problem. I learnt how to part it, clip it and then put on the wig and make sure it stayed in place.

But I could only do fairly basic hairstyles. My dancer friend Parijaat said, 'Chapal-da, in all your plays, you either have your hair open or tied in a loose bun. Let me make a proper bun for you this time.'

'A proper bun with my wig?' I asked.

'Just you see,' he said. He tied my own hair into two plaits, added extra length using something we called 'lot' and then combined it with the wig to create a grand bun. The whole thing was held in place with a silver pin with little bells which would tinkle as I walked. I was amazed.

'But I am going to need you to take it off' I said. 'Are you going to be there for that?'

'I'll be there.'

'And we'll need to change quickly as well.'

'Don't worry about that. I'll take it off in a jiffy.'

The biggest hair challenge was in *Plabon*, in which I played a Muslim woman who has fallen in love with a Hindu man, both part of a revolutionary group.

FATHER. Are you not ashamed? As a Muslim girl, you have fallen in love with a Hindu man. Have you no shame? That too a revolutionary. I will reveal everything about them. I will complain to the authorities.

GIRL. Father, you will not. I forbid you.

FATHER. I will. You cannot stop me.

GIRL. What? You will not listen to your daughter's plea.

FATHER. No, I will not.

GIRL. Then you can go to your grave. (*Takes out her pistol and shoots him, then goes to the police station.*) I have killed someone. Arrest me.

INSPECTOR. Whom have you killed?

GIRL. My father. He was going to reveal our group's activities.

INSPECTOR. Who is your group's leader?

GIRL. I will not tell you.

The police beat her and torture her and in one scene even pull her by her hair. So I had to make sure my hair didn't come off on stage. That time I had to do my wig differently. There was a little spring and a contraption to fix the hair to my head. I figured it out myself and told the wigmakers how to design it. After that, no matter how hard you pulled, it would not come off.

Mehboob, our old hairdresser, taught me how to take care of my wigs. 'Take two sachets of shampoo and soak the wig in cold water. Rinse well, the way a woman shampoos her hair. Then turn the wig inside out and keep it in strong sunlight for a little bit. Ultimately, though, you must dry it in the shade. When it's dry, oil it gently with whatever hair oil you prefer.' My standard was Keo Karpin.

Hair can really change the geography of your face. So many of our famous actresses like Hema Malini and Mumtaz had really broad foreheads but they used their hair to cover it. Sometimes when I look at myself in the mirror, what makes me saddest is that most of my hair is gone.

Breast Man

What is a woman without breasts? When I began, we just had little mounds of rags that were held in place by cloth and then tied at the back. We had no bras or bodices. But if you tied it correctly, it would not shift while acting. And you could wear a blouse on top of it.

But an actor once told me he hated to embrace me onstage. My breasts were too hard, they poked when he bumped against them. So I went to New Market to find the right kind of sponge and stuffed that in little pouches. It looked a bit like the masks people wore on their faces during Covid. Those became my breasts.

In *Satyashrayee*, I played Jharna, daughter of a minister in a royal court. She was in love with a military commander named Muktoporno. Muktoporno joins the service of a rival king and comes to fight against his former kingdom.

JHARNA. I thought you loved me. You have given my father your word that you will marry me. And now you have come to do battle against my father! Siding with the enemy. What kind of love is this?

MUKTOPORNO. Love is love. But I cannot go against my duty.

JHARNA. I will not stand for this. You cannot come against us like this. Let's make a wager. Let me see how many soldiers you can slay and let us see how many I can.

MUKTOPORNO. Jharna! What are you saying? You are a woman and you will come to the battlefield?

JHARNA. Yes, I will. And I will go in such a fashion that every soldier will be so dazzled by my beauty that they will rush towards me like moths drawn to a flame. And as they fight among themselves, I will kill them with my own hands.

What a scene that was! I made the sponge breasts a little larger than usual, exactly like two halves of a coconut. After I fixed them on myself with spirit gum, you could hardly tell they were artificial. I painted my body the same colour as the breasts, because I had to perform that scene bare-bodied. Then I draped a very fine red, almost sheer, Benarasi cloth around myself. So that if I leaned forward, the cloth would slip and reveal my cleavage. In those days, electric lights had not come to jatra. That cleavage lit by the glow of Petromax lamps would drive the audience absolutely wild.

This was not something I invented. All the great queens of jatra like Chhabi Rani and Babli Rani used this trick. I learnt it from them.

The Voice

When it came to playing a woman, though, my biggest asset was always my voice, naturally high and sweet. Chhabi Rani had the looks but his voice had no sweetness. Some actors like Babli-da would just try to imitate a woman's voice. Many actors continue to do that.

I once asked a young actor, 'Why do you all imitate a woman's voice like that?'

'We don't all have naturally high voices like you, Chapal-da.'

'Maybe not, but you need to talk naturally. Don't mimic. That will backfire. Your voice will get distorted, your vocal cords will get affected. Instead, close your eyes and summon up your femininity from inside you.'

'My goodness, Chapal-da, that all sounds a bit too profound for us.'

'But this is how we had to learn. This is how we had to train ourselves. You lot do not even know how to modulate your voices properly.'

Everyone thinks that, in order to play a woman, you just have to make exaggerated swishing movements with your hands and make your voice high-pitched and squeaky. That is caricature. Acting is about normality, not abnormality.

My own voice was weak when I started at Natta Company. But when you have no other choice, you learn how to do everything. Slowly, my voice gained power because the characters required it. I needed to be able to project my voice on stage whether I was shouting or screaming or doing a romantic scene. And I had to do it night after night. People always asked whether I had a special regimen for my voice, but I did not. I didn't gargle regularly or take any homeopathic pills. I liked my paan and chewing tobacco. I drank hot tea. When I caught a bit of a cold and it affected my voice, I asked Surya-babu what to do.

He said, 'Have some dry muri or puffed rice.'

'Muri? No medicine?'

'No, no, just dry muri.'

He was right. It somehow did fix my voice.

Initially, I would try to scream at the top of my lungs. But Surya-babu put an end to that. 'Why are you screeching, Chapal?'

'People are saying if I don't do that, the audience at the back won't be able to hear me. And it's jatra. Everything is at higher pitch.'

'Your voice is fine. People will tell you all kind of things, that doesn't mean you have to listen to everything. Look at my finger. See my knuckle. You are acting at this level. Dial it down a notch. Like to the base of the finger. You will see, people will understand perfectly fine.'

He was right. That's why he was my guru.

My voice gradually grew stronger. But thankfully it remained sweet. Once, when I was living with my sister, the phone rang. In those days, you would often get wrong numbers and cross connections. I picked it up.

'Hello.'

'Who is this?' It was a man's voice.

'Me? I am Teesta,' I promptly lied, making up a woman's name.

'Teesta? Where do you live? You sound lovely.'

'Why, thank you. So sweet.'

The unknown man started flirting gently and I flirted right back as Teesta.

Emboldened, he said, 'Will you meet me somewhere?'

'Where?'

'What about in front of Metro cinema? What will you wear?'

'I will be in a black silk saree with a black blouse. And I'll carry a handbag. I'm sure you will recognize me.'

'All right, then, I'll see you tomorrow?'

I quickly hung up.

My voice was my asset when it came to making me Chapal Rani. But as times changed, that same voice became my handicap.

'Look, the situation for actors like you isn't going to get better. More and more women are going to come in,' a well-wisher said. 'Why don't you see if you can change your voice?'

'How do I change my voice?' I asked.

'Go meet the ENT specialist, Dr Abir Lal Mukherjee. He is the best.' I knew of him. He knew my sister well and respected her a lot.

He examined me and said, 'Yes, we can do a surgery and change your voice somewhat. But why would you want to?'

'To help my acting career,' I replied.

'Don't you play female roles anyway?'

'That's why I want to change my voice. So that perhaps I can play male roles as well.'

Dr. Mukherjee looked thoughtful. 'It's possible. Tell me, has this been your voice from the beginning?'

'Yes.'

'A boy's voice usually starts to change around 12 or 13. Did that happen to you?'

'Not really.' It had not happened and no one in my family had been perturbed about it. My mother had just died. Our family was in shambles, everyone was trying their best to hold things together. No one had much time to pay attention to my voice.

Dr Mukherjee said, 'I understand you want to act in male roles. But as a doctor and as your well-wisher, I am advising you not to tamper with what you have. If we do an operation, there's a chance that it can go husky or cracked. Now, you tell me, which one you would prefer?'

I didn't know how to answer him. Seeing my confusion, he said, 'I say: forget about any operation. Try to speak more in a low voice. And gradually it might change on its own.'

But that was just not possible. How could I suddenly start speaking in a different voice? If you keep scrubbing a metal plate every day, it slowly gets more and more smooth. That's what had happened to my voice. And the more I played women, the more effeminate I became. There was no way around it. All those years of acting left their mark on me. And inside me. Day after day, year after year, I was putting those sponge balls into my bodice, and wearing a blouse over them. There were marks on my chest from that bodice. The string of the petticoat cut into my waist. There was no getting away from any of that.

The voice stayed high.

Labour Pains

When I joined jatra, people would give me all kinds of advice about how to play a woman. I had heard that some jatra actors trained themselves to always put their left foot forward first or use the left hand more, because women were said to be bama, favouring the left side. Rules like that made no sense to me. 'If a mad bull chases me, am I going to think about which foot I put forward first?' I asked. 'Anyway, some of these women I play, like Chand Bibi and Sultana Riziya, were very masculine as well. Which foot should they favour?' No one had an answer to that. I firmly believe that one had to do what came naturally.

What is more important is thinking deeply about the role—are you playing a mother or a coy young girl? If it's a mother, you have to figure out how to bring out that maternal feeling not just through your clothes but also through your expressions, your looks. You have to analyse the character and then express it on stage. Only then will the audience accept you. We were playing women, we were not playing men acting as women. You had to understand something about being a woman. I might not be able to bear a child, but I think I understand a bit about the psyche of women.

I believe firmly that a woman has a shakti, a force, an energy that men don't have. They can do many things a man cannot. Women are khetro, like a fallow field. Men are khetrogyo, as in those who know how to till that soil. Women have a sixth sense which men do not. Which is why, I often say half-jokingly, so many men have been duped by women. I may not have acquired that sixth sense, but I certainly have fooled my share of men.

Like the time I was playing a young woman being raised as an unmarried girl in her rich father's house. Then she finds out that she was once married, and that her husband is dead.

'Why did you not tell me I am a widow?' she asks her father accusingly and exits, then changes from the green silk sari into a widow's white cotton. The dresser would be ready in the green room to help me change quickly, put a white tika on my forehead, remove my jewellery and muss my hair.

At a performance in Jamshedpur, I was on my way to the green room to change my sari when suddenly I felt I was floating in the air.

Before I even realized what was happening, some strapping young Sikh men had grabbed me, picked me up and deposited me in their jeep. The organizers and stagehands came rushing out, shouting: 'Stop! Stop! What are you doing?'

The men had thought I was a real woman and decided to abduct me.

A tug-o-war ensued. The jatra people were holding on to my left arm while my lovestruck kidnappers hung tight to the other.

'I am going to take you home with me,' said one.

'Come with me, darling. Marry me,' laughed another.

'But this is our actor. He is a man,' protested one of the members of our troupe.

'No, no, that cannot be.' They were completely disbelieving.

Finally, I had to take off my wig to prove that I was actually a man. By then I was entirely dishevelled, my clothes were torn, my make-up a mess. Somehow I managed to pull myself together and finish my performance. After that incident, whenever the green room was at some distance from the stage, I would insist that someone accompany me there.

Another time, while acting in *Plabon*, blinded by all the lights, I tripped and fell and broke my wrist. I was rushed to Bangur Hospital in South Kolkata, groaning in pain. I was still in a sari because I had had no time to change. The medical staff took one look at me and tried to send me to the maternity ward, convinced I was having labour pains. I had to curse at them and scream for my wig to be taken off. Now it seems funny. At that time, it didn't feel that way.

Many actors who played women on stage have similar stories of men, fooled by their performances, trying to abduct them, woo them or proposition them. I am just one in a long line of actors who played women on the stage. All in their own ways made their mark. Chhabi-da, Babli-da, Haripada-da. I have seen some of them act and even acted in some of their roles. But though it sounds arrogant when I say it, I hope I brought something extra to those roles and that earned me a different kind of fame.

Keeping Up with the Girls

Voice, make-up, hair, costumes. I was riding high. The audience loved me.

I didn't know then that the same audience that had once raised me to the stars would one day bring me crashing to earth.

But for a while they were eating out of my hands, and I revelled in the adulation. There was a certain freedom that comes with acting as women, playing what I was not. A stranger would come and say, 'The scene where you lift your sari and show your calves as Chintamoni is out of the world.' He would give me a garland of jasmine flowers. That night I would wear the flowers in my hair, and when I'd lift my sari so the maid could line my feet with red alta, I would give my legs a good shake so that the bells in my anklets tinkled a little louder for my jasmine man.

Another time, I was performing at Durgabari in Ranchi city. I was wearing a deep-blue Benarasi silk sari. As I made my way to the performance space through a narrow passage, I noticed a few young men loitering. As I squeezed past them, I felt a tug on my sari. One of the men had taken out a blade and cut off a piece off my anchal! He draped it around his neck like a scarf, looked at me insolently and said with a sly smile 'Go, go and do your acting now.' I couldn't say a word. These men were the local toughs, they could shut down the show if they wanted. I had to digest their impertinence.

How convincingly one plays a woman varies from man to man. But from watching others I noticed something that often gave them away—their hands and feet, their wrists. That's why I have always taken great care of my hands and feet. I still massage them with cream or olive oil, so that I do not get dark patches. Swapankumar would marvel that my legs were as smooth as polished bell metal. I would use Anne French hair remover to get rid of all the hair from my underarms and legs. I needed to do it every week. It was a chore but it was important, especially in a jatra like *Sultana Riziya* where my legs could be seen. If you see Helen dancing in a Hindi film, she is barely wearing any clothes. But she never looks obscene. Now I see women dancing in sleeveless dresses but they don't bother to shave their armpits.

Once, I saw another actor playing Maxim Gorky's Mother. He asked me if he looked all right. I said, 'You are a well-known actor. You are playing the mother. But why did you not shave your armpits? Anyway, there's nothing you can do now. Just fasten the sari close to you with a safety pin and hope for the best.'

Even women didn't always understand why I was so particular about my make-up and accessories. Sometimes, actresses would look at my make-up box and ask, 'Where did you buy all this, Chapal-da?'

'From a shop, of course. It's not like I just came back from London. But you cannot go to just any store. You need to go to a brand-name store. Just being a woman isn't enough. You need to do your homework too.'

'You use all this for your make-up, Chapal-da?'

'Of course I do.'

'That's why you look so good. They just give us cheap Renuka powder. And coloured paints. How much can you do with that?'

'You should ask for better cosmetics. Or buy them yourselves.'

'The company does not buy all these for you?'

'Why would the company spend this much money on me? '

'Doesn't it bother you to spend your own money on this?'

'Why should it? I don't wear the company's wigs either. I spend my money to have them made because I have to keep up with you girls, after all. I need to look the best I can.'

Acting as a woman was my bread and butter. Wigs, make-up, everything was important. Everything had to be in the right measure. What worked for the queen in *Sultana Riziya* did not work for the middle-aged Punjabi mother in *Jallianwala Bagh*. You had to get it right. Otherwise you could become the object of ridicule on stage.

Many years ago, someone showed me a newspaper clipping and said, 'Take a look, Chapal-da, and tell me if you recognize this person. It's a famous jatra artiste.'

The person in the picture was truly beautiful.

'Who is this lady?' I asked in wonder.

'It's not a lady. It's a gentleman. Take a closer look.'

'Is that Chhabi-da?' I wondered. Chhabi Rani was known for his looks.

'No, no. Someone more recent. He created quite a sensation in a very short time. But I don't know where he is these days.'

'You are sure it's not a woman?' I could not be sure. Even in my heyday I don't think I looked that beautiful.

Then the man's wife and children started giggling. And he said, 'It's you, Chapal-da. It's your photograph! Can't you recognize yourself?'

It was from *Sultana Riziya*—but I had never seen those photographs. They would appear in newspapers and magazines, but I was so busy, I never had the time to pick up a copy.

Now time has washed everything away. Nothing is left, not even the photographs.

The Photograph in the Wallet

But once a photograph got me into so much trouble.

It was probably around 1956–57. I had not started in jatra then. I was acting as Bijoya in Sarat Chandra's play of the same name in an amateur production at a friend's house. The man who was playing Naren, the person to whom Bimala had been betrothed, was Titu-da. He was my oldest brother's friend. We were going to stage the performance during Durga Puja.

Titu-da was quite handsome. He was the one who persuaded me to act in the play in the first place. I didn't really want to do it, because my eldest brother didn't approve of me acting. He thought I should be paying more attention to my studies.

'Your brother won't say anything to me,' Titu-da said. 'Anyway, it's our home production.'

There is a scene where Naren has bought a microscope. Bijoya does not know how to use it. As she tinkers with it, he tries to show her, their heads bump against each other. And that's the beginning of their relationship.

Everyone was very happy during the rehearsals. Godai-da, Titu-da's older brother, told me, 'Oh Tuku, you are just splendid in this role. Your voice is just perfect.' Then he teased Titu-da: 'Titu, you had better up your acting game. Tuku is going to leave you in the dust.'

We would rehearse from the morning. They would cook lunch for us at the house itself. Then everyone would settle down with cigarettes and paan. I didn't smoke but would have some paan. Around three, we would start rehearsing again.

The girls and women of the house would sometimes come and peek into our rehearsal from the next room. Hearing my voice, some of them thought I was a real girl. They were stunned to hear I was actually a boy.

Titu-da, still unmarried, tall and handsome, was a great favourite among the girls. One day, he came up to me and said, 'Listen, Tuku, there is a request.'

'What?'

'The girls want to dress you as a bride and me as the groom, just like in the last scene, and take a photograph.'

'What nonsense are you saying?' I protested. 'How can we? Anyway, I am wearing a shirt now, how can I dress as a girl? We can't do all this.'

'No, no, they will make all the arrangements.'

'No, I can't just wear a saree here.'

The girls were insistent. They said, 'You can do this.'

I still kept making excuses. I don't have bangles for my hand, I said.

But they refused to listen. Someone got a red Benarasi sari and made me wear it. They made me pull it across my head like a new bride. My hair was long anyway at that time. They parted it and gave me a dab of sindoor. They had me roll up my shirt and pin it in place so it looked like a full sleeved blouse. One of the ladies of the house loaned me her gold bracelets. Someone found an old mukut, the white pith crown that brides wear on the wedding night. I protested but they said: you won't look like a bride without it. They found a pith topor that grooms wear on their heads for Titu-da. I was dying of embarrassment.

Then they made us pose like a real couple. When those photographs were developed, everyone was stunned. I was looking into his eyes, my faced upturned towards him, my own eyes limpid as he embraced me, gently holding my chin, At that time, I was still very young. My moustache had not sprouted fully yet. You couldn't make out that I was wearing my shirt as a blouse under that sari, everything was so artfully covered.

Titu-da showed me the picture and said, 'Look how beautifully they have come out. Just look at the two of us. What do you think? Should I show your brother?'

'Absolutely not. He'll kick me out of the house. I can't believe you took these pictures. What nonsense is all this?'

Soon I forgot about that picture. Titu-da and I acted again in another play. This time he was Emperor Aurangzeb and I was his sister, Jahanara.

After that, I left amateur theatre and joined professional jatra. Titu-da started working in a bank. He got married as well, but I could not go to the wedding because I was working that night.

One night, suddenly, Titu-da showed up at my house. At that time, there was a jatra festival happening nearby. Natta Company was staging *Chand Bibi* and I was playing the title role.

I took one look at him and said, 'Titu-da, what happened? How did you put on so much weight?'

'That happens when one gets married, Tuku, which by the way you did not attend.'

'I am sorry. It's very hard for me to go to these social engagements any more. I am always working. But it looks like you are happy in your marriage.'

'Well, you have to do me a favour. My married life depends on it. If you don't, God knows my wife might leave me. You can't imagine what's going on.'

'What are you talking about?'

He brought out his wallet, and said, 'Look at this. This is the source of all my problems.'

It was that 'wedding' picture of the two of us from that long-ago play.

Then he told me the whole story.

'Every day my wife gets all my stuff ready before I go to the office. She lays out my clothes and hands me my briefcase and wallet and handkerchief before I leave. One day, she said, "Here's your wallet," and then went silent. I was distracted and said, "Oh, aren't you going to give me the wallet?" She said nothing. I didn't think too much of it and left for work. When I came home, I found her standing silently by the window, looking out onto the street. Neither did she move, nor did she say a word.

'I went up to her and said, "What's wrong? Why are you standing like that? How come I didn't get a cup of tea today?"'

'She turned to me and said, "Why? Don't you have another place to drink tea? Why didn't you have tea there?"'

'I had no idea what she was talking about. Then she showed me this photograph which she must have taken from my wallet and said, "You didn't tell me you were already married once. Who is this woman?" I started laughing and she got even more angry. I told her it's a boy dressed as a girl but she refused to believe me. Now it's all up to you, Tuku.'

Now it was my turn to laugh. 'OK, Titu-da, we have shows for four days in Laha Colony. *Chand Bibi.* Please come there with your wife. I'll organize tickets for you.'

Titu-da and his wife showed up. Later, she told him, 'Who is this actress? She looks very familiar.'

Then it dawned on her. 'This is that lady from the photograph.'

Titu-da said, 'See I told you. These are not ladies. These are men who act as women on stage.'

'You lie,' she said. 'It's that same woman.'

At the end of the show, when Titu-da brought me to her, she was still upset. 'You had a relationship with my husband. You even married her. I remember those eyes from the photograph.'

I brought them to the green room, asked them to sit down, and then told her, 'Now sit and watch.'

Then I slowly started removing my make-up, my wigs, my ornaments and transformed back to Chapal Bhaduri from Chapal Rani. Years later, I would do the same in many plays on the stage, but this was real life.

She stared at me in amazement and then started laughing. 'Please forgive me. I am so embarrassed.'

'There is nothing to forgive,' I said. 'Anyone could make this mistake. This is my job. If I couldn't pull it off realistically, the audience would throw stones at me.'

'No, no, you look so beautiful. I was completely fooled. Please come and visit us. I hear you live in the neighbourhood.'

'Yes indeed. But, sadly, tomorrow we leave for Asansol. Once I am back, I will certainly visit.'

I did, and she was very hospitable and gracious. Later, I asked Titu-da, 'Why did you keep that photograph in your wallet?'

'I don't know,' he replied. 'Somehow, whenever I looked at it, I would feel a strange sensation. I would feel like getting married. And within six months I did get married. But I still kept that photograph.'

He was a very nice man, that Titu-da.

INTERLUDE

In Imagination

The Heroine

'Men still make the best women at least when it comes to jatra.'

If I got ten rupees for every time I heard that, I'd be a rich woman today.

Nowadays, I hear all kinds of titles attached to my name. Jatra legend, Jatra Queen, Jatra Lakshmi, Jatra pioneer. But it was no picnic being part of the first generation of women in jatra. No one rolled out a red carpet for us.

Instead, everyone listed all the reasons they could about why we shouldn't be there. Women's voices are too soft. If you are in a village and there are 5,000 people sitting all around the stage, how will your voice carry to everyone without mics? That last person in the last row in a crowd of 5,000 needs to hear you when you say, 'Maharaj, I am yours.' Jatras are on the road all year. They are creatures of the night. Which self-respecting family will let their daughter go around like a vagabond? Sometimes, there aren't proper places to stay. We go do our business in the fields. Can you do that? Do you know how rough it can get? We've had audiences try to kidnap the jatra ranis. Then they have to take off their wigs and saris to prove they are men. What will you do?

If women came into jatra, they said, it would be the beginning of the end. Newspapers said jatra would lose its way, it would lose its dignity and crass commercialism would replace artistic principles.

Brajen Day had written so many palas showing women standing up for their rights. In his pala *Upekkhita* [The Spurned], Amba questions the double standards of society and rebels against Bhishma when he abducts her and then spurns her. In *Akaler Desh* [Land of Famine], Matongo is shown as accepting his wife when she returns to him, refusing to question her purity.

That same Brajen Dey apparently said that if women entered jatra, they would sow the seeds of destruction. It angered so many of us, we wrote a letter to *Jatrajagat* magazine protesting his 'uncouth gesture.' We signed it—I, Jyotsna Dutta, Chhabi Roy, Bina Ghosh, all of us.

Later, his son said Brajen-babu was simply concerned about us. He thought the rough-and-tumble world of jatra was not ready to guarantee our security, that it would create too many problems for us. So they should continue with the male ranis till security for women could become foolproof. Which meant never.

Change never comes to those who wait patiently. You have to force the doors open.

We, the first generation of women in jatra, were there because we were desperately poor. All our stories sound the same, almost like a jatra script. Faridpur, Jessore, Barisal. These are the places we came from. Bijoygarh, Khidirpur, Naktala—these were the neighbourhoods of Kolkata we ended up in. I too came from a refugee family from East Pakistan. My parents had fled from there with nothing but what they could carry. We were dirt poor, starting out at the bottom. My father tried his hand at small businesses. All of them failed. I didn't get into jatra to become a star. I went into it because I wanted to put food on the table somehow. My schooling ended in Class 8 because there was no money. I could sing and dance a little and had acted in small child roles in amateur productions. Someone told me the jatras were looking for women. It sounded better than washing dishes in someone's house.

If anyone showed us the way, it was Jyotsna Dutta. We all came in her wake. We were the first generation of women in jatra. But jatra wasn't ready for us.

I remember the first jatra I was in. They set up a dressing room for us. And I went there and found Chapal Rani doing his make-up. I said, 'How can I change here?' The manager said, 'Well, where will he do his make-up then? He can't do it with the other men.'

'But he is a man,' I protested.

The manager said, 'No, he is a rani.' The manager was once a rani himself. It was clear where his sympathies lay.

They were the ranis, the queens. They were special. We were merely common women. At first, women were deemed not good enough for audiences used to the rani style of acting. It stung after I acted my heart out to see the audience throng around Chapal Rani, to hear them say that a real woman could not hold a candle to his mother role.

'Men still make the best women at least when it comes to jatra.'

Surya Dutta of Natta Company would say: when a man acts a woman, that is art. Meaning: when a woman acts as a woman, that's nothing special? It would make me furious. What was so spectacular about what these men did? It was just trickery of costume and voice modulation to me. If you just flounce your hands a little, do you become a woman?

I found out later that women were not such strangers to jatra. Some had acted in jatra troupes even in Sri Chaitanya's time, when jatra began. They played music and banged cymbals. Muktamani Kundu, the wife of a wealthy businessman in Nabadwip founded a jatra group in the 1870s. It became popular as Bou-Kundur Dol or Kundu's Wife's Troupe, though the actors were all men. Trailokyatarini of the Sonagachi district had her own troupe of both men and women. As did Katagolapi and Bhabatarini.

But these women are lost to history. By the time we came along, it was like starting afresh. We gritted our teeth and hung in there. We were young and poor and desperate. Maybe that's why we didn't give up. And let me tell you, some of those managers were bastards. Our security was their responsibility but some of them extorted their pound of flesh from us. At least, Chapal Rani didn't take advantage of us. We were safe with him. But some of the other stars? The less said the better.

Tapan Kumar was called heartbreaker by a rag of a magazine and he was proud of that title. So many stars had two 'wives' and two families. One actress had to return to her home in the red-light district after her 'husband' tried to make her abort their child. Some of us found money, but love? That was always so much harder to find. When Jyotsna Dutta wanted to marry Swapankumar, her own mother tried to sabotage their love affair, afraid she would lose her golden goose. His mother said he couldn't marry her because Jyotsna wasn't a Brahman girl. Her jatra troupe's manager, scared he would lose his star heroine, encouraged both families to oppose the relationship. In the end, he married Kaberi, a jatra dancer but at least a Brahman. Poor Kaberi did snag the famous Swapankumar, but she was so paranoid, she had spies in every troupe to see what mischief he was getting up to. And she would show up unannounced to try and catch him in the act.

All of Kaberi's spying came to nought. Their husband–wife drama just annoyed everyone so much that troupes decided to boycott Swapankumar despite him being a superstar. So he set up his own troupe, Swapan Opera, and promptly eloped with the newcomer actress in that troupe—Swapnakumari. Poor Kaberi!

In some ways, Brajen-babu was proven right. Soon every jatra pala found some excuse to have me molested and my sari unravelled, all in the name of raising awareness about the plight of women. The dresses got tighter and shorter. The necklines plunged deeper. When a man playing a woman showed off his cleavage between his coconut-shell boobs using some trickery of lighting, that was art. When we had to show our cleavage, that was a free peep show.

We had to really fight for our place. That's why, in 1975, Bina Ghosh and Jyotsna Dutta set up Jatra Abhinetri Parishad. There was no one else who would stand up for the women in jatra. It didn't last long, but it was a beginning.

In a way, the more things change, the more they stay the same. Chapal-da once told me his mother's brothers turned their back on her because she was an actress. She was no better than a prostitute in their eyes. Then, one day, that same brother showed up to ask her money. That story repeated itself so many times in all our lives.

Sahana Basu's uncle ridiculed her mother because she lived off the earnings of a jatrawali. Then when his own daughter was going to get married, he showed up to beg for money. Sahana never tired of telling us that story. The hypocrisy of the middle-class Bengali knows no bounds. They want their women to have college degrees but then sit at home and gossip. It's all about appearances.

Still, we did change things for the better. Though it was hard to get out of the shankha-sindoor-alta trap, those glycerine-soaked senior wife, middle wife, junior wife–type roles. But when Mamata Banerjee became the chief minister of West Bengal, did you see the number of jatra palas that told her story? *Banglar Kshamatay Mamata* [Mamata in Power in Bengal], *Banglar Masnade Mamata* [Mamata on the Throne of Bengal], *Matir Ghare Mamata* [Mamata in a Mud Hut] . . . That's empowerment too. We were not second fiddle to the men, living and dying by their whims. I feel Mamata understood the power of jatra more than most of the other city-bred bhadralok politicians.

I think it took women coming to jatra for jatra makers to realize we were always its real audience. Chapal Rani will disagree, but I think the '70s were the golden age of jatra. Everyone was pumping money into it. Managers were throwing money at us, trying to woo us from one troupe to another. There was so much buzz that the

newspapers had reporters who only worked the Chitpur beat where all the jatra companies were located. Our love affairs sold film magazines and newspapers like hot cakes.

But it was still hard to get respect from the Bengali bhadralok intellectuals who smoked cigarettes and drank coffee at Coffee House and talked about filmmakers like Satyajit Ray and Mrinal Sen with their black-and-white films that won awards abroad. The people in Kolkata gushed over *Pather Panchali* after the West hailed it as a masterpiece because it let them go to the real Bengal without getting their hands dirty. They forgot most of Bengal lived outside Kolkata. In the 'real Bengal', they didn't need to see *Pather Panchali*. That was their life already. There they wanted Swapankumar and Jyotsna Dutta doing *Agniparikhsa* [Trial by Fire].

Now some people point fingers at us and say we brought about the end of the Chapal Ranis and Chhabi Ranis. But we didn't. The times were changing and audiences wanted to see real women play women on stage. Those ranis had their age and now it was over. That wasn't our fault, was it?

I acted in several palas with Chapal Rani. I honestly thought it would continue like that. We would both have our place on the stage. I both admired him and resented him. It made me angry that ranis like him had made a certain kind of woman the norm, so much so that we who were real women had to fight to prove ourselves every step of the way. I was jealous of the attention he got. I still am. I am just one of a long line of forgotten jatra heroines rotting away in old age. Sometimes it upsets me when people like you come and do your wistful pieces about the female impersonators but ignore the struggles of the females who came after them.

But, yes, I was in awe of what Chapal-da could do on stage, how he could break the hearts of men who knew full well he was a man. I wish I had talked to him more about what it meant to be a rani. But we just circled around each other, both friends and adversaries. We could gossip about the men, about the dirty business that was part of any jatra. We would look out for each other. But deep down we knew he was the old guard and we were the new wave. I wish I had really talked to him, girl to girl, heart to heart. I could have asked his advice on so many things—on acting, on make-up and on love. On yes, love for sure.

I think the best ranis understood something about what being a woman meant. They straddled the worlds of both men and women. They switched from one to another, but some part of them lived in a shadowy place that was both. They understood the love stories between men and women the way very few did.

When a jatra actress married a man who had been a rani once, some of my friends tittered. But I said: perhaps she will be happier than most of us. Look at the mess our love lives are in. We chase the Swapankumars and Tapan Kumars and they dump us for the next young thing. We hope the sons of Kolkata's first families will give us status and respectability. But when it comes to marriage, all of them go crawling back to their mothers with their tails between their legs. The proprietor of a famous jatra company fathered a child, a girl, he even admitted to it when she confronted him years later. He offered her money but not his name. She refused to accept it. I know a heroine who married the jatra company cook just to get some respectability. I told my friends: perhaps this man who has played a woman for years will understand his wife better than others.

Chapal-da always said he understood the pain of being a woman. Once, he pulled up his kurta and showed me a line on his waist: 'See that line? It's from the petticoat string. All these years of playing women have eaten into me. I call it the mark of a woman.'

The day I heard they had thrown clay cups at Chapal Rani and driven him offstage, my heart ached for him. That's the day I finally felt like he was my sister-in-arms. He had been the queen of queens but now he was being tossed aside. As a woman, I understood what had happened only too well. I know only too well what it means to live in a world of men (and women) who will woo you, worship you and then spit you out.

Chapal-da didn't throw a fit, he didn't complain to everyone, he didn't have a tantrum. He just disappeared into silence. There must have been hurt, there must have been pride, there must have been disbelief at the ingratitude of the world.

If I had been there, I would have made him a cup of tea and said, 'Chapal-da, now you really understand what it means to live as a woman in this messed-up world. But wipe your tears now, drink the tea. You and I, we will both survive.'

8
Love

The Boy with the Goddess Face

Femininity has always been a part of me, ever since I was a child.

Other boys liked rough-and-tumble sports like football. My favourites were all indoor games house—ludo, snakes and ladders, chess, made-up games with the dolls I had inherited from my sister, a make-believe kitchen with a set of little pots and pans made of fired clay . . .

When we played outside, we would go to the park for blind-man's buff. Or chor–police. It was extra thrilling to chase each other, whooping and squealing, in and out of a real police station. The station was right next to my uncle's Srirangam Theatre. Srirangam is long gone but the Burtollah Police Station is still there, an old red brick building with POLICE HOVSE written over its door. Built in 1888, it's a police station steeped in history. Inside it, you can now see some of that history painted on its walls—Charak fairs under the old banyan tree where men tied themselves to hooks and spun around like whirligigs, roosters facing off in cockfights while babus cheered them on, dancing girls and palanquin bearers. When we scampered around the police station, the policemen would holler at us but it was all in good humour. My uncle Sisir Bhaduri was a big name in the neighbourhood, and the officer-in-charge was his friend. We knew we would not get into any real trouble.

I had only a few friends—the sons of neighbours whose names I do not remember any more. One of them invited me home for his birthday. I was probably his only friend. His mother had made prawns with cauliflower. Later, I realized they must have been of fairly humble means. In those days, prawns, unless exceptionally large, were regarded as poor man's food, something to give flavour to food, not a main course.

Other than that, I did not like to be with boys too much. When they came to the house and tried to drag me to their games, I didn't want to go. I was girlish, but, luckily, no one ever behaved too badly with Prabha Devi's little boy. My mother had a lot of stature in the neighbourhood as a famous actress. Also, I had three older brothers who protected me. They themselves would sometimes tease me but they always told their friends, 'You mustn't taunt Tuku when you see him out on the street. So what if he sounds a little girlish? He isn't hurting anybody.'

At most, once in a while, someone would gently pull my leg. 'You're so pretty. I want to marry you.'

'What rubbish!' I would retort.

But one young lad, rather sturdy, went a step further. One day, while we were talking, he suddenly grabbed me and gave me a kiss on the lips. I was both surprised and repulsed. It was a sensation entirely new and confusing—the roughness of his lips, his hands gripping me. I thought he smelt bad, and that made me feel queasy. At the same time, I liked it too. Confused by the swirl of emotions, I shrugged him off and ran away. I told no one about it and tried to put it out of my mind.

Then there was Deepti. He was a friend of my elder brother's, beautiful in a way few boys are. It was as if the face of Goddess Durga had been superimposed on a boy. This was the first time I realized that even men could be beautiful. His thick eyelashes were dreamy, longer than the false ones I would wear years later on stage. Yet he was not effeminate. Well-built and strong, he was a handsome young man who just happened to have the face of a goddess.

Deepti-da lived with his older brother and widowed mother in a couple of rented rooms in a house near our playground.

One day, he suddenly said, 'Tuku, come to our house today.'

'Why should I?' I said. 'Am I your friend?'

'If not friend, at least my young brother. Come along.'

His mother was very welcoming. She looked so calm and dignified, in a plain white sari with a green border. By then my mother had died and something melted inside me when she said, 'Come, sit, son. I've heard a lot about you.'

Deepti-da's brother, Arun, came out of the room and said, 'Oh hello, Tuku, what are you up to?'

'Deepti-da has dragged me here.'

'Why? Is he your new friend?'

'I'm going to treat him to parathas,' Deepti-da said. 'Parathas made by Ma.' I think they thought I needed a bit of mother's love. Indeed, it was a meal cooked with love, I still remember it so clearly. Warm whole-wheat parathas with a dollop of ghee, a simple potato stir-fry and some sweet semolina halwa. Simple homely food but to me it felt like the food of gods. Even now, decades later, I can taste it.

Then, one day, I suddenly heard that Deepti-da was dead. My first encounter with sudden death was my mother's. Then it was Deepti-da's.

'What do you mean Deepti-da is dead?' I asked my brother. 'You mean he'll never talk to me again?'

I just could not fathom it. He had no vices, no addictions, not even any love affairs that I knew of. He liked to play football which was why he had such a good physique. I was barely 13. He must have been 16 or 17, in the full flush of youth, so vigorously alive.

For some reason best known to him he had chosen to love me. And I had loved him back. It was a pure and innocent love, untainted by sexual desire. I didn't know how to verbalize it. All I knew was now there was a Deepti-da shaped hole in my world.

I don't remember how he died. Perhaps I never asked. I went to his house and wept. His brother, Arun, in the throes of his own grief, consoled me saying 'Don't cry, Tuku. This was in our fate. What can one do?'

One day, I heard that Arun and his mother had moved house. I never saw them again.

Of Girlish Boys and Boyish Girls

As long as Ma was alive, my world revolved around her and my sisters. All my stories and gossip came from them. I spent as much time as I could talking to them or eavesdropping on their conversations. Chhordi, though, was always playing with our brothers' friends, much to Ma's exasperation.

'Why are you always running around with the boys?' she would scold as Chhordi grew older. What was worse, Chhordi did not shy away from getting into fisticuffs with her friends, especially if anyone said anything nasty about our mother. If someone bothered me, I would run to her, sniffling. 'Who hit you?' she would demand to know, ready to take on the world. Sometimes she would shake her head and say, 'I should have been a boy, you should have been a girl.'

In the 1960s, the violent extreme-left Naxalite uprising was raging in Bengal. The police would pick up young boys in the neighbourhood on the suspicion that they were involved with the Naxalite movement. Even my own nephews were picked up on occasion. My sister would have to go plead with the police, pay a fine and get them released.

The jatra world was hit hard. The agents who came from out of town to book the shows were afraid to come to Kolkata and be caught in the crossfire between Naxalite youths and the police. Shobhabazar, where Natta Company had its office, was known as a Naxalite hangout. After sundown, the streets would be eerily deserted. No one wanted to step out. It was hard for us to come home after rehearsals. The Natta Company car would come pick me up and drop me off.

One night, around 11, there was a loud banging noise at the front door. When we opened it, uniformed police rushed in, claiming a local Naxalite youth named Hemen had been seen entering our house.

Chhordi did not flinch. She calmly told the police they were welcome to search the house if they thought Hemen was hiding there. What I did not know was that Hemen had indeed come to the house. My sister had sent him up to the roof. In our cramped neighbourhood, where the houses almost rubbed up against each other, the roofs of the houses were very close. So

Hemen was able jump from one terrace to another, and escape. Chhordi could have given him up but who knows what his fate might have been if she had done so. Perhaps that night she saved one life. She was a fighter, my sister, and a tomboy. Yet that same sister could play such a winsome Saudamini on stage in *Anthony Kabiyal,* the love story of a Portuguese poet who fell in love with a Brahman widow.

While Chhordi was a tomboy, running around the roof flying kites, I guess I was the sissy. My voice was always high like a young girl's. Perhaps people said things about me behind my back, but no one teased me much to my face. Years later, someone told me, 'You are a homo.' By then such words didn't bother me. I retorted, 'Yes, I am a homo. So what? I can go up on stage and act the part of a woman. Let's see if you can.'

Another time, I walking through Howrah Station when a man hissed at me and called me chhakka. By then I knew very well that was a derogatory term for a gay man, but I also knew it was the name of a vegetable dish. So I turned around and said innocently, 'Are you talking about pumpkin chhakka? I like that too.' The man stared at me a bit baffled and hurriedly walked away.

I didn't really know the words they used in English—gay, lesbian, transgender. Even if I had come across them, I had never focused on them. If there was a gay scene in Kolkata at that time, it was not something I was really aware of. Of course, there must have been something, even if it was hidden and underground. This is something that has always been there. A relationship between two people of the same sex is absolutely natural. There is nothing wrong with it. To me, it is a game, like any other love affair. What does it matter if it's between a man and a woman, or two men or two women, as long as both sides get pleasure out of it? I refuse to harbour any guilt about these things. This is not a sin or a crime. I am a man who has loved another man. And I refuse to apologize for love.

It's just that I didn't know the name for it. But I knew the ancient Greeks were famous for it. I knew it was common in the military, in hostels and in religious orders where the sexes were kept segregated. You cannot deny physical desire. It's entirely natural that you will want to sate that hunger. But it was not a scene I was looking for. I was so young when I got busy with work, I had no time to think about these things.

I am not innocent by any means. I never studied too far, I don't know English, but I read a lot. From books on religion to those dirty books that come wrapped in yellow covers, I have read them all. You could get those books from pavement booksellers near New Market. You had to ask for them surreptitiously. They were filled with raunchy sex stories where young boys discovered sex on hot sleepy afternoons with the older boy who worked in the house as well as the bored housewife next door. I certainly learnt a lot about from those books.

Same-sex desire to me was part of a great game. But very overtly gay behaviour would make me uncomfortable.

When I was acting in an amateur production of Sarat Chandra's *Bijoya* at Titu-da's house, one of the other actors was a boy who belonged to that house, a nephew or something. I was Bijoya, the lead character, while he was playing another female character named Nalini.

Even though he was a teenager, the young man's arms were really hairy, like a grown man, and he had a moustache. But when he talked, he sounded like a coquettish girl.

One day, we had been given kebabs as snacks. Biting into one, he asked me somewhat archly, 'How do you like it?'

'What is this?'

'It's called a shami kebab.'

'Oh, how do you make them?'

'You take minced meat and then make a fine paste of it . . . '

The way he talked had a real flounce to it, as if he was a flirtatious girl and everything was a double entendre.

Finally, I could not help myself any more: 'Why do you talk like that?'

'Like what?' he simpered, 'Does it bother you if I talk this way? You don't like it?'

'Actually, I don't. Does your uncle not mind that you talk like that? He is such a through and through gentleman.'

'No, my uncle does not say anything.'

'Well, good for you. But it bothers me. Please don't talk to me like that.'

Maybe I am old-fashioned. Once, a young man I know visited me at the old-age home. The person who works here asked me, 'Why is he so girlish?' I know there is nothing wrong with it, but I did not like hearing that. I played female parts but I never wanted my femininity to consume my life.

I didn't know gay men, but I would see the hijras ask for money on the streets. Oone day, one of them tried to talk to me as if I too was one of them. I was not going to have it. 'You are making a mistake. Please don't talk to me that way,' I said curtly. 'Just because I smiled and talked to you politely does not mean you can be over-familiar with me.' I am not belittling them because they are out on the streets, asking people for money. That is their way to make a living. I knew that the way I walked and talked marked me out as different from the other men I saw around me. But I have always been clear—I am not a hijra.

The Woodcutter and the Tree

During my amateur theatre days, perhaps around 1956–57, I met a doctor from R. G. Kar Medical College. At that time, the doctors' recreation clubs used to stage plays. That young doctor fell head over heels in love with me and contacted me after the play was over. He would ask me to visit him. We would meet up now and then. He would talk sweetly and embrace me and kiss me.

I remember saying, 'Don't do this. I am not sure I want to do this.'

'I am going to America,' he told me, 'Come with me. You can become a woman there and marry me.'

'No, I won't.'

'Why not?'

'I think we are fine the way we are. I can change for you, but how long will you still like me? Perhaps one year or two or maybe five. But then you might want another woman. Perhaps a biological woman. What will happen to me then? Who will I live with? Perhaps it works in stories and plays but I don't think it works in real life. You can leave me as quickly as you are now embracing me. I am fine the way I am.'

Years later, the film director Rituparno Ghosh also told me, 'Why don't you become a woman?' I said, 'Long before you, a doctor from R. G. Kar had made me an offer. I said no to him then. I am still saying no.'

Some men would openly say we could live together. But I didn't trust them. I feared that if a man could love a woman and then abandon her, they could just as easily leave me and move on to someone else. I read somewhere that the relationship between men and women is like that between a woodcutter and tree. There is pain and torment, even annihilation, but there is also a strange pleasure in knowing that the woodcutter wants to possess you so intensely. The tree gives everything to the woodcutter—her branches, her trunk, her all, even though he ultimately chops her down.

Passion . . . that fades in the end, a distance grows between lovers. desire flags. Even if it doesn't, you don't have the energy to act upon it. To put it crudely: it no longer arouses you.

That's not to say I was impervious to desire. Once, at a show somewhere, there was a man who was exquisitely handsome, the kind of looks where you think God must have sat down and made him with special care. He was a little hefty, but that was fine with me because I don't like girlish wispy men. I like my men to be manly, like Salman Khan or Hrithik Roshan, though my dream man is Russell Crowe in *Gladiator*. Even now, whenever that movie comes on TV, I cannot stop watching it. On stage, I always thought Shekhar Ganguly was a good hero for me—tall and handsome. Sujit Pathak didn't have the same effect, but I had to act his heroine's part convincingly nonetheless.

Anyway, after that show, this hefty young man took me home. I remember we would feed each other and cover each other in kisses, though it never went much beyond that. Once, he took a gold ring off his finger and put it on me. There were so many moments of great passion. But then, as it always happens, the mind wanders. The mind is a fickle thing, it does not like to stay still. Even the Bhagavad Gita says so.

As my fame grew, my suitors increased as well. Some were people besotted by my looks, some by my acting, some by both. Years later, when I was sitting at home with no work, and no prospect of work either, I would wonder if all of that had really happened to me. Was this me really that me?

An Astonishing Proposal

Once, we were acting in Siliguri in North Bengal. After the shows were over, when we were getting ready to leave, a man showed up to meet me. It was clear he was smitten with me. He would not stop talking.

'O bhai, our bus is about to leave. You need to get off now,' I told him politely.

'No, no, don't call me brother,' he said. 'Call me friend.'

'Friend? All right I will call you friend. But what kind of friend would that be? I don't know what kind of friend you mean.'

The man looked embarrassed and changed tack.

'Promise me you will come back here.'

'Of course, we will. Natta Company comes to Siliguri every year.'

'All right. Keep this please.'

'What is this?'

'Just keep it. Open it after you leave.'

It was a letter, a proper love letter. At the end, he had written 'Please reply to me at this address.'

As the bus got going, I threw that letter away. Someone in the troupe, who had been watching the whole exchange with amusement, said, 'What was there, Chapal?'

'A letter from that man who was annoying us. The reason why the bus could not leave on time.'

But the most astonishing proposal came when we were touring in Assam. We were staying in a local businessman's house in Bongaigaon. Manasi, the daughter of the house, had seen our performance. Oddly, Manasi looked rather like me when I dressed as a woman. She was tall like me and fair, not classically beautiful but attractive with a good figure and long thick hair.

The second day we were there, as I was trying to get water from the well in the house, she came up to me: 'Wait, let me do that for you.'

'Don't worry. I can manage,' I said. 'I know how to do this.'

'Please let me,' she replied and drew the water, chatting all the while. Later, she brought tea for us. I thought she was being hospitable. I did not read anything more into the incident.

The day before we were supposed to leave, she suddenly grabbed my hand and broke down in tears.

'I want to go with you. Please take me along.'

'Go where? What are you talking about?' I was stunned. 'And let go off my hand. What will people say if they see us?'

'Let them say whatever they want. I have fallen in love with you. Tell me you will marry me.'

I was quite scared. We can act out passionate impulsive romance as much as we like on stage, but this was real life. This girl had parents and brothers. If they saw us standing together like that in the dark, I could be in for a thrashing.

'Please compose yourself and go to you room,' I said as calmly as I could. 'Don't get so emotional. I regard you like a sister, just like my own sister at home. A sister has drawn water from the well for a brother. How can you turn that into romantic love?'

I somehow managed to get out there. It's the only time a woman proposed to me. Later, everyone in the troupe had a good laugh about it, but at that time I did not know how to react. A woman who fell in love with a man who acted as a woman. What could it even mean?

I did not need all this. If I had wanted to, I could have had many such lovers. But I was content with just one.

The X Factor

Let me call him X.

I was 18 and he was 22 or so when we met. He would come to our house often because he was friends with my younger brother-in-law, the one who was married to Chhordi. X even helped him get a job at his company. So I would see him all the time.

I don't know when and how that turned into romance and attraction. It just happened. Somehow, we were just drawn to each other. I was already deep in the jatra world. I already knew about what could happen between men. I had been approached by other men but had averted it. But what had to be had to be.

X and I went to Ghatshila, a beautiful little town surrounded by forests and hills, on the bank of the Subarnarekha river, and the inevitable happened. We had the kind of relationship a man and a woman have, a physical one. He suggested it. I hesitated at first, unsure whether it was right, but he persuaded me: 'There is nothing wrong in this, think of it as art.' I was not upset or surprised. When I think back, I feel we were in a state of intoxication, high on each other. And why not? He was a very handsome man, with a grand moustache slightly curled at the ends, well built and smart. His eyebrows were thick and he had a head full of hair. He reminded me of a police inspector, but handsome like the hunky actor Salman Khan.

He was also a good hunter. He had three guns, including a 357 Magnum. When he wanted to buy a rifle, his father refused to give him the money. So I said, 'I'll buy you one.' We went to J. Biswas & Co., a famous gun store in Esplanade, which has now been around for five generations. We bought a double-barrelled rifle. It was the early '60s, I think it cost 700–750 rupees, which he paid me back. Later, he bought himself another rifle. He gave me many gifts, like a transistor radio from Japan, the kind you could not get in Kolkata.

X came from a very good family and was well educated. Unlike me, he had been to college. When he spoke fluently in English, I would be floored. He worked for a well-known company in Kolkata, in the shipping and clearing department. His family had a large house in South Kolkata. It had a beautiful terrace garden with all kinds of flowers. He would spend hours on Saturday and Sunday tending to his roses.

His salary was 250 rupees a month, which was fairly respectable in those days, though I was earning 3,000 a month at one point. That impressed him. He would say he would not be able to earn money the way I did. On the other hand, I could not do what he did. Sometimes, he would come to see me perform. Afterwards, he would say, 'What's the point of seeing these plays?

Everyone looks like a dowdy servant next to you.' I would giggle and shush him: 'Don't say things like that. What will people think if they hear you?'

We grew so close that I could not live without him and I dare say he could not live without me. We could not imagine ourselves apart, such was the meeting of our hearts and minds. We never named this thing between us. In those days, we didn't use words like boyfriend. We just accepted what we had stumbled upon with each other with joy, we felt fulfilled from it. He made me feel complete and I think he understood that. But I never thought he should be mine and mine alone.

One day, maybe a year or two into our relationship, he told me, 'I am getting married.'

'Oh! Wedding. When will it be?'

He told me and asked, 'Will you be there?'

'I don't know. I have shows in Chandrapura where they have the power station. That's almost the next state. I can't go back and forth from there.'

And just like that he got married. I did not go.

The Married Man

Nothing changed between us despite the marriage. It may seem surprising but I did not resent it. After all, I could do everything a wife was supposed to do in those days. I could cook, clean, do housework, keep a man happy but I could not give him a child. I didn't care about the trappings of marriage. On stage, I was always wearing the shankha and sindoor that married women wear anyway. I had no need to go around offstage wearing them.

His wife was quite beautiful. It was sort of an arranged marriage, the families had planned it when they were both young. I knew her slightly because she lived in the neighbourhood. Her father, a football coach, used to come to our house occasionally. I liked his wife and she liked me. She knew about our friendship, but did not seem to mind. I do not know how much she knew exactly. Some things are just not spoken out loud. When they had their first child, I was genuinely happy for them. The child called me uncle.

It was enough for me that there was a meeting of both of our minds and bodies. I knew what he needed without him saying a word. This kind of mutual attraction happens with so few people, you can count them on your fingers. Your desire for each other is so fevered, you don't need those medicines and aphrodisiacs you see advertised of television to fire you up. It was not a one-night stand. Our friendship lasted 34 long years. And when the sex faded, as it inevitably does, I did not mind. The friendship remained.

People would make dirty insinuations and say: Chapal lives alone, so he can have the freedom to do whatever he wants with whoever he wants. But they didn't understand that I connected with this one person in every possible way—physical, mental, romantic. Even when our physical relationship had petered off, I did not feel the need to look elsewhere for anything. I do not think I could have ever got more than what I had with X from any other man.

He didn't just teach me about sex. He taught me how to talk to important people, how to conduct myself in fancy places, what kind of clothes to wear. He had a sports coat made for me, charcoal grey, in some kind of woollen material. He had no problem with what I did for a living but he never wanted me to wear women's clothes at home. Home was home. Outside was outside.

I was a good cook, so I would often cook for him. We never went out to restaurants on my birthday. There was no need. I could cook at home and feed him with love and care. There was a raw papaya dish I made that he was really fond of. Years later, whenever I made it, I would remember him.

CHAPAL BHADURI'S SAVOURY PAPAYA HALWA

Take a raw green papaya and cut it into large chunks. Scrape the seeds and discard. Soak the papaya chunks in water for a while to make it easier to shred finely. Mix salt and sugar with it and cook it on low heat the same way you would cook shredded coconut to make narkel narus.

Fry minced garlic, minced ginger and small shrimps separately. You can also use flaked boneless bhetki fish or even minced meat.

As you keep sautéing the papaya, it will cook in its own juices. Then add the other ingredients and mix together. It tastes so delicious, you won't even realize it's papaya. Though Chhordi would say: it's because you put so much stuff in it. She cooked it once with just soya-bean nuggets and said, 'Try this. What you make is like your jatra. It's over the top, like all your velvet outfits and brocade shoes!'

Both X and I were well-off at that time. At home, there were problems of privacy and other issues, so we loved to go away together after the jatra season was done. As the monsoons descended, we would go away somewhere, perhaps for 10 or 12 days, just to quench our pent-up physical longing for each other. The mountains always felt rather forbidding. But the sea was wild and free.

I loved to wade into the waves, to surrender to them, to feel them lift me and carry me away. And he would be right there, waiting for me. I didn't mind that we could not be together all the time like a married couple. There was a pleasure in the waiting, even the pain of his absence made me feel somehow more alive.

Sometimes we went to Ghatshila, the town where we had first consummated our relationship. Or a quick trip to the beaches of Medinipur, just a few hours from Kolkata. We would go up to the mountains of Darjeeling, or down to the mangrove forests of the Sundarbans where tigers lurked in the jungle and huge saltwater crocodiles sunned on the river bank. He loved to go to the forest because he liked hunting and was good with his rifle. He hunted birds, chital deer, sambhar, even bison.

During the jatra season, we would seldom be together, because I was on the road all the time. All we could do was write to each other. I would tell him my itinerary in advance. On such-and-such date in Bongaigaon, on this date in Tinsukia, on that date in Digboi and so on. As soon as I arrived somewhere, I would rush to the post office first and see if there were letters waiting for me. The only other person who would send me post-cards regularly was my father. He always ended them with the phrase Aa: Baba. He said that meant 'Aashirbaad [blessings], Baba'. X would sign off his letters simply: 'With love' or even 'Namashkar'. His letters were just full of news about his life—how his parents were, how his daughter was or that his wife was expecting. They was nothing racy or particularly romantic about them. But the man could be romantic.

Once, we were performing in Bandel, an old Portuguese colonial town famous for its church and cheese. When we got there, I found to my astonishment X waiting for me.

'What's the matter. How come you are here?'

'Don't you know I bought a jeep? I just drove here from Kolkata. I knew you would reach by 7. After you are done with your show, you can come with me.'

He had driven all the way from Kolkata just to spend that night with me. That passion floored me. I felt flattered and thrilled. Later, of course, that desire dulled but the memories remained.

I loved him like I love my own hand. He was a part of me.

Family Matters

Everyone in my family knew that I had a special relationship with X. Everyone at his home knew as well. No one, whether from my family or from my work life, ever tried to put any obstacles in our way. People at work knew us to be close friends. If they suspected there was more to it, they did not say anything to me. Now, I think, if someone had pushed me about the exact nature of our relationship, I might have said, 'So what if we are lovers? There is nothing wrong with that. I have fended for myself from when I was just a boy. I do not owe anyone any explanations.' But no one asked, and I didn't tell.

X's father, though, did not like me. He thought that I intended to sweet talk his son into giving me all his money so that I could start my own jatra company. But his mother was very fond of me. I do not know whether she understood the true nature of the relationship I had with her son. But I do know that she trusted me without reservation.

Once she said, 'Chapal, I am going to Varanasi with my daughter-in-law.'

'Isn't your son going with you?' I asked.

'No, he cannot take time off for office. His father is also coming with us. I am leaving my granddaughters here, though. I need someone who can look after my Shiva idol in my prayer room. Can you pour water over it every day?'

'Certainly. Do you trust me to do it?'

'Who can I trust but you? You call me Mother, you are like my son. And you are my son's closest friend. I will leave this whole house in your care.'

She really did trust me. They had another house which was rented out. She told me, 'When the tenant comes to pay the rent, you just take it and sign for it.' When I think back, I realize we had become a little family. When she died, not only I but even my sister went to the crematorium, something women didn't usually do in those days. Chhordi helped smear her body with ghee which you needed to do when you burnt the dead on wooden pyres. I had lost my mother when I was but a boy. This was another mother figure gone.

'Don't Touch Me'

Over the years, many men approached me, sometimes directly, sometimes indirectly. They would introduce themselves, ask for my address, write letters but I would not reply. I would always tell everyone the same thing: 'Sorry, this will not be possible for me because I don't think anyone will be able to match the passion, the pleasure, the utter madness that I have felt with my friend. So let us just be friends instead and not try to go beyond that.' Some of them were very handsome, and I will not lie, I was flattered, because who does not like attention. But, somehow, I never wanted to proceed further.

Some cold-shouldered me after that. Some did become friends. Of course, nothing I said stopped tongues from wagging. I worked in jatra. I played female roles. So people assumed I must be sleeping with many men. That's when I first heard people calling me a homo.

'He's a homo.' Those words confused me. I was in love with another human being. That was all there was to it as far as I was concerned. Perhaps I was a homo. But X was married, he had children. Was he a homo too? I didn't know what the terms really meant and there was no one there to explain them to me.

Relationships between men were not uncommon in the world of jatra which was all-male when I started out. We were on the road a lot, spent weeks away from home. It wasn't surprising that relationships developed along the way. I didn't understand how it worked at first, even though it was happening in front of my eyes. Many actors had a special boy who served them as a sort of assistant. Some of these boys danced in the sakhir dal, the background dancers.

Once, someone in our jatra troupe told me, 'Chapal, of all the boys you could choose, why have you kept Sona?'

Sona was a boy who also did female parts occasionally. He was a sweet-natured chap but nothing much to look at, a big burly chap.

'Oh, he helps with my cooking,' I said. Country chicken was cheap and plentiful when we were out on the road. I enjoyed rustling up a spicy chicken curry. I would send Sona back to my room in the afternoon and ask him knead the dough. At night, after the show was done, he would make parathas. Freshly made parathas with a lick of ghee and hot chicken curry was a treat.

Sona would help with the cooking, run errands for me, wash my clothes now and then and do other odd jobs. I didn't realize people assumed that, as my special 'assistant', he might be keeping my bed warm as well.

The person who asked me about him said, 'Oh, just cooking and cleaning? Many men in jatra keep a boy the way zamindārs would keep a mistress in the old days. That's why I was confused. I was thinking you could do better than Sona!'

Perhaps, if I did not have my own relationship and spent all my time with the jatra folk instead, I would have been more clued in about these goings on. I mostly kept to myself. I didn't like some of the things I saw, not because it was wrong but because it felt strange.

Later, I realized that in jatra, if an actor took a fancy to some young man, he could ask him to stay with him. Then he would be responsible for his food, his clothes, the cost of his entertainment. When the excitement wore off, the relationship ended as well. It was accepted practice and commonplace enough. I didn't want all that. And I still don't. It does not appeal to either my conscience or my sensibility, not then, not now.

People would openly propose to me while I was on the road. Some were very forward. 'Come on, dear. I am alone here as are you. Why don't you spend the night in my room?'

I would retort, 'Whatever for? They have given me my own room. Why should I stay in yours?'

'No, don't act coy. You understand what I mean.' And then he would touch me gently, suggestively, on my back.

'Take your hands off me,' I would say curtly. 'Don't touch me.'

At that time, I didn't know words like gay, but I knew there were men who had relationships with men. Little flings and short-term relationships, some that lasted merely a night, some that lasted a few weeks or a few months before they moved on to other men. Those I could see around me. But I was happy with just one man. Otherwise, it would not have lasted over 30 years. I didn't know anyone else who had a relationship like ours.

Love and Marriage

I do not mean to say that the men who acted as women were all homosexual. Not at all. Most of the men who had preceded me in female roles had wives and children. Chhabi Rani had three sons. Babli Rani also got married and had sons. But that does not mean they were all fully heterosexual either.

I remember telling Babli Rani that he and his wife made a very odd couple. His wife was very beautiful, like Goddess Jagatdhatri, and he was a short, fair, very effeminate man with a bald head and a rather blunt nose.

'Babli-da, why did you get married?' I asked.

'Why do you say that, dear?' By then his mannerisms were entirely feminine, whether he was on stage or off.

'Just take a look at your wife. You look very out of place next to her.'

He looked me oddly and said nothing. He was lucky that his sons took more after their mother than him.

Some ranis got married, but that did not change who they were. I knew their propensities, their attraction towards handsome young men. Someone got beaten up in his old age for trying to touch a young man inappropriately. That same man had a wife and several children. But I should not disparage him. At least he managed to build a house for them, even if it was somewhere in the outskirts. I didn't get around to doing that for myself.

A few of us remained unmarried. Banaphool, who brought me into jatra, and Bimal Rani lived together in a room they rented in Renu-ma's house. They were long-time friends and colleagues from jatra days. But who would rent to a man who did jatra, a man without wife and family? Renu-ma had a room to spare. They stayed there and did their own cooking. When times were hard for me, even I stayed with them for a little bit, paying my share of the expenses. I think Bimal once had family in Baharampur. By the end, though, he was without anyone in the world. At least, Renu-ma and her sons were there. Even if you showed up at 2.30 at night, she would open the door for us. Her sons didn't get married either. Perhaps they too didn't have the mentality to get married. Or maybe all those years of acting as a woman left their imprint on us. For a while, that place was a gathering spot for us jatra queens—Chhabi Rani, Babli Rani, me. We were all scrounging to make ends meet. Gradually, we lost touch and scattered to the winds.

Because I remained unmarried, I had to listen to some snide comments occasionally. In one production, the director asked me to supervise the women's performances. Another actor was put in charge of the men. Chhabi-da was in that production.

He told me, 'Oh, the women's performances? I wonder why just the women? Perhaps because you are . . . .'

'Listen, please don't judge everyone by your standards,' I said sharply. 'I am what I am. And I am not ashamed about it. At least this much I can say: I've never tricked anyone. And I've never hurt anyone by my choices.'

I was well aware of the fact that people would talk about me behind my back. Occasionally when we toured places like Siliguri, I would stay at the homes of friends and fans. They were just admirers of me as an actor, there was nothing inappropriate going on between us. Sometimes it was their mothers who would ask me to have dinner with them and stay the night. When I did that, members of our company would snigger knowingly and I would have to face a lot of mocking comments when I returned the next day.

At first, I would be hurt and angered by their insinuations. Then I learnt to stop caring. I would remember that Hindi saying my mother loved: the dogs bark, but the elephant keeps moving. I tried to make that my philosophy in life.

One day, Chhordi brought up the subject of my marriage. I must have been in my early 30s then. She said, 'Well, this has been a while. You have done a lot of jatra and made a name for yourself. But everyone you worked with has got married. Chhabi-da, Babli-babu. I think it's time you marry as well. I'll look for a girl.'

'No, I will not marry,' I told her.

'Why?'

'All these years of playing women has made me think a lot about what it means to be a woman. I don't think this is something I can subject a woman to. Also, I spend so much time on the road. I am away for months. What if my wife falls in love with someone else and goes away? Also not just my voice, my mannerisms are quite feminine. Why would a woman want that in a husband?'

'Well, Babli-da is also very effeminate, but his wife does not seem to care.'

'That's his luck. Mine might be different. Please don't ask me to get married.'

So many couples are unhappy in marriages despite all the talk of love and romance. Perhaps I understood all this because so many of the plays I acted in dealt with the issue of unhappy marriages.

Men and women are very different creatures and sex is a huge part of married life. There is no way I could close my eyes to that and pretend it did not matter. I might be alone now but I don't regret the choices I made.

My eldest sister fell in love with a friend of my brother's, though he was quite a bit older. He married my eldest sister, but she remained with us at our house on Dalimtala Lane. He would pay her expenses, his brothers would visit but he never took her home. Dalimtala Lane was where her children were born and where her oldest son was stricken with blood cancer and died. My eldest sister was not an actress, even though she had done a few roles here and there as a child. But she was still the daughter of an actress. That was enough of a scarlet letter for respectable families in those days.

My youngest sister Ketaki was a professional actress but she also dreamt of a traditional wedding and then moving into a new home, a house filled with in-laws. She fell in love with another friend of my brother's, Mohan Dutta. He was well educated, smart and handsome and came from a rather renowned family, the Duttas of Fariapukur. His father was a well-known lawyer. His elder brother used to come and play cards at our house, and taught Chhordi as well. They owned a huge bakery in Howrah as well as hotels. At one time, Dutta Bakery's bread was quite popular. But the Duttas didn't want their son to marry the actress daughter of Prabha Devi. Ma wasn't keen on the marriage either, unsure whether Chhordi would ever be accepted by her very respectable in-laws.

Mohan went against his family's wishes and married Chhordi secretly. Ma gave Chhordi away and my father filled in for Mohan's father. Chhordi's written in her memoir about how for seven days she stayed in seclusion, pretending she had cut her hand. She didn't want anyone in the business or the neighbourhood to know she had got married. After seven days, she removed the threads tied around her wrist as part of the marriage rituals and quietly returned to work, without telling anyone she was married. Like any other married woman, she still wore her sindoor, but just a little dab carefully hidden inside her hair.

They married out of love, but they paid a price for it. Mohan's uncle had arranged for a high-paying job for him at a well-known company. When the news of the marriage broke, the uncle said, 'Either you leave Ketaki or you leave this job. You have to choose.' Mohan stuck to his guns. He said, 'Would you abandon your wife for your job? I will leave the job. I will find something else somewhere. But I cannot abandon my wife.'

Those were brave words, romantic even. But it affected him. He did find other jobs but he was never happy in them. My sister found jobs for him through her contacts but I think by then he did not want to be known as Ketaki Dutta's husband.

Mohan had hoped that, with time, his parents would come around. In truth, his father was quite fond of Chhordi, but the rift caused by the secret marriage never quite healed. Chhordi never ever went to her in-laws' home as a bride. She had five children, but never got any recognition as the daughter-in-law of the Duttas of Fariapukur. Over time, she did build a relationship with some of the in-laws. One of them taught at a school where her daughters studied, and she helped them a lot. But Chhordi's childhood dream of marriage and in-laws remained a dream. She had wanted to be actress and have a traditional marriage and family. She realized soon that society would not let her have both.

Thankfully, times have changed. All of Chhordi's daughters married well and are well settled with their families. Chhordi was happy when all the Duttas of Fariapukur came for her youngest daughter's wedding. However, some things do not change. One of my nieces had an interest in acting. She could sing quite well too. But then love happened. And it's rare that a man will feel secure about his wife being an actress. Being the daughter of an actress was trouble enough. So my niece chose love and family over whatever dreams she might have had about acting.

Sometimes it seems the practical thing to do, to suppress your desires and put them aside. It happens to both men and women, though I have seen it more with women. We cannot tell from outside the pain that lies buried in them. But every now and then that unfulfilled desire flares up like an old ache. It never truly goes away.

It's Only Words

After my relationship with X ended, for years I did not get physical with anyone. It's not that I did not feel desire but more that I did not feel the need to act on it. It is not easy, sometimes it hurts but I have learnt to bear it. God has given me at least that much strength. It didn't matter that it had not ended well. That's a story for another day. But as long as it had lasted, it had been enough to fill my life.

Even now, in my 80s, I feel it. I still have sexual urges. If I see a handsome man, I can feel the shoots of desire. I am attracted towards beautiful women too, but there is no sexual desire there. I can appreciate a woman's beauty, but when it comes to men, the pull is entirely different.

A handsome, well-built man, say in his mid-30s, can still create a great turbulence inside me. Such a man remains my weakness. I am attracted to him but I've also learnt to remove myself, to create a distance, to stay in control.

I joke: at my age, what's the point in keeping the shop open when there are no goods left to sell? The customer will come and ask for this and that and I will have nothing to offer. Eventually, he will get frustrated and say, 'Why have you kept the shop open then?' and leave and go to another shop where he can get what he wants. Our lives are a bit like that shop. I remember what famous playwright Girish Ghosh once said, '*Deho pot, shoney not, shokoli haaray*'—this body, its clothes, all things go. My sister would repeat that all the time. Our acting lives are so much about our looks. As long as we can hold on to that, we are of value. Once it's gone, everything's gone.

Now that I am old and live alone in the old-age home, I sometimes wonder: did I go down the wrong path after all? I spent my whole life earning a living by playing women. The personal love story was but a small part and that is long over. When I was with X, I only thought of it as a relationship between two people. I didn't think about, know about or care about all the issues you read about now—like lesbian and gay. Now I know the Indian Penal Code had something called a Section 377 that criminalized homosexual acts. I didn't even know such a thing existed. I found out about it much later from people like Rituparno Ghosh. To be honest, even then I did not pay it much heed. What did it matter to me? By then I lived alone, had no friends from the gay community outside of a few people I knew through my work. X was history. There was no one in my life. What difference did 377 make to me?

Yet just because I did not know words like gay does not mean I did not live those lives. What people do not realize is that sometimes you don't need words, you don't need labels. There are other ways to tell the in stories of our lives.

Sometimes all you need is a betel leaf or paan. I love eating a dressed paan. Once, one of my admirers went off to fetch me a paan. But while he was gone, someone else offered me one. Without thinking too much about it, I accepted it. When my fan came back and saw I was already eating a paan, he got really upset.

'What! I go to bring you a paan and you take one from someone else!'

I said, 'What can I do? He gave it to me.'

'Dhyut saala!' He cursed and threw away the paan he had brought and stormed off in a huff.

What does this mean? This exchange could happen between a boy and girl. But when it happens between two men, what does it mean?

I did not have a name for it. All I know is I enjoyed it. As a man. I had no desire to be a woman. If I had wanted to, I could have fathered a couple of children. I am Chapal Bhaduri. I am not third gender, I am first gender.

INTERLUDE

In Imagination

The Admirer

My dear Rani (if I may call you that),

It has been merely seven days since Natta Company left town. But it feels like seven years since I last saw you.

Those four days you were in town now feel like a fevered dream. Ever since I saw you as Sultana Riziya, my dreams have been filled with you and only you. Until I saw you, I did not know a man could look so ravishing. The truth is, I have never seen a woman as beautiful as you either. It does not matter to me that you are a man in real life. You are Rani. You are Riziya and Kaikeyi and Purnima. When you wept as the wronged Queen Kaikeyi, my heart felt like it was going to burst. I wanted to rush on stage and slap that Vishwamitra who tricked you. It was as if he was wronging my own mother. But then when you came as Riziya, dressed in almost nothing, just some black cloth to cover your shame and that gauzy net skirt, I felt embarrassed to even look at the person sitting next to me, sure that he could read my overheated mind. How could the same person evoke such different emotions in me? You must be some kind of sorceress. But if this is black magic, I find myself craving more of it.

As I told you that night when I met you (and I waited almost an hour just to meet you), I am a simple man. I grew up in this small town where nothing much happens. Even the train from Kolkata only stops here every other day. My father was the headmaster of our school here and very respected for his knowledge of Sanskrit. He is dead now and I live at our modest home with my younger sister and my mother. I am BA Pass and studied history. That is why I went to see the jatra in the first place. Historical topics always interest me. I certainly did not expect to encounter someone like you.

History brought me to the jatra. But you are what brought me back every night. I wish I was one of those old zamindars who could tell Natta Company, 'Stay back and be my private jatra company.' Dear Rani, would that not be a dream come true? You and me, together, every night. I would read you poetry. Did I tell you in my spare time I like to write poetry? One day, I might write a poem for you. Would you like that?

I hope you will come back to our town again perhaps closer to Durga Puja. You have seen the festival in the big city but I can assure in small towns and villages it has a different charm. By then the monsoon has ended and the blue of the sky looks freshly washed, the clouds fluffy and white. The sunlight has a different quality. It feels like Puja. And all over the fields you will see the kaash flowers in bloom. When the breeze runs through them, they shimmer like a white blanket. How I would love to be lost in the kaash field with you, dear Rani, you and me and the white kaash flowers stretching till the banks of the river like our own private canopy. It would be our little refuge from the world.

Dear Rani, even though you only spoke to me rather formally, I cannot but dare hope that one day you might let down your guard a little. I promise I will never do anything to hurt your feelings. You know it took all my courage to ask if I could keep that flower you wore in your hair that last day. When you gave it to me, our fingers touched. Oh, if I could have made that moment last a little longer. I will dry that flower and press it and keep in my favourite book of poetry. Late at night, after everyone has gone to bed, I will open the book and the flower will remind me of you.

Though I fear that when I fall asleep, I will only dream of you in that net skirt. Do you think that's a bit naughty of me? Please, be assured, I am actually a decent sort. You would have seen that for yourself if you had accepted my invitation to come to our house for dinner. My mother would have been happy to cook for you. I am sure in Kolkata very rich people invite you to fancy feasts in their mansions and feed you ilish and golda chingri every week. Even then, you would have liked our simple food. My mother makes potatoes with poppyseed paste that everyone loves. And the taste of fish freshly caught from the pond is something else altogether. What fish is your favourite? I hope some day I can feed you what your heart desires.

Till then, I will make do with the flower you gave me. And the memories of four magical nights. And I hope to get a letter from you soon.

Yours ardently,

B

My darling Rani,

It has been over a month since you left town. Every day, when the postman goes by, I run to the door and ask him if there is a letter for me. Now, even before I can say anything, he tells me, 'Nothing today either.'

My dearest Rani, I know you are busy and the company is always on tour. So I worry that my letters are not reaching you. Perhaps they are waiting for you at the Natta Company office.

Rani, I have been thinking about us. Do you think if I got a job somewhere in Kolkata, we could be together? Or perhaps not Kolkata at all. Some place where no one knows you or me. We could live together as man and wife. I could be a teacher in a school, like my father. I dream of coming home from work to find you waiting for me. You would be freshly bathed and wearing a simple cotton sari like Sita in that play, and you would smell of Pears glycerine soap. When would you hand me my cup of tea, our fingers would touch like the time you gave me that flower from your hair, and a smile would play on your lips. No one in town would know our secret.

I have read that in some countries a man can do surgery and become a woman. Last night, I was lying in bed and thinking about that. If that could happen, we could build a life together, could we not, as man and wife? Is that too much to ask from the world, to just be happy with each other, without hurting anyone? These are not things I have thought about too much, but now these thoughts keep crowding my mind.

I must tell you, Rani, I have never had these feelings for anyone else, man or woman. But ever since I saw you, it's as if a forest fire is raging within me. My mother said the other day: 'What is wrong, Babu? Your mind always seems so far away.' She thinks I should start thinking about marriage soon. Dear, I hope you are not angry I am sharing all this with you. I am not trying to burden you with my problems. I just want you to know I think about you all the time.

Yours forever,

B

Dearest Rani,

Another two weeks have gone by and the emptiness in the mailbox mirrors the emptiness in my heart. I have no desire to eat or go out to drink tea with friends any more. My mother says I am growing thin. She worries I am sick. She keeps trying to entice me with my favourite dishes but I have no appetite.

How can I tell her I am sick with love? I crave a word from you. Is a letter too much to ask? Did all the plans and dreams I outlined in my last letter offend you? I apologize. Perhaps I got too carried away, planning a future far ahead of my reality. I am just a small-town person. You must have princes and industrialists falling at your feet. But while my fortune is not as big as theirs, I can promise you my heart is bigger. And if you can find some room for me in a little corner of your heart, I will never let you down. I would be a one-Rani man. That I can promise on my own mother.

I thought about getting on a train to Kolkata and finding the Natta Company office. But you might be touring somewhere else. Also, if I showed up unannounced, that might displease you further. Instead, out of sheer restlessness, I went to the railway station and just watched the train from Kolkata pull in. If this had been a film, just as I had given up all hope, you would have disembarked after everyone else, dressed in a silk sari, a suitcase in your hand, like Suchitra Sen returning from England in one of those films that are the rage of Kolkata.

In the end, the train pulled away, hissing and belching smoke, leaving more emptiness behind. I sat there, watching the platform empty out. The stationmaster returned to his little office, took off his shirt, hung it on a peg in the wall, and sat back in his chair to take a siesta. Seeing me, he asked if I wanted to have a paan with him.

But that only reminded me more of you, Rani. I remembered how at the end of the show when I went to meet you, you asked me if I could get you a paan. And then added 'It's my only vice.'

By the time I brought you the paan, you were already eating one. Someone else had given you one. I remember how angry and crushed I felt. My own feelings surprised me. This is new territory for me. I have never felt such strong emotions for a man. When you are on a stage, I do not think of you as a man. Yet when I saw you off stage, in your kurta and pyjama, I did not feel any less of a desire to be with you.

Anyway, I bade the stationmaster goodbye and walked out of the station, When I looked back, it was entirely empty, baking in the sun, except for a dog that had curled up in a patch of shade under the bench. One day, I hope your train will stop here for me.

Yours,

B

Dear Rani,

By the time you get this letter I will be a married man. My mother says marriage is the only cure for whatever ails me. My aunts agree. They say marriage will put my feet back on the ground and dispel the clouds around me. They have found a young woman from me. She is educated and passed her matriculation examination and is an acquaintance of my sister. They say she will be a good match for me because she likes to read books. They asked me if I wanted to meet her. I said it does not matter. If I cannot have you, then it does not matter who comes into my life.

I wonder sometimes what you do with these letters I send. Do you even read them? Do you tear them into bits and scatter them out of the window? Do you read parts out to your jatra friends so you can all laugh at the foolish daydreams of a history graduate in a small no-name town far away from your fancy lives?

A part of me still hopes that some day before the wedding you could land here like a hurricane and sweep me away from this little town where nothing ever changes. How strange is that? I, as a man, should be the one sweeping you away. But I wait for you like a princess trapped in a tower. But what can I say? Why did you come to this town with Natta Company and turn my world upside down and go away like a thunderstorm bringing an all-too-brief respite on a scorching summer day?

Please consider this the last letter from me if I do not hear back from you.

Sincerely,

B

Dear Miss Rani Bhaduri,

My name is Anima. Six months ago, I married Bhuvanesh Sen of Guptipara. While my husband seemed a pleasant and polite man, I noticed he was distant and a little formal. I put it down to shyness. One day, while dusting his things, I found a folder filled with unfinished letters and poems addressed to Rani.

That surprised me because my husband seemed a prosaic sort. Now I am more curious than angry about this woman in Kolkata my husband writes passionate love letters to. I am not sure what your relationship is since I have found no letters from you. Perhaps he has hidden them better or destroyed them.

I must admit that you intrigued me very much. I saw a small picture of you that he had saved from a newspaper. It was faded and yellowed but you seem to be a very beautiful woman. I cannot hope to compete with you in terms of looks. It also seems that you are an actress. That's very odd because I cannot see what a glamorous actress might see in a person like my husband from a small town like ours.

I do not want to confront him about these letters nor am I asking you to tell him that I found them. Perhaps you could tell him to pay more attention to the wife he has chosen to marry instead of the love he has to hide away in a drawer. I am asking you this as a favour, one woman to another.

I hope you will excuse my impertinence in reaching out to you.

Sincerely,

Anima Lahiri

9

The Wilderness Years

The Women

When I joined jatra, I knew of just one woman in it—Jyotsna Dutta. Like my mother, she had started out as a child artiste in a group of dancers. Her family had fled Barisal in East Pakistan after Partition and struggled to begin anew in Kolkata. She was a mere schoolgirl, the youngest child at home. She got into jatra to support her desperate family. She had a lovely singing voice and that helped her make a name for herself. When she grew up, she joined Satyambar Opera. One of their productions, *Sonai Dighi* [Golden Lake], became a big hit. In 1962, a jatra festival was held at Beadon Square. Most of the women in those jatras were still played by men. Jyotsna Dutta was the exception. And a handful more, like Chhabi Roy, Bela Sarkar and Firozabala. You could pretty much count them on one hand.

I always said that women would come to jatra when it was their time. There was no point in being upset or resentful about it. I certainly did not feel the slightest bit of jealousy. How could I? I had spent my life portraying so many different kinds of women—good, bad, but never ugly. I had fought as a queen, wept as a mother and seduced as a lover. I had tried to get into all of their minds. Somewhere, somehow, some of those characters must have rubbed off on me. I hope I can at least empathize with a part of the struggle of being women in a world where men make the rules. Women are not just meant to get married, have babies and then spend the rest of their lives cooking and cleaning. I grew up around working women. My mother and sister went out into the world to work, and that's what kept their families going. It would be downright wrong if I hated women for claiming their rightful place in jatra.

My dilemma was different. It was never whether women should come into jatra or not. Rather, it was: what do we do with those who played the female roles all these years? What about their plight? Their income will dry up. Where are they to go?

But no one gave a damn about that.

Women started trickling in from the early 1960s, but they were limited to the amateur companies that performed in Kolkata, not the big professional jatra companies that travelled up and down the state. Those companies didn't want to take women, and women didn't want a life on the road either. But change was in the air, and soon the trickle turned into a torrent. By the 1970s, the transformation was complete. Before I knew it, ranis like me were out of a job. In fact, we were out of a profession.

To be honest, the writing had long been on the wall, but we had been wilfully blind to it, to the world changing around us. I remember, during my last days with Natta Company, we had gone to Assam. By then, women had joined many jatra companies and those troupes were doing very well. Natta Company was one of the last holdouts. The booking agents would dourly warn us: 'Times are changing and you need to change with the times.' But Natta Company resisted obstinately, even though its ticket sales kept dropping.

By the time I joined Nabaranjan Opera, women were everywhere in jatra. Even Nabaranjan had women. But it didn't affect me, at least not then. Audiences wanted women but they also wanted me. There would be ten women in a troupe. And me. The women played the romantic heroines, but when it came to the mother role, and jatras had plenty of juicy mother roles, the company would inevitably turn to me. I was lulled into thinking that's how it would continue.

When I acted as Jahnavi, Michael Madhusudan's mother, in Cuttack, the students who had organized the performance mobbed me afterwards. 'Your performance as the mother was just unforgettable,' they gushed, 'The way you sang that song was beyond words. The women who played Henrietta and Devaki, they were certainly beautiful. But their voices were weak, their singing just so-so. To be honest, they didn't leave such an impact on us.'

I was flattered. Who wouldn't be? But I tried to be diplomatic: 'I have been doing this for so many years. Most of the women, on the other hand, are quite new. They are still learning the craft. They need time, they need experience. I am sure one day they too will leave their mark on you.'

But I realize now that some actresses were jealous at the sight of the audience showering me with such compliments, such adoration. It was only natural. Once, I had my tailor send some blouses to my sister. I would pick them up from her later. That day, an actress friend of hers, Dipika Das, paid her a visit. She noticed the blouse and said, 'Oh, this is lovely.' My sister said, 'Those are Tuku's. He does jatra, you know.' Apparently, Dipika sniffed contemptuously and immediately tossed the blouse aside, as if it was something dirty. 'Men acting as woman. Who cares about their taste?'

When I heard about her reaction, I wanted to tell her, 'Look, you work in theatre, I work in jatra. First you get to where I am today and only then throw around such airs.' Where is Dipika Das now? Who remembers her? How long did she last in theatre? Incidentally, years later, I saw a blouse like that again, tied with a knot at the back. The Hindi-film superstar Madhuri Dixit was wearing it in a dance number. I said, 'Look, that's my blouse from *Raja Devidas*!'

I admit sometimes that it did hurt when a woman got a part I was coveting or was picked for a role that had been mine back in the day. When an actress named Kalpana was selected to play the warrior queen, Rani of Jhansi, I sneered 'I didn't know the Rani of Jhansi was short and stout like a rosogolla!' Unfortunately, Kalpana overheard me and tore me apart. I deserved it, though. I really should have kept my mouth shut.

Some of the actresses, like Meenakshi Dey, did become good friends with me. I naively thought that jatra would have enough room for both the women and me. But that space quickly started to shrink until one day it simply disappeared. Chapal Rani, one-time queen of hearts, was thrown into the dustbin, discarded by one and all.

I am not trying to garner pity or be a drama queen. I was by no means the only one left out in the cold.

Requiem for a Queen

Some years ago, I had gone to a jatra festival. A man came up to me and said, 'Aren't you Chapal Bhaduri? I have a request. Did you know Rakhal Das? He died recently, and we are having a memorial service for him. It would mean a lot if you came to it and said a few words.'

'Rakhal-babu? You mean Rakhal Rani? Are you his son?'

'Yes, I am.'

'I have of course heard of your father but I never had the good fortune to see him on stage. He was very famous indeed, especially in East Bengal. Surya-babu and Makhan-babu of Natta Company often spoke about him with great fondness. I wish I could have seen him act. I have only seen his pictures and he was so very beautiful as a woman.' In fact, I had heard that when Rakhal Rani had gone to perform in the tea gardens of Assam, the European manager mistook him for a real woman and was so besotted, he even tried to kidnap him from the green room after the show.

Despite all that beauty and fame, his last days were very hard. Rakhal Das started out as an actor when he was still a child. His family was very poor, and thought that jatra would at least put food on the boy's plate. By the time he was seven or eight, he was already touring with a jatra company. Soon, he started playing female roles. There were no mics then. So he practised his lines by standing neck-deep in a pond in order to train his voice. The hard work paid off, and Rakhal Das became Rakhal Rani, the star. But after almost 40 years of acting, he had neither savings nor a pension.

To make ends meet, he took a job at a small neighbourhood grocery store, sold roasted peanuts by the riverside and then worked at a tea stall. That's where Brajen Dey, the man who wrote many of the scripts both Rakhal Rani and I once starred in, found him. Brajen-babu was shocked. In his play *Parasmani* [Touchstone], Rakhal Rani had played Manisha, a beautiful young woman who teaches the murderous king Raja Gaurishankar a lesson. Gaurishankar would lure beautiful women into marriage and then kill them. Until he met his match in Manisha. Audiences couldn't get enough of Manisha. Now that same Rakhal Rani was practically a beggar, hobbling about in ragged clothes.

Brajen Dey brought Rakhal Rani to the school where he was the headmaster and found some office work there for him. It didn't pay much, but at least it gave his last days some semblance of dignity. He and his family stayed in a small common room in the school until they could afford a place of their own.

At Rakhal Rani's memorial, I saw they had a framed picture of him, around which people had put garlands. They had also printed a small pamphlet about him. I saved it, relieved that at least in death Rakhal Rani had not been entirely forgotten.

The Blessings of Omkarnath

Rakhal Rani's acting days were over, but there were dozens of us female impersonators hungry for work. Suddenly, I had a stroke of luck. At that time, in the mid-'70s, the religious leader Sri Sri Thakur Sitaramdas Omkarnath would stage plays at his ashram. He had a huge following and built dozens of temples all across the country. There were many ashrams as well.

Omkarnath wrote more than 150 books on the Indian scriptures. He also wrote plays which he would stage at his ashrams. But women were not allowed to act in the ashrams. That was a godsend for all of us out-of-work female impersonators. Each of those plays was four to five hours long, with 10 to 15 characters. It was not just one performance at just one ashram either. We would go by train to different towns and cities, like the seaside town of Puri or the city of Waltair (now Visakhapatnam). Sometimes, even famous actors from stage and screen, like Satya Banerjee and Tarun Kumar, would come to act, because they all wanted the blessings of Omkarnath Thakur. I would do the direction, supervise the stage, mic and lighting arrangements, look after everyone's make-up and then play my part on stage. It was a lot of work but it kept me busy.

The roles were mostly of Hindu religious characters—Yashoda, Radha, Ratnabali, Mirabai, Sita. Many religious leaders from across India came to watch, and I had the good fortune to meet some of them. The spiritual leader, the Sankaracharya, once gave me the cloth he had wrapped around himself, printed with scriptures. Anandamayi Ma, the mystic who many believed was an incarnation of Goddess Durga, came to watch us too. That time I was playing Lord Krishna's mother, Yashoda. When Krishna leaves his home in Gokul to go to Mathura, I had to cry my eyes out. My 'Gopal, Gopal' cries were so heart-breaking that Anandamayi Ma told me, 'You are truly Yashoda.' It's a comment I treasure.

The parts were all based on familiar stories from our mythology but they were not without dramatic challenge. In *Nadianagore*, the play about the fifteenth-century saint Chaitanya Mahaprabhu, I had a small part, that of Satyabati, the devout wife of one Madhavacharya. She is so lost in her devotion that while chopping a bottle gourd, she cuts off her child's head by mistake and cooks it.

That's all well and good in a story, but how could we show it on stage? I figured out how to pull it off. There would be two dolls, one whole, and one whose head was loose and whose arms and legs could be pulled apart. It was just like a magic trick. I would sit with the doll on my lap, and when I cut the doll instead of the gourd, it would look like blood was spurting from its neck. When she cooked the child, the coal stove would glow red. It was all so realistic, a woman in the audience once fainted from shock in the middle of the performance.

Madhavacharya comes in and realizes what his wife has done.

MADHAV. Where is our son?

SATYABATI. Our son? Son?

Satyabati looks first at her lap which is empty but soaked in blood, then at her hands, also stained red and finally at the blade of the knife still dripping with fresh blood. She gets up, goes to the stove and turns to stone.

MADHAV. Go away, go away, Leave right now. And take that pot with you. I cannot bear to look at you. What is this you have done?

SATYABATI. No, I cannot leave. I cannot leave my beloved child. I want my child back.

MADHAV. How will you get the child back? Do you even know what you have done, you foolish woman?

SATYABATI. I will not go. I did not do this. I will go to Chaitanya Mahaprabhu and ask him, 'How could this have happened? Lost in the power of your name, I chopped up my own child and cooked him! Is this the reward for my devotion? Is this the power of your name? Answer me, my lord. Or return my child to me.'

Desperate, she puts holy basil leaves in the pot and starts singing Sri Chaitanya's name. After a few minutes, a child starts crying.

SATYABATI. Isn't that our son's voice?

Satyabati looks in the pot and finds her son restored, wrapped in a blanket.

He was quite a character, Omkarnath Thakur, with his flowing white beard and long dreadlocks, He would sit with his legs outstretched because he could not bend them properly. There was something childlike about him, an innocence that touched me. Once, he saw me peering at him as he was getting ready: 'What? Peeping at me? Look at me, I am dressing up just like you. Now when you all get dressed and put on your make-up, I'll come and peep at you.' His followers might have worshipped him as an avatar of God, but I saw him as a warm and kindly man.

Eventually, those plays petered out too. Omkarnath Thakur fell ill. The ashrams hosted fewer and fewer performances till they stopped altogether. And I was back to square one.

Occult and the Exorcist

That was around 1975 or so. I lived in a little room I was renting from a friend who had also acted in female parts on stage. The rent for my room was 68 rupees a month plus another 10 rupees for electricity. It wasn't exorbitant, but there was no income. Some friends, like the writer Abadhut, would help me out. But every month was a struggle. One day, my friend, the one I was renting from, said, 'I am going to get married soon and I will need this room. Anyway, you owe a year's rent and you don't have any work.'

He was right. I had no work and could see no prospects in my future either. I borrowed money from here and there and somehow paid my dues. I left all my furniture behind—the steel almirah, the bed, the dining table and an old dressing table with three mirrors. I packed up the rest of my belongings and went to the only person whom I could go to—my Chhordi.

She saw me standing at her doorstep and said matter-of-factly, 'Of course you can stay.' My sister didn't care whether I was earning or not. It didn't matter to her. We were family. We had no choice but to look after each other. But my nephews were less welcoming. They would taunt me. That would sting but I had to suffer those insults in silence. I had no income, but I was still getting two meals a day and a roof over my head. I couldn't complain.

I tried to keep to myself and busied myself in religious rituals. I'd roll out my mat and sit in a corner of the room with the little images of my gods, I would count my prayer beads, recite the Gita, a habit I had picked up from Makhan-babu of Natta Company. My nephews and their friends would poke fun at my singing and chanting, jeer at me.

After a couple of months, I could endure it no longer. I went to X.

'The situation is quite intolerable. I don't think I can stay there any more.'

'That's very sad, but how can I help?

'I don't know how I will manage any more. I have no income. And no prospects. I am at my wits' end.'

'I really don't know how I can help. I have a family, wife, children, parents. I have responsibilities.'

'But at least you have your own house. Will you let me stay in your house?' Actually, they had not one, but two big houses in Kolkata.

'That I have. But you know how my father feels about you. He thinks you want to get your hands on my money to set up a jatra company. He will go through the roof if I move you in the house. I cannot deal with that. He is still the head of the family.'

'Can you at least keep my things?'

'I don't know if Father will permit even that. He will ask whose things these are.'

X was going through a transformation as well. He had become increasingly interested in religion and spirituality. His wife had developed some psychological issues and sometimes behaved erratically, grinding her teeth, rolling her eyes and making strange faces. They already had two young daughters by then. No one knew what to do or how to handle her. She would sometimes have to be tied down like that character in the horror film *The Exorcist*.

In utter desperation, X went to see some religious guru. The guru said his wife had been possessed by some evil spirit. I don't really believe in all that, but X was desperate. Someone told him about a woman who lived in the suburban town of Barasat, reputed to be a medium and exorcist. So we took his wife there and left her there to be treated. I would take the bus and make the long trip to go and visit her.

The exorcist was a good-looking woman in her 40s with very large eyes. Her ramshackle house had a luxurious garden and a pond. Blood-red hibiscus flowers grew everywhere and she used them in her rituals. But she was quite poor and the family basically lived on dal and rice, sometimes throwing in a few small fish they would catch in their little pond. They didn't even have an electric connection. On moonless nights, it would feel eerie to be in that dark house, lit only by a flickering candle or a hurricane lamp.

On Saturday nights, a big night for those who believe in the occult, there were large crowds. She would light incense and burn mustard seeds. I remember the acrid smell of the mustard seeds and the smoke wafting everywhere. She'd sit in the middle of all smoke, talking in different voices and flinging red hibiscus flowers about. I don't know how much occult was happening, but as an actor I could see it was certainly full-on theatre.

I suspected that the whole spiritual business was just a ploy for her to try and make some money, even if meant preying on gullible and desperate people. She tried to use me as a medium in her seances. She would make me fast on no-moon nights, then bathe in the cold waters of the pond at midnight and then sit down with me to do a seance. I would go along with it but only because X really believed in her and I wanted to try and figure out what was going on.

I still don't believe there was anything magical or supernatural about her. Yet, somehow, X's wife slowly recovered. It took a good six months but she did eventually get better. She even bore X a son. All that only reinforced his faith in the woman. I remained sceptical but he dismissed me: 'What do you know about these things? You didn't even finish school.' I could see he had become utterly beholden to that woman. Her wish became his command. One day, she said, 'Oh, I really want to do a Durga Puja.' He promptly gave her the money.

'What are you doing? You shouldn't be selling off your possessions for this woman,' I protested.

'You just keep quiet,' he shot back. 'I will do whatever I think is fit. This is my money anyway.'

I fell silent. Even my own sister came under that woman's spell. She gave one of her heavy sacred utensils to that woman. I don't know what it did to my sister's fortune but the exorcist's fortunes turned around completely. The old rundown house was repaired, renovated and remodelled and she built an entire temple to Goddess Adya Kali.

Tara and the Rickshaw Driver

That woman was how X got connected to the world of spiritualist, exorcists and tantriks. One day, his young son swallowed a coin. Doctors prescribed all kinds of purgatives and laxatives. Nothing worked. The whole family was in an utter uproar.

X turned to me. 'Chapal, you must go to my guru, Lahiri Baba in Tarapith.' Tarapith was a pilgrimage spot, famous for its Tantric temple dedicated to Goddess Tara, some 200 kilometres outside Kolkata.

'How will I go? I don't know anything about Tarapith.'

X was having none of my excuses.

'Just go to Howrah Station and buy a ticket for Rampurhat. Take a local train and when you get down there, hop on to a cycle rickshaw.'

I got there around 2.30 in the afternoon, starving and thirsty. X's guru, Lahiri Baba said, 'What are you doing here in the middle of the afternoon? I don't have room for you to stay here.'

'I have not come to stay. X has sent me here. His son has swallowed a coin. He hopes you might be able to do something.'

'Swallowed a coin? What can I do? This is not a skill I possess.'

'Is there any way you can bring that coin out naturally?'

'No, I am sorry.'

I turned away disheartened. The whole trip had been in vain. It was late afternoon and the heat was scorching. The whole town seemed to have downed its shutters, as if hiding from the blazing sun. A cycle rickshaw stopped in front of me. The driver was a young man with long tousled hair, his skin the colour of polished mahogany. He looked like one of those marble statues you see in museums of javelin throwers or warrior princes, just dark not white.

'Where do you want to go?'

'Rampurhat Station. Will you take me?'

'All right, come with me. But you've come so far, and you won't go to the temple, to see Tara, Mother Goddess?'

'Isn't it shut now? It's late in the afternoon.'

'You can still go to pay your respects. Don't worry, I'll wait outside for you.'

The temple was of medium size, with many arches rising to a pinnacle. There was a sacred tank next to it where devotees could bathe before worshipping at the shrine. Some say those waters could heal the sick. I walked up to the temple and found, to my astonishment, the door wide open and a clear view of the goddess inside—like a headstone, the shape vaguely like a woman with a man suckling at her breast. The story goes that terrible poison emerged during the great churn of the cosmic oceans. Lord Shiva held that poison in his own throat to save the universe. His consort, Goddess Sati, in the form of Tara, breastfed him to relieve that intense burning sensation in his throat.

A priest saw me and said, 'You want to worship the goddess?'

'But I haven't brought anything with me. I didn't think the temple would be open at this hour.'

'That's all right. Take these flowers and some of the charanamrita, the elixir of life from the feet of the Goddess, back with you.'

'What will I take it in?'

'It does not matter. Anything will do. But let me tell you this. If you give it to someone to drink, everything will be OK.'

I looked at him quizzically, wondering what he was getting at. Perhaps it was the heat or the lack of food and drink, but I was in a kind of daze by then. Everything, even the priest seemed hazy, as if I was looking at the whole world through a sheet of glass.

The priest found an empty bottle, poured the charanamrita into it and gave it to me. When I came out, I found my rickshaw was gone. I went to a small shop, the only one that was open, next to the temple.

'Was there a rickshaw here?' I asked the owner. 'With a very dark strapping young man? If you saw him you would remember.'

'I didn't see anyone. But just walk towards that bridge. You will find other rickshaws there. It looks like you already worshipped at the temple?'

'Oh yes. Look here's the charanamrita and the flowers.'

'How strange. The temple is not open at this time. That's why most of the shops are also shut now.'

'I don't know. A tall priest appeared out of nowhere and helped me. He gave me the charanamrita and these flowers.'

The shopkeeper looked at me a bit strangely and shrugged, 'Never mind. Go on ahead. You will find your rickshaw.'

At the rickshaw stand, I described my rickshaw driver again. But all the men there just looked blankly at me and said they could think of no one who looked like that.

By the time I returned to X's house in Kolkata, it was past 11 at night.

Next day, his wife said excitedly, 'It was a miracle. As soon as he drank that charanamrita, he said he needed to use the bathroom very urgently. That coin came out with his waste.'

X was the one who had sent me to Tarapith. But now he dismissed the whole story, I think he did not want to acknowledge my part in it. So he said, 'No, no, I think it was because of the homeopathic medicine I had given him.'

'So you are saying I took all this trouble for nothing?'

'I had already started him on the homeopathic medicine,' he said dismissively.

I just kept wondering who that rickshaw driver, the colour of mahogany, really was.

Address Tarapith

But my connection with Tarapith had not ended. When I was desperately looking for a place to live, X had a brainwave.

'You go, live in Tarapith. For now, I'll send you 100 rupees a month. Then we'll see.'

Tarapith is now a bustling town. In those days, it was pretty much a village of thatched huts and fishing ponds. X's guru Lahiri Baba's real name was Hirendra Kanta Lahiri Chowdhury. He was quite elderly then but very distinguished looking, a tall imposing man. At one time, his family had been landlords in Mymensingh in what is now Bangladesh. He left it all and moved to Tarapith. His wife had refused to come with him. She said: I cannot go and live like a beggar over there, I would rather go live in my father's house. So he came on his own. His children were grown, the daughter a doctor in America. He did eventually get the compensation for the land the family had once owned—9,75,000 rupees. Until that came through, others in the ashram helped out. He kept detailed accounts of all their help, and paid every single person back when he came into that money.

Tarapith was full of empty houses that belonged to wealthy families who lived in cities like Kolkata. They had built these houses but visited only during the big festivals, especially the ones observed on no-moon nights. Otherwise, the houses remained empty but for the caretakers who would often rent them out on the side for some extra income.

One such person had built a big house in Tarapith with a thatched roof. He offered it to Lahiri Baba to live in and appointed someone to look after him. I asked if I could also stay with him.

'Two people, no, no. One is more than enough,' chuckled Lahiri Baba though he was quite fond of me. When he would see me going to the temple, he would tease me 'Where are you off to, Chapal? Are you going to the temple to put bel leaves on Shiva's head? Go on, do that and see if something good happens to you.'

'Why are you saying that? Don't you believe in it?'

'I tell you, Chapal, all ritual is meaningless.'

'How can you say such things? You are a sadhu, you wear the saffron robes of a renunciate and yet you talk like this. You even eat fish!'

'To me, it's all the same whether it's fish or beef. I observe no rules.'

But I knew his devotion was deep and true as was his knowledge. I told him about the exorcist and the mantra she had given me.

'Oh, you must immediately discard it. Go wrap that mantra in bel leaves, smear some red sindoor paste on it, pin it together with thorns and then throw it into the Ganga,' he said.

He told me to chant the Aum mantra instead, not aloud, just in my mind, uninterrupted and unceasing. 'I can't promise you will become a millionaire. Or that your deepest desires will be fulfilled. You may become a king or you may become a pauper. Don't blame me if something bad happens or nothing happens at all. Nor should you put up a picture of me and worship it if something good happens. This mantra was with me, now I am giving it you. That is all there is to it. No one is anyone's guru. The only real guru is your conscience. You must follow your conscience.'

Still, in my mind, he was my guru.

I met all kinds of colourful characters in Tarapith. Nagen Baba was one of the last surviving tantriks who had served the legendary Saint Bamakhyapa, whose shrine is right next to the Goddess Tara's own temple in Tarapith. By the time I met him, Nagen Baba was a toothless old man. He taught me the Gayatri mantra and told me to say it once a day.

I finally managed to find a place to stay at Tarapith: at the Ram Kanai Dharamsala, a boarding house founded by one Jamini Ranjan Ram Kanai Pal. Luckily, I didn't have to pay rent. The manager, another Lahiri, told me, 'As the manager, I have a room. You can stay with me.'

I said, 'If I stay with you, I should do something for you. I know how to cook. Why don't I cook for you?'

'That's fine,' he said. 'As long as it doesn't go against your dignity.'

'What dignity? I don't have any left. All that has long become dust.'

He offered me his bed and said, 'You can sleep here. I can make a bed for myself on the floor.'

'No, no. I am used to sleeping on the floor. That's where I will sleep,' I replied.

It still took some getting used to. The tantriks, with long matted hair and orange robes, smoked up all the time, sucking on their chillums. They would get high and create quite a ruckus. I would politely refuse whenever they would invite me to smoke with them.

'Are you insulting our ganja?'

'No, no. Why should I do that? The great Bamakhyapa, the famous saint of Tarapith, himself would smoke it. I revere him. How can I disrespect what he did?'

Every moonless night, they would gather to smoke up while I cooked huge amounts of meat and fish for them. They spent all night at the cremation grounds doing their rituals and ate early in the morning. I still remember the stench of marijuana, mutton curry and local liquor vividly.

'Eat with us,' they would say.

'Please excuse me,' I would reply. 'I already ate last night.'

Those drug-fuelled sessions would continue all day. Sometimes the sadhus would be so intoxicated I would have to carry them to the bathroom and seat them on the toilet. I have held them while they vomited, not caring that I was getting soiled. Later, they'd apologize. But I was still just so relieved to have a roof over my head.

Some days, I would sit with the poor and indigent and eat the food that was given to them as alms. In Tarapith, I had to learn to truly let go of my pride.

Someone to Watch Over Me

Occasionally, X would visit from the city. Then they would organize a big feast. Someone would get a huge bottle gourd and fish heads. We would rent big cooking pots and pans, and I would cook lau with fish head for everybody.

My routine was strange then. I spent so much time sitting in the cremation grounds, watching people bringing the corpses in. I learnt how to count my beads as a way to meditate. At one time, I could count from 50,000 to 1,00,000, even 3,00,000. Now my fingers are arthritic and I can't any more. I would sit late at night in the cremation grounds and look at the heavens. It would feel like the sky had covered the earth like a blanket, and that blanket was studded with pinpricks of light. I had never seen so many stars in Kolkata. I would lie on the ground and gaze at them for hours. I would feel strangely close to the sky itself, as if the heavens had come down to hold me. Now the town is so lit up, you can barely see stars any more.

Lahiri Baba told me to wear a sindoor bindi and meditate in the crematorium. He would joke that if I looked the part of a holy man, then people would leave me more money than I could ever imagine. One night, as I sat there, meditating well after midnight, I felt something on my thighs. I looked down and there were two huge dogs, one brown, one black, their eyes glowing like red coals in the dark. They were sitting there with their paws on my thighs. For a moment, I was petrified. Who knew what kind of corpse-eating dogs these were. Finally, I said very slowly, 'There's a good dog, please move your paws and let me go.' I don't know what they understood but they released me, I slowly got up and started to walk back to my room. When I glanced back, I saw them following me. But I didn't feel scared at all. I felt as if they were escorting me home safely.

Another time, a sadhu I was talking to suddenly said with a start, 'I should go.'

'What's wrong?' I asked.

'There seems to be someone behind you, a shadowy figure looming over you.'

'Are you trying to scare me?' I asked. 'I don't see anything.'

'I had better go,' he said hurriedly.

I like to think that perhaps it was actually someone watching over me and protecting me.

Tarapith was a curious place, drawing the poorest of the poor as well as the richest of the rich. They all wanted to appease the goddess in their own ways.

A man from Khidirpur in Kolkata once sponsored a huge crown for the goddess. The priests went into a tizzy. They didn't know where to keep it safely. Eventually, they asked if I could safeguard it in my room.

'It's not even my room,' I protested. 'The person whose room it is, he's not here right now. How can I keep something so valuable?'

'Please keep it in your room. We can't trust anyone else.' I was so nervous I was unable to sleep a wink that night. I stayed up staring at that huge crown—studded with emeralds, diamonds and rubies—and praying to the goddess. 'Dear Mother, they have left this in my care. Please don't let me down. Let nothing happen to this crown tonight.'

When they took it away in the morning, I felt as if a huge weight had been lifted off my shoulders.

At Tarapith, I got to see the rituals at the temple up close. I saw how they dressed the stone that represented Goddess Tara. They would put a sort of wrapper around it and then adorn it with her clothes and her ornaments. It looked like a person with a bald head till they put the hair on it and finally the crown on top. At that moment, she became the goddess. I laughed and said, 'Oh, this is just like us in the jatra. This is how we transform ourselves as well.'

Then, in 1978, there was a huge flood. I was sitting and cooking on my little stove when I saw it grow menacingly dark in the west. The wind suddenly went cold, and before long, the rain started coming down in sheets. It was a terrifying day. The rain was relentless. The Tilpara barrage burst and flooded everything. Our holy tank, the one we called Jibitakundo, overflowed and the muddy water started lapping at the steps of the main Tara temple in Tarapith. Everyone fled home. Until the waters eventually receded, it was a huge task to even conduct the goddess' daily worship.

From my room, I could see the water swirling around us. There was no kerosene for lamps, no candles. As soon as evening fell, everything got swallowed up by the inky darkness. It was hard to find even basic things like salt and sugar. The cremation grounds were under water. I had some puffed rice at home. I'd eat that with a little jaggery. Finally, someone started some sort of a relief camp.

There were poor backward castes in that area called Lets. I would go and eat at their homes. Some would raise eyebrows at a Brahman's son eating at the homes of the lowest of low castes. But after the floods, they were the ones who saved me. They came and said, 'You have not eaten, will you eat with us?' 'Why not?' I said. That stubby-grained rice, and little kundri gourds with poppyseed paste—that tasted like the food of the gods. It's never about the food, it's about the care with which someone serves you the food. I guess I always knew that, but I understood it once again at the home of the Lets.

It took almost a year and half for things to get back to normal.

The Housekeeper

Around 1981, X said, 'Come and stay with me.' By then, his father was quite ill. He had developed glaucoma and was barely able to see. 'Now, there will be no problem for you to stay at the house,' X said. 'In fact, it will even be helpful. You know my wife has health issues. You can help look after the house and the children, especially when I am away. I have been sending you money every month anyway. You might as well just stay in the house now.'

I moved in. 'Immerse yourself in our lives,' he advised me. 'Spread yourself all over this house and become part of this family. Take care of it as your own.' And so I became, to my own surprise, a housewife. At the beginning of every month, X would give me the money needed to run the household. It was my job to keep everything running smoothly. When his daughter got married, he said, 'You take charge. Here is 1.5 lakh rupees. You decide how to spend it. No one will overrule you.'

By then our physical relationship had ended. Perhaps I had been a way for him to fulfil some desires, and he did not need them to be fulfilled any more. Or perhaps, after a time, everything, no matter how exciting it was once, becomes boring and humdrum. But our deeper connection remained, a friendship that went beyond sex—and that was enough for me. It gave me peace of mind, perhaps more than the physical relationship ever did.

But it didn't last. At some point, men and women, even if they are married with children, can feel a strong urge for someone else. That happened with X too.

In his case, it was another woman, a widow with a child. I pleaded: 'Don't do this. You are married. You are a father. You have a young son now as well. How will this look?'

He said scornfully, 'Did I ask you for your advice? This is my house. I can do what I want here. You get to live here. What more do you want? '

At that moment, I felt I was nothing to him, even though I was the one who kept that house running. I looked after everything in it. And everyone. No one even knew his salary in that house. I did. All day long, I would be going up and down three flights of stairs. Sometimes, I would mop those stairs myself. I would cook for all of them, I would do the shopping, pick up the rations, go to the coal shop, everything. He would not eat before midnight, long after everyone had fallen asleep. By then, after a whole day's work, I would be falling asleep on my feet, but I still served him his food.

I didn't protest. Thanks to him I had a roof over my head. Every month, some money would be deposited into my account, so that I would have a nest egg. That was his way of guaranteeing my future.

Soon, his father passed away. Now there was nothing to hold him back. He moved his mistress and her son into an empty apartment in the lower portion of the house. His wife was devastated. For some reason, she had accepted my presence in their lives, she had even taken to me. But she could not accept another woman. She came to me in tears.

I felt like I had to say something to him.

'This is not right,' I protested.

'How can you of all people say that?' he retorted. 'You are no different from her!'

'This is a woman with whom you have an ongoing physical relationship. It is none of my business but isn't that something you need to discuss with your wife? Shouldn't you care about what she thinks? In my case, your wife knew all about us, but she still treated me with such respect and courtesy. There was never any bad blood between us. We're like brother and sister. But you're bringing this woman home now. A woman with a child. Your own son is not so little any more—he's 11 or 12 years old. What if he asks you about her? How will you answer him?'

In fact, the boy did ask me that very question. The children's nickname for me was C.

One day, he said, 'C, Father just bought a new car. He took that aunty on a trip to Ghatshila. How come he didn't take us?'

I looked away and said, 'I don't know. It's best you ask your father himself.'

The Used Sal-Leaf Plate

One day, the last straw broke my back.

I complained that I wanted to go away somewhere for a few days. 'Everyone gets to go. Only I don't.'

'That's fine,' X said. 'You go, take a trip.'

'All right. I will go to Ghatshila for 10 days.' He had rented a house in Ghatshila and would often go there, sometimes with the family, sometimes with that woman. He had taken me once as well in the early days.

'But you must come back in three days.'

'What do you mean?' I protested. 'You all go for seven to ten days. I get only three?'

'Well, who will look after things here? Who will look after my wife and children?'

'Is that what it's all about? Looking after your house and family?' I said angrily. 'My own needs don't matter to you?'

Things got worse from there.

When my jatra career had ended and I was struggling to make ends meet, X would give me 100 rupees a month. At that time, his salary was not huge but he did it for me. Later, I learnt he had sold off his rifles and cartridges to be able to spare the money for me.

Now he reminded me of all that and that too, in front of that woman. I had thought all that was our private affair. When he spat out everything in her presence, it was as if he stripped me naked in front of her.

I walked out of that house, that relationship, that life I had built up over so many years.

Years later in the play *Ramanimohan*, I had a line of dialogue: 'They threw me out onto the road as if I was nothing more than a used sal-leaf plate.' Every time I said that line, it was a flashback to the day I left X's house after 12 long years. Yet I can never say he threw me out. I left on my own. But I felt like a used sal-leaf plate nevertheless.

He called me back: 'Go, if that's what you want to do. But take your things.'

I said, 'I will come back and take whatever is mine.'

I left in the clothes I was wearing. I had no money with me but I didn't care. I didn't know what to do or where to go. Soon, it started to rain. I took shelter on someone's front porch, and that's when the enormity of what I had done hit me. After 12 years, I was suddenly homeless again. I started to weep.

A car pulled up in front of me. A gentleman, quite well dressed, emerged and said, 'Excuse me, but why are you sitting here and crying?'

"Am I blocking your doorway?' I replied.

'No, this is not my house. I am just surprised to see a well-dressed person like you sitting here and crying. What is wrong?'

'What is that to you? You don't know me, I don't know you. Please mind your own business.'

'Yes, of course. I understand. You looked like someone from a decent family. That's why I was concerned.'

'There is no need to be concerned. I am just sitting here enjoying the breeze. You go on now to wherever you were going.'

'Enjoying the breeze? In this rain? Can I give you a ride somewhere?'

'No, don't worry about me. Just leave me alone.'

The man went away. By then the rain had eased off as well. I realized I must look like a fool, a middle-aged man in a kurta-pyjama, sitting on the porch and weeping. I picked myself up and trudged down the streets all the way to Goabagan where my niece, Chhordi's daughter, lived.

She answered the door. 'What happened? Where did you come from? Why are you in this state?'

'It's not something I can even talk about yet,' I replied. 'I just need to stay here for a little bit.'

Eventually, I went back to my sister.

She opened her door: 'You never told us what you were doing. Had I asked you to leave? You didn't let us know anything. You didn't keep in touch.'

But she welcomed me back without reservations.

A few days later, I went back to my friend's house to pick up my things.

When I first walked in, he smirked.

'There you are. You had to come back, didn't you? Where can you go, after all? Who is going to provide you with a home? They all just kicked you out, didn't they? And you had to come crawling back to me.'

'I haven't come back to stay,' I replied tersely. 'Just for my things.'

But I could not find half the things that were mine. I said, 'Where are my photographs?'

He just shrugged. 'I don't know, and I don't have time to look for them now.'

He had all those pictures from my jatra days—Sultana Riziya, Chand Bibi, Kaikeyi.

'Just give me my pictures. And I will go.'

'I've given whatever I had.'

That is why I have no photographs any more, only memories.

As I left, he said gruffly 'Where are you going?'

'You don't need to know,' I replied.

He stared intently at me, his eyes burning holes into me: 'You are making a terrible mistake.'

'So be it.'

Sometime later, he came to my sister's house. Perhaps deep down I thought he was looking for reconciliation. But it was about money.

He said, 'All that money that was kept in your name. I need you to sign this form so I can withdraw it.'

'What will happen to me?'

'How is that my concern? You left on your own accord.'

'I didn't leave—I was compelled to do so because of the way you behaved.'

'I don't want to get into all that. Just sign this. It's my money, after all.'

'And if I don't?'

'I'll just rip it all up. No one will have it.'

We had met when I was 18 and he was 22. Now I was a middle-aged man. What was over was over. There was no point clinging to that money when not just the relationship but even the friendship had ended.

It was a lot of money, but I signed it away unhesitatingly. I told him, 'There is God above me. He will look after me. And if

He does not, that is also fine with me. What was truly mine will always remain with me.'

He left.

I never saw him again.

All Games End

Once, I had asked whether what we did in bed ever made him feel strange. He laughed and said, 'It's just sport, khela. You should treat it as play.' I had laughed with him but I did not understand then that one day the game would be over.

That was my great failing. I thought I would play a woman forever, that even when women came into jatra there would be room for me. I thought I would be with Natta Company forever. I thought I would be with this one man forever, that nothing would change anywhere. We would talk about how, after his children were all grown up and gone their own ways, we would grow old together. He had put aside that money for me so that if anything happened to him, I would be provided for.

The opportunity to have other relationships came up many times. But I never pursued them. I stopped at one relationship. Not because I felt bitter. Or because I thought those other relationships were immoral. I stopped because I did not think anyone else would've been able to give me more than what X and I had.

Years later, I was at a performance at Jogesh Mime Academy. Suddenly I heard someone crying out: "C, C, oh C!"'

I looked around with a start. It had been years since I had heard that name. It was X's daughter. Now she was stout and matronly, nothing like that young woman whose wedding I had helped organize many years ago. She was there with her sister.

She said, 'I read in the newspaper that you were performing here. That's why we came. We wanted to see you. It's been so long.'

I said, 'How have you all been? How is your father?'

'What can we say about Father?' she said with a sigh. 'He is what he is.'

'The woman who lived with him?'

'She's passed away.'

'And the house?'

'That's gone as well.'

After that, they would call me up now and then. I would ask after their parents. They would tell me about their health problems.

Sadly, that younger daughter died during Covid.

Her sister called and wept. I said, 'Don't cry, this is fate. And listen, please don't take this the wrong way, but do not call me any more. I know you care about me, but what happened between me and your father is no secret. That has never been resolved, and I don't think it will ever be. I have no desire to rake it up again either. Too many years have passed. So this is my request to you. Don't call me any more.'

She called me one more time not too long ago from her in-laws' place in Medinipur.

She said, 'Father has died. Today is the funeral.'

He was 88. I thought: in the end, all our arrogance becomes dust. We all end up as ashes.

INTERLUDE

In Imagination

The Cook

What do I know about anything?

All my life I've been a cook in people's houses. Ask me about when to use panchphoran or kalo jeere and maybe I can offer you some tips.

But I don't have the audacity to talk to you about Chapal Rani. That would be big words from a small mouth.

When Chapal Rani came to live in our house, I was caught by surprise. The mistress had said the master's friend, some Chapal-babu was coming to live with us. But when Chapal Rani showed up, you could have knocked me down with my own ladle.

A little older, a little less hair, but I would recognize him anywhere even if he was not dressed as Chand Bibi. Of course I knew who Chapal Rani was. I grew up in the village. There was no cinema in our parts. Jatra was the highlight of our calendar. I would try and not miss a single show even though when I was young and I would get thrashed by my mother for staying out late. But I didn't care. There were kings and queens, song and dance, stories about gods and goddesses. Four to six hours, dozens of songs, action, melodrama—what more could we ask for?

Weeks before the jatra arrived, everyone would be talking about it. I remember the names as if they were the ingredients in a recipe.

Chand Bibi, Sonar Bharat, Bilwamangal. Cycle rickshaws would roll in carrying someone shouting into one of those little hand-held mics 'Coming, coming, *Sonar Bharat* is coming' and throwing handbills in the air. We children would run behind it, hooting and shouting, fighting with each other to scoop them up.

There was a field in our village called the jatra field. During the monsoon, when no jatras happened, we would play in the mud. But during jatra time, a stage would be built with wooden planks in the middle of that field. They'd put up bamboo poles and make a roof of sorts with tarpaulin. Wooden planks on both sides were the ramps. That was our theatre. Big bulbs tied to the poles bathing the stage in a yellow glow—that was our lighting. One or two chairs. Byas, nothing else. No scenery, no props, no sets.

But on jatra night that was enough to create magic. The musicians would sit below the stage—drums, cymbals, bells, clarinet, harmonium, flute, maybe a couple of trumpets. When the music went pyan pyan pyan, people would start streaming in, from all the villages around us. A river of people, all jostling to find a seat, the women on one side of the stage, the men on the other three, and us children squeezed in wherever we could, all our faces sweaty with excitement. The actors' faces, caked with make-up and greasepaint, with white lead and lamp soot, shone in the light of the Petromax lamps around which hundreds of insects buzzed. My mother's favourite were the jatras about gods and goddesses. I had a weakness for the historical ones whether about kings and queens or English sahibs and freedom fighters. Those had more fighting. I liked that. But most of all I liked to watch the jatra queens. That was real magic.

We would hang around the makeshift dressing room and try to peep through the faded velvet curtains with the name of the jatra company written on them. Inside would be big metal trunks full of costumes. The actors would be sitting around gossiping, doing their make-up, some of them half-dressed, looking like half-kings and half-gods. I would fantasize about running away with them, travelling all over the country. How exciting that would be.

Someone would always come and shoo us away. But we kept sneaking back, because we really wanted to see how men became women. It would be the closest we could get to seeing a city lady naked. My friend Robi said those jatra ranis were really half-man–half-woman. We would dare each other to catch the rani when she put her on bra. Robi claimed he had once seen a rani in full make-up, standing bare-chested and smoking a bidi, then putting on her blouse. Her face was like a queen with lipstick and powder, he said, but her chest was full of hair. I didn't know whether to believe him, but the image gave me a strange thrill.

One day, after a show, someone told me, 'Can you get a paan? Chapal-da wants to have a paan.' I scurried off and got one. I gave it to him myself and he said thank you in English. I was beside myself.

When Chapal Rani came on stage, I would get goosebumps. Once he was a queen in armour. Another time he showed up in a dress to seduce some rebel chieftain. That had the men folk in the village whistling.

What shows they were! The trumpets would sound their fanfare. The drums would start beating. And Chapal Rani's voice would rise higher and higher, traveling to the end of the field, as clear as a bell. I have seen him as a princess and I have seen him as the queen mother. I have seen him crush men with a look and I have seen him cry his eyes out. I have even seen him die on stage as someone stabbed him with a knife. Suchitra Sen and Supriya Devi, the leading ladies from the films, were not our stars in the village. They might as well have been stars in the sky. The jatra queens were right there. We could almost smell the powder they used.

The thought that Chapal Rani would be living in our house was mind-boggling. Of course I didn't tell him I knew who he was. Our village was just one of so many villages he must have visited. There was no reason he would remember its pond with its dozing water buffalos, its thicket of banana trees, its paddy fields. It was no different from any other village. And there was certainly no reason he would remember the gangling teenaged boy who got him a paan. But I never forgot that moment. He was in kurta-pyjama, but his face was still made up like a woman's. I stood there and watched him eat the paan, the red juices staining his white teeth. Then he smiled and went back into the dressing room. My friends teased me 'Don't wash your right hand any more. It's the hand from which Chapal Rani took a paan.'

When Chapal babu moved into our house, I didn't know what to make of it. He was the master's friend but beyond that I knew little. What will he eat, I asked the mistress. Whatever we do, she said sharply. But after lunch that day I quietly gave him a paan.

'A paan?' he said, his voice still high like a girl though he didn't look like one in his kurta- pyjama. 'For me? How did you know I like paan?'

I didn't say anything.

Over time I realized he was not Chapal-babu or Chapal Rani. He was our housekeeper. He had the keys to the house. He would set the menu often, sent Hari to the ration shop and keep tabs on how much oil we were using. I had to be careful. All cooks siphon off a little oil here and there, we make a little money off the bazaar. But he would grill us. That caused some heartburn in the kitchen.

Purnima the maid would pull a face and say, 'Who does he think he is? Why does he lord over us like he pays our salaries?' As cooks and maids and drivers, we are paid not to say anything, but we notice everything. We noticed that the master relied on him to run the house. He had a special place in it.

But we also knew he was not one of them. Purnima would sashay like him and say, 'He thinks he is still queen, but we all know he is just living on our babu's charity. If the babu's father was in his senses, he would be out on his ass in minutes.' She said she had heard that many years ago he'd done some black magic on our babu and put him under his spell.

These ranis know tricks wives don't, she would say darkly .

That didn't bother me. In our village, I knew boys like him. They were girl boys, they could sing, they walked with an extra swing to their hips. Some of them ended up in jatra parties like Chapal-babu. They danced in the chorus. One of them had even run away with the jatra once. His father said, 'Good riddance.' But every time the jatra came to town, I would try and spot him. I never did.

I often wished I could talk to Chapal-babu about his jatra days. I would wonder what he would look like now in a sari and a wig with his face made up like a woman's. 'Ask the master,' Purnima would snicker. 'I'm sure he still dresses like that for him late at night, when the whole house has gone to bed.' I never dared ask Chapal-babu but sometimes, alone in bed, in the hush of the night, I would imagine it and it made me feel strangely flustered.

With us he was very proper indeed. Sometimes, he would act like the poor widowed sister who had been given shelter, straight out of one of those Sarat Chandra weepies. Sometimes, he felt more like the real mistress of the house. The master would come back late, often after midnight. It was Chapal-babu who would stay awake to serve him his dinner like a good wife. The real wife would be asleep, nursing a headache. When the children needed something from their father, they would go to Chapal-babu and ask him to put in a good word. When the daughter got married, you should have seen how he bustled around, the house keys jangling in his kurta pocket.

He knew all the accounts of the house, how much rice we needed every month, how much coal, how much ghee. If push came to shove, he even mopped the stairs. He went to the market and got the fish. I would look at him curiously and try to imagine the goddess I had seen in the village. But that Chapal Rani had been put away in storage somewhere.

We bonded over cooking. He would come to the kitchen and ask for a cup of tea. He would tell me about things his mother cooked with fish head and pui saak. One day he came to the kitchen and said he needed to cook something with papaya and small shrimps. I said: tell me what you need, I will make it. He said: no, no, I will make it. It's something your master loves. I didn't ask him how he knew, but as he chopped that papaya finely, I knew this was something he had done many times. It was like watching my mother chop vegetables. How fast his hand moved. If he had bangles on, they would have been singing a song. Later that night, he served it himself to the master. I don't know what the master said but that day Chapal-babu seemed happy, humming a song as he went about.

It all ended when that woman moved into the house. You know that story. There is no need to wallow in that ugliness. Men are like that. They move on from one flower to another, Purnima said.

One day Chapal-babu had a showdown with the master. And then, just like that, he was gone. We were not to mention his name again. Nothing remained. Only the paans in my paan box.

The master came to me one day with bags full of papers and said: go and sell this to the raddiwala, the fellows who buy old bottles and newspapers. When I peeped inside, I saw torn letters and documents and some old photographs of Chapal-babu, many from his days as Chapal Rani. I got rid of them as I was told to, but I must confess I kept the pictures. I felt like I saved a little bit of Chapal Rani that day, for myself at least if not for the world.

I never saw Chapal Rani again but I kept those photographs with me. I've heard even Chapal Rani does not have his old pictures any more. Perhaps I am the only person in the world who does.

Sometimes I thought I should seek him out and give them to him. But how would I explain why I had stolen them? Even I don't know why. The truth is: when I see them, I feel young again, like a teenage boy shyly offering a paan to a queen.

10
Performing the Goddess

A Ball of Happiness

I had a roof over my head thanks to my sister. But there was no work. That would eat away at my soul.

But Chhordi, bless her, gave me no grief about it.

'Look, an actor's life always has ups and downs. My own life has been quite a rollercoaster, hasn't it? There was a time you were so busy with work you barely had time to breathe. Now there's no work. It happens. But mark my words, Tuku, today you might have fallen to the ground. One day you will get up again using that same ground as your support.'

But I would still feel like a burden. I was living off my sister's charity, and my nephews' jibes would ring in my ears.

'Don't mind them,' Chhordi would console me. 'It's not your fault that you are not getting any work right now. Anyway, it's not like there are many jobs you can suddenly do. Our world is all about acting. What else do we know? You will just have to be patient.'

But I hated having to take money from my sister. I hated sitting at home all day with nothing to do.

Our house rose straight off the pavement on Girish Chandra Avenue. You walked up three steps and entered the house through a heavy collapsible gate. It's still there, a grey two-storeyed house, its slatted green windows faded by sun and rain. Three or four families lived in it. Now a big board outside advertises a dance academy. A moustachioed man in a fancy kurta brags that he's won 'Best Colourful Choreographer' in a TV competition. I am sure no one in that house knows that Ketaki Dutta and Chapal Rani lived there once.

The ration shop and little liquor store across the road are gone but the Kali temple down the street is still there, bigger and shinier and more orange than it used to be back in our day. Another small temple has sprung up at the other end of the block, its entrance decorated by an arch of strawberry-pink and snow-white artificial flowers. It looks more like something left over from a wedding than a temple. Half the pavement has been swallowed up by tea shops. The sign hanging overhead says 'Eat well, stay healthy' though the fare on offer is basic—butter toast, egg toast, Maggi instant noodles, alur dum and ghugni. A woman in a nightie boils water in a large aluminium kettle. None of that was there when we lived there but Girish Bhawan, the old house that belonged to the great playwright Girish Ghosh, was. The house was older than the street. When they carved the street out of the neighbourhood, they saved the house because of its history. Now it stands in the middle of the thoroughfare as if stranded on a desert island. A white statue of a dhoti-clad Girish Ghosh, his moustache drooping despondently, stands in front of it, a shawl draped over his shoulders, his hands clasped in front of him, looking ahead with great seriousness. The sign on the pedestal reads 'The Maestro of Modern Bengali Theatre, Great Actor & Dramatist, Girish Chandra Ghosh, Born: 28 February 1844, Died: 8 February 1912.' We could see the little house clearly from our front door. Some days I would sit on our steps and just look at life on the street. Sometimes I'd walk down to B. K. Paul Avenue.

But bad times attract bad friends and that happened to me as well. One such friend lived in nearby Bagbazar.

One day, he showed up with a dark little ball, the size of a marble. 'Eat it,' he said. 'Just try it and see.'

I did, and kind of liked it.

'What is it?' I asked.

'It's siddhi. Cannabis.'

I was no innocent. I knew about siddhi because I had lived with the tantriks of Tarapith who took all kinds of substances.

'Where did you get it?' I asked.

'There's a shop right here on B. K. Paul Avenue,' he said. 'But don't have the raw kind. Have majoon.'

'What's majoon?'

'It's a different form of the drug. They cook it and concentrate it, stirring it until it becomes dense like a Bengali sandesh, not the soft kind, but the harder korapaak kind. Then it's wrapped with tobacco leaves.'

It was a little costlier than the raw siddhi balls. But you could get a decent sized one for about one rupee. My sister would give me two rupees as pocket money. I would use one rupee for that and save the other by walking instead of taking the bus.

I ate the majoon. It was rather sweet with something hard in the middle. I chewed that up as well and drank some water.

In those days, I was always paranoid, suspicious that people were talking about me. When I had those wonder balls, I would calm down and sleep like a log at night. And my bowels were clear in the morning.

But my family soon realized something was off. My eyes were bloodshot. My niece said, 'Tuku-mama, what's wrong with you? Why are your eyes so red?'

'Wrong? Nothing's wrong with me. I am fine.' Unlike alcohol, siddhi didn't affect your speech. My words were clear, not slurred. But I would be in a stupor, because the balls would make me feel dizzy.

My family noticed that as soon as the clock struck seven in the evening, wild horses could not keep me at home.

'What's the time?' I would ask.

'Why?'

'I want to go out for a bit.'

'It's 6.45. Where do you want to go now?'

'I need to go somewhere.'

'All day you stayed at home. And now suddenly you need to go out after dark?'

But nothing could keep me away from that store, such was my addiction. Eventually, they figured it out and begged me to quit.

But I was adamant.

'How can I? It makes me feel normal. Otherwise nothing feels right. Only when I take it, I can get along with everyone.'

But even I could not deny that it was affecting my health. I could see how gaunt I had become. There were dark shadows under my eyes even though I slept soundly every night.

One day, I fell ill and went to see the doctor. He examined me and said, 'Do you drink?'

'No,' I replied.

'But you must be taking something. Your liver is in really bad shape. Are you sure you are not lying to me? I hear you used to be an actor. Don't many actors have a drinking problem?'

'At one time I did drink a little, at a party perhaps. But it was very little and very occasional. That's all long over now.'

'No, no, this is something that's been roosting in your body for a long time. Is there something else you take? Any drugs? Heroin, charas? Do you smoke up?'

'No.'

'What about cannabis?'

'That I have daily. Without that I cannot function normally.'

'Do you stir it in milk or something? The way people have it during Holi or Durga puja? With milk and crushed nuts?'

'No, I have it raw. Or sometimes it comes in this ball, like a sweet, with something hard at the centre'

'Do you chew that up?'

'Yes.'

'My God! You have to stop immediately. You are literally chewing your way to death.'

'How can I stop? At the dot of 7, I just have to go to this shop.'

'You are completely addicted. First off, I will give you some medicine to deal with that.'

I took the medicine, and after three days I no longer felt the craving to take those siddhi balls any more.

'I don't feel the need to go there any more,' I told the doctor.

'Good, but you must continue taking the medicine,' he replied. 'If you want have a drink, one or two pegs won't matter.

Just not on an empty stomach. But please don't take those drugs any more. You have no idea what that was.'

'What was it?'

'It's a kind of root—it's very dangerous.'

After that, I never took cannabis again. But I would pass by the shop all the time. It was always busy. All kinds of people would come there, rich and poor, looking for their ball of happiness. Once I too had been one of them. Now, looking back, I know I went there because I was depressed. Those balls were a way to forget my depression for a while. At that time, I had neither the language nor the wherewithal to understand that. I just knew that when I ate those balls, life became tolerable.

Slowly, the nightmare of the addiction receded. My looks returned as well. The dark circles disappeared from under my eyes. But I still got no acting jobs.

The Goddess of Smallpox

That was when I started thinking about Sitala, the goddess who wards off smallpox. It's an old tradition dating back to days when there were no vaccines. Sitala, or the Cool One, is the goddess who grants you relief from fevers and ailments. Her temples are everywhere, in villages and cities, small humble structures where women worship her every Tuesday. In one hand she carries a pitcher with holy water that heals the afflicted, in her other a broom with which to sweep away illness. In villages, she is often shown as a goddess without jewellery and silk saris. Perhaps that makes the poor people in the villages feel closer to her. She rides a donkey, an animal we think of as a beast of burden. But the ancient texts tell us that the milk of an ass helps fight smallpox. In Sitalar gaan, a man in a white sari went from village to village, carrying a whisk or chamor, singing the songs of Sitala. Some people gave him money, some gave him clothes.

The first opportunity to play Sitala came my way around the time jatra work started drying up. I had turned up my nose. I couldn't see myself performing on the street, singing the songs of Sitala, for pennies. But in 1992, I couldn't afford my pride any more. I went to my friend Raju who did Sitala.

'Help me,' I said. 'Teach me how to do Sitala.'

Raju said, 'How? Do you even know what you'll earn? After performing for four to five hours, we might at best make about 40–50 rupees. Then we walk home back home, because by that time in the night, the buses have stopped running. Do you think you can do this?'

'I don't know if I can,' I admitted. 'But I have to try at least. I need to survive. Somehow.'

Raju smiled, 'At one time you had said, "Have I no self-respect? I am not going around the streets, performing in slums, holding out a plate to people asking them for money." At that time, this work was beneath your dignity.'

'I know I said all that,' I said meekly. 'But things are different now.'

'OK, let me see what I can do. But there is nothing to teach, really. This is not like your jatra where some playwright writes a script and a director tells you what to do. Here, you just have to make it up as you go along. But you do need a good working knowledge of the epics like *Ramayana* and *Mahabharata*. Take those stories and incorporate them into your act. The more convincing you are, the more generous the audience will be with their alms when you go around with a plate at the end.'

'How much do they give usually?'

'Someone might give you 2 rupees, someone might give you 5. Or just coins. Anything goes, to be honest.'

'Is there a book or something where the Sitala story is written?'

'If you know a little bit of the *Sitalamangal* by Nityananda Das, that will help. We take chunks of that and mix it up with dialogues from different jatras and that becomes the performance.'

'Will you show me some day?'

'Sure. Come with us. We have a show in Barrackpore today.'

I went with him to the show. The man playing Sitala really looked like a majestic goddess, tall and rather hefty, his face full, the eyes made up to look even larger than they were.

'There's nothing to learn,' he assured me. 'You are an artiste. I am sure it won't be hard for you to grasp.'

Finally, one day, I got my chance at the Taltala Sitala Mandir in Central Kolkata. They promised me fifty rupees, five rupees bonus at the end and a conveyance fee.

The place was a like a large warehouse. I had to sit in the middle of that and put on my make-up and get changed. There wasn't much privacy. One of the actors said, 'Don't be embarrassed, Chapal-da. This isn't like the green room in your theatre.'

I somehow got dressed. There was one scene where Sitala takes on the forms of the ten Mahavidyas, like Kali, Tara, Shoroshi. You had to ad lib the dialogue as you went from one form to the other. Each version of the goddess had her own weapons, all of which were laid out but I didn't really know which one to pick up when.

Seeing me fumble, the people who had hired the troupe griped, 'Where did you find this Sitala?'

The manager of the troupe tried to stand up for me: 'Don't say such things. Do you know who he is? Do you know how famous he was back in the day?'

'What do we care? We didn't even see a trident in his hand when he stood tall as Goddess Durga! What kind of Durga is that? Your Raju was much better.'

One actor came to my defence. 'How will Chapal-da know all this? He's never done this before. You should have guided him, told him what to carry in each scene. You did no such thing and now you are complaining about what he didn't do!'

It was like Day 1 at Natta Company. That's how I always learnt—by doing, stumbling and then doing it again.

'Sitala Begs'

There's no way to disguise the hard truth. Sitala troupes beg for money. And not just money. People also brought saris and shawls, sometimes a bag of rice, as offerings to Sitala.

After the show, we would sell off Sitala's garland of 108 blood-red hibiscus flowers to the highest bidder.

The barker would start shouting: 'Sitala's garland is up for sale now. Who wants it? Who is the fortunate one who will take it home? How much can we get for it? Five rupees over there—5 rupees, one, 5 rupees, two—' Someone might say 10 rupees. Another person might shout 30. The price would go up steadily.

Finally, it would sell perhaps for 70 rupees.

'That's 70 rupees, one, 70 rupees, two, 70 rupees, three. Done. This lucky gentleman has bought the Sitala garland for 70 rupees.'

The buyer would come and bow to me. As Sitala, I would bless him and accept the money from his hands. But the owner of the troupe would be standing right next to me, waiting to snatch the money out of my hand. Sitala got nothing from the sale of her own garland. She begged for money, holding a little tray woven from cane in her hand. Whatever she made by begging, she got to keep half. The owner took the other half.

Once that led to a great fight. People kept bidding and outbidding each other. Finally, a young man won, bidding 251 rupees for the garland, a princely sum in those days. But he insisted the money should go to me, and only me.

The owner of the company grabbed his wrist and said, 'Why?'

'Why not?' the young man retorted. 'He did all the hard work as Sitala. This money is rightfully his.'

'No, no. It's my right as the owner.'

'I refuse to accept that. Look at him. He is a jatra star, now performing on the roadside like this. I insist on giving him this money.'

'Just give it to the owner,' I pleaded. I didn't want him to make a scene.

'No, it breaks my heart to see you going around with a plate begging for money. A mother goddess begging for money? Chhi.'

'That is the rule,' the owner said. 'Sitala begs. Now, you just tell me, who you will give the money to. Him or me?'

'What do you say?' the young man asked me.

'Just give it to him. That is the way it is. But the garland belongs to you now.'

He reluctantly gave the money to the owner but then he took out another 100 rupees and laid the money at my feet. And he returned the garland to me too: 'Keep the garland. I have nowhere to keep it at home. I only bid for it as a tribute to you.'

I almost wept when I heard that. It had been a long time.

Becoming the Goddess

We didn't just perform the story of Sitala. Our mythology is rich with so many stories from Manasa Puran or Padma Puran, Lakkhinder–Behula, Harish Chandra and Shaibya. We had to know the little details of all those stories. What kind of snakes were sent to kill Lakkhinder? What diseases does Nityananda Das describe in his *Sitalamangal*? Why did God Vishwakarma leave a slit the size of a needle in a snake-proof wedding chamber made of iron? A lot of the people who came to the shows knew these stories inside out, and they would grill us.

'Tell us, who was Padma Gokhra?'

'Who was Dhanyantari?'

'Which snake bit him on the crown of his head?

If you did not know, they would scoff, 'You don't know? Why are you even singing the songs of *Manasamangal* at all?'

At first, I felt offended by their remarks, but now I think they were right. One should know these things before one takes up such roles. These were not just any roles. They were about performing the goddess. Truth be told, I've been every goddess one can imagine. Sitala with her donkey, carrying her broom and her water pot. Manasa, the beautiful goddess of snakes, holding a snake and a lotus. The fair-skinned Saraswati with her veena and swan. The Kali of Kalighat, black as night, in a white sari with a red border, a garland of plastic hibiscus flowers around my neck, my skin blackened with shoe polish.

I did Sitala not because I was her devotee but because there was nothing else I could do. My life had come to a dead end. I had to make a living somehow.

But, as I started performing, I realized this was different than the queens and goddesses I had played on the jatra stage. There I was playing a role, Chapal Rani as Sultana Riziya, but for the people who came to see Sitala, I actually became the goddess. They no longer called me Chapal Rani. They said: 'Mother, bless us.' Women said: 'Mother, can I put a little sindoor in the parting of your hair?'

'But this is just a wig,' I protested. 'Women put sindoor on the heads of other women. I am a man dressed as Sitala. If you put sindoor on my head, won't your husband get upset?'

'My husband is the one who told me to do this. He said this is no longer Chapal-babu. This is the Mother Goddess Sitala. If you put sindoor in her hair, she will do the same to you and bless us with a long and happy married life.'

At the end of the performance, I would stand there, my black wig turned bright red from all the sindoor women would smear on my head. My forehead, my cheeks would be streaked with red. At first, it would unnerve me, but the other actors said, 'When you dress as Sitala, you become Sitala in people's eyes. They believe you are possessed by the spirit of the goddess. They can worship her, garland her, put sindoor on her just as they would to a goddess.'

Gradually, even I started to feel a transformation within me. As soon as I drew the divine third eye on my forehead, I stopped my usual banter. In my jatra days, once I was finished with my make-up, I would want to chat with everyone. But not when I was Sitala. Maybe somewhere inside me I was scared. This was the Goddess of Disease after all. No one should fool around with her. If someone tried, I would tell them, 'Not now. This is no ordinary goddess. She can curse you with a disease you will not be able to cure.' As I invoked her with the song '*Aaye ma, o ma din jay, kaal jaay, doya kore aay go ma*'—Come, O Mother, the day goes by, the age goes by, have mercy, O Mother, and come to us—a strange feeling would come over me.

Of course, in reality, it was a business, we were all trying to make a few bucks in our Sitala costumes. The money was paltry. You would work for hours and barely make 30–40 rupees, maybe 60–70 rupees on a good day. We would go from place to place by bus, lugging a heavy jute bag stuffed with Sitala's paraphernalia—her sari, her crown, her garland, her ornaments. Sometimes a performance would start at 9 at night and not end until 1 in the morning. There were no buses and trams that late, no taxis even. I would walk home through the empty streets, past beggars sleeping on the pavement while street dogs barked at me.

Once, a policeman stopped me at Shyambazar crossing.

'Wait. Where are you going? Why is your face made up? Is that sindoor in your hair? What's in your hand?'

'I am an actor. I'm just going home' I replied wearily.

'Actor? At this time in the night? What theatre gets over this late?'

'I was doing Sitala's songs.'

'Sitala's songs?' he asked mockingly. 'I hear all kinds of no-good useless boys act in those things. Are you of that type?'

'Hmm, you can understand what type I am by looking, can't you?'

'Open your bag.'

'Why?' I was carrying Sitala's garland of red hibiscus flowers in my bag. My friends had told me to always carry that with me. It was my insurance, a way to prove that I was indeed returning from singing Sitala's songs.

The policeman picked up the garland.

'Don't throw this,' I said. 'This is the goddess' garland. I am taking it home.'

'What else is in that bag? Show me.'

'Listen, you cannot talk to me like that. You cannot force me to open my bag like this.'

'I need to see what's inside.'

'I live right here in Bagbazar. On Girish Chandra Avenue. My sister is the actress Ketaki Dutta. I live with her.'

'Ketaki Dutta? The one who acts in *Barbodhu*?' That play had become a massive hit at that time, and created quite a sensation because in the very first act, Chhordi had to do a love scene dressed in just her brassiere and petticoat. Marketed as 'Love's Blow-Hot Play', it created history by running for 1,800 nights.

'Yes, I am her brother. My name is Chapal Bhaduri.'

'Chapal Bhaduri? Wait, wait. A long time ago, perhaps in the early '70s, did you act at the Shyampukur Police Station? I think the play was *Durgeshnandini*. Are you that Chapal Rani?'

'Yes, that's me.'

'And today you are doing this?'

'What can I do? At least I am doing honest work to make a living.'

'I am so sorry I harassed you. Please don't mind. I will have someone reach you home.'

'No, that's fine. I can go on my own.'

'No, no, these are bad times, and it's very late. Let us escort you home.'

The Season of Sitala

Our season was short—essentially the months of spring and summer when the dreaded smallpox was most common. It would begin with Sitala-snan in Howrah in the spring, when the Sitala idols from the nearby temples, the so-called sisters, would be brought for their ritual dip in the river. Then the season would be officially open for the next three months. We would perform almost every day, sometimes twice a day, perhaps 20 days every month, often travelling outside Kolkata. Once the monsoon set in, Sitala's songs would end, then our troupe would perform the story of Manasa, the goddess who protects us against snakebite.

I call them troupes, but they were not as formal or as professional as the jatra companies. These were much smaller, often cobbled together by one person. That's whose name was on the troupe: Mahim's Troupe, Naru's Troupe, Gopal's Troupe, Raju's Troupe. Raju was much in demand because he was beautiful. 'You should just become a woman,' I would tell him. He indeed thought of himself as one.

Not all of them came from the world of jatra. Some had taken up this line of work because their looks suited the part. Like Manoranjan, a tall, striking-looking young man. When he acted as Durga and killed the demon Mahishasur, everyone would leap to their feet and cheer. People would joke that he was like a strapping firefighter. They nicknamed him Durga of the Fire Brigade. Manoranjan managed to save some money and set up his own troupe. He would get old costumes, patch them and re-use them. It didn't make him rich but he managed to get by.

These were not very educated people. They were rough in their manners and unpolished. My sister was startled when one of them showed up at the door, hollering for me.

'Who on earth is that?' she asked me.

I came to the door, shushed him and asked what he needed. He immediately got down to business.

'We have two shows. One at Beleghata and then at Tangra. How much will you take?'

'Double show? Is this in full costume and make-up or just one-faced Sitala?'

'Full costume'

'All right then, 70 rupees'

'No, no, Chapal-da. Make it 60 rupees each, and 10 rupees for conveyance.'

We were haggling over a goddess as if over a prime rui fish at the market. It was very little money, barely enough to make ends meet. But someone must have been looking out for us because suddenly my life took a different turn.

Enter: The Seagulls

In 1999, I met Naveen Kishore. Sometime around 1997–98, a group of women theatre personalities were invited to a seminar at Seagull Books, a publishing house that put out many books on theatre. Chhordi went to the seminar. That's how she met Naveen Kishore and Samik Bandyopadhyay of Seagull.

One day, Samik-babu and Naveen visited our house in Bagbazar to interview Chhordi. That was the first time I saw

Naveen. Even at first glance, he looked like a man with a keen artistic sensibility. I was wearing my usual checked lungi while he looked so distinguished in his crisp kurta–pyjama. I still had traces of Sitala's red alta paint lining my feet.

My sister told me, 'Oh, can you make some tea, please?'

As I set the tea and biscuits down, Naveen looked at me and said, 'Thank you. You look rather familiar.'

I didn't know what to say. Samik-babu said, 'You've probably seen him as a woman. This is none other than that Chapal Rani from the world of jatra. Remember, I told you about him.'

'Oh, what do you do now? I hear there isn't much work in female roles for men these days.'

'Nowadays, I perform as Goddess Sitala on the streets.'

'I would love to see that. Can you take me one day?'

'This isn't a performance at the Academy of Fine Arts. How can I take a gentleman like you to Sreemani Market where we spread a carpet on the street and sing the songs of Sitala? That's not a place for someone like you.'

'That's not an issue at all. I can go anywhere.'

The next time I had a performance at the Taltala Sitala Temple, I took Naveen along. After the rundown mansions of the old merchant princes give way to shuttered movie theatres, across the street from the offices of the Communist Party of India (Marxist–Leninist), with portraits of its presiding gods—Marx, Lenin, Stalin and Engels—over its door, right next to dingy stores selling auto parts and rice (Rice Kings, established 1891), stands the marble block of Taltala Sitala Temple with its green wrought-iron doors and mosaics of peacocks and deities on its columns. The neighbourhood is quite Muslim. Men in skull caps hang around a nearby mosque and in the little shops on the street, but the temple remains very popular. Buses slow down in front of it, so that the conductors can throw a few coins inside as an offering to the goddess. Not one but four Sitala donkeys are lined up next to each other, some with white faces, some yellow, all draped in red and gold. The walls have memorial plaques from devotees in memory of dead parents. Even now, Sitala's songs take place here every year, though I doubt anyone remembers me.

I told the group's leader, 'Listen, this gentleman wants to take some photographs of our performance. I hope that's all right with you.'

'Why should we have any problem? No one gives a damn about us. Will those photos appear in a newspaper?'

I told Naveen, 'They are fine with it. But where will you sit?'

'I won't sit anywhere. Please don't pay any attention to me. Just don't look towards my camera. You do your thing and I will do mine.'

There was a little makeshift green room right there on the street, if you can call it that, just a naked 150-watt bulb and some wooden planks over the drains. We all sat there, dressing, changing, getting into character while Naveen kept clicking. I remember suddenly feeling shy, but we kept chatting as I carried on with my work.

'You just do whatever you always do,' Naveen told me. 'Don't look at me. Erase me from your mind.'

By the time it ended, it was quite late, well after midnight. Naveen stayed till the very end. Later, he invited me to the Seagull office to see the photographs from that night. He seemed rather pleased with them but I was a little bemused. Until now, all my jatra photographs had been in full costume and make-up. That was what I was used to. In Naveen's photographs, I was putting on my bodice, applying eyeliner, drawing my eyebrows, fixing my fake eyelashes. It showed me bare chested, my arm raised, putting on my blouse. You could see my body, my torso. When I looked at them, I felt strangely naked. Also, they were all in black and white. At a time when I was trying to make jatra feel more contemporary, those pictures felt rather old-fashioned.

Later, I realized he had done something very different with me, something no one had done until then. He had documented my transformation into the goddess. He had given my Sitala a whole new life. Some of those photographs went to an exhibition, and to my surprise, sold for a good amount of money.

He took colour pictures as well, but that was later, in my house.

Naveen helped take my Sitala off the streets and into theatres. I call it Ekmukhi Sitala or One-Faced Sitala. That means I would play the different aspects of the goddess using various props. Five people dressed in plain dhotis and kurtas would be my assistants, helping to keep the story moving. They used long veils of different colours to signify different characters and help me transition between various stories. I would say, 'I need to descend to earth now. Show me the way.' One of them would do that and lead me to the bedchamber of King Virat.

Then I would transport the audience to King Virat's bedchamber late at night, switching between all the parts by just changing my voice.

GODDESS. Virat, Virat, awake.
(*Sings a song*) Wake, O Virat, How much longer will you sleep?

VIRAT. Who is it? Who is there?

GODDESS (*in a quavering voice*). It's me. I am an old Brahman woman. I beg you for some alms.

VIRAT. It is the duty of the king to give. What do you want?

The old woman asks for different things and then finally makes her last demand.

GODDESS. Place piles of blood-red hibiscus at my feet.

VIRAT. What? How dare you? The blood-red hibiscus that I use to worship Goddess Sankari—you want me to give those to a beggar woman? Leave this place at once. Who do you think you are? Just who?

GODDESS. Listen, Virat. I am the One. I am without parallel. I am the Energy of the Universe. I am the all-powerful Goddess. I am Durga. I am Kali. I am Tara. I am Shoroshi. Sometimes I am Bhuvaneshwari. Sometimes I am Bagala. Or Chhinnamasta. I am Goddess Sitala.

Theatre audiences had never seen something like this before. It was received so well that Naveen asked me to work on it a little more.

'Think of how you can do this differently,' he said. 'Not with four or five people as you are doing it now. It has to be just you. With music of course, but it will be a one-person Sitala, you solo.'

'How will I do that?'

'Think over it. See what you can come up with. You have done so many roles. Maybe you can think of something that puts together the different bits somehow, like a puzzle.'

I felt both excited and nervous. I am no intellectual. I've only studied up to Class 8. But somehow Goddess Saraswati blessed me that night. I dug deep into my many roles in jatra and made a collage of them. I wrote a script with bits of many parts I had done, incorporating songs, some parts of the *Sitalamangal* epic poem. Until then, each jatra I had done had been its own entity. Now, suddenly, they became a patchwork quilt.

I stayed up all night, writing.

My sister woke up late at night and saw me bent over the table, working away. She said, 'Tuku, it's almost 3 in the morning. What are you still writing?'

'I have to write,' I replied. 'This is something I need to do.'

I took what was a three-hour production on the jatra stage and distilled it down to one-and-half hours.

Everything, goddess, crone, king, boy, queen, all had to be done by me, sometimes using simple tricks and sleight of hand. If I needed to transform into Goddess Kali, I turned my face away from the audience and quickly brought out a cigarette packet. Its inner flap had been painted red like Kali's blood-soaked tongue. My sari did not change. I didn't have black or blue Kali make-up. But that simple prop transformed me into Kali. In the next instant, I could become Goddess Chandi, slaying an imaginary demon while all around me rose a swell of voices reciting her prayers to the frenzied beat of drums. When I told the story of the fisherman, his wife and Sitala, I would have to do all three, switching between one and the other just using my voice and a simple prop,

We performed it for the first time in 1998 or 1999 in New Delhi. Seagull had set up shows at different venues, like the Kali

Temple at Chittaranjan Park, India Habitat Centre and Triveni Kala Sangam.

We took musicians from Kolkata with us to give the authentic feel of a jatra—a tabla player, a pakhwaj player, someone to play the violin and the harmonium as well as a well-known dhaki drummer from the Rambagan area. He could be counted on to give a rousing drum roll when I struck a dramatic pose as Sitala. That always got the audience on their feet. It was exciting but nerve-wracking. They had never dealt with a performance like mine. I had never done something like this.

Documenting the Whole Story

In 1998 or 1999, Naveen came up with a new idea—a documentary about me. I was nonplussed. Why would anyone would make a documentary about me? Although I became a star as Chapal Rani, no one had ever interviewed me about my life or craft. Newspapers interviewed my sister because she acted on stage and screen, but jatra stars like us didn't merit that kind of interest.

Chhordi said, 'Yes, I think you should do it.' To be honest, I had another more pressing incentive. I needed money. I had, in fact, gone to Naveen at the Kolkata Book Fair and said I needed a job, any job. I could make tea at Seagull, if need be. Naveen came up with the idea of a documentary instead. And told me I would get paid for it.

He shot in different venues, bringing together some of my old colleagues from that world, like Shekhar Ganguly and Phani Bhattacharya. Everyone was paid for their time. He went with me to the Natta Company office in Putulbari to meet Makhanbabu.

Makhan-babu said: 'Of course, I will help. I am delighted that Chapal is getting his due.' He showed us around the office, pointed out places where I would hang out, sometimes moping in a dark corner of the veranda because someone had scolded me, the place where we practised, the room where the actors who came from villages slept dormitory-style . . . We took many photographs in Putulbari, standing on the terrace and the balcony, looking out over the train tracks to the brown river flowing sluggishly in the distance.

Naveen said, 'Let us bring together some of the people you worked with and hire jatra musicians. We can re-enact bits of those plays in full costume in an old mansion like the Shobhabazar Rajbari.'

When I took Naveen to meet Aloknath Deb, the head of that Rajbari, all the women were so excited to see me after such a long time.

It ended up being quite an experience, a reliving of lost days. Queen Kaikeyi from *Bharat Biday*. Chand Bibi. Old colleagues reprised their roles. For one night, we had suddenly gone back to the glory days of Natta Company as I emerged from between those massive whitewashed pillars, walking towards the camera reciting those old lines. It was the old jatra, but without 10,000 people watching us.

We recorded a whole segment on the street as well in front of Srimani Market, an old rather dilapidated market in North Kolkata. I think there might have been some goddess immersion happening that day, I remember the plumes of smoke and the smell of incense.

There were long interviews as well. Samik Bandyopadhyay asked me question after question and I answered the best I could.

But something kept nagging at me. This was a film about my life and I was talking about my roles and career but I was omitting a huge part of my life.

One day, I went to Naveen and said, 'I wish to talk about something more personal. Should I?'

'Of course, you can,' he said. 'It's a documentary about your life. You can say whatever you like. But only if you wish to.'

I brought him back to my house because this was something that needed privacy. It was just Naveen and our filmmaker Pushan Kripalani with a handheld camera. I sat there, cooking the recipes that X loved, and for the first time ever, I told the world my love story. Naveen asked worriedly, 'Are you sure you want to talk about all this? Your nieces are here. Your lover's children are around.' I was sure. I had waited long enough.

A documentary has to document all the facts of my life, good, bad or ugly. How could I hide things just because society might not approve? Anyway, I had not done anything wrong. I had just loved another person. I had not murdered anyone.

That story became the heart of the film. Naveen had to throw out much of the other footage we had shot already, many interviews about my work.

When *Performing the Goddess* was screened at Nandan in September 1999, I felt a little embarrassed seeing myself blown up so large on this screen, saying all those things. Chapal Rani appeared before audiences in wig, sari, jewellery. Here I felt naked.

After the screening, a prominent journalist said, 'You revealed so much private stuff. Were you forced to do that? Perhaps in return for money?'

I retorted sharply, 'Absolutely not. That's a complete lie. There was no pressure to say something or not say something. This is a documentary about my life. And I refuse to apologize for it. Sharing this is my personal right and I don't really care what other people think about that.'

He said, 'We can't write about such things in our newspaper. Ours is a family paper.'

'That's fine with me,' I replied. 'But that is my story.'

That documentary brought me a lot of attention, though I don't know who from the jatra world saw it. If they did, they didn't reach out to me. My own connection with that world had ended long before. But now I was suddenly an object of media curiosity. It was as if Chapal Rani had sprouted wings or grown horns.

Performing the Goddess took me all over India. When Naveen sent me to Delhi, I took a friend with me. He was from a small village in Bardhaman and acted in female roles at one time. He too had no livelihood any more. I said, 'Come with me. You can spend a few days in Delhi. It won't be any trouble. Come.'

My friend confessed, 'I have never been to Delhi. In fact, this is the first time I have come anywhere so far from Bengal.' Such was the life of a female impersonator in jatra.

Around 2007–08, I had gone somewhere for a rehearsal. I saw someone was performing Sitala nearby. When I looked closer, I realized to my surprise it was Raju, the one who had first introduced me to the whole world of Sitala.

I stood quietly on the side, watching him. He spotted me and gestured with his eyes, asking me to wait. When it was over, he came to me. He was still carrying the kulo tray in which devotees placed their offerings. I placed a 100-rupee note in it and said,

'Take this. Once I also dressed as Sitala and went around with a kulo, asking people for money. This is for you.'

He said, 'Wait.' He carefully took off his third eye. Now he was no longer a goddess. Then he bent down, touched my feet and said, 'Chapal-da, *tumi Sitala ke kothay niye gecho jekhane amra keu pouchate pari ni*—You have taken our Sitala to a place which none of us could reach. We have remained right here where we started.'

I said, 'No, Raju. I could have started long before I did. By now I might have had my own troupe. But it's all right. Whatever has happened has been for the best. Ma Sitala raised me from the darkness and made me strong.'

But it moved me. Sitala is the stuff of our old folklore and myths. Poor people acted in those roles. Poor people went to watch it in slums and villages, on street corners and in ordinary little temples. I had been lucky enough to be able to take it to theatres and auditoriums far away from Bengal. But I always remember Raju's words. That was my ultimate reward.

In 2018, after I performed in Delhi, the newspapers called me Golden Girl.

Chapal Rani's age in jatra was long over. But Sitala opened up a new chapter for me.

INTERLUDE

In Imagination
The Sitala Performer

I have only had two goddesses I worship—Sitala and Chapal Rani.

I wanted to become the next Chapal Rani. But long before that, I knew deep down that I was not a boy like the other boys in my neighbourhood. When I saw the hair on their wrists, a tremor would run through me. When my own moustache started to sprout, I wanted to weep. I would look at my friend and wonder what it would feel like to kiss him, to feel his moustache bristle against my lips. I refused to get my hair cut and grew it so long that my mother threatened to chop it off with her scissors while I slept.

My friends were obsessed with Raveena Tandon singing 'Tip tip barsa pani' in a red chiffon sari in the rain. The boys wanted to have sex with her. I wanted to be her. I wanted to drive those boys wild with desire. I also wanted to be Madhuri Dixit in *Devdas* and line my eyes with tragedy. But I didn't have the words you have now to name that desire. Instead, I tied a towel around my head and ran around the house in my banian and shorts, singing those songs of love and longing, disguising my desire as caricature.

For a while everyone found it funny, but when my father discovered me wearing my mother's sari, he beat me to a pulp. He said: no son of mine will be a hijra. He got my brothers to hold me down and they took my mother's scissors to my hair. They hacked it away in clumps, leaving my head looking like a battlefield. See how he steps out of the house now, my father snarled. Later, my mother paid our local barber to come and shave my head. But I still wanted to wear her sari. They could not beat that out of me. In fact, it just made my desire stronger.

I wish I had been born in a different age, an age when boys like me could act on stage like Chapal Rani. I didn't want to be a hijra and beg at traffic signals. I wanted to be a queen. I wanted to wear blouses with sequins, and crowns. I wanted love scenes where my breasts would press against the chest of my hero and he would look into my eyes.

And I refused to be ashamed of my desire. I didn't want to hide the way my hips swayed. The same boys that called me names when I passed by would come to me secretly when no one was looking. 'Give me a kiss,' they would plead if they caught me alone at dusk in some corner of the park near our house. Sometimes I would, even though I knew they were no good. But they wanted me. At that moment, they were like putty in my hands. I could mould them into any shape I wanted. It made me feel like a goddess with divine powers.

Years later, one day, when I was visiting my grandmother's house in North Kolkata I saw an old man sitting outside their door, a frail man in grimy white kurta-pyjamas that had seen better days. But something about his gaze, his gestures gave me pause. My grandmother said, 'That's Kiron Gayen. He used to be a jatra actor once, but now lives off the charity of his neighbours. That's how you will end up if you don't forget this jatra nonsense.' I was working in a beauty parlour in those days, but I still dreamt of being a jatra star. When I talked to him, he seemed startled.I noticed his voice was high, lilting like a woman's.

This was no ordinary jatra actor. He had played women on stage. I was Kiron Bala once, he told me, but no one has called me by that name in years. That day, to my mother's horror, I brought him home . We didn't have much ourselves. How could I think of bringing home another mouth to feed?

What could I do? I couldn't just leave a rani on the streets like that. He was so grateful. He said he would scrub our dishes, chop our vegetables, mop our kitchen, none of which he had the real strength to do any more. 'Just tell my stories instead of your jatra days,' I told him. 'That will be more than enough.'

Kiron Gayen was losing his mind. Some days he did not know who I was. He would call me by the name of his long dead brother. He would eat and forget he had eaten and come to the kitchen and ask for his lunch. He would even forget to put on his pyjamas sometimes, and wander about in just his torn kurta, scandalizing my mother. But when he talked about the old times, his jatra days, he remembered every name, every detail, every costume.

He was the one who introduced me to Chapal Rani. And through Chapal Rani I discovered the world of the ranis of jatra. Unlike Chapal Rani, Kiron Bala had never been a big star. I would listen to Chapal's stories, my eyes wide like saucers. 'Tell me the lines again,' I would beg him. I would stand in front of the mirror and pose like Goddess Jagaddhatri. I wanted to be a goddess. I wanted to have men passing secret notes into my dressing room. I wanted to see my name on big posters.

'Show me how to do my eyes,' I would beg Chapal Rani. One year, for my birthday, he gave me one of his old wigs. 'I want to be the next Chapal Rani,' I told him. 'Be my guru.' He laughed and said, 'You think you can just wear my wig and become me?'

But we did share a stage once. It was just a local club production. We played two mythological characters. He was the older one. I was the younger. It was a dream come true for me, but I couldn't help feel that Chapal-da was not ready to pass on the baton. He still craved the limelight. When I was dressed as the young princess, and the local boys flocked around me like buzzing honeybees, he said, 'Well, you should have seen how the men went mad when I played Riziya. Those sniffing around you now, they are just riff-raff.' I think he was upset they didn't know who he was. They treated him with respect, not desire. They thought he was beyond desire, but desire has no age limit.

But offstage Chapal-da was so generous. He was the one who told me about the Sitala palas. 'That's one thing men like us still have,' he said. 'We still have Ma Sitala's blessings. And let me tell you, when it comes to Sitala, you must not take any short cuts.

Of course it is a business, but that does not mean the devotion isn't real. When I have a show, I don't smoke, drink or have sex. I don't even eat meat. We do not want to mess around with the goddess of disease and smallpox.

Sitala was born out of the cold ashes of the sacrificial fire. We worship her with cold food, dishes made on the day before her festival and offered to her without being heated. She rides an ass and carries a broom in her hand to sweep away all the germs. At one time, I would say: why did we get the goddess on an ass? Why couldn't I get the one on a lion?

But now I am glad I have Sitala, she is the goddess who has survived famine and pestilence. She fills us with dread and awe because she can take life and give life as well. She is an old devi struggling to get recognition and respect from the gods in heaven and the people on earth. That struggle for acceptance is something I understand only too well.

Here you see me in my backless blouse, my deep-red lipstick and sexy ways and you think of me as a creature of loose morals. But if you see me on the street as Sitala, you will forget this sexy person. There I am in my sari with its red border. People come and pin 10 rupees and 20 rupees on me. They buy garlands that carry their deepest desires for a good wife, a cure from some malady, a job, and put them around my neck. I sing my blessings to them. For that moment, just as Chapal Rani had told me, I truly feel I am some other person. Not a goddess perhaps but touched by one.

And for that time, brief as it is, I am comfortable in my skin. Nobody laughs and jeers at me for being a woman in a man's body. I become respectable. You would not be embarrassed to be seen with me on the open street. When it's over and the garlands are put away, I am back to being the girl-man I've always been. But I refuse to apologize for it any more. If you are embarrassed to meet me in public, that's your problem. Sitala has taught me that. Accept me as I am, with my donkey, my broom and my whisk. Once you become Sitala, on the open street, with buses and taxis honking around you, you learn to stop worrying about what people will think. And you understand that you too are worth something in this shitty world.

That's why when the man I loved said his family wanted him to get married, I told him he had to choose. I might have the parts of a man when the lights go out and I take off my clothes, but in my heart I was already a wife and he was my husband. He could not set up home and family with someone and then come to me when he was drunk and needed some fun. Chapal Rani might have made peace with sharing his man with a woman, but times have changed. I won't play second fiddle to anyone, man or woman. In the end, my man chose to get married. It hurt. For a week, I lay in bed and drank non-stop. It still hurts. But I am happy I did what I did. Whether I am first gender or third gender, I refuse to be second best.

Chapal Rani lived on his own terms in a way that poor Kiron Bala never dared to. Chapal Rani showed us, he still shows us, that it's possible to be yourself in a world that says you cannot. Kiron Bala didn't have that much courage. Times were different then. What he could be on stage was not possible off stage. I won't say it's easy for me, but I don't fear the world the way he did. Kiron Bala would curl into his shell like a snail, afraid the world would crush him. The world might still crush me but not before I tell it to fuck off.

'Dress up as Kiron Bala,' I told him once. He was so shy, laughing like a little girl. 'No, no' he kept protesting. 'Those days are over. Who wants to see this old crone in those saris and blouses?'

'I do,' I said. 'I do.'

I rode roughshod over his protests and dressed him to my heart's content. I drew his lips and eyes the way Chapal Rani had taught me. And then placed Chapal's wig on Kiron Bala's head. 'Stop, stop,' he said. 'Someone will come, someone will see.' But when I took a picture of him with my mobile phone, he said, 'Show me.' As I watched him look at my phone, I saw his eyes grow soft. The wig hid his bald head with its straggly hair, the blouse was slipping off his scrawny shoulders, the necklace with its fake rubies and emeralds hung heavy around his wizened neck. But it didn't matter. 'Show me the picture once more,' he pleaded all day like a small child with a new toy.

But he didn't have the courage to step outside our house as Kiron Bala. When Kiron Gayen died, I dressed him like the Kiron Bala he had once been. I painted his eyebrows and drew his lips. I dabbed rouge and compact powder on his cheeks. I bought him a sari and draped him in it. I wish I could have done more for him. Perhaps if I could have afforded better medical care, he would have lived longer. But at least I gave him a send-off as a queen.

Later that day, I bought a small bottle of whisky and went to visit Chapal-da. I needed to be with my own people. Chapal-da was surprised to see me, my face made up like a woman, dressed in a sari with rainbow stripes. I talked to him about the men who had loved me and wondered if I would ever find the kind of love I wanted. He told me about his great love story but refused to tell me the man's name. I tried to coax him into revealing it but he protected that name like a yaksha demon guarding his treasure. Perhaps if he had a couple of drinks they would have loosened his tongue. But he didn't touch the drink I had brought with me.

As I left, I noticed the woman who worked in that old-age home looking at me disapprovingly. 'How do you know Chapal-da?' she asked tersely. 'What do you do exactly?' 'I act,' I replied. 'I am his protégé.' 'You don't look like the kind of person who would be his protégé,' she said, raising her eyebrows. I did not know what she meant. I just shrugged and walked away.

I might have had a little too much to drink that night. Perhaps I had been a little loud. Perhaps I should not have gone to him in the sari. But the next time I met Chapal-da, he seemed a little distant. 'Why do you talk like that all the time?' he told me sharply. 'Why do you exaggerate your mannerisms so? You are not on stage. Why do you laugh so loudly, so shrilly? There is no need to act like a woman all the time. Don't call everyone girlfriend or sister.'

I understood that woman who worked there must have told him something. Perhaps I embarrassed him, but my womanliness was not something I could just switch on and off. I was too trashy, too loud, too queeny for that old-age home.

But there is nothing I can do about that. That's who I am now. Take it or leave it. I might have made Chapal Rani feel uncomfortable in that middle-class old-age home yet I will always maintain it was Chapal Rani who made me possible. He was the one who marched to the sound of his own drum when few dared to do so. By being himself, he helped fashion the world in which I could be me.

People like us rise from the ashes. We burn the person we are born as and emerge as someone else.

How can I go back?

11

Rebirth and Resurrection

Off to Canada

One day in 2001, as soon as I came home, even before I'd taken off my shoes and washed my face, Chhordi shouted: 'Listen Tuku, call Seagull at once. Naveen had called for you.'

When I called Seagull, Naveen told me that I had been invited to Canada as part of a festival called *A Dialogue with India*, along with many artists, writers and filmmakers, like Nalini Malani, Vivan Sundaram, Anand Patwardhan and Atul Dodiya. My Ekmukhi Sitala performance would be the opening act of the festival, to be performed at the Roundhouse Community Centre in Vancouver. They would also screen the documentary about me. Chhordi was over the moon. She had always wanted to go abroad, but it had never happened. By the time she finally got the opportunity, she was too ill to go.

My mother had been to America as part of Sisir Bhaduri's theatre troupe around 1930. It was not exactly a resounding success. In America, they expected their actresses to be like Claudette Colbert and Greta Garbo—beautiful, fair with slim figures. But my mother was quite dark and, since she did not take proper care of her health, rather stout. The theatre company struggled to connect with the American audience. The businessman who had organized the tour reneged on the money he had promised them. One day, they realized they were stranded, without even the money for the return fare. Ma was also pregnant. The shipping company refused to let her on board, saying if there was a miscarriage or some accident on the ship, they could not take responsibility for it. Finally, Shotu Sen, whose son Tapas Sen became one of our great lighting designers, helped them return. They had to sign some bonds to get on that ship . . . They were in dire straits, they had lost a lot of money and were utterly devastated by the entire experience. Soon after Ma returned, my sister was born, Sagarika, named after that ocean voyage. But she was not in this world for long, alas.

I was excited when I heard I might travel to Canada but also scared. I had not even finished school. My English was almost non-existent, and dried up in an instant especially when it came to conversation. And now I was being asked to go to Canada where they all talked in English all the time! I could not imagine how on earth Chapal from Dalimtala Lane would even survive a day there, let alone a 10-day trip.

When I went to New Delhi to get my Canadian visa, the officials had so many questions. Why was I going? What did I do? What was I planning to do in Canada? It made me weak at the knees before I had even set foot in Canada. Sunandini Banerjee, an editor at Seagull Books, was going to travel with me. 'What on earth am I going to do there?' I told her. 'What am I going to say to anyone?'

'You don't have to do anything,' she said, 'As soon as anyone says hi, you promptly say hello. I will handle the rest. Don't worry.'

She was indeed my crutch.

Everything was new to me. It was my first time on an airplane. As we sat down in our seats, Sunandini said, 'Take off your wristwatch. The time will keep changing as we fly. You won't be able to match the time, and it will drive you crazy. Once we land in Vancouver, then we will set our watches.'

I kept peering out of the window to see what we were flying over. As we flew over snowcapped mountains, I felt both thrilled and afraid. Before the trip I had feared I would feel sick and nauseous while flying but it was an extraordinary adventure unlike any other. I kept staring out of the window trying to figure out the lands passing below us, trying to remember the maps I had seen from the atlases of my geography class in school.

We landed in Vancouver at the dead of night. And I promptly had my first mishap. I tried to put my shoes back on and realized my feet had swollen on the flight. There was no way I could fit my feet into my shoes any more. 'There is nothing to do. Just carry your shoes in your hands,' Sunandini told me. 'When the swelling goes down, you can wear them again.' Thus my first steps in the first foreign country I had ever been to, besides Bangladesh next door, were in my socks.

There was more in store for us. Sunandini's suitcase had not arrived. What a pair we were, one in socks, the other without her luggage. She refused to sleep in one of my brocade-bordered silk saris though truly I would not have minded. I even offered to lend the poor thing one of my petticoats at least. Finally, being a female impersonator was to be of some use. I had quite a few things to lend her in that crisis.

A tall man named Peter White, one of the festival organizers and curators, received us at the airport and bundled us into a taxi cab. It was very different from the taxi cabs I was used to India. The seats smelled different, foreign in a way. But the driver, to my surprise, was a Sikh man.

We drove to a very tall apartment building in Vancouver. As soon as we unlocked the doors to the flat, the lights came on, automatically! There was a huge living room and two large bedrooms. The beds were as soft as the beds in a five-star hotel. I was afraid I would feel claustrophobic in the room with all its windows shut but I ended up feeling like a child, exploring every closet, every corner. Inside the closet, I saw a row of coat hangers. Naveen had got me a coat before the trip. Now I had a place to hang it.

There was a microwave in the kitchen. 'Put the container in. Close it. Press the button,' Sunandini told me. 'Listen to the buzzing noise. Wait till it stops buzzing and then open the door and take out the food.'

When I walked out onto the balcony, I felt like a chunk of ice had fallen on my head. It was a kind of cold I had never experienced before. I stood there pinching myself. This was happening to me. I was staying in an apartment in Canada. I wondered what my sister was doing right now, so many thousands of miles away in Kolkata. I felt like a pioneer, the first one from my family walking into such uncharted territory.

Canadian Queen

Vancouver was beautiful. The city was hilly and the roads went up and down. There was a huge park in the middle with enormous old trees, so many trees it felt more like a forest than a park. The city was on the Pacific Ocean. I had only seen that on maps.

I was awestruck. I had never been to a place like that with hills and sea and forest altogether, a city where snowy white seagulls with yellow beaks floated in the sky instead of crows, their strange mournful cries echoing through the air. The city was very green, the air was clean and the sunshine was bright, even though it would get bitingly cold. It was a different kind of cold than I was used to. The monsoon rain of Kolkata is warm, but here the rain was cold and stinging, like a barrage of icy needles. The organizers had given me a raincoat and an umbrella, so I could walk about and see the city a little, though my bad knees got in the way. Still, I walked where I could, despite those steep streets. Taxi cabs were expensive and my few dollars were precious.

The first few days we were busy—workshops during the day, rehearsals in the evening. A production in India is one thing, the same production abroad was another creature altogether. I hadn't brought the usual weapons I carried as the goddess. Someone told me: you'd better not carry such things on the plane. Instead, I drew them on paper and they made me beautiful replicas out of wood.

The music was another challenge. At that time, there was no Internet, I could not show the musicians any samples on YouTube. I had carried a CD with all my music instead. Some of the volunteer musicians knew Indian classical music, but jatra music wasn't about sitars and tablas. How would they know the fanfare that accompanies the arrival of the goddess?

The musicians looked at my hand movements and eyebrow wiggles to figure out what music was needed where. Was it a moment of anger or divine retribution? When the homely folk goddess becomes installed in the Hindu pantheon, does that call for a triumphant musical flourish? I had to guide them every step of the way: 'No, not like that. You are not hitting the right notes on the clarionet. Make it more pyan-pyan.' Sunandini wrote and rewrote the cues for them. She explained, listened, conferred, corrected and then explained again late into the night. There were many cups of coffee needed on those rehearsal nights, many coffees indeed.

Then there were the workshops. I had no idea what that really meant, because I had never conducted a workshop before. I knew what 'work' meant and I knew what 'shop' meant. But what was this 'workshop' I needed to do with these women? I was an actor. A director would tell me to do this or that, and I would do it the best I could. I fretted about what I could show these people. I was nervous. Would people find me interesting? What could I tell them that they would find useful? Would anyone be interested enough to return the next day? What if they felt it was all a giant waste of time? But I knew I would be paid for each and every workshop and that was incentive enough. In Kolkata, you got paid nothing or very little for such things, sometimes just car fare and food. Luckily Amir Ali, the program director at the Roundhouse Community Centre, a tall man with a warm personality, could speak some broken Hindi. He explained what I needed to do. Sunandini, as usual, was reassuring. 'Don't worry. This is very simple. These women want to see how you act, how you sing and dance. And they will try to emulate you and learn from you.'

Six women showed up on the first afternoon. Some worked in theatre, some were dancers, some wrote plays. Some of them were out of work because the theatres had folded, a pain I understood all too keenly. They were very attentive, they listened to the music carefully, watched my poses with rapt attention and then imitated me. Since many of them came from a theatre background, they could pick it up easily despite the language barrier.

We had to make it up as we went along. One day, we showed the documentary. Another day, I showed them how to do make-up, especially how to draw the eyes of the goddess. I demonstrated the dance steps and they copied me. And they kept asking questions. What is jatra? What is puja? Who taught me to act? What was my childhood like? Who is Sitala exactly? What's her position in the family tree of gods and goddesses? How did I become a goddess?

The women asked why I did not wear female clothes offstage as well. I told Sunandini, 'Tell them that I convey my femininity through my acting. I know there is a strong feminine feeling within me and that I can feel a strong attraction to a man. I can certainly appreciate a woman's beauty, but it's a different feeling when I look at a man. But I get what I need through acting. I don't need anything further. I know there are people in India who like to live 24x7 as women. But I am not like them. I am fine the way I am. If you come to me and say: Chapal-da you need to become a woman, then you have to give me an hour to get ready. Then I will become mother, daughter, sister, but all through my acting, my make-up, my costumes. But when I get off the stage, I will be Chapal-da again.'

In Canada, I also met men who dressed as women even though they did not play female roles. One of them was very tall, dressed in women's clothes but so masculine in appearance, I could not find an ounce of femininity within him. He too was very curious about me. He told me, 'You look so beautiful in women's clothes. Why do you not wear women's clothes all the time? Why do you not live as a woman?'

I said, 'This is my job. I do this because of the way I look, the way I sound. Why should I dress as a woman day and night, wearing saris and bangles and wigs? What pleasure will I get from that? What benefit? I have never done that and never will.' But I also wanted to make it clear that my drag was not about caricature. 'I play a woman on stage,' I told them. 'But I don't do it for laughs. I cannot make myself the butt of jokes.'

People would tell me I could get surgery done. I would retort, 'I know. But I don't need it to play a woman on stage. I know how to become a woman through my acting, my make-up and my persona.'

I am Chapal Bhaduri. Female impersonator. No apologies.

The show thankfully was a success. At the end of the performance, I did something I had never done onstage in India. I sat on the stage and slowly transformed myself back from goddess to woman to man. I removed the jewellery, piece by piece, slowly wiped off the make-up, took off my Benarasi sari. Behind me, a slideshow showed the reverse transformation through Naveen's photographs—from man to goddess. At the end of the slide show, I had become Goddess Sitala on the screen, but on stage, in front of the audience, stood a bare-bodied ageing man in his pyjamas, his hands folded in a namaste. The air felt electric.

So many people came to see me that night. Bengalis who were settled there had heard about the performance and showed up. They were all curious about this man from Kolkata who became a woman on stage. There were gay people who had read about the show in the papers and had all kind of questions about sexuality and India. There were performing artists interested in a fellow artist from across the world and academics from different colleges and universities. I had to pinch myself. These people were so cultured, so educated, and then there was me, I who had been born in a dingy alley in North Kolkata and never even finished school. I could still hear those voices in my head: '*Jatra kore fatra lokey*'—those who do jatra are rubbish people. And here in Canada, these people were all shaking my hand and saying things like, 'Amazing. Incomparable. Bravo.'

People kept coming up to me to offer their congratulations and Sunandini had to translate everything for me while I just smiled and nodded. It was an experience like no other.

One day at the workshop, Sunandini said, 'The women are saying that they want to dress like you and act out some of your roles, like Sitala.' They wanted me to paint the third eye on their foreheads and teach them how to wear a sari though of course we did not have anything like the Benarasi saris I was carrying with me. They had also brought whatever jewellery they could find. Naturally, they didn't have golden ornaments like I did. But we managed. I drew the third eye and explained its significance and they all carefully copied me.

We had no language in common but sometimes when we speak to each other through our hearts, we understand each other. We all became friends, even though I could not really talk to them directly.

I had a photograph of myself surrounded by all these women. I think there were seven of us that day. I am in full goddess costume, wig and all, wearing a deep orange-red and gold Benarasi sari and shiny golden blouse, a crown on my head, holding a pot in my hand. The women are all dressed the best they could manage with whatever they could find, Rajasthani-print skirts, salwar kameezes, or a sari wrapped around their sweaters, held together by pins. But all seven of us in our own ways were performing the goddess. That day we were all Sitala.

The Solo Traveller

One day the phone rang while Sunandini was out. Someone started talking to me in a burst of English. I, of course, understood nothing. They found someone who could speak some broken Hindi and managed to explain that some women had come to meet me in the lobby.

My heart sank. I had never gone anywhere without Sunandini. I stepped out nervously from our apartment. It was completely hushed and silent, an endless carpeted corridor. I managed to get to the lift. At least I knew that I had to press G to go to the ground floor. Suddenly, the lift stopped and a large black lady got on. She told me something. I just nodded and smiled, praying that we would get to the ground floor before she said anything more.

A group of Canadian women were waiting for me downstairs. Again I smiled and nodded without understanding anything they were saying. Luckily, at that moment Sunandini walked in. Seeing her, some life returned to my body.

'Why are you feeling so nervous?' she asked me.

'I cannot talk to them in English. Nor can I understand what they are saying.'

'Don't worry. They all know you cannot speak English. Just use your hands. Aren't you an actor?'

The women took me out to explore the city. It was crisp and cold but the sunlight was brilliant. We walked around the streets. There were benches on the pavement where you could sit and have a cup of coffee. The coffee was very strong and came with hard biscuits which I didn't really care for but I had them anyway. There were fountains that danced and people threw coins and made wishes. It all felt magical.

The women gave me so many little gifts. Someone gave me a necklace, another gave me a lovely pink wrist band. They were not expensive gifts perhaps, but gifts are about love and affection, not money. One girl kept admiring my red veil. I gave it to her. I gave away other things too—a necklace, some clip-on earrings. It was about saving a memory of each other, of the little time we had spent together. Peter gave me a camera.

One of the women, Anna, recorded her own songs and presented me with a cassette before I left. She told Sunandini, 'Don't let Chapal buy any cosmetics. We want to present him with some.' She kept her word, but the cosmetics there confused me, because the shades all came with numbers that were different from the ones I was used to. I gave away some of the lipsticks they gave me as gifts when I returned to India.

Amir Ali, the program director, invited Sunandini and me over for dinner one evening at his lovely little house built on a small hill. I met his wife and sons, drank red wine and ate turkey for the first time. I had never seen such a big bird served up on a dinner table. There was so much left over, we brought it home and ate that for the next two days. I also got used to not eating rice with every meal. There were so many kinds of meats, fruits and chocolates, I certainly didn't go hungry though I was not quite as adventurous as Sunandini who would always say, 'Eat this. Try that.' One of the women invited us out to dinner at a restaurant. It had raw fish and I could not manage to eat that. They had to get some fried rice for me.

Some nights, I craved the Maggi instant noodles I was used to in Kolkata. But where could I find them in Canada? Off went Sunandini to the grocery store three blocks away and returned with a bag full of noodles in cups she'd managed to locate at an Asian supermarket. All you needed to do was add hot water and voila, you had a cup of soupy noodles just like the Maggi noodles from home. It was a wonderful experience, like a dream almost. I can never forget my time in Canada.

One day, Sunandini said, 'Chapal-da, from tomorrow you will be on your own. I am leaving for San Francisco. I have made all the arrangements for the rest of your time here, just a day and a half, but you will have to go back to India on your own.'

That had always been the plan, but my hands and feet still went cold. In India I could travel everywhere on my own. But this was not Bhagalpur. Without English, how could I ask someone when my plane was leaving, where I needed to go, what I needed to do, whether I was on the right plane even?

Amir Ali's father came to drop me to the airport. His Hindi, even though it was Punjabi Hindi, helped calm me a bit. But when I got to the airport, my heart was thudding again. The airport was so vast, I felt like I was falling into outer space. Luckily, there was another Punjabi family going to London—our flights to and fro had been via London—as well and I just attached myself to them.

As the plane kept flying, I just kept remembering the mantra Sunandini had given me. 'Don't worry about anything. Just close your eyes and go. Only remember to read the gate number, like I showed you on the way in. Everything will be fine.'

In London, I somehow managed to locate the gate for the Kolkata flight. There was a young man sitting next to me on the plane. He had the window seat and I had the middle one.

I said, 'Are you Indian?'

'Yes, I had come to visit London. I live in Kolkata.'

A Bengali! Relief washed over me. At least, he could help me fill those immigration forms. When I finally got out of the airport in India, all I could think was nobody in my family had ever been as far as I had flown.

Back to the Stage

As new audiences started discovering me, it felt like a rebirth. Now I was doing shows in places jatra had never taken me—Prithvi Theatre in Mumbai, Habitat Centre in New Delhi. When Sujoy Prasad Chatterjee organized a three-day monologue festival in Kolkata in 2012, I performed alongside legends like Saoli Mitra and Pranati Tagore. Both Janardan Rani and I, two of the last remaining ranis, were felicitated at that same festival.

It was hard work and physically taxing. I would sit down to do my make-up at noon and give back-to-back interviews at the same time. Then, finally, at 4, I would be ready to do a double show, each show lasting an hour and a half.

Once, in Mumbai, right before the second show was ready to start at 6, the manager told me, 'Will you give me a little more time?'

'But why?'

'A lot more people have heard about the show, they want to come.'

I was overwhelmed. I don't think in Mumbai they knew much about Goddess Sitala. They probably thought I was the goddess Santoshi Mata but it didn't matter. They were coming to see me.

All this caused some heartburn among people I had worked with in my jatra days and as Sitala. I would hear catty comments. 'Goodness, Chapal, when the tide is in your favour, even your piss can light lamps.' I ignored them. Chapal Rani's name was back in currency. That's all I cared about.

I started my career in theatre with Ma before my life took a turn towards jatra. Oddly, it was my own niece, my mother's granddaughter, who brought me back to the world of theatre. At that time, I was done with jatra, or more accurately jatra was done with me.

My niece, who was part of an amateur theatre club, was acting in a production of the play *Meghe Dhaka Tara* at the Boys Own Library Hall in North Kolkata. Suddenly, the woman playing the mother, fell ill. As they desperately looked for a replacement, one of the actors told my niece, 'Your Tuku-mama can do that part.'

I said, 'Are you all crazy? Your show is at 6.30. It is already 10.30 in the morning.'

'If anyone can, you can. Please do this for us, Tuku-mama.'

Somehow, I pulled it off. At least no one threw clay cups at me that day. Rather, people asked 'Is this that Chapal Rani?'

I didn't take any payment. 'Just invite me home and feed me something good one day.' But it felt good to be back on stage. And word got around.

Sometime, in 1999, a man named Bharganath Bhattacharya came to meet me: 'Chapal-da, I run a theatre group called TheaLovers. You need to act again. We are doing a play, and I want you to be in it.'

'A play?' I was hesitant. 'Do you think I can manage a play?'

'Actors can manage everything,' he said confidently.

The play was *Khola Janala Bondho Chokh* [Open Window, Closed Eyes]. The story was about a beautiful theatre actress named Malini Roy Chowdhury being felicitated for a career spanning 30 years. But nobody knows she is actually a man. For 30 years, she had been pulling the wool over everyone's eyes.

As another actor sits down to interview Malini, she tries to confuse him by giving misleading details, throwing out dates that do not add up.

INTERVIEWER. If your acting life was 18 years, then does that mean you were acting from when you were very young?

MALINI. Oh yes of course, at that time I didn't know anything. I was just a child.

INTERVIEWER. But you said in that year you . . .

MALINI. Oh, you must be mistaken. That year I did not act at all. I think I had a lot of health problems that year.

INTERVIEWER. Didn't you have a relationship with Monotosh?

MALINI. Oh, don't ask about all that any more. That man is gone now. Why drag him into all this?

INTERVIEWER. No, no, we are not trying to drag anyone into anything. I was just thinking that there was never a proper explanation for his strange death. It was an unnatural death, was it not?

MALINI. I don't know about natural or unnatural. All I know is Monotosh was very fond of me. Though he made a proposal one day that was impossible for me to keep.

INTERVIEWER. What did he propose?

MALINI. Oh, please don't ask me that. We can't go into those murky waters now.

INTERVIEWER. But what could it have been? Was it something scandalous?

MALINI. He wanted to establish a physical relationship. He wanted me to be the mother of his child. I didn't like all that. Later, he hanged himself.

INTERVIEWER. But that was not how he died. He was indeed found hanging but the autopsy showed he had been killed before he was hanged.

MALINI. Is that so? I wouldn't know anything about that. Anyway, listen, let's talk about you. You are an actor too. I remember that jatra where you and I acted together. You played the prince. It was marvellous. Why don't you say those lines? I am sure the audience will want to hear a bit of that.

INTERVIEWER. That was a long time ago. I don't remember those lines any more.

MALINI. Of course, you do. As soon as you start, it will all come back. The audience will love it. Please all of you, encourage him to do this. I need to just step outside for a couple of minutes. I will be back in two minutes.

Malini exits the stage, changes out of the demure sari and then re-enters in a very revealing seductive outfit with a red veil wrapped around her.

In that jatra, Malini plays the queen of Magadh. She is the king's fourth wife, a very attractive woman who has sexual designs on the king's son by the first wife.

PRINCE. Please do not do this. O Queen, I have called you mother.

QUEEN. Mother, what mother? How long will it take to forget that word? Forget it. Forget this world, forget the skies, the stars. Remember only the throb of our hearts, rising and falling, rising and falling. (*Prince tries to get out of her embrace.*) What if I open my hair like this? What if I rend my clothes? And leave my nail marks all over my body and tell the king you came here to this isolated place to satisfy your lust? Then how will you respond?

PRINCE. You cannot do this. You cannot do this.

Finally, Malini decides she will not accept the award to honour her for 30 years of acting. That leads to much speculation and many questions. In the climactic scene, Malini starts to undress on stage. She removes her hair, rips off her blouse and sari, wipes off her lipstick, all the while laughing maniacally. Finally, she rips off her petticoat and tosses it away. By the end, I would be in just a bodice and leggings, my whole body painted to give the illusion of nudity. Thankfully, I still had the physique to pull that off.

> MALINI. Now do you recognize me? I am no longer Malini Roy Chowdhury. I am Sudhakar Mukherjee.

But this time the voice was completely a man's. That was always challenging for me because my natural voice is feminine.

We only had 18 days to rehearse, but the play ran for 40 nights straight. The audience was not aware at the beginning that Malini was a man. They assumed that it was Chapal Rani playing a woman on stage just as I had done for years. That was the great difference between my roles in jatra and in plays like *Khola Janala Bondho Chokh*, *Ramanimohan* and *Sundarbibir Pala*. In jatra I played women. Now I was playing a man who played women.

Chapal Raja

At one time, I would always complain that I didn't get enough publicity. Surya-babu told me, 'You will be so famous one day, people will come and touch your feet to ask for your blessings. This is my blessing.'

That happened, but long after I had left jatra. In 2006, a man named Prakash Bhattacharya came to meet me. He had a well-known theatre group called Nandipat. He wanted my guidance for a play they were putting on.

It was about a man named Ramanimohan, now 62, the father of five grown children with families of their own. At one time, this man had acted in female parts in theatre. Now he eked out a living running a small grocery store in the neighbourhood, but the acting bug had not quite left him.

Prakash said, 'The person who is doing it can't get the feminine bits quite right. If you could show him how to act a little girlish, that would be very helpful.'

I said, 'Look, there is nothing called girlish acting or boyish acting. Acting is just acting, whether it's male parts or female parts. When a man is doing a female part, he cannot overact or do exaggerated gestures. No, he must act naturally. I was taught by Surya Kumar Dutta of Natta Company. He would say, "Why are you acting so affected? It does not matter whether you are a man or a woman. Just speak normally and clearly." I never forgot that advice.'

Then I told Prakash, 'I have an idea. Instead of showing you how to do that part, what if I acted in that role? Would that be all right with you?'

'Oh, that would be wonderful,' he said, quite overwhelmed. 'But we cannot pay you what you are used to.'

'You pay what you can,' I replied. 'I would love to sink my teeth into a character this tempting.'

It was indeed a great role. At the beginning, all that the audience knows is the man whose name is Mohan used to work in jatra but for some reason lost that job. He had never paid much attention to his studies and his father had thrown him out of the house. He did not know where to go or what to do, but he could sing very well. He ended up with a jatra troupe in the village. That's where he started to act in female parts, and it suited him so well that his name became Ramanimohan or Young Woman Mohan. At one time, men and women would both fall head over heels in love with him. But those days were long gone. Now he was an elderly man running a small grocery store, selling dal and rice and soap.

One day, he learns his neighbourhood is putting on a variety show. He tells the organizers, 'Look, you have all kinds of acts in the show. I too acted at one time. Would you give me a chance to show you what I can do?' They say, 'Why not? After all, we have all these warm-up acts that are just crass comedy. Maybe you could bring a different flavour to things.'

The play opens with Ramanimohan dressed as Mughal empress Noor Jahan reciting a long dialogue from that play. As Noor Jehan exits the stage to applause, someone announces, 'That was Empress Noor Jehan. In reality, he is someone from our own neighbourhood. His name is Ramanimohan Dutta.'

In the two minutes it took to make that announcement, I had to change from the Mughal Noor Jehan to Behula, the devoted wife from Hindu mythology. Underneath my Noor Jehan costume which came with handy zippers, I already had on a white sari with a red border and bangles. Underneath that Behula sari, I wore the pyjamas I needed to transform myself into the man named Mohan Dutta.

As soon as that scene ended, four dressers would quickly help me change my costume in the wings and then I came back on stage with: 'Namaskar, I am Mohan Dutta. But my full name was once Ramanimohan Dutta. How that first bit got deleted is a sad story. I will not bore you with it today. Some other day perhaps, if the opportunity arises. You have just seen Noor Jehan. Now please listen to a song from a character from our myths, the famous Behula. This is the song she sang as she carried the body of her husband Lakkhinder on a raft down the river to beg the gods for his life after the Kalnagini serpent bit him.'

In the next scene, Ramanimohan is returning home after the performance, laden with gifts . . . a bouquet of flowers and a tote bag with a cake in it. At that time, I had not had my cataract operation and so I could see next to nothing in the dark. The assistant told me, 'Don't worry. Go exactly 10 paces and then stand still.'

I would walk 10 paces, go through a door and wait. When the stage light lit up, my face the audience would see we were now in his house where his wife was sitting and sewing.

RAMANIMOHAN. Suprabha, O Suprabha

SUPRABHA. What? Oh my goodness. What are you doing? Are you getting older or younger? Walking around in a sari! Couldn't you just change wherever you dressed like this?

RAMANIMOHAN. No, no. Hold these things please. It's been quite a day. Let me tell you what happened.

While he talks, Ramanimohan starts taking off his female clothes and removing his make-up. There was no timing gap at all between Ramanimohan's different avatars.

The wife knows about his old career. While she does not approve of it, she has made her peace with it. But the youngest son humiliates his father whenever he gets a chance, calls him a hijra. The father retorts, 'Well, then explain to me how did I manage to produce not one, not two but five children? What kind of hijra does that make me?'

That line always got a lot of applause.

SON. Are you not ashamed of yourself, Father? Dressing as a woman and performing like some two-bit slattern! You just humiliated me in our own neighbourhood. How will I show my face here ever again? And if you were such a good actor, why were you shown the door? Why were you thrown out onto the street?

MOTHER. Stop it, son. Just stop. Why are you saying all these things?

RAMANIMOHAN. Wait, Suprabha. Since he has brought this up, let him listen to what I have to say.

Then he recounts the story of what happened. Ramanimohan did not just lose his job. He was kicked out of the company because the owner wanted to bring in women. To do that, they resorted to underhand means. Someone doctored his food, to make him lose his voice right as he was going on stage as Sita. Obviously, that performance was a dud.

As Sita tells Urmila, 'Sister, if my husband spurns me, I will still cling to his feet. I will go to my Ram, because my Ram will forgive me,' Ramanimohan starts to choke. When he clutches his throat in distress and cries, 'What is happening? Why can I not speak? Aargh,' the audience throws stones at him.

The role certainly had a lot of parallels with my life even though I did not know the playwright Sekhar Samaddar. It was a story that many of us, the former queens of jatra, could relate to. Many ranis had their careers end in ignominy. They would go to work and be told, 'You don't need to come from tomorrow.' They had been replaced by a woman.

It seems Sekhar had seen me in *Khola Janala Bondho Chokh*. When I changed my outfit on stage, it shook him. In a way that inspired *Ramanimohan*, though when he wrote it, he had no idea that one day I would act in it myself. When I met him, I told him I thought people had forgotten me. *Ramanimohan* brought me back to the limelight.

Our first show was in Jaipur, Rajasthan, during Durga Puja. It was such a roaring success that we recouped all our expenses within 10 shows. *Ramanimohan* ran for 70 nights, something that does not happen often in theatre. I do not know how I pulled off that role. I am neither the father nor the mother of a son. But, somehow, I had to play a husband and a father of five sons. What did I know about how a man behaves with his wife or talks to his sons? I guess that is what is called acting. That is what my mother had said all those years ago. Acting is to be what you are not.

I acted my heart out for that role. I stopped dyeing my hair. I acted in the freezing cold wearing only thin cotton pyjamas and kurta. I performed with 102-degree fever. The role required me to change my voice within minutes. One moment I would be gasping and choking as I recounted the Sita scene that spelt Ramanimohan's downfall. The next moment it had to come back to normal. And I had to do it night after night, show after show.

But I have to say, whatever I put in, Nandipat returned to me double. If I could do Ramanimohan again, I would. Even if I died trying to do it, I would have no regrets.

After that play, the director said, 'Chapal Bhaduri has proven that he is not only Chapal Rani—he is Chapal Raja too.'

Curtain Call

Sekhar, the man who had written *Ramanimohan*, worked with me on another production—*Sundarbibir Pala*. In that play, Sekhar himself played Aniket, an intellectual theatre director who wants to bring the old folk traditions of Bengal, like Jhumur and Nachni, into modern theatre. He decides to stage a Vidya–Sundar pala, the kind that was such a rage in the early days of jatra. In the Vidya–Sundar romance, the go-between was always Heera Malini, the legendary flower girl who could charm the pants off anyone. Even the great Bankim Chandra recreated Heera Malini in his novel *Durgeshnandini*. Aniket decides rather than have a woman play Heera Malini, he wants a female impersonator. 'Heera is no ordinary woman,' he says. 'She gives her word, then fools everyone with her charms. Then she herself gets tricked when she believes in Sundar. A dialectical character! I wish we could get one of those old-time actors who used to play women . . .'

That was me. I played Sundar Haldar, once famous as Sundar Bibi, a Domni folk artist from Malda in northern Bengal. In Domni groups, boys called chhokras still play the female roles, telling the stories of the joys and sorrows of ordinary poor people through song and dance.

Sundar Haldar was famous once but now he is an old man, a widower. His son has no contact with him. But in the villages of Malda, where Domni folk theatre was popular, the name of Sundar Bibi still means something. When Aniket approaches him, Sundar Bibi jumps at the chance to play Heera Malini.

The story of Sundar Haldar wasn't inspired by me. Shekhar was moved by the story of Jiten Ghosh, who once danced as a woman in Domni performances but in his old age had been reduced to scrounging a living by selling cheap lottery tickets. But he wrote the role with me in mind because by then we had become friends.

At the end of the play, everything goes haywire. Some people try to woo Sundar Bibi away by offering to make a film about him. Aniket tells him they only want to milk his life story and not his talent. The nachni folk dancer from Purulia who plays

Vidya calls him a hijra, much to his anger. He in turn calls her a whore, one who sells not just her body but her art.

When it all falls apart, Sundar Bibi cries, 'Who is Sundar Haldar? What is he worth? If people remember anyone, it is Sundar Bibi.' In anguish, he cries out 'I will act. I will act with all my heart and soul. Start up the band. Begin the song.'

It was well received but somehow people did not gush 'Sundar Bibi, Sundar Bibi' the way they would go 'Ramanimohan, Ramanimohan'. But I was paid whatever I had been promised. I have no complaints about that.

There is no way I could not love theatre. My mother was from the world of theatre. My uncle Sisir Bhaduri was a legend in theatre. My sister acted on stage. Theatre is in my blood. I love jatra too, but at some point, I fell out of love with it the way it often happens even in the most passionate love stories. Now when I see what jatra has been reduced to, it inspires no love, no respect. There are a few good actors, but jatra has lost its sheen. It's forgotten its history. I might sound like a bitter old man nostalgic for my glory days, but no productions are becoming the stuff of legend the way they did once. All we have are tawdry cheap imitations of potboiler films and television serials.

Sisir Bhaduri had great respect for jatra. He would say: it is not enough to just know your lines. Every day it's different, so every day you have to be on your toes. You have to be aware of the composition. You have to remember that the audience is sitting all around you and can see you from all sides. You act with almost no props, no sets. You have to know where the light is. My great fault was that I constantly failed the light. The light man would complain: 'Where will I give the light? As you play Draupadi, when you sit down suddenly, the light is no longer on your face.' You have to pay attention to the light, you have to pay attention to your position, you have to pay attention to your acting—only then can you do justice to your role.

In the theatre, there's the stage, the wings, footlights, then another two or four feet of space, then finally the seats for the audience. There's no contact with the audience the way there is in jatra. That's why the acting style is different. There is a distance from the audience that is built into it. But in jatra, we're right there with them, we physically mingle with the audience.

There is also a difference in style and pitch. I had to learn how to act on stage after so many years in jatra.

Once, when I was rehearsing my lines for *Khola Janala Bondho Chokh*, my sister overheard me and said, 'Are you back to doing jatra?'

I said, 'No, I was just going over my lines for *Khola Janala Bondho Chokh.*'

She said, 'Why are you reading those lines as if they were in a jatra? Going really high and then very low? Is the director all right with that?'

'I guess so. He occasionally corrects me when I make a little mistake.'

'Little mistake? Hmm. Show me the script.'

She skimmed over it for a few minutes and then looked up. 'My goodness, this is a wonderful character.'

'But it's difficult. Because it is not a woman. It's a man who pretends to be a woman.'

'Shall I say the lines? Your throwing is off. You are doing them like you are in a jatra. Jatra and theatre are not the same.

But how would you know? You have never had the chance to do real theatre.'

'Show me,' I said meekly. She did, I listened carefully and picked it up somewhat.

Next day, at rehearsal, the director was mystified.

'What happened? Yesterday you said your lines one way. Today they sound so different . . . I am sure Ketaki-di has something to do with this.'

'Yes, I was practising this bit yesterday and my sister said it was not working. She showed me what she thought sounded right.'

The director told my sister, 'That was amazing. Please guide Chapal with the rest of the role.'

My sister laughed: 'I don't have that much time. I just pointed him in the right direction so he could understand the difference between theatre and jatra.'

I always kept that in mind.

But theatre paid you far less than jatra did. You got fame and respectability, but not much money. You might get 300–500 rupees per show. When I did *Sundarbibir Pala*, I was paid better: 1,500 a day. At least it covered my medical expenses.

Most importantly, my sister came to see the play and she loved it. That meant a lot to me. After my mother died, she was my everything.

Sister Act

We had a funny relationship, my sister and I. When we were children, we would fight all the time. We were always rubbing each other the wrong way. On top of that, we started our acting careers around the same time. We were friends, siblings and rivals. Like me, she too would sit in the wings and watch our mother act. That's how she knew entire plays by heart. When no one was around in the afternoon, she would go up on that empty stage and act her heart out. That's where Sisir Bhaduri spotted her and asked Ma to train her properly. That led to a fight with my oldest brother who wanted her to focus on her studies instead. But Ma had her way.

At seven, my sister acted in her first film *Propaganda*. In 1941, she acted in her first play *Shah Jahan*. In *Siraj-ud-Daulah*, she played Lutfa, an adult, even though she was just thirteen. They made her put on four or five dresses to make her look older and had her wear high heels for it. She would joke that she was Uttam Kumar's first heroine, because in the film *Drishtidaan*, she played the heroine Sunanda Devi's young version while Uttam Kumar (then Arun Kumar) played the hero Asit Baran's younger self. Many artistes, male and female, got a lot from Ketaki Dutta. I won't name them here but most of them never acknowledged that debt.

I always wanted to compete with her, to outshine her when we were young. I would wear her clothes and imitate her. She would get annoyed: 'Why are you copying me? Don't copy my voice. That's not right. You need to find your own voice.' She was my first drama teacher. I learnt how to sing, dance, act, dress even how to move on the stage from her. But, for a long time, I would not go to watch her on stage because I was afraid I would end up imitating her. I didn't want her shadow to fall on me.

We would find faults with each other constantly. 'What do you understand about acting?' She would sometimes say scornfully. She also had a way of looking at me that made me shut up instantly, no matter how much I had been shouting moments before.

We fought, we squabbled, we argued. But we could not do without each other. We were each other's support. In 1988, we left the house we shared on Girish Avenue and moved in together into the flat she got in Belgachia Villa from the government via the West Bengal Theatre Academy. She felt it would be better that way. The flat had three bedrooms and two bathrooms and a big kitchen. We could live on our own, her sons could live on their own. Her daughters were worried: 'Will you be able to manage?'

She said, 'We won't have any problem.'

Chhordi herself acted in jatra too but around the end of her career. They used her name but not her talent, wasting her as the fourth female lead. Or they made her dance, something that wasn't seemly at her age. It made me furious. It felt humiliating to me that the person I had seen acting in a play like *Anthony Kabiyal* was reduced to this cheapness.

One year, I had gone to Siliguri to act in *Chand Bibi*. When I got there, someone told me, 'Your sister is also here with a play.' She was acting in a play based on Sarat Chandra's *Nishkriti*. I was amazed. That was a role that had been made famous by our mother.

I took a cycle rickshaw and went to her hotel. It was quite a scene. She was cooking for the entire company. She just loved to cook. She saw me and said, 'Tuku, where did you come from?'

Her co-actors said, 'He also has a big production here—*Chand Bibi*.'

I said, 'I've come to see you. What a lovely coincidence. Both of us are here at the same time—you with your play, I with my jatra. But goodness, you will do the role our mother did on stage? You certainly have guts. I cannot imagine doing that.'

To be honest, I too had always wanted to act in a role which our mother had made famous. It would have been a way to pay tribute to her and connect with her so many years after she was gone. But I never got to. The closest I came was when I once read a few lines of her dialogue in a stage show. But my sister played Siddheswari in *Nishkriti* and made a huge name for herself. Sadly, I never got to see it. Our jatra went on for 3 hours and 15 minutes. Her play was only 2 hours and 10 minutes. But I did send someone to watch it. They said she was marvellous. She didn't let our mother down. I did not feel jealous at all. That day I just thought, 'Wow, my sister has gone very far. She would have made our mother proud.'

Later, I got to see her in a solo performance at Girish Manch. She left me awestruck. After the show, I went to the green room and touched her feet. I couldn't't help myself. She had not even taken her make-up off at that point. Surprised, she said, 'Tuku, what's going on? You've never touched my feet before.'

I said, 'I have no choice. There is nothing else I could do after that bravura performance on stage today.' I had tears running down my face.

She laughed: 'We are from the Bhaduri clan, after all. We can do everything. You didn't quite get the same chance as I did, that's all. Listen, if worse comes to worst, I will beg a harmonium from someone and go and sit on the river bank and sing songs and earn a few pennies that way. Can you do that? You could sing too, though you've not kept it up.'

Looking back, I realize I craved her approval. Sometimes, I was lucky enough to get snippets of it. One day, she came to see me in a group-theatre production. I caught her looking at me oddly afterwards. I said, 'Why are you looking at me like that?' She said, 'It's nothing. I was just thinking about what our mother had said. If only you had been a girl, you would have been one of our great actresses.'

We finally acted together in a play called *Nijabhumey* [On Their Own Ground]. That was towards the end of her career. By then her star was fading. It was an autobiographical play written by Salil Sarkar that he put together under a banner named after our mother—Mancha Prabha. In it, Ketaki Dutta became Kusum Dutta. Chapal remained Chapal, and like the real Chapal, this one also travelled around, singing the songs of Sitala. It opens with Kusum Dutta's memorial service and then goes back in time and the audience discovers who she really was. It was a way to present a collage of some of Chhordi's most iconic characters. It was not bad, but it was not great either. It ran for a few shows in Girish Mancha in 1997, and later in a few different theatres, but then Chhordi fell ill.

She had not told any of us she was ill. I had noticed she was having problems with her voice but she kept acting, because that's what we actors do. In 2003, she had gone to perform in Ranaghat, but got so sick that everyone wanted to cancel the programme. She insisted on doing it, gritting her teeth through the pain. She had to be hospitalized the next day.

One day, her body finally could not take it any more and she collapsed. The doctor said there was nothing anyone could do. I heard she had vomited blood a few times while singing. But she had told no one at home. By the time they diagnosed it as lung cancer, it was too late. It had spread everywhere. She barely had four months left.

Chhordi didn't understand what was happening. She asked me, 'Tell me, Tuku, What's wrong with me? Why is no one telling me? I have had so many illnesses before. I've come through them all. Why are they not letting me eat?'

I said, 'What do I know, Chhordi? I don't really know anything.'

But she looked at me with those piercing eyes that could see through you. And I knew that she understood I was hiding something. I looked away. She did not ask me again.

One day, she pointed at a guava that had come from a tree we had planted in our house. By then, she could barely talk. But she kept pointing at the guava and gesturing that we should cut it and give everyone a piece. I didn't know it then, but that might have been our last interaction.

She was born on 13 July 1934, the 28th day of the monsoon month Aashaar. She died on 8 July 2003. She suffered a lot in the end. When death came, it was a relief. But I felt like I had lost my mother all over again.

After she died, I wrote in the newspaper: 'Today, I remain me in my own land, nijabhumey. But my Chhordi is gone.'

Fish without Water

Chhordi tried to keep acting and singing till the day she died. I wish I could have as well but fate willed otherwise. Now age and health do not permit me to act any more.

When people came and said, 'Are you sure you cannot do this at all any more, Chapal-da?' I would say, 'My legs aren't what they used to be. Perhaps if you write a character with a broken leg, maybe that will work.'

I sometimes joke that perhaps we could tweak *Ramanimohan* a bit. In the play, his character gets a thrashing. Perhaps they could make it so that, after that beating, he can only limp around. Then this Chapal can still act as Ramanimohan. My body will not support me, but that desire to act doesn't leave me either.

The way a fish cannot survive without water, it's hard for a true actor to survive without acting. I am luckier than many. I got to explore so many worlds when it came to acting.

Jatra was one world. The songs of Sitala were another. And group theatre was yet another. God has given me the opportunity to be part of all these worlds.

There remained only one more world left to explore—the world of film and television.

INTERLUDE

In Imagination
The Drag Queen

I can't explain how excited I was to meet Chapal Rani.

Moira, my academic friend in Canada, told me about him. She found out that Chapal Rani was coming to do workshops and performances in Vancouver and said I should come. I had never heard of him but I booked my tickets right away. Why? I'll come to that story later. I came all the way to Vancouver from the American Midwest just to meet him. Or should I say her? Or them? I don't know. At that time, we didn't have preferred pronouns. Somehow, I don't think Chapal Rani cares about pronouns anyway.

I thought I would feel an instant connection with him because I am Bengali too, albeit half-Bengali. I don't know the language and have never been to that part of the world, but my Bengaliness is very important to me. I had grown up in the cornfields of the Midwest in a small university town with one Dairy Queen and two McDonalds. There were a few drag queens around, but no one with roots in South Asia like me. I would joke that I was a freak among freaks.

I settled on Bang La Dish as my drag name, because my mother's family came from Dhaka. My father was standard-issue European mutt, German, Irish and goodness knows bits of what else. I thought I was the only gay in the village while I was growing up. But I was luckier than many. At least our town had a gay bar, a grungy one but it was better than nothing. Its name changed over the years—Lonely Hearts, Faces, Wonderland. A small dingy place with a pool table in the corner. The dim lighting hid the grime on the walls. But at least it had a small stage with tatty red velvet curtains, and on weekends, I could put on my wig and long curling eyelashes and strut about on it in my heels as Bang La Dish. None of the patrons really understood the joke. They just called me BLD for short.

We were a very steak-and-potatoes kinda family. My mom occasionally cooked dal and rice and chicken curry, though she mostly stuck to pasta, burgers and mashed potatoes. But she would watch old Hindi films when she could, because she loved the song-and-dance bits. There was one international store in town run by some Patels. They sold garam masala and gulab-jamun mix and had a lending library with pirated copies of Bollywood videos. The cabaret numbers were my favourite. I adored Helen, the queen of item numbers—all those spangled slit dresses and amazing pointy breasts. The way she sashayed, she could put many a drag queen to shame. I don't know if she is a queer icon in India, but she was surely my drag fairy godmother. I even wanted to get boobs like her. I am proud to admit my drag look was really inspired by her, though of course no one in Wonderland understood that.

Except once an elderly Indian woman in a saree got lost and walked in. She was visiting town because, many years ago, she had lived here with her husband, a graduate student. We drank Bombay gin and tonic and danced to 'Mera Naam Chin Chin Choo' together. I really had the best time bumping hips and sashaying up a storm. We brought the house down. I dropped her home in my Oldsmobile and gave her my number, but I never heard from her again. I don't think her son approved of her little late-night adventure. From the way she described him, he sounded like he had a stick up his ass. But I've never forgotten that night. It was as if my worlds had come together for a moment. I often wonder what happened to her.

I think that's what pushed me to meet Chapal Rani. Like that woman, he too was from Kolkata. But unlike her, he came from my world. A man who performed as a woman. I thought I would find my soul sister in him. I had read that, in South Asia, transgenders were called hijras and really respected. They had their own communities with gurus, and were an important part of birth and marriage ceremonies. I wanted to ask him all about it.

When I first saw Chapal Rani in make-up and full costume, I was speechless. He looked so imposing in that red-and-gold sari, with all those golden ornaments. The Patel store in our town didn't have anything like that. I wished I had gone shopping in Little India, on Devon Avenue in Chicago, before coming to Canada. It would have been so fabulous to have a girls' dress-up night with Chapal. The way he painted his eyes and lips was really a masterclass in drag. When he painted the third eye on his forehead, I swear I got goosebumps. It seems a little silly now, but I thought that Chapal Rani would connect me somehow to a heritage dating back centuries, far older and far richer than anything in the nightclubs in Chicago or New York. I hoped to return transformed, in touch with my true transcontinental translineage. I saw him as a torchbearer of something ancient, and hoped he would impart that wisdom of the ages to me.

I couldn't have been more wrong. When I asked him if he had a drag name, he said, 'Why should I need another name? My name is Chapal. Everyone called me Chapal Rani on stage. Like Babli Rani and Satadal Rani.' I tried to explain my name to him, but he just looked at me quizzically. Then I asked him about hijras, and his eyebrows shot up. He regarded me with real annoyance and said, 'I am not third gender. I am first gender.'

I too came of age at a time when we just said gay—gay bar, gay pride, gay rights. All this LGBTQI++ alphabet soup was yet to happen. But times have changed. We talk pronouns now. Even gay is not enough. You have cis gay and cis het. Heck, you even have aromantic, which I always misread as aromatic, like Basmati rice. It's hard to keep up with this identity churn. And I'll be honest. Even I have been scolded for putting a foot wrong now and then. I sometimes feel these young people spend more time coining alphabet monikers for themselves than getting laid. If we all got laid a bit more, the world would be a happier place. But I digress.

If you asked what letters of the alphabet fit Chapal Rani, I honestly wouldn't have a good answer for you. I guess now I would just say Chapal was a cis gay man who cross-dressed on stage. At first, I thought he was a drag queen, plain and simple, but then he threw me a real curveball. He said that when he puts on his make-up and draws his lips, something changes inside him. He feels like a woman, not just a man dressed as a woman. 'Every month, I feel something inside, just like a woman does when she has her time of the month.' That knocked me for a loop. Moira who teaches gender studies said it was probably a case of gender dysphoria. I had to Google it to know what that even meant.

It's funny. I came to meet him hoping to find answers to who I was, but I left with more questions about him instead. When I asked him if he had ever wanted gender-reassignment surgery, he scoffed at me. He said he saw no reason to change anything about himself.

One day at the workshop, I showed up in a dress I had found in a used clothing store. He said, 'That's a nice dress.'

'Don't you ever want to wear a sari when you are out on the street?' I asked.

'I don't feel the need to wear women's clothes off stage,' he replied. 'Being a woman is something I do onstage. When I am off-stage, I am happy being a man. And let me tell you, all my man parts still work just fine.'

Then he turned around and asked me, 'When you walk around the street like that, don't people call you names?'

I shrugged: 'I guess I have a thick skin by now. I call them names right back.'

He shook his head and said a female impersonator had once told him that boys teased him a lot. He said, 'I told him that if you keep long hair like a woman, wear lipstick out in public like a woman, do your eyes and eyebrows like a woman, of course people will say things. You have to be prepared for that.'

I thought perhaps something was getting lost in translation since he was speaking in Bengali. How could he compartmentalize his life like that? Putting Chapal Rani in one box, and Chapal Bhaduri in another? Was this some kind of denial about his sexuality? What was really curious to me was that he was happy to exchange make-up tips but absolutely not interested in my coming-out story at all. There was no BIPOC sisterhood. Zilch.

I grew up as a boy who liked to experiment with his mother's make-up. When I asked Chapal whether he had been the same, he told me he would only watch his mother do her make-up, never put any on himself. For him, make-up was something to put on when he performed on stage. You would think he was like Dame Edna or Eddie Izzard, one of those cis het men who do drag for entertainment. I play women on stage, he told me, I don't do caricatures. That's when I realized my mistake. Chapal Rani wasn't a drag queen at all. He acted as women in all seriousness. There wasn't a hint of camp anywhere.

Was I disappointed? I suppose I was. I thought I would find a queer elder. I had imagined we would become penpals. But he didn't care about identity. If he belonged to any tradition, it was the tradition of men who acted as women on stage. That was a profession more than an identity.

For me, coming out had been all about identity, finding community, finding the letter of the alphabet that fit me. Whenever someone who looked mildly desi, whether the colour of milky latte or strong Americano, walked into Wonderland, I would strike up a conversation with them. That's how I made friends with that elderly lady who walked in, though she wasn't L, G, B or T. But Chapal Rani didn't feel he belonged to any LGBTQ movement and moreover he didn't even want to.

'Do you want to go to a gay bar with me?' I asked him.

'No, no,' he said, almost shocked. 'What will I do in such a place?' I told him about Stanley Park in the middle of Vancouver. Late at night, men hide behind the trees there, looking for other men in the shadows. He shook his head: 'There are parks like that too in Kolkata. It's all play you know. Just play.'

To be honest, I had felt more of a connection to that grey-haired Indian lady who had wandered into Wonderland than to Chapal Rani. One day I told Chapal about her. It was the first time I felt him being really interested in anything I said. Excitedly, I told him the secret she had confided in me, something I had never shared with anyone—that she had discovered after her marriage that her husband had a male lover. I thought Chapal would be shocked. But he simply shrugged and said, 'What's surprising about that? I have known way too many men like him. Many of them were my colleagues. My lover got married too. And I still stayed with him for years.'

'Did you go to his wedding?'

'No, I was working. But it didn't change anything between us. I got along quite well with his wife. His children called me C.'

'They knew?'

'Everything does not have to be spelt out.'

'Didn't you get jealous about his wife?'

'Why should I? She could give him children. I couldn't. I could satisfy him in every way except that.'

If he said that to Moira's gender studies class, I think they would all spontaneously implode. I mean, where do you fit Chapal Rani in queer theory where we are always talking about the intersection of identity, gender and sexuality? 'How do you locate someone like Chapal?' Moira asked me later. I had no answer. 'Is he dismantling patriarchy or finding his own corner in it?' I had no answer for that either.

Perhaps he didn't wish to be located. I did. I was looking to belong. He was not. He was happy being himself. Or perhaps he was resigned to being singularly himself. It didn't matter. Much later, I thought of a letter of the alphabet that fit him. He was R—romantic for relationship. That's what defined him. He was not trying to define himself as an individual. He defined himself via his long relationship with that married man.

He wouldn't tell me his name. But he told me how he liked his men. Tall, strapping and handsome. 'Manly men,' he said his eyes shining. 'Can you bring me Russell Crowe?'

The day before he left for India, I went to see him. 'I want to give you something to remember me by,' I said. 'I want you to have this necklace. They are not real pearls, but they look real, don't they?'

He laughed: 'Everything I wear is fake. But I am not fake. I am the real thing.'

Then he said, 'But I don't have anything to give you. Here, take this red sari. Perhaps you can wear it on stage. And remember me.'

That touched me. He taught me how to wear the sari. We giggled and laughed as I messed up the pleats. I made him drink a glass of red wine. Then we watched *Gladiator* together, and he oohed and aahed over Russell Crowe. Afterwards, he taught me how to walk in the sari. When I added a sashay, he giggled.

I felt I finally had my sister-in-drag moment with Chapal Rani.

12

Silver Screen

The Vigil of Chapal

By 2003–04, my life had changed entirely. After 20 years of sitting around, then performing Sitala in streets, slums and villages, Chapal Bhaduri was back in demand.

My small-screen life began with a man named Asit Basu who was from the world of group theatre. He wrote plays and directed as well. He found me through another actor named Amit. Amit did me two great favours. He put me back in touch with Makhan-babu of Natta Company when Makhan-babu was ill with cancer. And he connected me to Asit Basu.

Asit Basu happened to mention to Amit that he was making a telefilm called *Shabarir Protiksha* [The Vigil of Shabari]. It included a bit that was set in the world of jatra.

'I wonder what happened to Chapal Rani,' he said. 'Wouldn't it be great if we could track him down for the jatra bit?'

Amit said, 'I can get in touch with him for you.'

Then Amit paid me a visit: 'Chapal-da, do you want to act in film? They will pay reasonably well.' It was not a lot, but every bit helped.

Shabarir Protiksha was set in pre-Independence India. Shabari was a young woman who had fallen in love with a man involved in the freedom struggle. As the police are closing in on him, he has to flee, but he promises Shabari 'Wait for me. One day I will be back. I promise.' So Shabari keeps waiting, hoping that one day they will be together again. Meanwhile, a jatra troupe arrives at her village. They perform the story of another Shabari, this one from the Indian epic the Ramayana.

In that story, Shabari is an old woman, an ardent disciple of the great sage Matanga. When Matanga is about to die, Shabari wants to accompany him to the 'abode of peace'. Matanga tells her to wait for Lord Ram instead, the incarnation of God Vishnu. If Shabari waits for him with true devotion, Vishnu will surely grant her a vision.

Shabari goes out every day with her walking stick and collects jujube berries for Lord Ram. She nibbles each berry to see if it's sweet enough to be worthy of Ram. She puts the ones that pass the test into her basket and throws away the ones that are too sour or too bitter. Then she returns home and waits. If anyone asks her what she is waiting for, she says with unshakeable confidence, 'My Ram will come.'

One day, Ram finally passes by the hermitage and meets Shabari. Some say he came to her because he had heard of her devotion to him. Elated, she touches his feet. He pulls her up and embraces her.

She says, 'You have come to my humble hut. What can I offer you? All I have are these berries I saved for you.'

'Give them to me,' he tells her. She rushes off to pluck some, and as was her wont, takes a bite from each one to make sure it is sweet. When she puts the half-eaten berries into a bowl made of leaves and offers them to Ram, his companions scold her. How dare she give half-eaten berries to Ram?

But Ram ignores them: 'Nothing can equal these berries, offered with such pure devotion. Whosoever offers a fruit, a leaf, a flower, or water with such love, I take it with great joy.'

'Today your waiting is over,' he tells her and blesses her.

I played that Shabari, the one from mythology whom the other Shabari watches on stage. Shyamal Ghosh, a big name from the world of group theatre, played Ram.

In the Ramayana, Shabari is an old woman by the time she meets Ram, bent over with age, walking with a stick, her hair white. But in the jatra version we staged, she was still young. After all, I was still young enough at that time and had not lost my looks. I remember, we went to the old Surul palace near Bolpur for our shoot. It was a magnificent old building, almost 300 years old but quite well maintained. It had these little temples with intricate terracotta carvings of gods like Jagannath and Shiva and Ram. The shoot was in the courtyard of the old palace. That was where they set up the jatra performance. Asit Basu kept checking with me anxiously to make sure he was getting the little details right. 'Is this how it was in those days?' he would ask. He really did not need to check. He had enough experience of the world of jatra because had been part of Utpal Dutt's theatre group.

It was like going back to the old days when we began to perform, lit by hissing Petromax lamps. The story was set in a time when electricity had not yet arrived at the village. Shyamal Ghosh and I performed the story of Shabari while the real Shabari watched us from the audience. For me, though, the real excitement was not with the set but what I saw when I got there—excited crowds gathered around the palace. Word had spread that jatra queen Chapal Rani was coming! As our car approached, a buzz spread through the crowd. I could hear people shouting 'Chapal Rani has come.' I could barely get out of the car as they started pushing and shoving for a better look at me. The handlers pushed them aside and cleared a passage for me to get down and walk into the palace.

I had long forgotten what that kind of adulation felt like.

Bird in a Cage

After that came *Ushnatar Jonno* [For Warmth], I think around 2003. I was still performing Sitala's songs and occasionally acting in group theatre when one afternoon I got a call.

'This is Kaushik Ganguly,' said the voice on the other end of the line.

'What I can do for you?'

'Have you acted in any telefilms?'

'I just did a film called *Shabarir Protiksha*,' I replied. 'But I know the basics about acting in film.'

'Good,' he said. 'Do you think you would be able to act in a telefilm I am making?'

'I am an actor. Why should I not be able to act, whether it's in play or a film? But what is it about?'

'We'll discuss that later,' he said. 'Why don't you come and meet me?'

'How will I do that? I don't know where you live. I live in North Kolkata.'

He thought for a moment. Then he said, 'Do you know the department store called Pantaloons near Gariahat? Why don't you come there? I'll send someone to fetch you.'

This was all sounding more and more mysterious. But in the days before mobile phones, that's how we organized meetings. On the appointed day at the appointed time, I dutifully came to the store. As I stood there waiting, a short smiling man approached me. I looked at him quizzically. 'I think I know you from somewhere,' I told him.

'You do,' he grinned. 'I used to know your sister, Ketaki. I've been to your house several times. I'm the one who passed your contact to Kaushik Ganguly. Come. Let me take you to him.'

He hailed a taxi and we went to an apartment which occupied one floor of a big house. We walked into a well-appointed living room with a nice sofa. When Kaushik walked in, though, my heart did a somersault. He was a large man, quite formidable in his appearance, and most disconcertingly, his eyes looked in different directions.

Much later, when I got to know him well, I confessed how hard it was for me to know when he was talking to me. He laughed uproariously: 'Oh you mean my eyes? Don't even start. That's a legacy from my childhood days. I was playing football and the ball hit my head.'

That day, he greeted me with great courtesy and told me what he needed.

'I am directing a film for television called *Ushnatar Jonno*. And there is a role there which I think you would be perfect.'

'A female part?' I asked.

'No, a man. But one who plays a woman out of necessity. Not unlike your own story. But, first, tell me what are you doing these days?'

'I go around singing Sitala's songs. Some days, I get a call from some amateur theatre group. Nothing serious, to be honest. A bit of this and a bit of that.'

'Imagine a character whose life is also something like that. But it's all in the character's past. That's where the real story is.'

'I don't understand.'

'It will be as clear as mud. And you are the one who will have to play this part. The person who wrote the story wrote this part with you and only you in mind. She said, "Only Chapal Bhaduri can do justice to the role of Saralaranjan. There is no one else." '

The script had been written by Sunetra Ghatak. Later her son, Parambrata Chatterjee, became well known as an actor and director in Bengali films. Her uncle was the great filmmaker, Ritwik Ghatak. She had apparently said that no one else should play that part because it had a lot of parallels with my life. That amused me no end. Other people seemed to know more about my life than I did.

'I have the script here. I can give it to you to read,' Kaushik said. 'But tell me, what about the money?'

'I have no idea how it works in film,' I confessed.

'You can get a package contract, or a daily wage. Which one would you prefer?'

'I have no clue. Just make sure I don't feel taken advantage of.'

We decided on a contract. He gave me an advance and said, 'You don't have to worry about anything else. My wife Churni is in the film, as is Rupa Ganguly. You will get the same perks and benefits they receive whether it be food or transport or accommodation. You have my word.'

It was a good story. Rupa Ganguly and Churni Ganguly played two women who shared an apartment. At some point they get into a romantic relationship. Then, one day, Churni's character decides she no longer wants that life. So she leaves Rupa and gets married to a man. But Rupa's character, Suman, stays the same in terms of her romantic preference for women.

I played Saralaranjan, an ageing actor with a jatra troupe who once played female parts. He too had fallen in love with a co-actor, the one who played the hero Ram to his Sita.

The story made sense to me. These kinds of attachments were commonplace in jatras where you spent eight to nine months on the road. Saralaranjan is coy around that leading man, like a lovelorn girl, but he does not realize, or is in denial of the fact, that their relationship can lead nowhere. After all, he cannot bear him a child. When a young woman joins the troupe, she gets involved romantically with the leading man. One day, Saralaranjan hears his lover tell the young woman to wait for him near the pond. Saralaranjan realizes that the leading man plans to elope with the woman and leave the company in the lurch.

Saralaranjan is devastated, but he has nowhere to go and no one to go with. He knows nothing outside the world of jatra. So he stays on with the troupe at the mercy of the abusive manager/owner of the company.

The actor who played the leading man was very young and handsome. I would feel quite embarrassed doing intimate scenes with him. He would say, 'What's there to be embarrassed about Chapal-da? This is just acting. And see, I call you Dada like an elder brother. You are so much senior to me.'

'That's right,' I said. 'I am much older. And certainly not as good looking any more.'

In fact, there was one love scene that made me acutely uncomfortable. I eventually told the director, 'Look, this is a flashback scene. My character is supposed to be really young then. I am too old for this scene. I feel very awkward. Why don't you try and find someone younger for this bit? I am happy to play the older Saralaranjan.'

Thankfully, they found someone to play my younger self in those scenes.

Fast-forward to the present. In the film, Suman, who is grieving her lost relationship, comes to interview Saralaranjan, now a middle-aged man. They sense a kindred spirit in each other and Saralaranjan opens his heart to her. Suman starts feeling a strange empathy for him as well, and both realize their lives had run on parallel tracks, many years apart.

Our outdoor shoot happened at Jhargram Rajbari, home to the old Malla Dev royal family, a huge mansion with Italian and Islamic architecture, beautifully laid out with lawns and gardens. But it was in the middle of June, and blazingly hot—the height of summer, without a monsoon cloud in sight. My character would wear pyjamas and a loose shirt-vest, and they would be drenched with sweat every day. We would iron our costumes dry and resume the shot from wherever we cut.

Kaushik took great pains to get the details right and recreate the feel of jatra days of yore. He got Petromax lamps and hired a concert party from some village as the orchestra. I made sure they had all the old instruments, so we could have the authentic jatra sound—the drums like pakhawaj and dholak, the behala violin and flute, the khadtal hand cymbals and the clarionet with its distinctive pyan-pyan noise, which to my ears is the sound of jatra.

One rarely hears these instruments any more, but I cannot imagine a jatra without them.

The heat was difficult, but Kaushik Ganguly kept his word. He treated me on par with his leading ladies. I travelled with them, sometimes in First Class in trains, sometimes by private car. When Churni finished her shoot, her room would be allocated to me.

In the film, after Suman leaves, we see Saralaranjan sitting alone in the courtyard of his little mud hut, clutching an envelope she has left him. It's late afternoon and the light is golden.

The manager of the jatra company sees him sitting there pensively.

MANAGER (*sharply*). Goodness. They drove us mad. Did they give some money or just took everything for free? After all, you didn't work for days because you were too busy yakking with that woman. Words are empty promises. If we don't act how will we eat?'

SARALARANJAN (*wearily*). I am old now. Why are you holding onto me? Let me go.

MANAGER. What nonsense. Where will I get someone to sing and act the parts of Draupadi? Anyway, have those annoying people finally left?

(*Saralaranjan sits as still as stone.*)

I didn't like that Suman. She acts like a man, wears men's clothes. What kind of woman behaves like that?

SARALARANJAN. Why are you picking on her? After all, I act like a woman too.

MANAGER (*laughs*). Tell me, did they pay you or not?

(*Saralaranjan mutely hands over the envelope which he has not even opened. The manager snatches it, tears it open, peers inside and starts to count the wad of notes.*) Small mercies. Not bad. We need the money, Sarala. We need to do a lot of repairs around here, not that you would notice anything or care.

The manager takes the money and moves to throw away the empty envelope. Saralaranjan stops him.

SARALARANJAN. Give me the envelope. Please.

MANAGER. It's just an envelope. What will you do it?

SARALARANJAN. You know all those newspaper and magazine cuttings from my old performances that I keep in that trunk, those old reviews? I will keep them in that envelope. I will keep this envelope as a symbol of Suman's love.

MANAGER. Hmmph, ridiculous sentimental nonsense.

He tosses the envelope at Saralaranjan who picks it up.

SARALARANJAN (*holding the envelope close, murmurs*). What will I do? What *will* I do?

There was a cage above my head with a little bird. Just as we shot that scene, the bird started to flutter as though it was trying to break free. I remember Kaushik noticing it, and signalling to the cameraman to continue filming and not cut the shot. It was not planned, but it became a perfect metaphor for Saralaranjan's life, struggling for air and freedom but stuck in his little cage. His eyes well up, but before a tear can roll down his cheek, the film ends.

A year or so later, I was in Puri, walking by the sea. A group of young people walked past me. Suddenly they all turned around and looked at me, then they came up and one of them said, 'Aren't you Chapal Bhaduri? We saw you in that telefilm. It was amazing. How did you bring that kind of feeling to the role? How do you play a woman so convincingly? Was that real money in that envelope?'

I laughed and said, 'Don't you know that's acting? Everything is fake. They just put pieces of paper in there to make it look like money.'

But it felt good. Instead of the sea or the temples of Puri, these people were more interested in talking to me. I felt like I still mattered. A new audience was noticing my work.

Something Big

After *Ushnatar Jonno*, I went back to doing Sitala's songs. Sometimes a theatre company like Nandipat would call if there was demand for a call show somewhere.

A few other offers came my way—small roles, almost cameo appearances. Like in a telefilm based on Rabindranath Tagore's *Atithi* [The Guest]. In it, a little boy has run away from home. He wanders into a field where a jatra is setting up. He sees a man sitting in front of a mirror and doing his make-up, putting on his wig. The man spots the boy in the mirror and says, 'Who are you?'

'I am Tarapada,' replies the boy.

'That's a pretty name.'

'You look pretty too.'

'I do? Do you want to look pretty? Do you want to dress like me? Come, let me dress you.'

The boy giggles and runs away. It was just a tiny scene, but they paid me well and we went back to Jhargram Rajbari for the shoot.

In another telefilm, they needed someone to do Sitala's songs. It was just a day's work, though. Now, I cannot even remember the name.

Then a tele-serial came my way. It was my first, and was supposed to last for at least 100 episodes. It was called *Ghare O Bairey* [At Home and Outside], but it had nothing to do with the famous story written by Tagore. Again, Kaushik Ganguly was at its helm.

I had to play a servant named Dhananjay. But because it was Chapal Bhaduri playing Dhananjay, I had to dress as a woman. Though I did not have to do the full make-up I usually did for my jatra roles. Dhananjay runs away with the son of a zamindar and sets up home in a slum in Kolkata's Khidirpur. There he lives as a hijra and raises the boy. The well-known actor Santu Mukherjee played the zamindar, Laboni Sarkar and Churni Ganguly played his two wives.

I was still quite slim and rather androgynous. No one was quite sure of my gender in the slum where we shot the serial.

In one scene, the hijra is being tortured in the police station. Policemen are dragging her by her hair—and the wig comes off. An officer asks, 'Where did the boy's mother go?' as if I had been impersonating a 'real' mother. And then my character is sent to jail.

It was hard for me to get into the rhythm of a serial. I would show up at the set at 9 in the morning. At 10, they would serve us breakfast. Around noon, someone would hand me a sheet of paper with three or four lines of dialogue written on it. 'When will we shoot?' I would ask.

'Don't worry. We will,' they would say reassuringly. 'After lunch.'

Lunch would come and go but nothing would happen. At some point, I'd corner an assistant and say, 'What happened? You said we'd shoot after lunch.'

'Let me find out,' he would reply and promptly vanish. At 4, someone would bring us tea and biscuits. Then, perhaps at 4.30, we would do a spot of rehearsal and finally shoot the scene for which I'd been waiting all day. There would be just a couple of takes and then it would be OK-ed. I'd pick up my money and go home and wait for the next call. Perhaps the next day I would have two pages of dialogue instead of one . . . It was hard to sink my teeth into the role.

Ghare O Bairey was not bad as a serial, but it didn't get the TRPs. Eventually, it was discontinued. At that point in the story, my character was still in jail. The cameraman joked: 'Chapal-da, we could not get you out of jail.'

One day, Kaushik Ganguly called me over to his house. He said, 'How long will you go from door to door doing a little bit of this and that? You need to do something big.'

'Well, there's nothing wrong with going door to door. Especially in these times.'

'You really need to do something much bigger. Let's organize some major funding. We should do a feature film about your life.'

'I have written about it. There's a small booklet out. You can read that.'

'I've read it.'

'And there is a documentary that Seagull made about me.'

'That's what I'm talking about. The more personal stuff. Will you write that story down for me?'

I said, 'I suppose I can, but I cannot name certain names.'

He said it was all right if I did not.

Not Just Another Love Story

I sat down and wrote my story and gave it to him. That became the film *Arekti Premer Golpo* [Just Another Love Story]. In structure, it was similar to *Ushnatar Jonno* but with a man–man angle rather than a two-women one.

Abhiroop, a documentary filmmaker, is in a relationship with Basu, a bisexual cinematographer married to a woman. Abhiroop comes to interview jatra actor Chapal Bhaduri, once known as Chapal Rani. Once upon a time, Chapal Rani had a relationship with Kumar, a married man. The film switches between the present life of Abhiroop and the past life of Chapal Rani, and compares the course of their love lives. Some of the same actors appear in both the past and present timelines to drive home the parallels.

I kept hearing it was going to be a big-budget film, and that celebrated director Rituparno Ghosh would play Abhiroop. Rituparno was already famous for his films like *Unishe April, Bariwali* and *Chokher Bali*. He had won many awards, and everyone was hailing him as the saviour of Bengali cinema, for bringing audiences back to the theatres. His name gave our film a lot of buzz.

But I never really saw the final script. Every time I asked, they would say, 'Yes, yes, soon' but it never happened. When I was given my costume, I complained it was too big and too thick. I only wore fine cottons, I said. They said, 'No, this is your character's costume.' I didn't say anything but I was realizing slowly that Chapal Rani the character was me but not me either. They kept the bit about my character making a living singing Sitala's songs, but many other things had been changed. Some of it I didn't understand at the time.

We shot many of the Sitala scenes at Aurora Studio. We did a few outdoor scenes in North Kolkata. There was also an outdoor shoot in Bolpur, at the royal palace where we had done *Shabarir Protiksha*. But all that was cut out of the eventual film. In the end, the film that everyone saw was entirely different from the film I thought we had been making.

Rituparno Ghosh was supposed to be my interviewer. Suddenly, shooting stopped for a few days. I do not know what transpired, but then I was told 'Your work ends here.' And that was that.

In the film, there is a scene where I am returning home early in the morning after performing Sitala's songs. The tram trundles past behind me. That's where my role ends in the film. All in all, I probably did eight or nine days' work on that film. I dubbed my part, but I had no idea what happened in the rest of the film.

I must admit they paid me exactly what they promised, no matter how much or how little work I ended up doing. They kept their word financially, but I was cheated when it came to the story, my story, that ended up on screen.

That's why I prefer theatre to film. In theatre, what you see is what you get. In film, you can act one way but it can be edited to look completely different on screen. In theatre, no one is editing your scenes.

When Sekhar Samaddar wrote *Sundarbibir Pala*, I was asked to play Sundar Bibi. I agreed because I needed the money. My friends when to watch it and were very disappointed, 'What is this play? There's so much talk about Sundar Bibi but you barely see anything of her.'

I shrugged, 'It is what it is. What can I do?'

Yet the same Sekhar Samaddar also wrote *Ramanimohan* and that was such a wonderful role.

Arekti Premer Golpo might not have been the film I thought it was going to be, but Kaushik Ganguly was an out-and-out gentleman, very diligent about payments and never making any attempt to shortchange me. His team really took good care of me. They would send cars whenever needed. If I had to take a train to Bolpur, I would travel First Class. I enjoyed working with the other actors too. It was the first time I met Jisshu Sengupta, with whom I had a few scenes. He was very polite and respectful. I became great friends with the actress Raima Sen. One day, Raima's mother, Moon Moon Sen, came to visit the set. She was radiantly beautiful. I told her I had once seen her mother, the legendary Suchitra Sen, on set but had been too shy to say anything to her.

Raima and I had a scene in which we are talking next to a window while it rains outside. I was concerned we would get wet. But everyone said, 'Don't worry. Nothing will happen.' We sat at the window while someone poured water through a strainer outside. Through the camera it looked exactly like rain. I was amazed—this is how cinema tricks us all. In theatre, you can't get away with as much.

Rituparno Ghosh was also very courteous on the set. At that time, he was a novice in many ways. He didn't know how to do his make-up properly, how to put on false eyelashes. He would look at me, wide-eyed, and say, 'Goodness, Chapal-da, how beautifully you can dress in those outfits.' I had met Rituparno earlier when he hosted a television show titled *Ebong Rituparno*. We had talked about acting and my career. I knew he was trying to push me when he said, 'Is there anything else you want to talk about? Anything personal?' At that time, I just said: no.

But I could sense a change coming over him while we shot *Arekti Premer Golpo*. One day, we were doing a scene together where I kept having trouble with one line. Rituparno got irritated and snapped, 'You can't do even this little bit?' I was so offended by his tone. Something rankled about the way he talked to me that day, the expression on his face. After that, I kept my distance.

When I saw the final film at the premiere at Priya cinema, I realized much had happened after the day they told me my work was done. In the film I saw, Rituparno was no longer Abhiroop, the character he had been playing in the film. He came to interview me, and then *he* became Chapal Bhaduri.

Many events that had happened to me in real life were still there, but as part of Abhiroop's story. Such as, my time in Tarapith. Who stayed there? I did, but in the film it's Abhiroop, with some made-up incidents that happened to him there. Who sat and washed dishes like a maid? I did. But I never squatted on my haunches, with a gamchha tied around my head the way Rituparno does in the film. As I watched Rituparno sitting in front of a big dressing-table mirror doing his make-up, I couldn't help but think that I'd never had such a grand dressing table in all my years in jatra. Also: Chapal Rani never acted while drunk. There is nothing wrong with drinking. I have drunk alcohol. But that does not mean I sat and drank while putting on my make-up or went on stage drunk. And I certainly didn't go around in a sari when I was off stage. I had no wish to whatsoever.

These were not what I had written and given Kaushik when he asked me to put down the story of my life. Yet this was still my story unfolding on screen. I was watching my life, but Rituparno's character had taken it over.

I must admit it hurt. Had I been replaced because I was no longer young, because I no longer had the looks you needed for a film star? I understand films need sell-able stars. But then someone else could have done it all. Why involve me? Why take my story? My story could have ended with that shot of me coming back home. Why did they continue, turning my story into a part of another person's life? I wished that all that work I had done as Chand Bibi, Sultana Riziya and Chintamoni had been captured somewhere, so I could show them to people, so that I could tell the world that I mattered.

Another actor, one of today's heroes, was sitting next to me at the screening. He said, 'But what happened to Chapal Bhaduri?' I said, 'I am right here next to you.' He said, 'No, no, I mean in the film. It's a very interesting film. I was watching it carefully. But what happened to your character?'

I just said softly 'You should ask the director that.'

There was no Chapal any more in the film, only Rituparno. Many of the scenes I had shot with Raima and Jisshu had not been included. I know these things happen while editing, but to me it felt as if the film had been cut and cut till it became all about Rituparno Ghosh. I know he is far more educated and learned than I, but I feel he was greedy for fame. Originally, he was playing an entirely different character in the film. But it was as if he saw the potential in my character and seized it for himself, and as a result my character's arc was made to abruptly end. That experience made it hard for me to truly respect him any more. I feel I was offed in the film that was supposedly based on my life to make way for Rituparno Ghosh.

But I said nothing at that time. I sat through the premiere and thought: these people have given me a lot of respect and affection. They have paid me everything they owed me, down to the last paisa. The producer even gave me an expensive Nokia phone. Until then, I'd never owned a mobile phone. And he was so thoughtful, he pre-charged it for the whole year.

At the end, Rituparno came and asked, 'Is everything fine, Chapal-da?'

I just said, 'Yes. Everything is fine.'

But those who knew me and knew my life story knew everything was not fine. They said, 'Where did Chapal go? All the events that happen after the character in the film come home from singing Sitala's songs—all that happened to Chapal. They are part of his life story. But where did he go?'

I have to admit I felt used. Even though they paid me well and treated me with great respect. The film happened—but what happened to me?

After that, I never met Rituparno Ghosh again. For a while, I turned down many profiles, interviews, even book proposals. Part of it might have been a certain wariness after that whole experience.

Even Kaushik Ganguly's son called me once with a proposal for some kind of student film. But I turned it down. I said, 'I don't work without pay. It doesn't matter whether it's big or small, school or college.'

I told myself: it's OK if everyone thinks I am snooty, that I have too sharp a tongue for my own good. It does not matter. As long as I have the sky above me, I will find my shelter.

One Last Film

After *Arekti Premer Golpo*, I did only one other film—*Maya Mridanga* by Raja Sen. It was written by Sahitya Akademi award-winning writer Syed Mustafa Siraj. A rather daring story about the lives of the chhokras, or the young boys who played female roles in travelling-theatre groups called alkaap, and the ustads who were their mentors and lovers.

I told Raja, 'Please don't ask me to dress as a woman again.'

'Oh but you must,' he said, 'But I will take care to do it sensitively.'

I agreed because Raja seemed to be a good person, very polite and well mannered.

In *Maya Mridanga*, I play Kalachand, an old artiste, once a female impersonator who now has no income. Once he was the pretty boy who sang and danced. Now he just dusts all the musical instruments and takes care of them for a pittance.

Deb Shankar Haldar plays the star, Jhakshu Ustad, a folk musician who, as a child, had known Kalachand. Ranjan Bose, a modern-day female impersonator, also acts in it and performed very well.

In the opening scene, Jhakshu hears Kalachand's voice and says, 'Who is that? Who is that speaking? I know that voice.'

'It's me,' I reply. 'Can you not recognize me? When I was younger, you certainly knew me well. You were just a boy. And my beauty knew no bounds. Now I am old. Your singing, though, is just spectacular. Amazing. Here, keep these 10 rupees. That's from me.'

Slowly it dawns on Jhakshu that he knows me from a long time ago.

I tell him, 'Ha, I might have lost my looks. But the voice is still the same. That I could not change. I always played a girl, now, look I've become a man. But keep these 10 rupees. It's a token of my appreciation for your song.'

'So how do you support yourself? How do you make a living?'

'Dusting. I do the dusting.'

'Dusting? What do you dust?'

'Before the session begins, I am the one who dusts the harmonium and all the other instruments. Then I recite a little prayer, so they don't let the musicians down.'

'For real?'

'Well, it's just for show.'

Later in the film, Jhakshu wants me to do something for him: dress up as a woman as I had done in my heyday.

'Kalachand, do you think you can?'

'Not a problem. My voice is still feminine. It's all I have left. I can dress up and do this. Wait and see.'

I liked the way Raja Sen used me in that film. He played to my strengths. He used both aspects of my personality—male and female. But he was also very sensitive to my handicaps.

At one point, the script required me to go to Canning, a town on the Matla river, and shoot on a boat. I told him, 'I don't think I can manage that. My legs are not what they used to be. I have gout.'

He said, 'Yes, yes, I should have thought of that. Let me see what I can do.'

He then rewrote the script so there was no need to drag me to Canning.

In another scene, I had to run up to someone in a cycle, warn them about something and run back. I told Raja I didn't think I would able to run like that. Even though it was meant to be one shot, he worked around it. When I saw it on screen, I was amazed. It really looked like one shot. But I had not been the one running. In close-up, I was the one panting, but the person running was someone else altogether. These little gestures made me really admire him as a director. I enjoyed that film.

After that, few offers came my way. Perhaps a part of me had hoped that *Arekti Premer Golpo* would open more doors for me. But I guess people had no need for me any more. By then I was getting older but my voice was still feminine. I assume there were not enough characters that fit me physically any more. But whenever people praised my acting, I would wonder why no one wrote other roles that suited me.

I did what I could. I might have done it because I needed the money or I might have done it for the sake of art. But I have turned down almost nothing that came my way, whether it was jatra, theatre or cinema. Only when my body would not allow it, only then did I say no.

Upal or Chapal?

There was one more role left but it was back to the stage again. Nandipat, who had staged *Ramanimohan*, wanted to do a play based on my life. I agreed, but said I have nothing new to say.

Whatever I have to say is already out there. You can use that. But make sure you start with my mother, because that's where it all started for me.

The play was called *Upal Bhaadury*, and its script begins with an old man watching a performance. He is about to be felicitated, something that had become a regular event in my own life. A Tagore song starts up, and he is suddenly overwhelmed because it reminds him of his mother. Then the play goes back into the man's life, the great roles he played, like Kaikeyi and Chand Bibi, roles that truly had once been mine. The older Upal sits on stage while a younger Upal re-enacts them. At one point, the two Upals have a face off, their voices rising higher and higher. One says, 'There is no Upal Bhaadury.' The other says 'But Upal Bhaadury exists.' 'No he does not.' 'Yes he does.'

I liked the script, but for some reason Nandipat did not. Then, several months later, another group called Dum Dum Shabdamugdha took it up. Its founder, Rakesh Ghosh, said they would do it. But they would do it their way, so he rewrote it to make it his own.

Rakesh was a good director, knowledgeable about theatre. I admired him. I had acted in an earlier play for him, *Rajkulogatha*, a reworking of the Mahabharata. And Ranjan who acted with me in *Maya Mridanga* and *Rajkulogatha* played the younger Upal. It was my life story but we changed the names. It was easier that way, gave us more license. Thus Chapal Bhaduri became Upal Bhaadury, Makhanlal Natta became Madhav Natta. Upal is the water that runs over the stones on a mountain, not a bad name for me.

But they took many liberties as well. In real life, Surya Dutta liked his special tobacco from Gazipur, his hubble-bubble, but he was not a drunk. He hated alcohol as did Makhanlal Natta. And Makhan-babu was a perfect gentleman, refined and well educated. In the play, he is shown as a drunk man, a man of bad character. I protested, but they said they had to change things to make it work on stage. I had to accept that. I was a professional actor who had committed to do the part, and I did it the best I could. We staged it in several important places. Unfortunately, when we went to stage it in Asansol, I fell and hurt my arm and leg and never really recovered properly. Then Covid happened, and put an end to everything.

While it lasted, the play did reasonably well. It was staged at the theatre festival organized by the National School of Drama. We even won a few prizes. I won several, Ranjan won a few, sometimes we won together. Once, I just gave my prize away to Ranjan, saying he was the real Upal Bhaadury. And I was the fake one. Perhaps we were both fake Upal Bhaadurys. Sometimes I feel that like *Arekti Premer Golpo*, this was not my story either . . . that all these stories were just disjointed fragments of my own.

Ornament of Bengal

My mother had done some cinema too. In 1938, Sailajaranjan Mukhopadhyay made *Shahar Theke Doorey* [Far from the City] based on his own story. It starred my mother alongside stalwarts like Dhiren Bhattacharya and Molina Devi. It was a huge hit. Bangles and saris, as worn in the film, showed up in the market. I think they were called 'Maney Na Mana' saris. The film went on to have a silver jubilee, then a golden and even a platinum. All the artistes got gifts for each jubilee. I remember my mother received gold rings with *Shahar Theke Doorey* engraved on them.

Ma had to change her style entirely for cinema. She was queen of the theatre, but film was a different medium altogether. In theatre, one day you might ace the part, the next day you might come up a little short. Another day, you have to tweak it. Imagine: there is a dialogue where you say, 'Here flows the river. And look, beyond that is a mountain. We must go to the top of the mountain.' One day your hand might come up higher than another day as you point to the mountain. Each day is slightly different. One day a line might garner applause. Another day it might not. You have to keep adjusting your performance, reading the audience, all the while trying to get the applause. But in cinema it's different. Until you do everything exactly as the director wants, down to the right expression on your face, they will not OK the shot. Until then, it's always NG, NG, NG—not good. In cinema, it's ultimately a lot about what the director and the editor do. In theatre and its jatra, it's all about me, the actor. The line rises or falls with me. There is nowhere to hide. That's probably why the stage will remain my first love.

But I do understand that if you are a true artist, you need to know how to adjust to each medium. Those who went from theatre to cinema would sometimes be too theatrical while those who came from cinema to theatre could be accused of being too cinematic.

Each medium has its own rewards. But jatra, despite its popularity was always the step-child, the one nobody deemed worthy of honours. That changed finally around 2012–13. I got a letter from Mamata Banerjee, chief minister of West Bengal. The government wanted to give me a Banga Bhushan award, something she had instituted to honour personalities in various fields for their contributions to arts and culture.

I have met the chief minister a few times at events. She has always been warm and courteous. She even sends me birthday greetings. Once, at an event, she pulled me aside and told me to let her know if I needed anything. I thanked her but I could not really say anything because there were so many people around clamouring for her attention. I think Buddhadeb Bhattacharya, her predecessor as chief minister and a Communist, was also very interested in culture, but it was a more elite intellectual culture. However, he did help my sister secure an apartment. Mamata Banerjee is more down-to-earth. She spoke very nicely to me. I could sense that she had a soft spot for artistes. I have no comment on her politics, but I have to say she has done quite a bit to help folk arts in the state—jatra, folk music, folk crafts, things that really needed some attention from the state.

Under her tenure, I have received many awards from the state and organizations affiliated with the state. I keep getting invited to convocations and being handed these fancy scrolls. I once told one of the organizers half-jokingly 'You all are giving me this scroll, you are calling me a celebrity. Everyone is supposedly entranced by my talents. Yet I don't have a house to call my own. Thank you for these honours, but what will I do with all these scarves and mementos and scrolls?'

Then I always remember what the great saint Sri Ramakrishna would say. 'If you need to eat a mango, eat a mango. There is no need to ask how many mangoes there are in the tree, what kind of mangoes they are, who planted the tree. Just eat the mango that's there in your name.' I try to live by that philosophy. As Ma always said, 'Just focus on the good instead of the faults in people. It will help with your peace of mind.'

Eventually, I did write to Mamata Banerjee. As jatra artistes, we get nothing like a pension. As a theatre artiste, my sister would get something, but as a jatra artiste I would get barely 1,500 rupees a month. I wrote a letter to the chief minister and requested her help in the matter. After that, it was eventually raised to a more respectable 5,000 rupees a month. Some would say that as artistes we should get even more. An apartment would have been nice, but, ultimately, we get what is written in our fate.

At least I got the recognition. Though even that proved a double-edged sword. The Banga Bhushan was indeed a great honour, but, ironically, it was also one of the reasons I ended up in an old-age home.

INTERLUDE

In Retrospect

Kaushik Ganguly

When you see Chapal Bhaduri, it's hard to think of him as Chapal Rani. He is quite a tall, large-boned man, his build isn't slight at all. His face is broad. It's not a face that's pretty in a womanly way. When I saw him in his kurta-pyjama, he was a man, very much a man.

But when he put on his costume, something shifted. The way he walked, the way he talked, everything changed. His demeanour changed. There was not a trace of that old man. Now he could not meet your eyes, a coyness had seeped into his gaze. His very being became filled with a sweetness that I still find hard to explain.

An hour before, we might have slapped him jovially on the back and said, 'Hello, Chapal-da, how are you? Sit down, have a cup of tea.' We might have pulled him by the hand and sat him down on the chair. He is a genial man, and he inspires joviality in people around him. But when he dressed as a woman, we would keep our distance from him. It was as if we, even the most boisterous members of the unit, suddenly felt shy about touching him. Then the outfits would come off, the make-up would be wiped away and a limping old man would emerge once again. It was a strange and splendid transformation, and I am at a loss to find the words to explain it.

I didn't know Chapal Bhaduri at all until we made *Ushnatar Jonno* together. I had heard about him because I had an interest in jatra and had researched it as a subject. I had read a bit about Natta Company. So I knew of him. I knew his sister was the renowned actress Ketaki Dutta. But I had no direct contact for him. Then somehow I got hold of the landline number for their home in Belgachia Milk Colony. I reached him and he came to meet me at a studio in South Kolkata.

Ushnatar Jonno was about a lesbian relationship. One of the women is making a documentary about an ageing female impersonator who had once been involved with the leading man of the jatra company. That relationship did not last. Neither did the lesbian one. The stories, one in the present, the other in the past, unfolded in parallel. He was so excited when I narrated the story to him and more than ready to do it. He was truly eager to do something different and happy to share the story of his life.

And what stories they were. Sometimes we didn't know whether to laugh or cry. We could not include all the stories in the film because many of them just could not be shown on film. Some, he declared, should not be shown. Many of the people who were part of those stories were still living, or their families were around. His own family might have been uncomfortable if he had let it all hang out. But this much was clear to me. Chapal Bhaduri had certainly been used and abused by people around him, over and over again. Many of those stories are in our film, told as honestly as possible.

In the end, he was happy with the script we wrote. He was so excited to go and shoot in the old Jhargram palace. It was all like a great picnic for him. It was as if he was back on the road again, like the good old days of the touring jatra company. He would be dressed and ready and raring to go every day. 'When are we going to shoot?' he would keep asking. 'Are we set yet?' He was like a child, eager to show us how he could transform himself to Draupadi or Riziya. Nothing but nothing made him happier than that act of transformation. But, more than anything else, I think he was rather overwhelmed that a feature film had been fashioned around his story. There had been articles and a documentary, but this was a movie.

For a telefilm, *Ushnatar Jonno* certainly made waves. We even had a press conference for it at Peerless Inn, one of Kolkata's five-star hotels. A press conference for a telefilm was unheard of, yet the room was bursting with journalists. This was around the year 2003. Everyone was agog with excitement that a topic like that had been addressed on Bengali television. Those were heady days indeed.

None of that would have been possible without Chapal-da. That time we spent together brought us very close to each other. When I made the mega serial *Ghare o Baire*, I fashioned a role keeping him in mind. It was not the best role, one might even say it was a bit of a stereotype. But it was regular work, it kept Chapal-da in circulation. More importantly, it gave him some financial reassurance. I felt that it was the was the least I could do as a friend.

Years later, I reworked *Ushnatar Jonno* and fashioned a feature film out of it. *Arekti Premer Golpo* became even more famous. It had bigger name stars in it. But if you want to see the true glory of Chapal Bhaduri, I will ask you to watch *Ushnatar Jonno,* and not *Arekti Premer Golpo.*

In *Arekti Premer Golpo*, Rituparno Ghosh was the star. If Chapal Bhaduri feels that Rituparno Ghosh took his story and made it his own, he is not quite right. That story was Chapal Bhaduri's and his alone. No one could take it from him. But Rituparno Ghosh certainly took his light. It's as if there was a 100-watt bulb that suffused the room with warm light. Then one day someone installed an LED in that house. It was only 28 watts, but everyone was so dazzled, they paid no attention to that old 100-watt light any more. Modernity can be cruel like that. Rituparno was an incandescent star, but without Chapal Bhaduri there would have been no film.

Rituparno had many things Chapal did not. He was well versed in art and culture. He was cosmopolitan and educated and a brilliant communicator. His knowledge was wide and deep. He had a social status that Chapal did not. He was a bona fide star, and he certainly regarded himself as one. Chapal Bhaduri might have once been a star in jatra. But that was then. When we made the film, he was a star no longer. Yet the film was about Chapal Bhaduri's story. That was a predicament for Rituparno Ghosh. Chapal Bhaduri was the legend. Rituparno Ghosh was the star. The star collided with the legend.

I had a scene in that film where the two characters, Rituparno and Chapal, are sitting next to each other in a car. I thought it would have completed the arc of their stories. But Rituparno objected. Don't keep that scene, he told me. He felt the two people were different and needed to be kept separate. It was as if he did not want to share the same seat with Chapal-da.

I think that hurt Chapal-da. He felt erased. Indeed, he was in many ways. Though he dubbed his part for the film, what most people do not realize is Rituparno re-dubbed those lines later. Little bits survive in Chapal-da's voice, but most of what we hear in the final cut is actually Rituparno. It made sense in some ways, because the voices of the two characters had to be close. But I can see how Chapal-da must have felt slighted.

This is not to say Chapal Bhaduri was denied anything. He got his pay, his perks, his food, his tea. But he knew he was not the star. A star can act as a gardener or a farmer in a film but he is still the star. There are 21 people running after him. Every time, he walks there are four people holding out umbrellas for him. He drinks fruit juice in a glass wrapped in silver foil and through a plastic straw while the others drink tea from clay cups. When the media comes on set to interview the actors, they mostly want to talk to the star. And there's Chapal-da, the person on whose story the film is actually based, sitting quietly in the corner. A director and a producer can never assuage that hurt.

In the end, we are creatures of the same ecosystem. With Rituparno Ghosh, we would worry about every little detail. Was the food OK? Where should we order food from tomorrow? Did the car come on time? If Ritupano was upset with something, he could storm off the set, saying 'Call me when you are ready. I can't sit around waiting for you.' We would get annoyed, but deal with it. Later, we would laugh and tease him, 'Ritu-da, what drama you can create.' But Chapal Bhaduri was not in a position to do that. If Rituparno told Chapal-da something cutting, he was not in a position to retaliate. He just bore it stoically.

That's why ,when we did press conferences for that film, we did not include Chapal Bhaduri. It was a deliberate decision because he would have felt excluded, an afterthought. I could not say anything. Rituparno had 17 feature films under his belt. His words carried weight. I was just a greenhorn in the world of cinema, a man who had then made only a few telefilms. Rituparno's clout helped that film get made. But today I can say that *Ushnatar Jonno* was a celebration of the life of Chapal Bhaduri. *Arekti Premer Golpo* merely used his life story.

But what a life story! Chapal Bhaduri had two films and a documentary made about him. I don't know any other living personality in Bengal who can boast of that honour. And I am so proud of both films. Today, we talk so much about sexual orientation and LGBTQI+ rights. We respect those rights, we speak about them publicly even though we still have a long way to go and we must still protest and agitate and demand. Nevertheless, we cannot deny society has opened up. That gives me joy.

Rituparno Ghosh certainly had his struggles, but he didn't have to go through what Chapal Bhaduri did. By the time Rituparno came around, we all knew of Chapal Bhaduri. The world was by no means perfect, but it was far more aware. And Rituparno had the celebrity status and education to stand up to the bullies, to answer back, to cut people down to size. Chapal had none of that. His fight to make space for himself was far more raw. Even in the '70s, jatras were using men like him for laughs, making them objects of ridicule, using them as comic relief like a man who stutters or a woman who is obese. If the Chapal Bhaduris had not fought to survive, the Rituparno Ghosh-es would not have gotten the lives they did.

Rituparno had to struggle far less to get *Arekti Premer Golpo* compared to the decades of struggle Chapal put in to get *Ushnatar Jonno*. In the end, Chapal grew up on the jatra stages and open fields, Rituparno grew up in advertising studios and drawing rooms. There is a difference.

Arekti Premer Golpo will undoubtedly survive as a landmark film. It was, and remains, my pride and joy. But the Chapal-da I knew and loved, in the end he was just an actor named Chapal Bhaduri in that film. When he came on set, we talked and laughed, we cracked jokes and drank tea, he did his scenes with sincerity and diligence. And when they were done, we let him go.

I feel that living Chapal Bhaduri's life on screen had deeply affected Rituparno. He had made 17 films before *Arekti Premer Golpo* but in not one had he dealt with the issues of his sexuality. But after *Arekti Premer Golpo*, he acted in *Memories in March* and directed and acted in *Chitrangada: The Crowning Wish*—both films that dealt explicitly with sexuality. I don't believe that was an accident.

Chapal Bhaduri brought Rituparno Ghosh out of the closet.

13
The Old-Age Home

Looking for a Home

The Banga Bhushan award came with 100,000 rupees from the government.

My oldest nephew wanted some of the money to start his own business. I told him frankly that I did not think he knew the B of Business. I had seen other business ideas of his fail resoundingly. I feared he would fritter away my hard-earned money. I wanted to save it, not spend it on some hare-brained scheme. One does not get a Banga Bhushan twice. I refused to budge from my stand, he refused to give up either.

Sadly, things got ugly between us. One day, I was unable to get into the flat because no one was home. I was stranded outside, my legs aching because I cannot stand for long periods. When my nephew got home, I said, 'I wish you had left the keys behind, since you knew I was out.' Perhaps I had raised my voice a little that day, my annoyance had been a bit too visible. I would like to think that as an uncle I had that much right, but he erupted in rage and complained to his sisters.

Finally, he issued an ultimatum. 'This cannot go on. Either he stays or I. We cannot both stay under one roof.'

I said, 'This is your mother's flat. She got it from the government. After she died, it passed on to your father. And after him, it belongs to you. When the neighbourhood club comes around to collect donations for Durga Puja, I am the one who pays on behalf of all of us. But it is still your flat. Undeniably so. You must stay here. I will go. I am sure God will provide for me somehow somewhere.'

When my sister got that flat in Belgachia from the government, she and I had moved into it. Her sons had stayed back at the house on Girish Avenue. At some point, though, they had to give up that house. Chhordi asked them all to move into the flat in Belgachia. I remember telling her, 'I understand that when you moved here, you couldn't just dump me. But I am not sure whether moving your son in here is wise. I think it would be better for us to be here and them to be there.' But a mother's heart pines for the son, no matter what kind of son he is. What would I know? I am neither a mother nor a father. I have only played them on stage.

In the end, it all panned out just as I had predicted. Sri Ramakrishna has said: if you stir the weeds covering the pond, they will float away. But slowly and inevitably, they will all return. Our lives are like that as well.

I told my nephew I would leave. Despite my brave front, in my heart I felt like the sky had fallen. I asked my nieces where I could go. The youngest, Sunita, said, 'I don't think you can stay all alone any more.' She found me an old-age home in North Kolkata.

Cat under a Hot Tin Roof

My old-age home is on a winding street where many of the houses still look like the ones I grew up in, faded walls and wrought-iron balconies, though they all sprout dish antennae now. It still reminds me of the Kolkata of my youth—the rickshaws, the little blue mosque, the haircutting saloon with its swinging doors, the houses with old-fashioned names, like Ma Kojagori Kutir and Chand Kutir. During elections, they string little party flags on ropes that stretch across the street from house to house. Hole-in-the-wall shops still sell cigarettes and chips and multicoloured lozenges that have to be plucked out of thick glass jars. Cats prowl, slipping from house to house. Someone lays out food for them on the street every day. One of the sweet shops is even older than me. It's still doing good business.

But change is afoot. At the head of a street, a chain bakery has opened an outlet, full of fancy cookies and cakes. An old house has been turned into a restaurant, its stained glass and plaster columns trying to evoke an old Kolkata palace, but it's all fake. Right next to it a signboard advertises a palace, but Bimala Palace is no palace either, just a glorified marriage hall, much like the Ganesh and Ajanta Opera jatra troupes were no operas.

If you walk past all this, you will come upon a shiny golden bust of reformer saint Swami Vivekananda. Sometimes, street dogs curl up at his feet. A few doors down, and past the century-old sweet shop is a squat pink building. It used to be a maternity hospital but these days it's an old-age home. The room I live in now was once an operating theatre. My niece was born in it!

About fifty of us live here. The rooms are plain, some in need of repair, the stairs are steep. But I have my own room and bathroom, and hot water whenever I need it. At my age, I cannot ask for too much more.

When I moved in, only a room on the roof was free. It had a tin roof, and we knew it would get scorchingly hot in the summer. Sunita, my niece, said, 'Why don't you move in here for the time being? Let me talk to the owner and see whether something else will open up soon.'

When a room freed up on the first floor, I moved in there. It's a small room, the window looks out onto the wall of the house next door. But when I lie in bed, I can see a sliver of the sky. The 'attached' bath is actually across the corridor. There are broken TVs and packing boxes piled outside my door. But at least I am spared summers under a hot tin roof.

After I moved in, my niece said, 'Tuku-mama, I feel torn about having put you in an old-age home. I know it's your own money. But I still worry whether I did the right thing by you.'

To be honest I never imagined either that I would land up in an old-age home. But I told her, 'Why worry about all this? God will take care of me. And it's not very far from you. You can come whenever you like by bus number 240. Or a taxi. Or your husband's car.'

My nieces do come to see me. Though she has a car, Sunita sometimes just hops onto a bus and comes by to drop off the month's spending money. When I started having trouble with my vision, she pushed me to get my eyes checked and have my cataracts removed. I was terrified, but she said, 'Don't worry I will take care of everything.'

Once, I had gone for a haircut when my niece called. I didn't hear the phone ring. She panicked and called her sister. When they finally got through to me, I got a big scolding. Now I am the child and they are my guardians. I don't have children of my own. But I treated those nephews and nieces like they were my own. I may not have breastfed them, but I cleaned their bottoms, washed their sheets, fed them and bathed them. My nieces tell me, 'You are not just our uncle, you are also our mother and our father.'

Whenever they come to visit, they bring me some food and it's never store-bought. They are all excellent cooks, they can even make ice cream at home. What I really love though is to see them lie next to each other on my bed and reminisce about the old times. 'Remember when . . . Tuku-mama, do you remember . . . ?' Those little girls I had bathed and cleaned and fed now have grey hair and bad knees themselves. They show me videos of their grandchildren on their phones. These three nieces of mine, Shanta, Chumki and Sumita, are all I have left when it comes to family. How strange I feel when I think of how full the house once was on Dalimtala Lane.

Still, I am so much luckier than most people who live here. Many never have any visitors.

Sometimes, old friends and colleagues from the world of acting call. The other day, an actor named Suman called: 'Chapal-da why don't you come and stay a few days with me?'

'Don't take it badly,' I said, 'But I really cannot go to your place.'

'I'll organize a taxi.'

'Please don't mind, but I cannot go any more. Why don't you come visit me instead? We can sit and chat.'

'But you used to love to eat, and my wife loved to cook for you.'

'Those days are over.'

Most of those who I had worked with, who professed great admiration for me when we worked together, never bother to call any more. Some of them just used me, and discarded me when they were done, when they got whatever they wanted.

A House for Mr Bhaduri

I do regret that I never built a small house for myself. Around 1960–61, we sold the house my mother had bought. It was a bit cramped and dark, but it had been ours. After my father died, my eldest brother said, 'The house is falling into disrepair. It's too expensive to maintain. Who knows, the roof might collapse during the next monsoon. Let's just sell it off.'

I was already working with Natta Company. I knew nothing about finance, but I had heard that some jatra artistes took loans to buy or build homes and then paid them off every month. I told Makhan-babu, 'My brothers want to sell our house.'

Makhan-babu said, 'No, no. Don't do that.'

He discussed the matter with my sister. She said, 'I am not sure what to do. Wherever I go, I will need three or four rooms because I have children. One agent has identified a house. Though it might still take 3,000–4,000 rupees to move in.'

'Don't do anything about that now,' Makhan-babu told her. 'I am lending Chapal 10,000 rupees. Why don't you see if you can arrange the rest from somewhere and buy this house from your brothers? Then we will see what happens.'

But my brothers refused to sell their share to us. They said, 'What's decided is decided. Let's not change plans. Let's sell it off, and divide the proceeds.'

I tried to argue, but it was to no avail. My mother had done her bit in making sure that her children would have a roof over their heads even when she was not there. But we children could not hold on to it. We got just about 30,000 rupees for that house. That was divided into six parts. Five thousand rupees was not nothing in those days, but it was not enough to buy something new either. From that day, I became beholden to my sister. I was the youngest and had nowhere to go when our family scattered to the winds.

Now, in my old age, I feel I should have built myself a little house. It could have been in the suburbs, a modest four-room affair perhaps, but enough for me. Many people in jatra who earned far less than me, like Babli Rani, managed to do that. I didn't have that much sense or foresight. Truth be told, I didn't think about the future. Obsessed with my looks, my make-up, my outfits and my acting, I assumed my life would just carry on the way it was, forever. I didn't think about what would happen when I grew old. At least, my sister got a small pension from the West Bengal Theatre Academy. But she was a theatre actor. There was nothing like that for us jatra artistes. That is why when people call me a celebrity, I say, 'What kind of celebrity am I? If I am a celebrity, would I be living in one room an old-age home?'

A Room with No View

It's a small room, pink like strawberry ice cream. It had one cupboard. I brought in another one myself. I had a big mirror, but I gave that away. There is no place for it. The full-length mirror on the wall outside is enough. The folding table is my own, as is the bed. It is a bit narrow. One night, I fell off the bed and then had to really struggle to get up. After that I kept a chair near by, so I could hold on to it when I got up at night.

All my mementos, awards, scrolls and medals are in a big trunk that I have shoved under the bed. I have no space to display them properly. As for those shawls and scarves I got as gifts at award ceremonies, I have given many of them away, some to the husbands of my nieces. I've given away some good kurtas as well. I don't think I am every going to fit into some of them again.

There's only one photograph of me on the wall. It's a recent one, taken on the roof of this very building. There's little else on the wall other than a calendar and a picture of Sri Ramakrishna whom I revere. Someone gave me a bust of myself as an award recently. I have no desire to display it. I think I shoved it in the back of the cupboard. But I hung the lifetime achievement award they gave me at the Bengal International Film Festival on the wall.

Some nights when I cannot sleep, I turn on the television and watch whatever is on, mindlessly scrolling through channels. I pay for cable, because I do need some way to pass the time. Once, I chanced upon a channel late at night where they were showing an adult film. I could not believe my eyes. There's nothing wrong with sex. It's an itch that must be scratched. I watched it for 10 minutes and then switched channels hurriedly, worried that if I kept watching, my mind would wander off to God knows where. I pulled the covers over me and tried to fall sleep instead.

The Daily Routine

I wake up at 5 in the morning when the sky is just turning light. I heat some water on my electric kettle and make myself a cup of tea. The tea they give us at the old-age home tastes like wrung out water from a towel. My niece sends me tea leaves so I can make my own tea.

After that, I go to the bathroom. If it's a good day, my stomach is emptied, but I cannot say the same holds true for my mind.

I used to worship my gods, but these days I don't have the energy. Instead, I just say God's name quietly in my mind. Sometimes I listen to Lata Mangeshkar singing Tulsidas' devotional bhajans. I used to light incense, but the smoke bothers me in this little room.

Around 8.30 they give us breakfast—two slices of bread, which they toast on the stove, not in a toaster. So they are always charred rather than toasted, and smell of kerosene. Alongside are some sautéed potatoes and beans which smell of nothing and taste of nothing as well. It's rounded off with a cup of tea without milk or sugar, though sometimes there's a small sweet.

Later in the morning, it's time for fruits. Some days it's apples or bananas, some days it's cucumbers. I ask them to cut the cucumber into smaller pieces because I have problems with my grip, though I don't like to pester anybody. Sometimes I just keep the fruits with me for later.

Lunch arrives around noon—rice, dal, perhaps a little bit of vegetable with poppyseed paste and some watery gravy with a piece of fried fish dunked in it which passes for a fish curry here. Even when money was scarce, the food we made was tasty, even if it was just potato peels with a little mustard paste and turmeric and chili. Here they cook for 60–70 people, but nothing has any taste.

After lunch, I take a nap. Around 4, another cup of tea and two biscuits. At 5, we get a bowl of curdled milk chhana because I am not allowed sweets except on special occasions.

Dinner is at 8. Some days it's egg curry with sautéed vegetables, some days chicken. I eat it right away, before the roti gets tough and chewy. Occasionally, we get diced potatoes and boiled carrots which I loathe. The egg curry I like. I used to like to eat and to feed people but those days are gone. Now, I have had to make my peace with the food here.

Sometimes visitors come and give us fruits and biscuit packets as part of their social work. At first, I would refuse but now I keep them.

After dinner, I take my pills and try to turn in by 9.30. I used to take psyllium husk for digestion but that doesn't do the trick any more. I need Digene pills. I also have my vitamin pills, my blood-pressure medication, something for my prostate, a sleeping pill, sometimes two.

Even then I can no longer sleep the whole night through. I keep waking up, because I need to go to the bathroom. Then, often, I cannot go back to sleep. When that happens, time hangs heavy. My niece tells me, 'Don't worry about it. It happens when you age. I have seen it with my mother-in-law and father-in-law. Do not obsess about it. Let it go. If sleep doesn't happen, it doesn't happen. You might stay up all night, watch the sky turn light, the sun come up. It's OK. Take a shower and go on with your day, maybe take a nap in the afternoon.'

But I am terrified that if I do that, I will again be up all night. It's not easy, growing old.

Sounds of Silence

In my dreams, I want a little house, really just a room of my own with its own little kitchen where I can cook for myself. And an attached bathroom. That's all I need. I would decorate that room with all my trophies and awards. But I don't have the ability to live on my own any more. So I try and remember what Saradama, lifetime companion of Sri Ramakrishna, said: '*Johkhon jemon tokhon temon, je jemon taakey temon*'—adjust to the whatever whenever, deal with everyone according to the situation. That is the key to equanimity.

I hardly eat much any more. I always had a sweet tooth. Whenever I ate a rosogolla, I would ask for extra syrup. Now, when someone gives me sweets for my birthday or at one of these award ceremonies, I distribute them among the people who work at the old-age home and the residents, at least those who are allowed to have sweets. I have even learnt to eat okra, a vegetable I always hated with a passion. One adjusts to everything.

People tell me, 'Chapal-da, you don't look your age.' But whether I look it or not, I know the body has aged. I feel it in my bones. Sometimes someone calls from the press. The interviews are tiring because they all ask the same questions. This caged bird has sung this song way too many times. I am grateful age has not erased my memories, that my mind remains alert. But that is also why the memories and thoughts and regrets crowd my mind. My mind knows what the body cannot do any more. It remembers everything. It feels the loss.

The residents all know who I am, but no one asks me anything about my life or shows much curiosity about it. The sound of old age is really silence. I read books, especially the Gita. I watch television. I listen to songs on my Carvaan music player. But how much will I listen to the radio or watch television or read books? I watch the news programmes, but some days I cannot bear hearing about murder rape and mayhem. The anchors scream, the panelists fight. I switch to films, but the films they show are completely mindless as well.

I had many friends, many companions but I have not really made any friends here. More than the residents, I talk to the women who work here. Some days, it is tough. I always enjoyed my own company, but in the old age home it does get lonely.

Drinking Games

I have put on a lot of weight. Some people insinuate that it's because I sit at home and drink every day. I have nothing against alcohol. I know some of the residents drink, because I can smell it sometimes. After all, I come from the Bhaduri family. We know our alcohol only too well. I can recognize it by just a whiff. I have had my fair share—from local Bangla hooch to foreign liquor, Vat 69 whisky to red wine. But I don't drink any more. Once, during my acting days, my friends said, 'Chapal, have a little.' Carried away by their enthusiasm, I had some and then some more. It was cheap alcohol of some kind, but I quite liked it. Then, when I got up, everything was swaying. I was shocked. 'What did I do? I drank that much? I have this much greed?' But what is the point of repentance once the deed is done? But I learnt my lesson that night.

I think around 2016–17 was the last time I bought a bottle of alcohol for myself. I had gone to a dentist in Bagbazar. As I was coming back home, I went past a liquor store. After a long time, I was tempted to have a drink. I thought: it's been a while, I live alone, I am not answerable to anyone. For a moment I worried what my niece would say, but then she does not live with me. So I went into the shop and bought a bottle of whisky.

After dinner, I settled down for a drink. I wasn't worried about getting drunk. I know I can hold my liquor. There was no chance I would be staggering around the corridor like a jatra actor. That night, I didn't take my usual sleeping pills. But strangely, I just could not sleep despite the alcohol. Restless and anxious, I stayed up till the crack of dawn. That day I decided I was done with alcohol.

I put away the bottle in the back of my cupboard. I could neither drink it nor toss it. I could not give it away without people asking where it had come from. I could flush the alcohol down the toilet, but I would still have to dispose of the bottle. I didn't want to give it to the attendants. I felt like someone trying to get rid of their black money.

I know there are many in the acting world who cannot get up on stage without two pegs in them. They claim their natural flow does not come without it. But I remember how humiliated I was by my father's addiction to drink. I would constantly hear snide comments, like 'Tuku's father is a drunk'. I was always afraid that when the car came to pick me up, they would see my father inebriated. One day, I told him, 'I have gained some reputation now in the world of acting. They come to pick me up in a car. I would request you to stop your drinking.' He looked at me and said, 'You are asking me to stop? All right. I won't drink any more.' And he did stop. He died soon after. Sometimes I wonder if I did the right thing. He was an addict. Perhaps he should not have stopped so suddenly like that.

Once, in 2010, when we were doing *Ramanimohan* in Delhi, I remember hearing a knock on the door of my hotel room. I opened it and saw Sanjib, part of our troupe, standing outside.

'What is it, Sanjib?

'No, I mean, um,' he stammered.

'What?'

Finally, he managed to say that they had smuggled in a bottle of alcohol and wanted me to join the cast and crew for a drink.

'Sanjib, listen. Your hair has gone grey, you have a bald patch now. As do I. Our time to do these things is long past. But you have gone out of your way to get this, so I will join you for a drink.'

There were a lot of young men in the cast and crew. Truth be told, I enjoy the company of good-looking young men. It's not like I behave inappropriately with them. But I like being around them.

I joked, 'What impertinence you boys have, offering me alcohol like this. But since you have gone and done it, come on, let's begin the party.'

We all had a good time that night, eating, drinking, laughing, singing, joking. That was it. I don't think I really drank after that.

Paan is the only addiction I have left. I still have a jaanti to cut my own betel nuts. Though even paan I eat less now since I can't go to the paan shop any more.

An Evening in Paris

The biggest loss for me is that the body does not allow me to act any more. I remember pages of dialogue almost verbatim from long-ago jatras. But the physical body betrays me.

Acting is like oxygen for us actors. Without it, we struggle to breathe.

A theatre group called Manthan was putting on a play called *Ardhek Akash* [Half the Sky]. There was a small part in the last scene which involved the goddess of dance. They pleaded with me to do it.

But I said, 'Sorry, I can't stand that long. My legs won't hold up any more.'

They said, 'But we want to felicitate you too, that day. The great actor Soumitra Chatterjee's daughter Poulami is supposed to be present on the occasion.'

'I can come for that,' I said. 'But you will have to organize my transportation and make sure I don't have to deal with too many stairs. I do not know if I will be able to perform.'

In due course, someone appeared with a formal letter of invitation. I agreed to go and said I would attempt to do the part of the goddess of dance as well. There wasn't much dialogue, but there were some dance steps. She comes and sits on the stage and watches various kinds of classical dances. Then she gives her anklets to a dancer who gives them to another who gives them to someone else, thus showing how tradition is passed down from guru to disciple.

They paid me a small stipend, modest but enough to cover my medicines for a month at least. The dancer Mamata Shankar was there, and they gave both of us small busts of ourselves, made of some kind of white stone. I told Mamata Shankar I had seen her father Uday Shankar dance in the film *Kalpana* and been mesmerized by the way he could make the muscles of his arm ripple, as if a current was passing through. She was impressed by how well I remembered the little details.

Later I wondered why I did it, whether it was worth the exertion and effort. Even a small role like that feels taxing now. Perhaps I was tempted because I live alone, with only myself for company. I thought even if it was physically arduous, it would break the monotony of my days in my old-age home. I would be around other people for a little while. And I was not wrong. I felt a little more alive that day.

Covid put an end to all my travels and performances. When that passed, my health no longer permitted travel any more. It's been a few years since I have acted on stage. The other day, someone came to invite me to yet another felicitation. I thought to myself: do you really need yet another plaque, yet another scarf, yet another bouquet? There's no space in my room to display the plaques. The money, if there is any, is usually fairly modest. Then why do I make the effort to go? I guess I still haven't been able to shrug off the hypnotic pull of the stage. It is maya. I remain in its thrall.

Some admirer, besotted with my looks or perhaps my talents, it does not matter any more, gave me a bottle of perfume. I think it was called Evening in Paris. It was such a beautiful dark-blue bottle. Long after the perfume was finished, I kept that bottle for years. I could not bear to part with such a thing of beauty. Then one day I sold it off. Perhaps I got 20 rupees, which was not bad for an empty bottle. But holding onto that bottle was also about maya. Beauty has its own maya. And it is hard to let go of it. Even now I want to look at myself in the mirror, but these days I often stop myself. All I can see is how much hair I have lost, how much weight I have put on. Luckily, there is no room for a full-length mirror in my room any more.

But when I lie in bed and close my eyes, I can only see the Chapal Rani I used to be.

The Legacy

There are a few actors who still try to make a living going around playing Sitala or other mythological parts like Lakkhinder–Behula or Sanaka. I have given them my wigs, my saris and my make-up boxes. They will be of more use to them than to me.

But it's hard to let go of the attachment entirely. A few things remain special. The Benarasi sari, a deep rani-pink one, which I took with me to Canada to perform as Sitala there, the gold jewellery I wore with it. The border of the sari is frayed. Its blouse does not fit me any more. The gold jewellery is fake. But there are memories and sentiments wrapped up in them. I have held on to some of the gifts I got over the years, like a pink bracelet someone gave me in Canada. A few wigs that looked absolutely natural on me. They were once my livelihood. Now I think I must let them go too. They need to find new homes where they will be loved.

Many have said, 'I will be the next Chapal Rani.' I always say that they are welcome to try. But I also say, 'If you want to be the inheritor of Chapal Rani's legacy, then a pair of earrings and a nose ring and a sari is not enough.' A young man named Kanchan, whom we called Moni, took on many of my roles, but it didn't really work out. Ranjan Bose performed very well as a female impersonator in Raja Sen's film *Maya Mridanga*. These are the young men who say they are the inheritors of Chapal Rani's legacy. But times have changed. Even Chapal Rani would not be the same Chapal Rani now.

I was 16 when I began acting. And I acted for more than 60 years. Now the need for people like us has gone. I didn't realize it then, but when I entered the scene, that age was already ending in jatra. I was lucky I caught its tailwind. I was fortunate I had mentors like Surya Dutta and Makhanlal Natta to teach me and guide me, and playwrights like Brajen Dey to write roles for me.

All of them are gone, and with them that age is gone as well. I give these new actors my blessings. I hope they will become somebody, but it will not be easy. You cannot turn back time.

Chapal Rani didn't just happen. I had to learn the hard way how to act as a woman. Some days I felt my vocal cords would just tear from the strain I put upon them, but I kept at it. I had to use my head, sometimes fight my directors, sometimes acquiesce to them. So much sweat and tears goes into every character. If anyone asks me for advice, all I can say is: for that time you are on stage, you cannot imitate a woman—you have to be one.

Once I acted on a stage, open on all sides, surrounded by thousands of people. Now Chapal Rani's stage is this room, closed in on all sides, with an audience of none. My last shot in the film *Arekti Premer Golpo* has me walking down a narrow street in North Kolkata and entering a house. They chose that street because they liked the look of the old houses lining it. At that time, I didn't know my old-age home would end up being a stone's throw from where we shot that scene. It's as if I exited that film and entered my old-age home. Life works in curious ways.

The old-age home is also a short walk from the house where I grew up. Around the corner from me is the house where my mother's old friend Renu-ma lived, the one who had given me my first lessons in Morjina. If my legs were still strong, I could cross the busy main street, pass by the Burtollah Police Station and what used to be the great Srirangam Theatre, and go back to our old house. My life has always circled these streets. Now, after all these years, I have come back to my old neighbourhood, to the streets where it all began, where my memories still roam like ghosts.

In my dreams, I can walk back home again.

Epilogue

One day, in October 2024, as I was taking a bath, I felt an electric current run through me. My left side tingled and grew heavy, I could not move it. It was as if it had turned to lead. Somehow, I dragged myself back to my room, scared, wet and unclothed. The people at the old-age home called my niece.

I have travelled in bullock carts and boats, steamers, trains, planes. But never an ambulance. Now I have managed to check that off my list as well. Since then, life has changed for me. I need physiotherapy. The left side of my body does not obey me. I need an assistant to help me with the simplest things. How strange that, as a child, my assistant too had acted in jatra, playing the roles of little boys. Now here we are together in this old-age home, a man who acted as a woman being looked after by a woman who acted as a boy.

There are no roles left for Chapal Rani except for the final curtain call. I don't fear death. It is just another stage in our lives. I only hope and pray that it happens without too much suffering. I have suffered enough, and I have borne it all stoically. I have gone without food, I have begged, I have asked people for hand-outs, I have washed dishes, I have done things that I disliked. Somehow, I have managed to survive.

I have seen videos of the great female impersonators, like Bal Gandharva from Maharashtra or Jaishankar Sundari from Gujarat. I really am nothing compared to them. Still, I was Chapal Rani. I have received so much love and adulation from my audience. I have got humiliation from them as well.

In the end, though, I have no regrets. I was a boy from a small lane in North Kolkata who never finished school. Yet I became a queen.

ACKNOWLEDGEMENTS

This book began its life as an idea from Naveen Kishore, publisher at Seagull Books, and Bishan Samaddar, editor of its Pride List. In my naivety, I thought Chapal Bhaduri would talk, I would translate and transcribe and the book would be done in a few months, at best a year.

It ended up being very different, and a very different book emerged slowly, over weeks and months and eventually years over many cups of tea with Chapal-da.

My deepest thanks to Anwesha Deb and Soham Chatterjee who patiently transcribed the reams of Bengali interviews.

Few of Chapal Bhaduri's contemporaries are around any more, but my gratitude to Ananda Lal, Kaushik Ganguly, Naveen Kishore, Debojit Majumdar, Sekhar Samaddar and Rakesh Ghosh, who took time out to speak to me about their experiences with Chapal Bhaduri.

Natya Shodh Sangsthan was a valuable resource with a treasure trove of carefully preserved newspaper and magazine articles about jatra and Chapal Bhaduri. My thanks to Madhuchhanda Chatterjee, Chanda Samaddar and Gitasree De for facilitating my access to the material. My great regret remains that we were unable to source any photographs from Chapal Bhaduri's early days in jatra. I am grateful, however, to Parama Ghosh, Debojit Majumdar and Babulal Das for so generously sharing the images they had in their possession, and to Bishan Samaddar who photographed what remains of Chapal Bhaduri's old neighbourhoods.

The first reader of the first chapter of this book was my mother. She had been born a stone's throw from Chapal Bhaduri's old-age home and remembered the neighbourhood and that period well. She was my first 'proofreader'. She didn't get to see the final book, but she did get to see the wonderful cover designed by Sunandini Banerjee.

But none of this would have been of any use without Chapal Bhaduri himself. His astonishing memory and zest for life is ultimately what made this book possible. For me, the greatest gift this book has given me is the time I spent listening awestruck to Chapal Rani recite pages of dialogue from memory, from jatras he had acted in more than half a century ago, most of whose scripts are now long out of print. That performance cannot be captured on the page. It will remain in my memory.

This book is for Chapal Rani. Truly a queen, forever.

APPENDIX

CHAPAL RANI: JATRA REPERTOIRE AND ROLES

1959–1967: Natta Company

Pratishodh – Chameli
Kohinoor – Kohinoor
Satyashrayee – Jharna
Raja Devidas – Anjana
Prayashchitto – Shankhiya
Maharaj Parikshit – Ira
Lohar Jaal – Tatini
Plabon – Zinnat
Samrat Jahandar Shah – Jahrat
Patiter Bhagaban – Malati
Chitor Lakshmi – Lakshmibai
Mahatirtha Kalighat – Kali Mata
Sonar Bharat – Purnima
Chand Bibi – Chand Bibi
Bilwamangal – Chintamoni
Mayur Singhasan – Rahmat-un-Nissa
Bharat Biday – Kaikeyi
Sultana Riziya – Riziya
Dudh Sayarer Deshe – Roshni

1968–1970: Nabaranjan Opera

Michael Madhusudan – Jahnavi

Devgiri – Kamalabai

Anarkali – Kadambini

Nekrer Thaba – Karali

Rashtrabiplab – Sudipta

Notun Prabhat – Paribano

Nyaydanda – Shubhabati

Raktalekha – Nibhanani and Bishu

1970–1971: Satyambar Opera

Jallianwala Bagh – Mahinder

Sati Ekabati – Shobhana Begum

Sipahi Bidroho – Ma

1971–1972: Ambika Natya Company

Narakasur – Prithibi

Aami Siraj – Ghaseti Begum

Rami Chandidas – Yashoda

Rakte Ranga Kashmir – Shamim

1972–1973: Arya Opera

Louho Kopat – Kuti Bibi

Nihoto Golap – Tarini Bariwali

Ramzaner Chand – Rupmati

1973–1974: Kamala Opera

Bipradas – Dayamayee

Durgeshnandini – Bimala

Source: Chapalrani, *Abhinetrir Bhumikay* (Tandra Chakraborty ed.) (Kolkata: Natyachitra, 2002).

BIBLIOGRAPHIC SOURCES

The interludes following each chapter draw on the following sources.

BANDYOPADHYAY, Debjit (ed). *Binodini Rachana Samagra.* Kolkata: Patra Bharati, 2014.

BANDYOPADHYAY, Samik (ed). *Ketaki Dutta: Nijer Kothay, Tukro Lekhay.* Kolkata: Thema Books, 2006.

BANDYOPADHYAY, Surajit. *Jatray Swapankumar.* Kolkata: Thema Books, 2011.

CHAPALRANI. *Abhinetrir Bhumikay* (Tandra Chakraborty ed.). Kolkata: Natyachitra, 2002.

DE DAS, Moumita. 'An Interview with Ranjan Bose'. *Theatre Street Journal* 5(1) (March 2021): 147–55. Available at: https://theatre-streetjournal.in/wp-content/uploads/2021/05/I1_Moumita-De-Das.pdf (accessed 20 November 2025).

DEY, Brajendra Kumar. *Sultana Riziya.* Kolkata: United Publishers, n.d.

DUTTA, Dipankar (dir.), and Debojeet Majumdar (writ. and prod.). *Chena Kintu Ajana* [Known Strangers]. Documentary film, 2014. Available at: https://www.youtube.com/watch?v=f839_qQfbj8 (accessed 20 November 2025).

GANGULY, Kaushik. Interview with Sandip Roy, Kolkata, 18 February 2025.

GARGI, Balwant. 'Jatra—Folk Theatre of India', *Yakshagana.* Available at: https://yakshagana.com/jatra-folk-theater-of-india-by-balwant-gargi-continued/ (accessed 20 November 2025).

'Jatra, a Bengali Tradition'. NY/NJ Bengali, 2014. Available at: https://nynjbengali.com/jatra-a-bengali-tradition/ (accessed 20 November 2025).

KUNDU, Manujendra (ed). *Women Performers in Bengal and Bangladesh: Caught Up in the Culture of South Asia (1795–2010s)*. New Delhi: Oxford University Press, 2023.

MUKHERJEE, Tutun, and Niladri R. Chatterjee (eds). *Nari Bhav: Androgyny and Female Impersonation in India.* New Delhi: Niyogi Books, 2016.

ROY, Sandip. *Don't Let Him Know.* London and New Delhi: Bloomsbury, 2015.

Scan the adjacent QR code to view the documentary *Performing the Goddess: The Chapal Bhaduri Story* (1999), directed by Naveen Kishore.

ILLUSTRATIONS AND CREDITS

Figure 1. Chapal Bhaduri and the author in front of the house on Ananda Prasad Street (earlier Balakhana Street) in which Chapal was born. Photograph by Bishan Samaddar.

Figure 2. A recent picture of the house on 13/1C Dalimtala Lane in North Kolkata where Chapal grew up. Photograph by Bishan Samaddar.

Figure 3. The house on Girish Chandra Avenue in which Chapal lived with his elder sister Ketaki Dutta. Photograph by the author.

Figure 4. The street outside the old-age home where Chapal now lives. Photograph by Bishan Samaddar.

Figure 5. Town School on Bidhan Sarani where Chapal studied. Photograph by Bishan Samaddar.

Figure 6. The house of Noti Binodini off Bidhan Sarani. Photograph by Bishan Samaddar.

Figure 7. A statue of Sisir Kumar Bhaduri that stands before the site of the former Srirangam Theatre, now replaced by a modern residential apartment building on Raja Rajkrishna Street. Photograph by Bishan Samaddar.

Figure 8. Prabha Devi, Chapal's mother. Reproduced from the book *Ketaki Dutta: Nijer Kothay, Tukro Lekhay*, courtesy of Thema Books, Kolkata.

Figure 9. Prabha Devi (left) with her young daughter Sagarika on her lap in the film *Annapurnar Mandir* (1936). Reproduced from the book *Ketaki Dutta: Nijer Kothay, Tukro Lekhay*, courtesy of Thema Books, Kolkata.

Figure 10. Sisir Kumar Bhaduri (second from left) and Chapal's father Tara Kumar Bhaduri (extreme right) in the play *Sita*. Courtesy of Natya Shodh Sangsthan, Kolkata.

Figure 11. Ketaki Dutta (second from left) and Saralesh Bhaduri (third from left), Chapal's sister and brother respectively, among others, beside the body of their father, Tara Kumar Bhaduri. Reproduced from the book *Ketaki Dutta: Nijer Kothay, Tukro Lekhay*, courtesy of Thema Books, Kolkata.

Figure 12. Sisir Kumar Bhaduri (left) and Prabha Devi (right) in the play *Reetimoto Natok*. Courtesy of Natya Shodh Sangsthan, Kolkata.

Figure 13. Chapal playing a female role (Anjana) in *Raja Devidas*. From *Rangavarta* magazine, courtesy of Natya Shodh Sangsthan, Kolkata.

Figure 14. Chapal playing a rare male role (Bishu) in *Raktalekha*. From *Rangavarta* magazine, courtesy of Natya Shodh Sangsthan, Kolkata.

Figure 15. Chhabi Rani. Courtesy of Debojit Majumder.

Figure 16. Janardan Rani. Courtesy of Natya Shodh Sangsthan, Kolkata.

Figure 17. Babli Rani. Courtesy of Natya Shodh Sangsthan, Kolkata.

Figure 18. Chapal Rani in an unidentified role. Courtesy of Natya Shodh Sangsthan, Kolkata.

Figure 19. Sunil Kumar Maiti. Courtesy of Natya Shodh Sangsthan, Kolkata.

Figure 20. Maiti as Satadal Rani in *Chandimangal*. Courtesy of Natya Shodh Sangsthan, Kolkata.

Figure 21. Rakhal Chandra Das. Courtesy of Babulal Das.

Figure 22. Das as Rakhal Rani playing Kubeni in *Bangabeer*. Courtesy of Babulal Das.

Figure 23. Chapal without make-up (*c.*1960s). From *Rangavarta* magazine, courtesy of Natya Shodh Sangsthan, Kolkata.

Figures 24–25. Chapal on the balcony of Putulbari, North Kolkata, 1998. Photographs by Naveen Kishore. Courtesy of Naveen Kishore, Seagull Books.

Figure 26. Makhanlal Natta (left) of Natta Company with Chapal in Putulbari, 1998. Photograph by Naveen Kishore. Courtesy of Naveen Kishore, Seagull Books.

Figure 27. The roof of Putulbari, 2025. Photograph by Bishan Samaddar.

Figure 28. Outside Putulbari, 2025. The statuary on the top survives, although the first-floor balcony was bricked up sometime after 1998. Photograph by Bishan Samaddar.

Figure 29. The courtyard inside Putulbari, 2025. Photograph by Bishan Samaddar.

Figure 30. Bengali sign inside Putulbari: 'Natta Company Jatra Party—Office Upstairs'. Photograph by Bishan Samaddar.

Figure 31. Surya Kumar Dutta, long-time manager of Natta Company. Courtesy of Babulal Das.

Figure 32. Brajendra Kumar Dey, prolific writer of jatras. Courtesy of Babulal Das.

Figure 33. Cover of the jatra script *Bharat Biday* by Brajendra Kumar Dey. Courtesy of Natya Shodh Sangsthan, Kolkata.

Figure 34. Cover of the jatra script *Bilwamangal* by Brajendra Kumar Dey. Courtesy of the author.

Figure 35. Diamond Library bookstore on Rabindra Sarani, which still sells jatra scripts. Photograph by Bishan Samaddar.

Figure 36. The jatra neighbourhood of Chitpur in North Kolkata. Photograph by Bishan Samaddar.

Figure 37. Swapankumar, the King of Jatra and Chapal's male co-star. Courtesy of Natya Shodh Sangsthan, Kolkata.

Figure 38. Arun Dasgupta, Chapal's male co-star, applying make-up for the Natta Company production *Vidyasagar*. Courtesy of Natya Shodh Sangsthan, Kolkata.

Figure 39. Shekhar Ganguly, Chapal's male co-star. Courtesy of Natya Shodh Sangsthan, Kolkata.

Figure 40. A Bengali newspaper advertisement for Nabaranjan Opera's *Michael Madhusudan*, starring Swapankumar along with Chapal Rani. Courtesy of Natya Shodh Sangsthan, Kolkata.

Figures 41–51. Chapal transforms into and performs Goddess Sitala at the Taltala Sitala Mandir in Central Kolkata; a photo essay by Naveen Kishore (1998). Courtesy of Naveen Kishore, Seagull Books.

Figure 52. Chapal with his elder sister, actress Ketaki Dutta. Reproduced from the book *Ketaki Dutta*: *Nijer Kothay, Tukro Lekhay*, courtesy of Thema Books, Kolkata.

Figures 53–55. Scenes from the play *Nijabhumey* (1998), in which Chapal acted alongside Ketaki Dutta. Photographs by Naveen Kishore. Courtesy of Naveen Kishore, Seagull Books.

Figure 56. A report by Sunandini Banerjee in the *Statesman* about Chapal's trip to Canada in 2001. Courtesy of Natya Shodh Sangsthan, Kolkata.

Figure 57. Playbill for *Ramanimohan* (2006). Courtesy of Natya Shodh Sangsthan, Kolkata.

Figures 58–60. Scenes from *Ramanimohan*; photographs featured in its playbill. Courtesy of Natya Shodh Sangsthan, Kolkata.

Figure 61. Playbill for *Sundarbibir Pala* (2012). Courtesy of Natya Shodh Sangsthan, Kolkata.

Figures 62–64. Chapal in the make-up session and scenes from the documentary *Chena Kintu Ajana* (2014) in which he recreates some of his iconic jatra roles. Courtesy of Debojit Majumder and Sanjay Singha, researchers for *Chena Kintu Ajana*.

Figures 65–68. Chapal in a photo shoot for designer Parama Ghosh (2023). Photographs by Debarshi Sarkar for Parama Calcutta. Courtesy of Parama Calcutta.

Figure 69. Chapal on the strand by the river Hugli in front of Putulbari in North Calcutta, November 2022. Photograph by Bishan Samaddar.

INDEX